What Color Is Your Parachute?

2002 Edition

What Color Is Your Parachute?

A Practical Manual for Job-Hunters & Career-Changers

by
Richard Nelson Bolles

TEN SPEED PRESS
Berkeley Toronto

This is an annual. That is to say, it is substantially revised each year, the new edition appearing each November.

Those wishing to submit additions, corrections, or suggestions for the 2003 edition must *submit them prior to February 1, 2002, using the form provided in the back of this book.*

(Forms reaching us after that date will, unfortunately, have to wait for the 2004 edition.)

PUBLISHER'S NOTE

This publication is designed to provide accurate and authoritative information in regard to the subject matter covered. It is sold with the understanding that the publisher is not engaged in rendering professional career services. If expert assistance is required, the service of the appropriate professional should be sought.

The drawings on pages 94–95, 158, 165, and 206–07 are by Steven M. Johnson, author of *What the World Needs Now.*

Distributed in Australia by Simon and Schuster Australia, in Canada by Ten Speed Press Canada, in New Zealand by Southern Publishers Group, in South Africa by Real Books, in Southeast Asia by Berkeley Books, and in the United Kingdom and Europe by Airlift Book Company.

Library of Congress Catalog Card Information on file with the publisher.
ISBN 1-58008-341-2, paper
ISBN 1-58008-342-0, cloth

Published by Ten Speed Press, P.O. Box 7123, Berkeley, California 94707
www.tenspeed.com

Typesetting by Star Type, Berkeley
Cover design by Thomjon Borges
Printed in the United States of America

1 2 3 4 5 — 2002 2001

www.JobHuntersBible.com

This book has a companion Web site, which began on the site of the *Washington Post* in 1996, and now has its own URL. Everything on the site is completely free (you don't even have to register). Much material supplementing this book, can be found there. It is an award-winning site; for example, from Dr. Randall S. Hansen at www.quintcareers.com:

QUINTESSENTIAL CAREERS SITE AWARD, 12/4/2000:
JobHuntersBible.com

"Quintessential Careers honors one career or job site each issue of *QuintZine* with the *Quintessential Careers Site Award* in recognition of quintessential efforts in helping jobseekers.

"We got a little lost on this site, and not because navigation is difficult, but because there's so much interesting stuff here to check out. Richard Nelson Bolles, guru behind the phenomenally popular *What Color Is Your Parachute?*, is also the brains behind this helpful Web site.

"We've always felt that Bolles' approach in *Parachute* was particularly well suited to career changers, perhaps even more than to entry-level jobseekers. And his JobHuntersBible.com is true to form, offering abundant information to those seeking to leave one career for another.

"The site consists of Bolles' guide to job-hunting on the Internet along with a collection of articles written by Bolles and two other experts. Many of the articles are excellent for career-changers, and the site also offers an advice column by Bob Rosner called 'The Working Wounded' to help people cope with the problems they face in their current jobs.

"Few experts are as uniquely qualified to offer career guidance as Bolles is, so his site is a 'must-see' for career-changers and, indeed, all job-seekers."

Contents

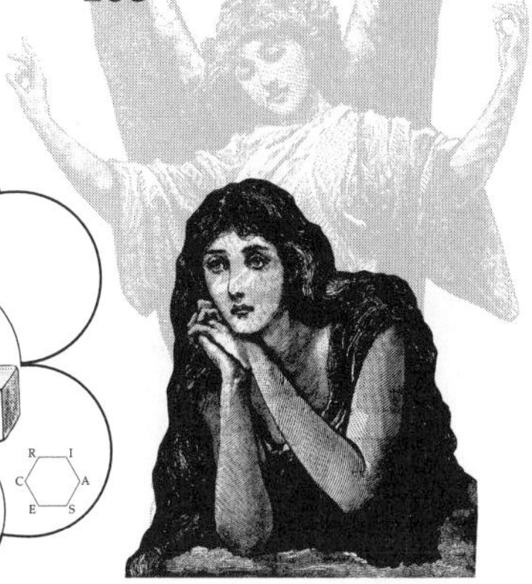

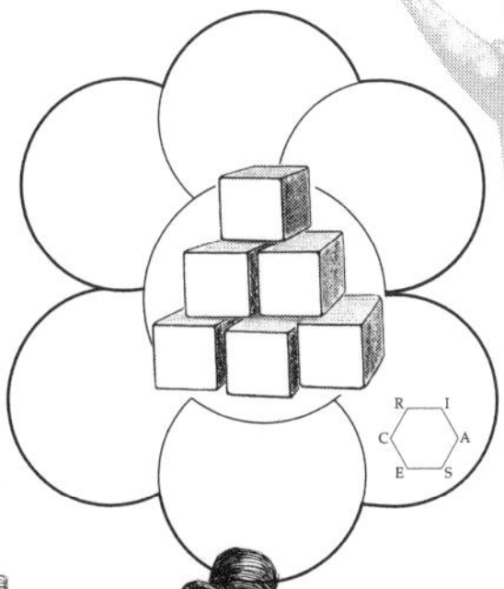
R
I
C
A
E
S

To Carol Christen,
The love of my life,
Now and always.

Preface to the 2002 Edition

I am not, essentially, a career counselor. I come, rather, from a journalism family. My grandfather, Stephen, was the editor of a daily newspaper (*The Janesville Gazette,* from Janesville, Wisconsin). Don, my father, was an editor for the Associated Press. Don, my brother, was a famous investigative reporter for *The Arizona Republic* in Phoenix, Arizona, who was assassinated in 1976 when malefactors put a bomb under his car at high noon in downtown Phoenix, and blew him up.

Though I myself have technically never been a journalist, I do have all the instincts and training of an investigative reporter, because of this family history. Hence, when friends of mine many years ago begged me to assist them with their job-hunt, I went and investigated "the job-hunt" as a reporter would, and reported back to my friends (in a 1970 self-published book) what they were 'up against' in the job-hunting world: I wanted them to know the reality vs. the illusion.

It was The W.E. Upjohn Institute for Employment Research, then in Washington, D.C., that very kindly gave me an office where I was able to do much of my research. There I first met Sidney Fine, Harold Sheppard, A. Harvey Belitsky, and some of the other original researchers in this field.

Seven million copies later, and throughout all the subsequent annual revisions and updating of this book, I have labored to keep this book factual and accurate, as any good investigative reporter would.

However, as this book has been found by readers in other countries around the world *(it is now in over 10 languages, and used in dozens and dozens of countries)* I have had to be content with digging up statistics from one country only, and that is my own, the U.S.A. Readers from other lands would of course like me to include statistics for their country as well, but I am just one investigator, who toils alone, and I have neither the time, space, or staff, to do multi-country research. I take comfort, as you may too, in the fact that this is basically a practical job-hunting manual, not a *world almanac.* And statistics, here, are not intended to *prove* anything, but merely to *illustrate* the general themes and strategies that I am discussing. For that illustrative intent, any example -- even just a U.S. one -- will do.

As I have uncovered problems with the job-hunt, I have of course labored to find solutions. Some of these solutions, over the years, have been mine, such as the concepts of *informational interviewing, trioing, The Party Exercise (of John Holland's work),* and so forth. But mostly the solutions have come forth from other people, and I have merely synthesized their ideas, into one broad system and one small book. The six thinkers who have had the most influence on me, over the years, have been Sidney Fine, the original *father* of the *Dictionary of Occupational Titles;* John Crystal, my earliest mentor in this field, who died in 1988; Daniel Porot, inventor of the system called *PIE,* and my colleague and co-teacher for over 20 years past, who is one of the most original thinkers and best trainers about the *nitty-gritty* of job-hunting that I have ever run into; John L. Holland, inventor of *The Holland Code* system of vocational choice; and -- lastly -- two of my own former students, John Webb and Debra Angel, both of whom have come up with some of the most original and ingenious *twists* upon my ideas (and those of my co-teacher, Daniel Porot) that I have ever seen.

As the years have gone by, I have never tried to "pass the baton" (as they say); but there have sprung up spontaneously over the years (I prefer to say, *God raised up*) a number of my former students who are doing truly wonderful work, based on the ideas in this book, in this and other countries. The ones I rely on most heavily are: John Webb and Madeleine Leitner in Germany, Brian McIvor in Ireland, Debra Angel in Australia and the U.K., Marie-Carmelle Roy in Canada; and Jim Kell and David Bennett in the U.S. There are other unsung heroes in those and other countries, too numerous to name here; but many of them may be found listed in the back of this book (on pp. 371ff).

I conclude this Preface, with my annual bunch of heartfelt thank you's -- gratitude that never grows old:

• My thanks first of all to all my readers, and most especially to the two thousand or so, who write me each year. I deeply regret I can no longer answer each individual correspondent, which I did in my younger days. But with the invention of eMail, I am inundated, and can no longer keep up. I still *read* every one of the letters that come in, whether by the postal service (P.O. Box 379, Walnut Creek, CA 94597-0379), or by fax (925-837-5120) or by eMail (**RNBolles@aol.com**) -- and feel that no author could possibly ask for more loving, and appreciative readers -- not in a million years. So if you write me about how this book changed your life, or *whatever*, you can be absolutely assured that I will read what you have to say, and ponder it well, though I cannot acknowledge or answer your kind letter. However, if you have a question that needs answering, and it has to do with job-hunting problems, you can eMail my devoted friend and job-expert, Jim Kell *(a saint if ever there was one)* at **jkell@texas.net,** and he has volunteered to answer as many such letters as he possibly can, without charge. Alternatively, you can contact any of the counselors who live near you, listed on pp. 371ff.

• My thanks also to the many other leaders in this field, all of whom are friends of mine: I think specifically of Howard Figler, Arthur Miller, Dick Lathrop, Dick Knowdell, Dean Curtis, Paul Tieger, and Martin Yate -- plus the six I saluted earlier, along with many of my own former students. Our exchange of ideas with each other is true *community* at its best.

• I have a thousand friends, and family, and from among them I want to single out one of my sons, Gary Bolles, consultant and columnist in the whole Internet field, former editor-in-chief of *Network Computing* magazine, former editor-in-chief of *Inter@ctive Week* magazine, former TV host on TechTV, etc., for all his counsel and advice about online job-hunting. While I spend hours and hours per week on the Internet myself, sifting through all the media 'claims' about the wonders of the Internet vs. job-hunters' actual experience with the Internet, I have had to rely on him again and again for his expertise, which is as great in his field as mine is in mine. He generously gives me hours of his time, month after month, so I (and you) are greatly in his debt; and also in the debt of Pete Weddle, Mary Ellen Mort, Margaret Riley, and John Sumser, for their counsel too, about the Internet and the job-hunt. Needless to say, none of them are responsible for any of the opinions I express, or the statistics that I use; if any of these grieve you, it is I alone who am responsible.

• More thanks -- this time to all the folks over at Ten Speed Press in Berkeley, California, who labor so hard to get this book out, each year: Bev Anderson, my brilliant friend and layout artist for all of the past 30 years, Jackie Wan, my eagle-eyed proof-reader for almost as long, Aaron Wehner, my friend and liaison at Ten Speed, Hal Hershey, the production manager at Ten Speed, Linda Davis, my typesetter, and Kristin Casemore, my publicist.

• My thanks to my extended family, near and far: my sister, Ann Johnson, of Mt. Holly, New Jersey; my four grown children, Stephen, Mark, Gary and Sharon, and my dear stepdaughter, Serena -- they have been wonderful to me; as has my faithful staff and secretaries: Norma Wong, Suzanne Anderson, and Loretta Walsh. I thank God for their devotion and dedication to helping people.

• I lost four dear people out of my life this year, one by divorce (my beloved wife of fifteen years, Carol) and three by death in the arms of God: my ninety-seven-year-old aunt, Sister Esther Mary, of the Community of the Transfiguration (Episcopal) in Glendale, Ohio, who taught me to serve the Lord, from my youth up; a famous psychic and dear friend of mine for many years, Jack Schwarz, of Ashland, Oregon (we used to go white-water rafting together); and last, but hardly least, a beloved colleague of mine in this field, Yana Parker, author of *The Damn Good Resume Book,* who died after a long battle with cancer. I thank God for all of them -- their example, their lives and their love.

• In closing, I'd have to be an ingrate not to mention my profound thanks to The Great Lord God, Father of our Lord Jesus Christ, and source of all grace, wisdom, and compassion, Who has given me this work of helping so many people of different faiths, tongues, and nations, with their job-hunt, and with finding meaning for their lives. I am grateful beyond measure for such a life, such a mission, and such a privilege.

Dick Bolles
P.O. Box 379
Walnut Creek
California 94597-0379
Wednesday, September 12, 2001

My Annual Grammar & Language Footnote

I want to explain four points of grammar, in this book of mine: pronouns, commas, italics, and spelling. My unorthodox use of them invariably offends unemployed English teachers so much that they write me to apply for a job as my editor.

To save us unnecessary correspondence, let me explain. Throughout this book, I often use the apparently plural pronoun "they," "them," or "their" after *singular* antecedents - - such as, "You must approach *someone* for a job and tell *them* what you can do." This sounds strange and even *wrong* to those who know English well. To be sure, we all know there is another pronoun - - "you" - - that may be either singular or plural, but few of us realize that the pronouns "they," "them," or "their" were also once treated as both plural and singular in the English language. This changed, at a time in English history when agreement in *number* became more important than agreement as to sexual *gender*. Today, however, our priorities have shifted once again. Now, the distinguishing of sexual *gender* is considered by many to be more important than agreement in *number.*

The common artifices used for this new priority, such as "s/he," or "he and she," are - - to my mind - - tortured and inelegant. Casey Miller and Kate Swift, in their classic, *The Handbook of Nonsexist Writing,* agree, and argue that it is time to bring back the earlier usage of "they," "them," and "their" as both singular and plural - - just as "you" is/are. They further argue that this return to the earlier historical usage has already become quite common *out on the street* - - witness a typical sign by the ocean which reads "*Anyone* using this beach after 5 p.m. does so at *their* own risk." I have followed Casey and Kate's wise recommendations in all of this.

As for my commas, they are deliberately used according to my own rules - - rather than according to the rules of historic grammar (which I did learn - - I hastily add, to reassure my old Harvard professors, who despaired of me weekly, during English class). In spite of those rules, I follow my own, which are: to write conversationally, and put in a comma wherever I would normally stop for a breath, were I *speaking* the same line.

The same conversational rule applies to my use of *italics.* I use *italics* wherever, were I speaking the sentence, I would put *emphasis* on that word or phrase. I also use italics where there is a digression of thought, and I want to maintain the main thought and flow of the sentence. All in all, I write as I speak. Hence the 'dashes' (--) to indicate a break in thought.

Finally, some of my spelling is *weird.* (Well, some might say "weird"; I prefer just "playful.") I happen to like spelling it "eMail", for example, instead of "Email." Fortunately, since this is my own book, I get to play in my own way; I'm so grateful that seven million readers have *gone along.* Nothing delights a child (at heart) more, than being allowed to play.

P.S. Speaking of "playful," over the last thirty years a few critics (very few) have claimed that *Parachute* is not serious enough (they object to the cartoons, which find fun in almost *everything*). A few have claimed that the book is *too* serious, and too complicated in its vocabulary and grammar for anyone except a college graduate. Two readers, however, have written me with a different view.

The first one, from England, said there is an index that analyzes a book to tell you what grade in school you must have finished, in order to be able to understand it. My book's index, he said, turned out to be 6.1, which means you need only have finished sixth grade in a U.S. school in order to understand it.

Here in the U.S., a college instructor came up with a similar finding. He phoned me to tell me that my book was rejected by the authorities as a proposed text for his college course, because the book's language/grammar was not up to college level. "What level was it?" I asked. "Well," he replied, "when they analyzed it, it turned out to be written on an eighth-grade level."

Sixth or eighth grade -- that seems just about right to me. Why make job-hunting complicated, when it can be expressed so simply even a child could understand it?

R.N.B.

*The Inquiring Reporter
asked the young woman why
she wanted to be a mortician.
"Because," she said, "I enjoy
working with people."*

The San Francisco Chronicle

CHAPTER ONE

What Are You Looking For?

WHEN IT IS TIME for you to go job-hunting, you may think you have no choice. But you do. And that's because there is more than one kind of job-hunt. Two, in fact. And you get to choose which one you want to pursue.

The choice is between doing **a traditional job-hunt**, or **doing a life-changing job-hunt**. At some times in your life a traditional job-hunt will be all you need. At other times, a life-changing job-hunt will look a lot more desirable. It just depends on what you're looking for -- at that, *or this,* particular time in your life.

You get to choose. And you get to make this choice at least eight times in your life, because that's how many times the average person gets to go job-hunting -- at a minimum. And each time you face the job-hunt, there's that choice again. *"Shall I do just a traditional job-hunt? Or shall I embark on a life-changing job-hunt, this time?"*

It would probably help if we begin by laying out the difference between the two.

The Two Kinds of Job-Search

Traditional The Traditional Job Hunt is A Matching Game	Life-Changing A Life-Changing Job Hunt is An Exploration
Overall, you are looking to stay in the same line of work as before.	Overall, you are looking for a new kind of work.
Wanting basically to put bread on the table.	Wanting basically to put a sense of mission into your life.
Wanting to get this job-hunt over as quickly as possible, and with minimal effort.	Wanting to do this job-hunt right, even if it takes longer and requires more effort.
Relying primarily on your resume, seeking to match it to employers' ads or job postings.	Relying primarily on homework, research, and contacts to find a new career.
Looking for organizations that are known to have vacancies.	Looking for organizations that you would like to work at, whether or not they are known to have vacancies.
Looking for a match between your resume and some job that employers are already advertising.	Looking for a place where you (like a flower) can grow -- even if you have to talk them into creating a job there, that matches your skills and passion.
Since a traditional job-hunt is a matching-game, this means that the Internet is usually the best place to do this kind of job-hunt; and you can do it from the comfort of your own home.	Since a life-changing job-hunt is a kind of intuitional search, this means that hitting the streets and going face-to-face is most often necessary. It requires you "to get off your duff."
In fact, the Internet excels at performing this matching-game for you. (Comparing your resume to some employers' job listings is a very left-brained, structured activity.)	The Internet does not excel at doing an intuitional search, for you. (This is a very right-brained, unstructured search.) The Internet can be an aid, however.
If you're undecided, you try to learn as much as possible about the job-market and what it wants, since if you do decide to change your work, that will be the determining factor.	If you're undecided, you try to learn as much as possible about yourself and what you want, since if you do decide to change your work, that will be the determining factor.
It ends up with you staying on the same path, in most cases, postponing your dreams *(unless you already have them, of course).*	It ends up with going down a new path, in most cases. You have gone after your dreams, at last.

The contrast between the two main kinds of job-hunt is not necessarily so stark as this chart would suggest. It is of course possible to mix and match -- mixing some elements from one column with some elements from the other. You end up, in fact, with an infinite array of ways in which your job-hunt can be conducted.

Nonetheless, experience has shown that it is immensely helpful to get these two *main* "types" of job-hunting clear in your mind, before you decide what you want to do. Hence the chart above. And my comments that follow.

YES, THERE'S A CERTAIN AMOUNT OF PRIDE IN BEING A SELF-MADE MAN, BUT TO TELL THE TRUTH, IF I HAD IT ALL TO DO OVER AGAIN I WOULD GET A LITTLE HELP.
THAVES

1997 Thaves/Used with permission. Newspaper dist by NEA, Inc.

THE TRADITIONAL JOB-HUNT IN ITS SIMPLEST FORM

Its simplest form is found, not surprisingly, on the Internet. Even if you don't use the Internet, it's important for you to understand what is happening there. For, on the Internet, over the last ten years the traditional job-hunt has evolved into a form so simple you could almost call it "mechanical." *"Mechanical?"* Yes, on the Internet the old "matching game" (matching employers' vacancies/ads/postings against job-hunters' resumes) is done not by a human but by a "robot" -- a piece of software that's also called a "job-search agent" or a dozen other delicious names.

Here is how it works, at its simplest:

1 **You prepare your resume.** Your resume is a summary of your experience, thus far, in the world of work. It describes where you've worked, what you accomplished there, and what skills you thereby have proved you have. It's essentially *an argument*, from your past, as to what you'll be able to accomplish for them in the future. ("*Them*" means "*prospective employers.*")

2 **You post your resume** on some Internet site that a) allows you to do that; and b) has ads that are put up by employers on that same site; and c) has some "robot" or "job-search agent" (as the software is called) that will compare your resume to all those employer ads. *Incidentally, I find the word 'robot' too capable of being misunderstood, so I prefer to call them "search while you sleep" programs.*

3 **When the "search while you sleep" program finds a match** of keywords (same keywords in the employer's ad as in your posted resume) it notifies you or the employer or both by eMail that a match has been found. If you are interested, you contact the employer; or they contact you. It's all, as I said, *mechanical*. The match can be (and is) done by a piece of software. The personal element only really begins when you start talking to each other by eMail, or phone, or have a face-to-face interview thereafter.

I'll say more about each of these steps in detail, beginning on page 21. But, for now, let us simply note that the *advantage* of the traditional job-hunt done in this simplest of all possible ways -- on the Internet -- is obvious. It is quick, requires a minimum of effort, a minimum of thinking, and if things work out well, it can match your resume to some employer's ad (or "*job-posting*" as it's called on the Internet) a lot quicker than you ever could on your own. Sometimes the matching is *lightning-fast.* Moreover it enables you to match against the ads, or job-postings, of a large number of employers, and over a wide geographical area. Potentially, the world.

The *disadvantage* of the traditional job-hunt (even in this simplest of all its forms -- the Internet) is that it only works *sometimes,* and for certain occupations, and in certain areas of the country or world. And it doesn't work very well at all, if you're trying to radically change the direction of your life.

THE SECOND ALTERNATIVE: A LIFE-CHANGING JOB-HUNT

A job-hunt is just a job-hunt until we come to that point in our lives where we want to set our feet upon a new path. Then the traditional job-hunt -- the *almost-mechanical* matching of resume to vacancy -- doesn't work very well at all. A life-changing job-hunt requires a different approach.

You're contemplating radically shifting direction. This is called by various names. Sometimes it's called "Finding Your Dream Job." Sometimes it's called "a career change."

> **U.S. Statistics**
>
> In the most recent year for which I have statistics, a survey found that 45% of all U.S. workers said they would change their careers if they could.[1]

1. The survey was done by the Roper Organization for Shearson Lehman Brothers, in 1992. I think its percentages hold true, even 10 years later. I've seen these same percentages since 1970.

In point of fact, each year about 10% of all U.S. workers actually do. In the most recent year surveyed, that equated to 10 million workers who changed careers that year. Of these:

5.3 million of them changed careers *voluntarily*, and in 7 out of 10 cases their income went up;

1.3 million of them changed careers *involuntarily*, because of what happened to them in the economy, and in 7 out of 10 cases, their income went down;

3.4 million of them changed careers for a *mixture* of voluntary and involuntary reasons (such as needing to go from part-time to full-time work, etc.), and there is no record of what happened to their income.

Despite the *myth* that career-change is primarily a mid-life phenomenon, in point of fact people can and do change careers at *all* ages. In this study, only one out of ten career-changers was actually in mid-life.[2]

WHAT PUSHES US TO DO A LIFE-CHANGING JOB-HUNT?

We make this decision to not just do a traditional job-hunt, for one of several reasons:

- We made a bad choice when we first chose our career, and now we've decided to set it right.
- We've been asked to do the work of three, and we feel stressed out, angry, exhausted, burnt out, and grumpy; we want a job or career that is a little easier on us, so we'll have time to smell the flowers.
- We've decided we want to go into business for ourselves. We want to be self-employed (12% of all the workers in the U.S. are self-employed).

2. The year was 1986. The survey was published in the *Occupational Outlook Quarterly*, Summer 1989, and in the *Monthly Labor Review*, September 1989. Not all that much has changed, since, I'm sorry to say.

- We are not earning enough, and we need a life change that pays us more money -- more of what we're worth.
- We had a dream job, but our much-beloved boss moved on, we now find ourselves working for 'a jerk,' and our former dream job has turned into 'the job from hell.' We not only want a new employer, we want a new career.
- We had been hardly stretched at all by our previous work, and we'd like something that offers a real challenge and 'stretches' us.
- All we wanted from a job, in the past, was money; now we want *meaning*. Indeed, if truth be told, most of us are engaged in a life-long search for, and journey toward, *meaning* - - a process in which a life change is mandated.
- We're looking more and more for 'our mission in life,' and while we don't yet know what that is, we do know for sure that what we're presently doing *isn't it.*

ARLO & JANIS reprinted by permission of NEA, Inc.

- We got fired, and we can't find our old work any more; we *have* to 're-tool.' (Twenty years ago, if you were let go, laid off, sacked, 'made redundant,' 'downsized,' or fired, it was universally assumed it was because of your job performance (i.e., *you were the only one 'let go,' and you deserved to be sacked*). Now, it is almost universally assumed that it was not your fault (i.e., *these days, employers decide to reduce their work force* en masse *at the drop of a hat*).

For any or all of these reasons, you may be at a place in your life where you don't just want a traditional job-hunt; you want a life-changing job-hunt.

WHAT ARE THE STEPS IN DOING A LIFE-CHANGING JOB-HUNT?

There are three steps in doing a life-changing job-hunt, just as there are three steps in doing the traditional job-hunt, in its simplest form:

1 **It begins with your defining just exactly what it is that you're looking for,** by way of change. There are six possibilities: a) You may be looking for a change in occupation, which is to say, job-title (and tasks). b) You may be looking for a change in field. c) You may be looking for a change in the kinds of people you work with. d) You may be looking for a change in your work environment. e) You may be looking for a kind of work that is more in keeping with the goals and values you have set for your life. f) You may be looking for a change (sometimes a great change) in salary. You may be looking for one of these, several of these, or all of these. The two most common ones in a life-changing job-hunt are: a change in occupation, and a change in field. They add up to what our culture calls a "career-change."

2 **You must consider the four pathways to a career-change,** if that is what you're looking for. It is widely assumed that there is only one pathway. It is widely assumed that the only way to make a career-change is to go back to school and get re-trained in a new occupation. But this is simply not true. It is *one way*, but it's not *the only way* by a long shot. Millions of people make a career-change each year without going back to school. That's because

there are three other pathways to career-change, which are illustrated in the following diagrams:

Types of Career-Change Visualized

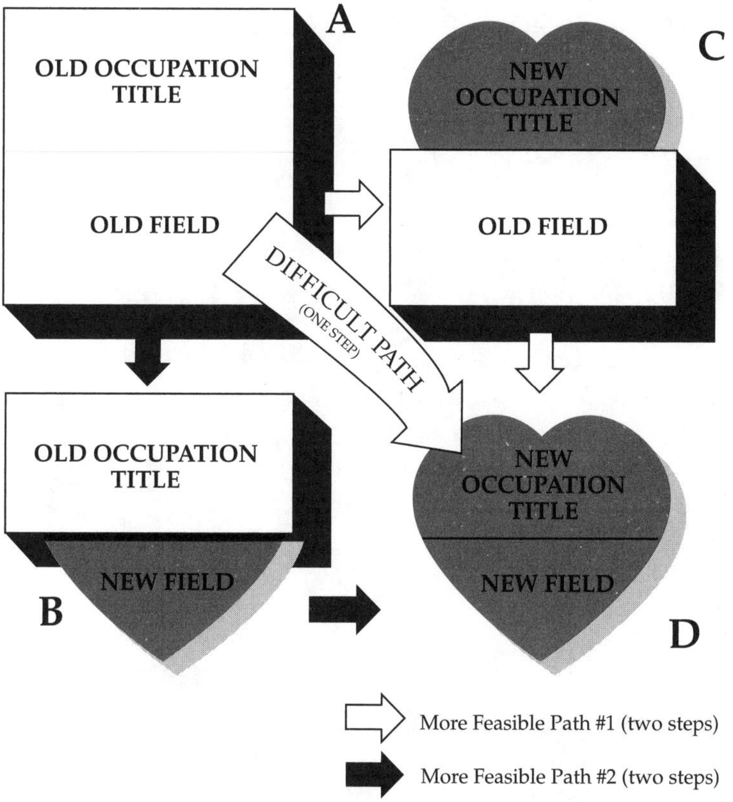

As we see here, if you want a career-change, you can change just your occupation; or just your field; or you can change both your occupation and your field. If you choose to do the latter, there are three pathways you can take:

a) *You Can Do It In a Single Bound* (The Difficult Path): The move can be made all at once by going from A to D (above) in a single bound.

b) *You Can Do It One Step at a Time* (More Feasible Path #1): Here, the move is made in two steps, as indicated by the two white arrows, where you first change only your occupation, but not your field; then, later, your field as well.

c) *You Can Do It One Step at a Time* (More Feasible Path #2): Here, the move is made in two steps, as indicated by the two black arrows, where you first change only your field, but not your occupation; then, later, your occupation as well.

Types of Career-Change Visualized

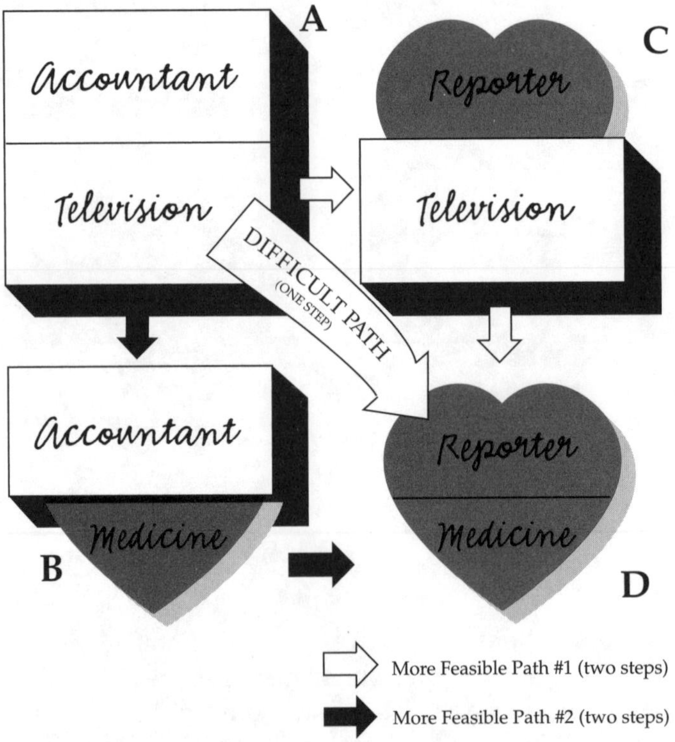

3 **You must do a certain amount of homework on yourself, to define exactly what is the occupation and what is the field you want to go into; and then go find it.**

This homework has three steps: WHAT, WHERE, AND HOW. They go like this:

***What:* You must decide just exactly what you have to offer to the world.** This involves identifying your gifts, or talents -- which is to say, your favorite skills, in order of priority or importance to you. Experts call these your transferable skills, because they are transferable to any field/career that you choose, regardless of where you first picked them up, or how long you've used them in some other field.

> Once you know your skills, you have the building-blocks of your *occupation*; and with these building-blocks, you can define an occupation that you love to do.

***Where:* You must decide just exactly where you want to use your skills.** This involves identifying your favorite subjects or fields of interest, as well as your geographical preferences, which you then explore through research (in books or on the Internet), and personal informational interviewing. *Where* is primarily a matter of the fields of knowledge you have already acquired, which you most enjoy using. But it also has to do with your preferred working conditions, what kinds of data or people or things you enjoy working with, where you'd most like to live, etc.

> Once you know your favorite subjects, you have the building-blocks of your *field*; with these building-blocks, you can define a field that you would love to do your occupation in. Also, you can now put occupation and field together, and voila! you have defined a new career.

How: You must go after the organizations that interest you the most, whether or not they are known to have a vacancy. 'Going after them' means using your contacts -- anybody you know -- to get an appointment there; specifically, to get an appointment with the one individual there who actually has the power to hire you for the job that you want to do. (Of course, you must have done a little research on them first, to find out just exactly who that is, not to mention other valuable information about the organization's goals, etc. Here the Internet may be helpful, as its research function and usefulness is sometimes superb.)

I'll say more about each of these steps in detail (pp. 156ff) But, for now, let us simply note that the *advantage* of a life-changing job-hunt is obvious. It prods you to do a lot of thinking about who you really are, what you really want out of life, what you have to give to the world, and what you want to accomplish with your life before you depart this world. It often changes your life, completely.

The *disadvantage* of the life-changing job-hunt, of course, is that it is not quick, it requires quite a bit of effort, and it requires a maximum of thinking -- just the opposite of the traditional job-hunt (at least as done on the Internet).

IN CONCLUSION

As I said at the beginning, when it is time for you to go job-hunting, you may think you have no choice. But you do. And that's because there is more than one kind of job-hunt. Two, in fact. And you get to choose which one you want to pursue. Traditional, or life-changing.

Furthermore, you have another choice. You can choose to just *find a job*. Or you can choose to use this particular job-hunt as a *way to master the job-hunt process* for all the rest of your life. The average person goes job-hunting at least eight times in their life; so it is likely that you will be going through this experience, again and again. You can choose to just look for a job, or you can choose to master the job-hunt *now*, so that at all times in the future you know how to avoid not only *unemployment* but also *underemployment*.

If you set this as your goal, it can have a rich payoff. For, as job-expert Richard Lathrop observed long ago, the person who gets hired is not necessarily the best person for the job, but the one who knows the most about how to get hired.

Well, yes, you do have
great big teeth; but, never mind
that. You were great to at
least grant me this interview.
Little Red Riding Hood

Chapter Two

Job-Hunting At Warp Speed

EATING UP THE MILES AND MINUTES

Back in 1985, the late John Crystal used to describe the ridiculousness of our traditional job-hunting 'system.' A job-hunter, he would say, would be walking down a street, despairing of ever finding the work he wanted; and, brushing past him, with a hurried, "Excuse me," would be an employer who was hunting desperately for exactly that man or woman with exactly those talents and experience. But that would be the last they would ever see of each other. Both job-hunter and employer would end the day frustrated and baffled, because -- John said -- our job-hunting 'system' has not come up with any good way for them to ever find each other. They had passed 'like ships in the night.'

But now it is the year 2001, or later, and we have fixed all that. We have invented the worldwide Internet -- first for military purposes, then for educational and research purposes, and now for every purpose under the sun, including job-hunting. Job-hunting is very big, these days, on the Internet, and more particularly, on that graphical part of it called 'The Worldwide Web' (www).

No one agrees on the *number* of Internet sites currently devoted to job-hunting -- some experts say 1,000; some say 5,000; some, 10,000; some 40,000; and some, 100,000 or more. But all agree on the *purpose* of Internet sites devoted to job-hunting. And that is, to make it easier for job-hunter and employer to find each other. It is, indeed, far far easier than it was back in 1985.

Also faster. *If* you play your cards right, and *if* there is a favorable wind, and *if* the stars are moving pleasantly in their courses, it is now *possible* for you and an employer to find each other in one day -- sometimes, even, in one hour.

That is, if you have access to the Internet. Many people don't, but would like to have it. And then there are people who choose not to have it, who would, in fact, rather be tortured than ever go on the Internet.

For all those who lack Internet access or interest, I'll have more -- much more -- to say, later, about how one does the traditional job-hunt *without* using the Internet. (pp. 69ff.)

THE GROWING IMPORTANCE OF THE INTERNET IN THE TRADITIONAL JOB-HUNT

For now, we must notice that Internet access is available to more and more job-hunters, month by month. Of course, *having access* and *actually using it* are two different subjects. Countless millions of people have access to a movie theater, but that doesn't mean they are in the theater in any particular period of time. *Access* speaks only of an opportunity, that may or may not be taken advantage of.

But, let us speak in terms of opportunity. Currently, in the U.S. at least, more adults have access to the Internet than don't. Of regular users, some can access it from their home; the remainder, from work. But, except in remote and undeveloped regions, many more *could* access it if they wanted to.

Internet Access

If you don't have access at home or work, you can usually find it by going to one of the following:

- One of the increasingly popular commercial *Internet cafes.* These are known by a different name in virtually every city, village and hamlet, around the world--a list of more than 4,000 of them, in over 148 countries, can be found at `www.Netcafes.com/`
- Your local public library; additionally, many librarians have time and are willing to take the trouble to show you how to use the machine, if it's brand-new to you
- Your local state or government employment centre
- A local large bookstore
- Internet kiosks in all kinds of places: airports, bookstores, stationery stores, coffee shops, and local print shops (such as *Kinko's*), plus places you'd never think of, like: rest areas along freeways, etc.

I will say this a dozen times, throughout this book: all statistics are confined to the U.S. All statistics are outdated before you can even put them on paper, but currently as I write, this is how things stand.

The Percentages in the U.S.

At least 58% of American men now have Internet access.
At least 54% of American women now have Internet access.
At least 66% of parents with children living at home now have access.
At least 75% of those age 18–29 now have access.
At least 82% of those with college or graduate degrees now have access.
At least 82% of those in households with income exceeding $75,000 now have access.[1]

1. Source (for this and following percentages): *The Pew Report,* 2/18/01.

The Numbers in the U.S.

Approximately 100 million American adults have Internet access as of June 2001.

58 million American adults were online on a typical day (December 2000).

The average American user spent 4.2 hours a week (November 2000)[2] or 16.5 hours a month (November 2000)[3] online.

Elsewhere

In Europe, the countries with the most Internet users are the UK, Germany, France, Italy, Spain, Denmark, Norway, and Switzerland.[4]

Wild Life by John Kovalic, © 1977 Shetland Productions. Reprinted by permission.

Now, let us turn from *opportunity* to the subject of *actual use.* The 58 million American adults who were online on a particular day, weren't there necessarily to do job-hunting. In fact, we know that 48 million were there to read or send their eMail,[5] among other things. Okay, so how many were also there to do job-hunting -- or are likely to be, in the future?

---

2. Source: PricewaterhouseCoopers.
3. Source: Nielsen/NetRatings.
4. Source: CyberAtlas, at Internet.com, 4/8/01.
5. Source: *The Pew Report*, 5/21/01.

Job-Hunters Online

Again, any statistics about the Internet or the Web are outdated before you can even put them on paper, but currently as I write, this is how things stand:

Traffic to job-hunting Web sites increased 80% from 1999 to 2000.

67% of all Web users expect to conduct their next job search online.[6]

40% of *new* Web users come online specifically to look for employment opportunities.[7]

These are not necessarily the young, as one might expect. In fact, the age group most represented among online job-seekers are people with 21 or more years' experience in the workplace.[8]

Where do they go, once online?

According to one survey, 95% of online job-seekers visit three or more sites; "they know that no single site can do everything for them."[9]

67% of online job-seekers visited corporate sites, to do research.

50% of online job-seekers visited non-corporate sites, like government sites, Dotcomfailures.com, Hoovers, etc.

43% of online job-seekers used the Web for salary research.

37% of online job-seekers looked for a technology-related position.[10]

21% of online job-seekers searched for administrative jobs.

6% of online job-seekers sought executive positions.

---

6. Source: A study by Greenfield Online.
7. Source: Headhunter.net, as reported in *WEDDLE*'s, July 2000.
8. Source: *WEDDLE*'s, September 2000.
9. Ibid. (for this statistic and the following ones).
10. Source (for this statistic and the following ones): Computing Canada, 3/2000.

PLAYING THE GAME

So much for background. Now, let us suppose you either have or could have Internet access, and you want to do your job-hunting at warp speed (as it were). What do you do? We saw the *basic* outline in our previous chapter *(unless you skipped our previous chapter)*:

1 **You prepare your resume.** Your resume is a summary of your experience, thus far, in the world of work. It describes where you've worked, what you accomplished there, and what skills you thereby have proved you have. It's essentially *an argument*, from your past, as to what you'll be able to accomplish for them in the future. ("*Them*" means "*prospective employers*.")

2 **You post your resume** on Internet sites where employers go to look. For job-hunting at warp speed you most particularly want sites a) that allow you to post your resume; and b) that also have ads put up by employers on that same site; and c) that have some 'robot' or 'job-search agent' or 'job-agent' (as the software is variously called) that will compare your resume to all those employer ads.

3 When **the "search while you sleep" program finds a match** of keywords (same keywords in the employer's ad as in your posted resume) it notifies you or the employer or both by eMail that a match has been found. If you are interested, you contact the employer; if they are interested, they contact you.

It *can* all happen very fast, for you. Warp speed.

But, of course, it *can* also happen very slowly, for you.

And, oh sad but true, it *can* happen not at all, for you. So, if a match isn't appearing quickly, you will want to supplement the 'warp speed' job-hunting by doing a methodical search, on your own, of employers' vacancies as posted on the Web.

THE RULES
OF JOB-HUNTING
AT WARP SPEED

1. Prepare Your Resume

Easier said than done. Of course! No one was born knowing how to write a resume. It's a craft, that has to be mastered. If, over the years, you've become good at putting together a resume that works, then proceed! If not, and you're kind of new to all this, well, mercifully there is help readily at hand.

Advice on the Web

Organizations that want you to post your resume on the Web (more particularly, on *their* site), have of course made sure there's loads of free advice there about how to write the kind of resume they want to see.

> "Resumes make sense: there is no way a harried executive or department head can set aside the time to interview every inquiry about employment that is made to his or her organization; there is not enough time."
>
> *(Anon.)*

124,696

Best advice on the Internet about how to write your online resume? Canadian job-expert Gary Will asked himself that very question, so he combed the Web, searched for such articles, and then put together an excellent list of the ones he felt were the best at that time (new ones, after all, appear weekly on the Internet--sometimes in some very obscure places). He even gave the articles various *star ratings*. I agree with his opinions and I like his ratings. The url currently is: **`http://members.nbci.com/worksearch/reswri.htm`**. If that url changes by the time you get this, just pull up a meta-search engine like Metacrawler (**`http://www.metacrawler.com/`**) type in the three terms "Gary Will resumes" and in the resultant list, the new url should appear. Alternatively, if Gary's site ever goes 'belly-up,' for whatever reason, you can do your own research. Just type in the search words: 'how to write a resume' and see what turns up. Good articles will say something about how you employ 'key words' in your online resume, so as to get employers' (and their search engines') attention. Either way, find the articles, read the ones that sound interesting, make notes, then write your resume. *Cost of this help to you: $ 0.*

Help from Friends

Alternative method: You ask every friend you have if they are good at writing a resume that works. Friends who merely say they're good writers don't count. A resume is "good writing plus." Acid test: did their resume actually help them (or help a friend) get a job? If you find a friend who's good at writing resumes *that work*, ask them for help in writing yours. *Cost of this help to you $ 0. Just take them out to dinner afterward.*

Advice in Books

For those who prefer to have a book at their elbow when learning a new craft like writing a resume, there are hundreds. The best? Gary Will says, "My picks for the best resume writing books are **Kate Wendleton's** ***Through the***

Brick Wall and **Donald Asher's *The Overnight Resume.*** Both will give you **excellent advice** that isn't yet matched by articles available through the web." (Donald Asher's book, now in its second edition, is available from: Ten Speed Press, Box 7123, Berkeley, CA 94707. Kate Wendleton's book is available from Career Press/New Page Books, 3 Tice Rd., P.O. Box 687, Franklin Lakes, NJ 07417.)

Need more book suggestions *(on the theory that "one person's meat is another person's poison")?* Here are some of my favorites:

- Richard Lathrop, *Who's Hiring Who?* 1989. Ten Speed Press, Box 7123, Berkeley, CA 94707. Richard describes and recommends "a qualifications brief"-- the idea that in approaching an employer you should offer him or her a written proposal of what you will do in the future, rather than "a resume" or summary of what you did in the past.
- Yana Parker, *Damn Good Resume Guide.* 1996. Ten Speed Press, Box 7123, Berkeley, CA 94707. Yana died last year; her good advice remains. This book describes, in ten steps, how to write functional and chronological resumes. A section on employers' comments upon resumes in the book which actually got people jobs, is especially helpful. Yana's other resume resources, available from Ten Speed Press, Box 7123, Berkeley, CA 94707, are: *The Resume Catalog: 200 Damn Good Examples* (1996); *Blue Collar & Beyond: Resumes for Skilled Trades and Services* (1995); *Ready-To-Go Resumes Software* (1995).
- David Swanson, *The Resume Solution; How To Write (and Use) A Resume That Gets Results.* 1991. JIST Works, Inc., 720 North Park Ave., Indianapolis, IN 46202-3431. (Dave was on staff at nineteen of my two-week workshops.)
- Tom Jackson, and Ellen Jackson, *The New Perfect Resume.* 1996, revised. Anchor Press/Doubleday, Garden City, NY 11530. This has always been Tom's best-selling book, and with good reason. One hundred + resume samples and some good career advice.

You can find these books either at your local bookstore, or on the Web (at, for example, `www.amazon.com/`) or directly from the publisher. *Cost of this help to you, typically: $ 20, or less.*

Help from a Live Expert

If *friends*, the *Internet*, and *books* don't help you, or just aren't "your cup of tea," there is always a live professional resume-writer, who -- for a fee -- will write a resume for you (better yet, *with* you). Where to find such a person? The Yellow Pages of your local phone book, of course: look under *Resume Service.* Also the Web has sample directories of resume writers: for example, at the National Resume Writers Association site (`www.nrwa.com`); and at the Professional Association of Resume Writers and Career Coaches site (`www.parw.com/`); and at `www.resumewriters.com/`.

Just remember: shop around before signing up with *any* professional resume-writer. Ask to see resumes they have written *that have actually helped a person get a job.* Indeed, ask to talk to those past clients. I remind you again: beautifully written resumes are not what you're looking for. You're looking for resumes *that work.* You're looking for a job. And don't think that because you pay for resume help it will automatically get you a job. It's a gamble. Your money may be going to a good cause, and then again it may not. *Cost of this help to you, typically: anything from $60 on up.*

Okay, that's it in the resume-advice department: *Web, friends, books, professionals.* Take your pick.

What you want to end up with is a resume which cites your relevant past accomplishments, taking care in each case to cite:

a) what the problem was
b) what especial obstacle (timewise, or otherwise) you had to overcome
c) what means you used to overcome the obstacle, and solve the problem
d) what the results were, of your actions, stated as concretely as possible in terms of things accomplished, money saved, money earned, etc.

It should essentially be a written proposal that looks forward rather than *(as the typical resume does)* backward. You are not asking them to do something for *you*; you are offering to do something for *them*. And citing your past accomplishments as proof that you can do, in the future, the things you claim you can do.

Final word here: don't spend *forever* putting your resume together. Otherwise, as job-expert Amy Lindgren has sardonically put it, "If you plan things just right, you will have a perfect resume by the time you're old enough to retire."

2. Search Those Sites Where Employers Go

You've got your resume; now what? But of course, you post it on one or more Web sites. Ah, and here's the tricky part: which Web sites? There are, after all, thousands. Well, if it's the traditional job-hunt at warp speed that you're looking for, then you want a Web site that:

a) *allows you to post your resume*; and

b) *has ads that are put up by employers on that same site*; and

c) *has some 'robot' or 'job-search agent' (as the software is called) that will mechanically compare your resume to all those employer ads. (As I mentioned earlier, I prefer to call them "search while you sleep" programs.)*

At this writing, some of the more prominent job sites[11] that have this "search while you sleep" capability, and will eMail you when a match is found, include:

www.monster.com
www.hotjobs.com
(now owned by Monster.com's parent, TMP)
www.flipdog.com
www.headhunter.net
www.careerbuilder.com
www.salary.com
www.jobs.com
www.joboptions.com
www.eurojobs.com

11. I'm a wee bit reluctant to mention specific sites in print since -- as job-expert Mary Ellen Mort observes -- trying to catalog the Internet is like trying to catalog a mudslide. These days, every mention of a particular site, every description of that site, every url for these sites, should come with a warning label (as it were): subject to change or may disappear without warning. Sites merge, get bought out, downsize, and vanish in the twinkling of an eye, never mind during the shelf-life of a book.

But, on the chance that my favorite sites *will* survive long enough for this book to reach your hands, I am listing particular sites here and throughout this book.

3. Wait to Be Contacted

In *job-hunting at warp speed,* once you've posted your resume on one (or more) of these sites, all you have to do thereafter is "sit back in your nice comfy armchair and let the jobs come to you," as one site puts it. "Each site will match your resume with job openings posted by employers or recruiters on the same site. Whenever there is a match you will be automatically notified by e-mail of this opening and you can respond directly."

When the **"search while you sleep" program** finds a match of keywords (same keywords in the employer's ad as in your posted resume) it notifies you or the employer or both by eMail that a match has been found. If you are interested, you contact the employer; if they are interested, they contact you. Things proceed to an interview (by phone or face-to-face) if both of you so wish

MY! HOW THINGS HAVE CHANGED!

And so we see, the Internet clearly has done a marvelous job of making it possible for an employer and a job-hunter to get together, in a way that was rarely possible even a decade or so, ago.

The evidence that this can work lies not in the theory but in actual practice -- in countless anecdotes from one job-hunter after another who have successfully conducted their job-hunt online. The media are filled with such stories.

One job-seeker, a systems administrator in Taos, New Mexico, who wanted to move to San Francisco posted his resume at 10 p.m. on a Monday night, on a San Francisco online bulletin board (*Craigslist.org*). By Wednesday morning he had over 70 responses from employers.[12]

Again, a marketing professional developed her resume following guidance she found on the Internet, posted it

12. Source: *San Francisco Chronicle*, 4/28/00.

to two advertised positions she found there, and within seventy-two hours of posting her electronic resume, both firms contacted her, and she is now working for one of them.[13]

It is not just the media that are filled with such stories. So is my mail. Here's a letter that I just received: "On May 1, 2001, I was very unexpectedly laid off from a company I was with for 5 years. I was given a copy of your book by a ministry in our church that helps people without jobs. I read the book, and it was a great source of encouragement for me. The day I was laid off I committed my job search to the Lord. He blessed us, provided for us, and gave me peace of mind throughout my job-hunt. The Internet was my lifeline in finding the right job. I did 100% of my job search and research via the Internet. I found all my leads online, sent all my resumes via email, and had about a 25% response rate that actually lead to a phone interview or a face-to-face interview. It was a software company that laid me off, and I am [now] going to work for a publishing company, a position I found online.

"[Thanks to the Internet], I found what I believe to be the ideal job in [just] 8 weeks -- a great job with a great company and great opportunities (and great compensation)."

13. Source: Freda Turner, Toolbox, *Business Journal of Jacksonville, Florida*, 12/28/00.

CONCLUSION

I receive testimonial after testimonial like this. It is obvious that, were John Crystal still alive, he would no longer need to complain about job-hunter and employer being condemned to simply pass each other on the street, 'like ships in the night.'

The Internet now permits encounter between employer and job-hunter, *at warp speed.* Hallelujah! And, ain't life grand!

*"It ain't what you don't know
that gets you in trouble;
it's what you know for sure
that ain't so."*

Mark Twain

CHAPTER THREE

But What If That Doesn't Work?

EVERY JOB-HUNTING book should answer two main questions: "What is it I'm supposed to do, in order to get a job?" *And,* "But what if that doesn't work?"

It's the second question that is *the killer*. And yet, no job-hunting plan is complete until you've got an answer to that question. That includes job-hunting on the Internet.

We saw in the previous chapter how online job-hunting has changed the whole *potential* for job-hunter and employer to find each other, around the country and around the world. I would now love to report[1] to you that this potential has been fully realized -- that job-hunting on the Internet works just as I described, and works like a charm 100% of the time. Unfortunately it does not. In fact -- alas and alack! -- it only works a depressingly small percentage of the time. For a host of reasons, most jobs are not filled through the Internet.

1. My own educational background is not only in vocation and counseling, but also in physics (at Harvard) and chemical engineering (at the Massachusetts Institute of Technology). As a 'techie' then, I always hope that technology will work as advertised, and get no joy in having to report that it does not.

To demonstrate this, I can offer you some statistics.[2] They are of course only from one country (the U.S.). And they will, of course, be outdated before I even write them down, but they will give you some insight into why online job-hunting so often goes awry.[3]

96% Two studies illuminate how small a number of jobs are found through the Internet. Forrester Research, in a study of 3,000 Internet-using job-seekers, found that only 4% had actually landed their most recent job by going online.[4] The other 96% found their job off the Internet. (Some other percentages: *40% of online job-hunters found their job not through the Internet, but through personal referrals or by direct application. And 23% of online job-hunters found their job not through the Internet but by responding to newspaper ads. The remaining 33% fall into 'miscellaneous.'*)

In a parallel finding, Employment Management Association's 2000 "Cost per Hire and Staffing Metrics Survey," discovered that only 8% of employers' "new hires" were derived from the Internet.

In other words, 96% of all online-job-hunters finally found their job in ways other than on the Internet. And employers find 92% of their new employees in ways other than through the Internet.[5]

2. These must, of necessity, be U.S. statistics, as nine out of every ten copies of *Parachute* are sold in the U.S. I have neither the staff nor the space to list statistics for the other 30 countries where *Parachute* is bought and read.
3. In the U.S. at least (though with similar ratios likely in many other countries).
4. The study, called "The Career Networks" was released by Forrester Research in the spring of the year 2000.
5. This survey was reported in *WEDDLE's*, 8/1/00.

Oops! What went wrong? What's going wrong? Why doesn't job-hunting on the Internet work like a charm, 100% of the time?

Various studies turned up these reasons.

74% According to one study, 74% of online job-hunters experienced some degree of failure in applying for a job online, and 40% ended in complete failure; that is, they couldn't apply for the job that *especially* interested them.[6] As one job-hunter put it, *"It just don't work the way it's s'posed to."* Poorly designed job-sites were often the problem: broken links, pages that won't open, navigation systems that just don't work, and (often) when you fill out the form presented, and try to send it, your computer just 'hangs.' Not all the time, of course, of course, but 'way too much' of the time.

And even if your job application does go through, it can take an organization *forever* to work its way through the follow-up hiring cycle. As recruiting expert Pete Weddle puts it, online job-hunters must face "a recruiting process that moves at warp speed online and at a slug's pace offline."[7] In many cases, the slug's pace turns out to be anything up to 81 days. . . . *that job-hunters are kept waiting for an answer.* I know that's unbelievable, but it's true.

45% Some online job-hunters don't start with employers' job-postings. They start by posting their own resume online -- optimistic, hopeful, and impatient. But as Charlotte Li, senior analyst at Forrester Research, and author of a Forrester study entitled, "Online Job Sites Work, Just Not Well Enough," reported: "Of those [job-hunters] who placed resumes online, not very many of them actually got responses. Forty-five percent received no

6. Source: Creative Good, reported in *WEDDLE*'s, 2/15/00.
7. Source: *WEDDLE*'s, 8/1/00.

responses at all... They're not [even] getting responses to their resumes when they submit a resume to a company."

Next depressing statistic?

35% Job-hunters can, of course, go online for reasons other than job-postings or resume-postings. There are, as it turns out, five ways in which the Internet can help you when you are job-hunting: 1. **Testing** and **counseling**. 2. **Research** -- of fields, jobs, organizations, and salaries. 3. **Networking** -- establishing contact with people, as sources of information, contacts, and referrals. 4. **Job-postings**. And of course 5. **Resume-postings**.

Some of these -- research, and counseling in particular -- work so well, that the 74% dissatisfaction we saw earlier with respect to just job-postings, is cut in half overall -- to 35%. It's a smaller figure, but take no false comfort in that! It keeps getting worse, each year. 10% were dissatisfied with their online job-hunting experience in 1998, but that figure rose to 22% in 1999, and to 35% in the year 2000. What it will be at the end of 2001 or 2002, one can only imagine.

Okay, so what specifically are online job-hunters dissatisfied with? Five things, as it turns out:

1. Many job-hunters are dissatisfied with the overwhelming amount of competition a job-hunter faces on the Internet. Experts say there are now over 16 million resumes floating around the Internet, many of them competing with yours. Incidentally, that figure was just 25,000 back in 1994.[8]
2. Many job-hunters are dissatisfied with the overwhelming amount of *Data smog*, as author David Shenk puts it. We're drowning in too much information. Currently, some experts claim that the number of job-postings left up on the Internet for *who knows how long* totals over

8. Source: eMarketer, quoted in *WEDDLE*'s, May 2000.

90 million.[9] Maybe that number is way too high. But whatever the number, it's undeniably overwhelming. That's a lot of job-postings to be searched through.

3. Speaking of which, many job-hunters are dissatisfied with the poor mechanisms the Internet has, for searching through all those resumes and job-postings. The most popular Internet search engines as I write[10] are Yahoo *(technically an index, and a portal, not an engine)*; Google and its stepchild iLOR; Ask Jeeves; Northern Light; HotBot; Dogpile; Go.com; Fast Search; Direct Hit; Infoseek; Excite; Alta Vista; Webcrawler; Lycos; Looksmart; AOL Search; MSN; Netscape Search; Flipdog *(now owned by TMP)* and Hotjobs *(also owned by TMP)* and NBCi (formerly *Snap*). A lot of engines. And yet, experts claim that no one of them covers more than 25% of the Internet's total content.[11]
4. Many job-hunters are dissatisfied with the time it takes to search for jobs. Job-hunters bring their impatience with them when they approach job-sites. (The duration of the length of time people spend looking at a page of content is about 50 seconds, some experts say.)[12]
5. Many job-hunters are dissatisfied with the partialness of the information that employers post, about their open positions. Even when interesting job postings are found, those sites often don't have enough information about the job in question.

9. Source: *WEDDLE's*, July 2000.
10. For sure, by the time you read this, this list will seem a little quaint. Search engines are born, merge, and die, at an alarming rate.
11. However, some meta-search engines, like Metacrawler, survey a number of search engines, all at the same time (in Metacrawler's case, 13 others).
12. Source: Nielsen/NetRatings, as reported in *WEDDLE's*, July 2000.

THE THREE ENEMIES OF A SUCCESSFUL JOB-HUNT

Why such obsession, here, with statistics? After all, they are only for the U.S. and even there, they're bound to change. Yes, but the basic ratios, and the basic lessons to be learned from these ratios, *won't* change. For as long as I've been in this field (that's thirty plus years) I have seen these same kinds of ratios, even back in the days of mainframe computers. I think it must have something to do with human nature, not *the latest technology*. In any event, I have become convinced that statistics are important to every job-hunter, because they help us overcome three enemies of a successful job-hunt: hype, low self-esteem, and misplaced energies. Let's look at each, in turn.

Hype

First of all, statistics help us overcome **hype**.

Hype: Exaggerated or extravagant claims made especially in advertising and promotional material.
Reality: The domain of actual or practical experience.
Webster's

It is in the land of reality that all job-hunting must live, if it is to be successful. But in the case of online job-hunting particularly, the *hype* about it is so pervasive, and so persuasive, that often sanity can only be restored by means of cold, hard statistics. Relying on just anecdotal evidence to fight the hype, is fruitless. If forty of *my* friends have had a bad experience with online job-hunting, and I tell you so, but four of *your* friends have had a good experience, you're not going to believe a word I say.

A lot of online job-hunters out there are definitely unhappy with their online job-seeking experience, and in everyday conversations they tell their friends so. But the warnings don't have much effect at all on new starry-eyed Internet job-seekers, who think the Internet is going to solve all their job-hunting problems. They are so hypnotized by the hype they read all the time, that it is almost impossible to get them to face reality.

Many job-hunters cling, and I mean *cling,* to the belief that the Internet has magically transformed job-hunting. Witness this letter (and many others like it) that I receive: "I manage/facilitate a Job Finding Club (in Canada). I myself have experimented with job searching online and posting resumes which I have created to be very generic, yet attractive to potential employers. *I have yet to be contacted by employers or have any 'matching' web site make a match for me.* But many of my Club members become confused when I tell them that the Internet is one of the most *ineffective* ways of job searching, despite all the media hyping of the wonders of the Internet and how it can work miracles."[13] Given this hypnotic influence of the *hype,* only statistics can splash cold water on our face.

Rejection Shock,
Resulting in
Low Self-Esteem

Secondly, statistics help us overcome **low self-esteem.**

Many if not most people find at times in their lives that the job-hunt is nothing but a long dreary process where, at the end, you may indeed find acceptance (a job). But prior to that it's a series of seemingly endless rejections.

My friend Tom Jackson (in his now-out-of-print *Guerrilla Tactics in the Job Market*) has written a depressingly-accurate description of many job-hunts *(where you go from employer to employer, asking, "Will you hire me?").* The answers you hear, are:

NO NO NO NO NO NO NO NO NO NO NO NO NO
NO NO NO NO NO NO NO NO NO NO NO NO NO
NO NO NO NO NO NO NO NO NO NO NO NO NO
NO NO NO NO NO NO NO NO NO NO NO NO YES.

Long before you reach the "yes," you go into what I call 'rejection shock.' You thought this was going to be easy, you thought this was going to be fast, but you're *striking out* again and again. Consequently, you experience 'rejection

13. From Cyberspace, 5/25/00. The italics are mine, added for emphasis.

shock' -- caught totally by surprise by the difference between the vision you had, and the way in which it's actually unfolding, and feeling that there is something totally wrong with *you.*

Typically, job-hunters fight 'rejection shock' by lowering their expectations, sinking into depression, feeling a real desperation and despair. Rejection shock can assume all the proportions of a major crisis in your life, your personal relations and your family, leading to withdrawal (often), or estrangement (frequently) -- where divorce is often a consequence and even suicide may be contemplated.[14]

And you learn -- oh, how you learn! -- that the worst outcome of a job-hunt is not what you thought it was. You thought it was that you wouldn't find a job. Now you know differently: the worst possible outcome of a job-hunt is that you lose your self-esteem (even if it was in pretty good shape, to begin with).

So, how do you preserve your self-esteem, through all of this? Well, great help can be found from knowing what the odds are, in the game you are playing. Let me illustrate with a 'game' outside the job-hunt.

Suppose you decide to participate in a lottery or sweepstakes, and someone tells you that ninety-nine out of every one hundred people in the lottery win some money. *That doesn't happen to be true, of course, but suppose you believe them.* Thereafter, you play the lottery a number of times, and each time you play, you fail to win. What do you think is happening to your self-esteem along the way? Well, you know what is happening: in most cases your self-esteem will be sinking like a stone.

Self-esteem falls *when you think everyone is winning, except you.*

14. My first introduction to this was when the front page of our local newspaper described a job-hunter who tied a plastic bag over his head, with a suicide note that said "Even a genius can't find a job." (He was a member of Mensa.)

Learn the real odds, and everything changes. In this case, suppose you learn the real odds *against* your winning run around 76 million to one. And suppose that thereafter you *(in a 'what-the-heck' mood)* play the lottery anyway -- a number of times, and each time, you lose. Now, what's happening to your self-esteem? Well, in most cases the losing hasn't lowered your self-esteem *because you knew what the odds were, going in.*

As with the lottery, so with the job-hunt.

1. Job-hunting is a game. (Or, at least, very much *like* a game.)
2. The most important thing you can lose in the game is your self-confidence, or self-esteem.
3. In order to avoid losing your self-confidence in the job-hunt, you must know the odds that you are working against, each time you choose a particular job-hunting strategy.
4. That way, if that strategy doesn't work, you can know it wasn't *you,* and move on to another strategy that has better odds -- with your self-confidence still high.

Misplaced Energy

Lastly, statistics help us avoid **misplaced energy.**

I refer to our spending a lot of energy looking in the wrong place, or places, for the job we want. "Place" suggests "address," of course. Great word! Jobs that are put on the Internet by employers obviously have an address. The address runs something like:

`http://www.brassring.com/jobsearch/`

Since the Web came into being, I have found it useful to think of *every* job vacancy as having *some kind* of address. Hence, the secret of successful job-hunting is:

Find your job's address.

Go there to meet it.

THE JOB WITHOUT AN INTERNET ADDRESS

If the particular job you're looking for doesn't have an *Internet* address, then what might its address be? Where could that job be found? Well, job-hunters typically guess their future job's address might be:

1. The Internet, of course -- but which *site*?
2. At the local newspaper.
3. At a private employment agency or search firm.
4. At a Federal/State agency.
5. Among an employer's friends.
6. Among an employer's present workforce.
7. On an employer's desk.
8. In an employer's mind, conceived but not followed up on, yet.
9. In an employer's mind, not even conceived yet -- except as a vague need or possible budget item, if the right person appears out of thin air.

Each time you choose a particular job-hunting strategy, you are trying to find what your future job's address might be. Guess wrong, you have a useless strategy. Guess right, you have a useful one. Let me illustrate.

THE MAN WITHOUT A TELEPHONE

I had a friend who moved to another city. We lost touch with each other. But two years later I found myself in that city, and I decided to look him up. How to find him? Well, I assumed everyone had to have a telephone, so I looked him up in the phone book. No listing. I thought maybe he had an unlisted number, so I called 'Information' and asked. Nope, not even an unlisted number. Consequently, I gave up. I concluded he had moved on to yet another city.

It turned out that I was wrong. He was still in that city; he just didn't happen to have a telephone. I had adopted the wrong strategy for finding him. I had assumed *everyone* would naturally have a telephone. Wrong! In the U.S. only 94% of all households have telephones. The other 6% don't. He was among that 6%.

I eventually found my friend. I contacted his former church, and found friends of his there who knew exactly where he had moved to. *Old friends* succeeded, where *telephone listing* failed.

And the moral of this tale?

There are only so many friends you can find, using the telephone.

There are only so many jobs you can find, using a particular job-hunting strategy, like the Internet. When that strategy doesn't work, the remedy is clear:

Change your strategy, find a friend.

Change your strategy, find a job.

There Are Always Vacancies. Organizations are born, organizations expand, workers become restless, quit, change jobs, move, become ill long-term, or become handicapped, retire, or die. There are always jobs out there waiting to be filled. The fact that you can't find those jobs only means the vacancy hasn't been advertised, or you're not using the right method to find it. When the Internet or job-postings, or agencies, or ads, or resumes, don't work, there are other ways of turning up the job you want. So, if you're coming up 'empty', you need to change the search method you've been using.

Now, what exactly do statistics have to do with all of this? Well you only have so much energy that you can give to your job-hunt. Experts say one out of every three job-hunters in the U.S. becomes an unsuccessful job-hunter, *because they abandon their job-hunt prematurely.* And if you ask them why they abandoned it, they say, "I didn't think it was going to take this long. And I ran out of energy."

Given that anybody's energy and enthusiasm for the job-hunt is limited, statistics can guide you as to *where* it is wisest to *invest what energy you do have,* and what strategy is most likely to pay off your investment of energy in it. It all comes out looking like this:

The Five Worst and the Five Best Ways to Look for a Job

The Five Worst Ways to Hunt for a Job. The five worst ways to try to find a job, listed in order from worst worst to least worst *(awful grammar!),* are:

1. **Using the Internet.**

As we have sadly seen, the success rate of this method turns out to be about 4%. That is, out of every 100 job-hunters who use the Internet as their search method exactly four of them will find a job thereby, while 96 job-hunters out of the 100 will not find the jobs that are out there -- if they use only this method to search for them. 4% is, incidentally, the summary of *a range.* If you are seeking a technical or computer-related job, an IT job, or a job in engineering, finances, or healthcare, the rate rises: I would estimate it to be 10%. But for the other 10,000 job-titles that are out there, the success rate appears to drop to around 1%. Let me remind you, before you use any job-hunting method, know the odds. That way, if you know ahead of time that the odds are really bad (as here, with online job-hunting), and subsequently you find out the method doesn't work for you, you won't take it so personally.

2. **Mailing out resumes to employers at random.**

This search method is claimed to have about a 7% success rate. That is, out of every 100 job-hunters who use this search method, 7 will find a job thereby. 93 job-hunters out of 100 will not find the jobs that are out there -- if they use only this method to search for them. I'm being generous here with my percentage. One study showed that outside the Internet only 1 out of 1470 resumes actually resulted in a job. In other words, here resumes had a 99.94% failure rate. Another study put the figure even higher: one job offer for every 1700 resumes floating around out there. If all of these figures still seem like good odds to you, here's a way to put them into perspective. Would you take an airplane, if you knew only one out of 1700 got through, to its destination? Let me remind you again: before you use any job-hunting method, know the odds. That way, if you know ahead of time that the odds are really bad (as here, with resumes), and subsequently you find out the method doesn't work for you, you won't take it so personally.

3. **Answering ads in professional or trade journals, appropriate to your field.**

   This search method, like that above, has a 7% success rate. That is, out of every 100 job-hunters who use this search method, 7 will find a job thereby. 93 job-hunters out of 100 will not find the jobs that are out there if they use only this method to search for them. I remind you again: before you use any job-hunting method, know the odds. That way, if you know ahead of time that the odds are really bad (as here, with professional and trade journal ads), and subsequently you find out the method doesn't work for you, you won't take it so personally.

4. **Answering local newspaper ads.**

   This search method has a 5–24% success rate. That is, out of every 100 job-hunters who use this search method, between 5 and 24 will find a job thereby. 76–95 job-hunters out of 100 will not find the jobs that are out there -- if they use only this method to search for them. *(The fluctuation between 5% and 24% is due to the level of salary that is being sought; the higher the salary being sought, the fewer job-hunters who are able to find a job -- using only this search method.)* The usual reminder applies.

5. **Going to private employment agencies or search firms for help.**

   This method has a 5–28% success rate, again, depending on the level of salary that is being sought. Which is to say, out of every 100 job-hunters who use this method, between 5 and 28 will find a job thereby. 72–95 job-hunters out of 100 will not find the jobs that are out there -- if they use only this method to search for them. *(The fluctuation is for the same reason as noted above. It should also be noted that the success rate of this method has risen slightly in recent years, in the case of women but not of men: in a comparatively recent study, 27.8% of female job-hunters found a job within two months, by going to private employment agencies.)* The usual reminder applies.

[*Others:* For the sake of completeness we should note that there are at least four other methods for trying to find the jobs that are out there, that technically fall into the 'Least Effective' category. These are:

Going to places where employers pick out workers.

This has an 8% success rate. *(Less than 15% of U.S. workers are union members, but it is claimed that those among them who have access to a union hiring hall, have a 22% success rate. What is not stated, however, is how long it takes to get a job at the hall, and how long a job typically lasts -- in the trades, that may be for just a few days.)*

Taking a Civil Service examination. This has a 12% success rate.

Asking a former teacher or professor for job-leads. This also has a 12% success rate.

Going to the state/Federal employment service office. This has a 14% success rate.

For all of these, the usual reminder applies.]

Now, let's look at the other side of the coin:

The Five Best Ways to Hunt for a Job. The five best ways to try to find a job, listed in order from lowest success rate to best, are:

1. **Asking for job-leads from: family members, friends, people in the community, staff at career centers -- especially at your local community college or the high school or college where you graduated.**

You ask them one simple question: do you know of any jobs at the place where you work -- or elsewhere? This search method has a 33% success rate. That is, out of every 100 people who use this search method, 33 will find a job thereby. 67 job-hunters out of 100 will not find the jobs that are out there -- if they use only this method to search for them. This is one of the five best ways to look for a job, but it should be noted that no job-hunting method is 'bulletproof.' No method works all the time and for everybody. 67 job-hunters out of 100 will still not find the jobs that are out there - - even if they use this method to search for them.

2. **Knocking on the door of any employer, factory, or office that interests you, whether they are known to have a vacancy or not.**

   This search method has a 47% success rate. That is, out of every 100 people who use this search method, 47 will find a job thereby. 53 job-hunters out of 100 will not find the jobs that are out there -- if they use only this method to search for them. This is one of the five best ways to look for a job, but it should be noted that no job-hunting method is 'bulletproof.' No method works all the time and for everybody. 53 job-hunters out of 100 will still not find the jobs that are out there -- even if they use this method to search for them.

3. **By yourself, using the phone book's Yellow Pages to identify subjects or fields of interest to you in the town or city where you are, and then calling up the employers listed in that field, to ask if they are hiring for the type of position you can do, and do well.**

   This method has a 69% success rate. That is, out of every 100 job-hunters or career-changers who use this search method, 69 will find a job thereby. 31 job-hunters out of 100 will not find the jobs that are out there -- if they use only this method to search for them. Again, this is one of the five best ways to look for a job, but it should be noted that no job-hunting method is 'bulletproof.' No method works all the time and for everybody. 31 job-hunters out of 100 will still not find the jobs that are out there -- even if they use this method to search for them.

4. **In a group with other job-hunters, using the phone book's Yellow Pages to identify subjects or fields of interest to you in the town or city where you are, and then calling up the employers listed in that field, to ask if they are hiring for the type of position you can do, and do well.**

This method has an 84% success rate. That is, out of every 100 people who use this method, 84 will find a job thereby. 16 job-hunters out of 100 will not find the jobs that are out there -- if they use only this method to search for them. Again, this is one of the five best ways to look for a job, but it should be noted that no job-hunting method is 'bulletproof.' No method works all the time and for everybody. 16 job-hunters out of 100 will still not find the jobs that are out there -- even if they use this method to search for them.

Reprinted with special permission of King Features Syndicate, Inc.

5. **Doing A Life-Changing Job-Hunt.**

This method has an 86% success rate. That is, out of every 100 job-hunters or career-changers who use this search method *(explained in chapters 6–10)*, 86 will find a job or new career thereby. It should be noted that this method's success rate is 12 times higher than the success rate for resumes. But it should also be noted that no job-hunting method is 'bulletproof.' No method works all the time and for everybody. 14 job-hunters out of 100 will still not find the jobs that are out there -- even if they use this method to search for them.

WHAT IF YOU USE MORE THAN ONE METHOD?

Ah, how brilliant you are, to have thought of that! Thanks to the studies that have been done, we happen to know the answer. In general, as you might suspect, the answer is that the greater the number of job-hunting methods any job-hunter uses, the greater his or her success at finding a job. That fact was uncovered in a study that was done over 25 years ago.[15] Makes sense, of course.

But, there's a strange twist to this, that no one could have foreseen. A more recent study uncovered the fact that the likelihood of your uncovering those jobs that are out there *increases* with each additional method that you use, but only *up to four.* If you use more than four methods, your likelihood of uncovering those jobs that are out there, starts to *decrease.*[16]

I have pondered this bizarre finding, and concluded that the explanation may lie in the fact that if you try to do more than four methods you will end up not doing any of them very well. You will give each method less time than it deserves and needs, if it is to be effective.

DON'T JUST USE ONE METHOD

Well, then, why not use just one job-hunting method, and do it exceptionally well?

The answer lies in the fact that for years and years in the U.S. as well as other countries the job-hunt has lasted two

15. The study was made a number of years ago, in Erie, Pennsylvania, by A. Harvey Belitsky and Harold L. Sheppard. It was published under the title *The Job Hunt: Job-Seeking Behavior of Unemployed Workers in a Local Economy* (now out of print). If you want to know why this and subsequent studies cited here are so old, and why they haven't been updated, it's because researchers have discovered that job-hunting is basically the same from decade to decade. The substance rarely changes; only the outward shell (e.g., the Internet). 5% of job-hunters found a job through an employment agency thirty years ago; same percentage today.

16. Steven M. Bortnick and Michelle Harrison Ports, "Job search methods and results: tracking the unemployed, 1991," *Monthly Labor Review,* December 1992, p. 33.

to four months, *and* during that time one-third of all job-hunters simply *give up*. Often, of course, the job-hunt lasts even longer -- from six months to two years or more -- during which time many more job-hunters also abandon their job-hunt.[17]

Why do we give up? It turns out the 'why' is related to the number of methods you use. For example, studies have discovered that out of every 100 job-hunters who use only one method of job-search, 51 of them abandon their search, by the second month.

On the other hand, out of every 100 job-hunters who use *several* job-search methods, only 31 abandon their search, by the second month.[18] The logic seems to be that if you use only one method -- say, resumes -- and it doesn't turn up anything rather quickly, you tend to give up hope. But if you are using two, three, or four methods, your hope tends to stay alive -- *surely, one of these will pay off* -- and so, you keep on looking.

The moral of our tale, then, is this: avoid using just one job-search method, because if it doesn't pay off almost immediately, you may quickly become very discouraged -- since you have no *'plan B.'* However, if you use more than one method (on up to four) you tend to keep hope alive.

Beyond numbers, you want of course to choose one or more of these from the Five *Best* List, above -- and not pick *all* of them from the Five *Worst* List. *(Among the Five* Worst, *stand resumes -- and I am assuming you will not give up that misplaced faith in their effectiveness, no matter what I tell you. Okay, okay. Just be sure to supplement them with one or more methods from the Five* Best *List.)*

17. "How Long Does Unemployment Last?" by the late Robert G. Wegmann, *The Career Development Quarterly,* September 1991. The median for unemployed workers in the U.S. was 13.7 weeks in 1994; currently as I write, 1,300,000 U.S. job-hunters have been unemployed for 27 weeks or longer.

18. Steven M. Bortnick and Michelle Harrison Ports, "Job search methods and results: tracking the unemployed, 1991," *Monthly Labor Review,* December 1992, p. 33.

CONCLUSION

What you do with all these statistics is up to you. At the very least, they underline in triplicate the fact that there are a *number* of different strategies available to you, even when you're doing a *traditional* job-hunt. This revelation runs counter to the popular perception that there is only one job-hunting strategy (resumes, ads, and agencies) and if no jobs turn up, that means there are no jobs *out there.*

They also tell you that some of these strategies are much more effective than others. That serves as a guide to you, if your energies are limited, as to which are the best strategies to put your energy into, and what else you might try, if the strategy you're working on doesn't produce any results for you. We now see that when job-hunters say: *"I can't find a job"* that tells us nothing, until they tell us *how* they have been looking for it. The method one uses, is everything! Indeed, put this up on your bathroom mirror:

> The major difference between successful and unsuccessful job-hunters is not some factor out there such as a tight job-market, but the way they go about their job-hunt.

You also want to notice comparisons. As mentioned, studies show that 47.7% of those who knock on doors find a job thereby, while at best only 7% of those who send (or post) their resume, do. *In other words, by going face-to-face you have an almost seven times better chance of finding a job.*

But the best method is still the so-called **life-changing job-hunt**. This method leads to a job for 86 out of every 100 job-hunters who faithfully follow it. Such an effectiveness rate -- 86% -- is *astronomically higher* than most traditional job-hunting methods.[19] That's why when nothing else is working for you, this is the method that you will thank your lucky stars for.

This is also the method you must turn to, if you've decided you would like to find a new career -- and you'd prefer not to have to take years out of your life to go back to school and get retrained with a new degree, etc., etc. It is described in great detail later (pp. 153ff).

Of course, of course, you'll probably still try a resume first. You'll probably want to try the Internet first. But at least now you know what to do if *that* doesn't work.

▶ Change your strategy, find a friend.

▶ Change your strategy, find a job.

19. I speak of individual job-hunting strategies. Group strategies, such as Nathan Azrin's 'job-club' concept, Chuck Hoffman's Self-Directed Job-Search, Dean Curtis' Group Job Search program, etc., have achieved success rates in the 84% range, using telephone approaches to employers.

I decided not to wait a long time,
To wait for the mercies of God;
I simply took a broom in my hand,
And started sweeping.

A Russian Jew, an aeronautical engineer, upon immigrating to Israel.

CHAPTER FOUR

How Employers Hunt For Job-Hunters

THE PARABLE OF THE FISHES WHO WANTED TO BE CAUGHT

I DON'T KNOW WHY, but when I think of this whole *game* called "job-hunting," I always think of a large, exotic fishing pond. You know, the kind where you rent a fishing pole and bait, and see how many fishes you can catch.

I have often wondered what kind of game it would be if the fishes actually wanted to be caught *(let's say they knew they would be guaranteed a plush existence in a grand swimming tank for the rest of their lives, if they let themselves be caught).* Could be a win-win situation. Fishes who want to be caught, and fishermen who want to catch them.

But it's not. That's because the whole game *in both fantasy and reality* is rigged in favor of the fishermen, and not the fish. And how do we know that? Because the pond is always stocked with many more fish than the fishermen could ever catch. That large number is necessary, in order to be sure each fisherman *(or fisherwoman)* goes home a winner. But this unequal ratio means that the majority of the fishes in that pond are destined to remain uncaught, and so, to lose their reward.

I first thought of this parable about three years ago, when I saw some statistics about resume-posting on the Internet. Job sites have become wary since, of letting this kind of information out of the bag, so it's impossible to find any up-to-date statistics of this kind. But here's what the figures looked like then:[1]

The Fishes and the Fishermen

Resume-Posting Sites Online	No. of 'Fishes' (Job-Hunters' Resumes)	No. of 'Fishermen' (Employers Coming To Even Look at the Resumes In a 90-Day Period)
Site One	26,644	41
Site Two	40,000	400
Site Three	59,283	1,366
Site Four	85,000	850

You get the *comparative* idea. And since at least 1970, when large computers were first pressed into service for job-hunting purposes, you could always count on this kind of ratio showing up: lots of *fishes* (resumes), a much fewer number of *fishermen* (employers). Today, some things have changed -- the *numbers,* for one, keep expanding. But the basic *ratios* have remained unchanged for thirty years.

Why is this? Why so few employers, compared to the number of job-hunters (resumes)? That's easy! It's because fishing through a huge number of resumes is not most employers' idea of 'fun.' Nor is it their favorite way to find job-hunters. Recent surveys of recruiters have revealed that

1. Source: The sites themselves (here anonymous) as first reported by Peter *WEDDLE* on the Web site of the *National Business Employment Weekly* (which, incidentally, is no longer in existence). Used with the kind permission of Nbew.com, Copyright © 1998.

some of them spend as much as 16–20 hours per week online searching for job-hunters.[2] And still, as we have seen, in the case of many employers, this only yields 8% of their new hires. That's a lot of work, for very little reward. In many cases, employers and recruiters would do almost anything to get out of it.

Going Face-to-Face

I know job-hunters who have used this fact to their advantage. One job-hunter whom we'll call *Elsa* saw a Monday ad for a hostess position at a hotel's sky-top restaurant. Instead of answering the ad, she went over to the hotel a day or two later in person, sat in the lobby and watched to see what floor the hotel employees went to when they took the elevator. They went down, she observed, to level 3 in the basement. Boldly, she stepped into an elevator, punched 3 down, and got off there. Wandering down the hallway, she saw several open doors, and inside one of them she saw a woman combing through a truly huge stack of resumes on her desk. Sticking her head in the door, Elsa said, "Are they for the hostess job you guys advertised earlier this week?" The woman nodded. Then Elsa made her pitch: "You know, I can save you the trouble of going through all those resumes; I'm the perfect person for that job." The woman, with a sigh of relief, took Elsa in to meet the person-who-had-the-power-to-hire. She was hired, the very next day.

2. Source: *WEDDLE*'s, 5/1/00.

FOLLOW THE MONEY, FIND THE POWER

So, what do we have? We have a job-hunting 'system' which *should be* loaded in favor of both job-hunter and employer equally -- *but is not.* We have a job-hunting 'system' where the people who write the rules of the game should be advocates for job-hunter and employer equally -- *but are not.* The old adage about the world of business -- 'follow the money, find the power' -- applies to the job-hunting *business* tenfold. For it is a *business,* like any other. Lots of people make a living off it: Web site owners, newspapers, employment agencies, recruiting firms, counselors, executive search firms, etc. And it is employers' money, not yours, that maintains all this apparatus. It is employers, not you, who represent repeat business. It is employers' money, not yours, that maintains online sites, newspaper advertising, etc. It is employers and employers only who 'call the shots,' and determine 'the rules of the game.' This explains those parts of the whole job-hunting 'system' that drive job-hunters *nuts.* For example, why *you* are obligated to send in a resume, but employers are not obligated to answer those resumes, or even acknowledge they ever received them. If *you* made the rules, you would *require* employers to at least acknowledge you exist. But, dear friend, you *don't* make the rules. Nor do I.

It is employers who 'call the shots' in the traditional job-hunt. This doesn't make employers necessarily 'bad,' or you necessarily a victim. It's simply *the way things are.* But if you realize that, if you understand *whose* game you're playing in, then you can push your own job-hunt toward success, by following this simple rule:

> To meet up with employers, study what employers do, go where employers go, adapt your behavior to theirs.

THE MAJOR STUMBLING-BLOCK: THERE IS NO SUCH THING AS 'EMPLOYERS'

The problem in trying to do this is that there is really no such thing as 'employers.' The generalization implies that they are one large, unified group, one tribe, who all move along the same track, see the world in the same way, and have the same values and preferences. They don't. In actual fact, one employer may be as different from another as *night* and *day.* Therefore, every generalization you try to make about 'employers' as a group, will always die a horrible rattling death.

We are reduced, therefore, to speaking of employers *in general,* or *on average,* or *in the majority* -- with probably a thousand exceptions to every generalization we make. However, that said, there *are* some general broad statements we *can* make, using the phrase: *many if not most* employers.

MANY IF NOT MOST EMPLOYERS HUNT FOR JOB-HUNTERS IN THE EXACT OPPOSITE WAY FROM HOW JOB-HUNTERS HUNT FOR THEM

As I said, to meet up with employers, study what employers do, go where employers go, adapt your behavior to theirs. That's the rule, but the degree to which this rule is *not* understood by most job-hunters, can easily be illustrated with the following diagram:

The Traditional Job-Hunt

The Way a Typical Employer Prefers to Fill a Vacancy

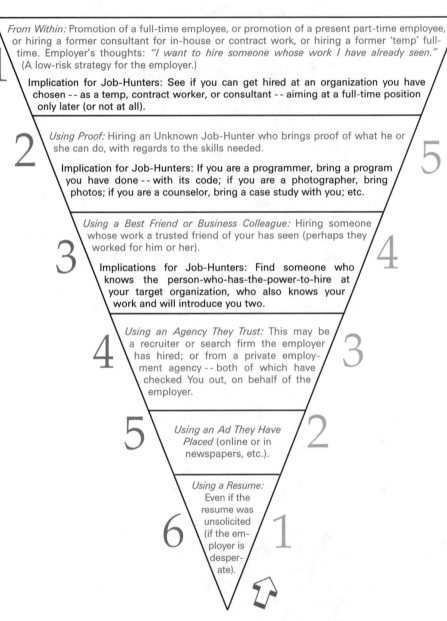

1 *From Within:* Promotion of a full-time employee, or promotion of a present part-time employee, or hiring a former consultant for in-house or contract work, or hiring a former 'temp' full-time. Employer's thoughts: *"I want to hire someone whose work I have already seen."* (A low-risk strategy for the employer.) 6

Implication for Job-Hunters: See if you can get hired at an organization you have chosen -- as a temp, contract worker, or consultant -- aiming at a full-time position only later (or not at all).

2 *Using Proof:* Hiring an Unknown Job-Hunter who brings proof of what he or she can do, with regards to the skills needed. 5

Implication for Job-Hunters: If you are a programmer, bring a program you have done -- with its code; if you are a photographer, bring photos; if you are a counselor, bring a case study with you; etc.

3 *Using a Best Friend or Business Colleague:* Hiring someone whose work a trusted friend of your has seen (perhaps they worked for him or her). 4

Implications for Job-Hunters: Find someone who knows the person-who-has-the-power-to-hire at your target organization, who also knows your work and will introduce you two.

4 *Using an Agency They Trust:* This may be a recruiter or search firm the employer has hired; or from a private employment agency -- both of which have checked You out, on behalf of the employer. 3

5 *Using an Ad They Have Placed* (online or in newspapers, etc.). 2

6 *Using a Resume:* Even if the resume was unsolicited (if the employer is desperate). 1

The Way a Typical Job-Hunter Prefers to Fill a Vacancy

You will probably already have noticed one strange thing about this diagram: employers and job-hunters use the same strategies, but they use them in a completely different order of priority -- in fact, and this is weird, *they use them in exactly the opposite order of priority, step by step.* Employers' *most* favorite strategy is job-hunters' *least* favorite strategy. And job-hunters' *most* favorite strategy is employers' *least* favorite. And so on. And so forth. No wonder it's hard for us to hook up with each other. This traditional job-hunt has job-hunters and employers running in opposite directions trying to find each other.

TWO DIFFERENT WORLDS, WE LIVE IN TWO DIFFERENT WORLDS

The employer is running one way; you're running another way. The job-hunt is a strange world. *Two* different worlds, in fact -- that of the employer, and that of the job-hunter.

You want it to be a hiring game; but the employer regards it as an elimination game -- until the very last phase.

You want the employer to acknowledge receipt of your resume; the employer feels too inundated to have time to do that for you.

You want your resume to be *all that gets weighed;* the employer regards your whole job-hunting behavior as *significant.*

You want the employer to be taking lots of initiative toward you; the employer prefers that it be you who takes the initiative. For example, the fact that your resume is "up" somewhere, on the Internet, doesn't mean a thing. Some employers have time to go looking for it, but most employers don't. The employers will instead post a vacancy on their own Web site, and maybe on a couple of major 'job-boards' like Monster.com or Headhunter.net or Careerbuilder.com, and perhaps in the newspaper -- and then count on you the job-hunter to carry the ball, from there, responding by posting your resume on their own site.

They want job-hunters to have done their homework on what this organization does, and what its present challenges are, before they come in for an interview.

HOW EMPLOYERS HUNT FOR JOB-HUNTERS

1. Many if not most employers, prefer to begin with resumes. Though *what kind of resumes* is the big question. People will tell you there is a standard format for resumes *(implying that all employers like this form).* Not true. The resume one employer loves, another employer will hate. I used to have a hobby of collecting 'winning' resumes -- that is, resumes that had actually gotten someone a hiring-interview and, ultimately, a job. Being playful by nature, I delighted in showing these, without comment, to employers whom I knew, over lunch. Many of them didn't like the winning resumes at all. "That resume will never get anyone a job," they would say. Then I would tell them, "Sorry, you're wrong. It already has. What you are saying is that it wouldn't get them a job *with you.*"

The resume reproduced on the next page is a good example of what I mean. (*You did want an example of what I mean, didn't you?*) Jim Dyer, who had been in the Marines for twenty years, wanted a job as a salesman for heavy construction and mining equipment thousands of miles from where he was then living. He devised the resume you see, and had fifteen copies made. He mailed them out (rather than posting them on the Internet). "I mailed out," he said, "a grand total of seven before I got the job in the place I wanted!"

E. J. DYER Street, City, Zip Telephone No.

I SPEAK
THE LANGUAGE
OF
MEN
MACHINERY
AND
MANAGEMENT
. . .

OBJECTIVE: Sales of Heavy Equipment

QUALIFICATIONS

* Knowledge of heavy equipment, its use and maintenance.
* Ability to communicate with management and with men in the field.
* Ability to favorably introduce change in the form of new equipment or new ideas . . . the ability to sell.

EXPERIENCE

Men and Machinery

* Maintained, shipped, budgeted and set allocation priorities for 85 pieces of heavy equipment as head of a 500-man organization (1975-1977).
* Constructed twelve field operation support complexes, employing a 100-man crew and 19 pieces of heavy equipment (1965-1967).
* Jack-hammer operator, heavy construction (summers 1956-1957-1958).

Management

* Planned, negotiated and executed large scale equipment purchases on a nation to nation level (1972-1974).

Sales

• Achieved field customer acceptance of two major new computer-based systems:
  — Equipment inventory control and repair parts expedite system (1968-1971)
  — Decision makers' training system (1977-1979).
* Proven leader . . . repeatedly elected or appointed to senior posts.

EDUCATION

* B.A. Benedictine College, 1959. (Class President; Editor Yearbook; "Who's Who in American Colleges").
* Naval War College, 1975. (Class President; Graduated "With Highest Distinction").
* University of Maryland, 1973-1974. (Chinese Language).
* Middle Level Management Training Course, 1967-1968 (Class Standing: 1 of 97).

PERSONAL

* Family: Sharon and our sons Jim (11), Andy (8) and Matt (5) desire to locate in a Mountain State by 1982, however, in the interim will consider a position elsewhere in or outside the United States . . . Health: Excellent . . . Birthdate: December 9, 1937 . . . Completing Military Service with the rank of Lieutenant Colonel, U.S. Marine Corps.

SUMMARY

A seeker of challenge . . . experienced, proven and confident of closing the sales for profit.

Like the employer who hired him, I loved this resume. Yet, other employers have criticized it for using a picture, or for being too long (or too short), etc., etc. In other words, had Jim sent his resume to *them,* they wouldn't have been impressed enough to invite him in for an interview. So, don't believe anyone who tells you there's one right format for a resume, or one style that's guaranteed to win.

All employers are different, and in terms of "the right form," let me say that after four thousand years, we've still gotten no further than the *ink-blot* stage in resume-writing, where your resume means one thing to one employer, but something quite different to another.

To some employers, all resumes are *death.* They hate them. They break out into a rash, if they see even one in their mail. Hence, oftentimes a brief individual letter, summarizing the same stuff, is preferable to sending these employers your resume.

Trouble is, you don't know which employer likes *what.* Therefore, when you post your resume on an Internet 'job-board' or on an employer's very site, or when you mail it to an employer of your choice, you need to essentially become a man or woman of prayer: "Please, dear God, let them be an employer who likes a resume, and let this resume appeal *to those employers I care about."*

2. Many if not most employers, want *you* to come find *them.* And where do you go to find them? Your instincts may tell you to go to the most *popular* sites -- the ones with the largest number of unique visitors. After all, wouldn't they afford you the most opportunities?

The answer is: Yes, *if* a lot of employers go there. But "unique visitors" doesn't tell you that. If the unique visitors total 85,850, is it 85,000 job-hunters' visits and 850 employers' visits, or is it 85,000 employers' visits, and 850 job-hunters'? You don't know. And, it makes a big difference.

"Popular sites" is not a reliable guide. "Employers' favorite sites" is. *That's* where you should be. And according to a recent survey, these turn out to be (as I write):[3]

3. Source: *WEDDLE*'s, May 2001.

First preference of employers: *to look at "for fee" commercial job-boards* (either to search the resume database there, or to post their job-openings). $64,000 question: *which* commercial job-boards? Turns out five are/or were employers' favorites, at the time that I write:

- `Monster.com`
- `HotJobs.com` (now owned by Monster's parent company)
- `Headhunter.net`/CareerMosaic *(they merged)*
- `AmericasJobBank.com`
- `Careerbuilder.com`

Second preference of employers: *to look at their own Web site.* (This, incidentally, is backed up by 51% of college seniors surveyed by `Vault.com` who said visiting company Web sites was the most helpful way to find a job. By contrast, 44% said visiting online job-boards was.)

Third preference of employers: *to look at "free" commercial sites* (either to search the resume database there, or to post their job-openings). Which free sites? Not revealed.

Lowest preference of employers: *to look at newsgroup sites* (either to search the resume database there, or to post their job-openings). As a group, the employers surveyed said that going to newsgroups was generally the least helpful online matching technique.

3. Many if not most employers, see their subsequent dealings with all the resumes they pick up as a *screening out* process, rather than as a *hiring process.* They need to eliminate as many job-hunters as they can, before proceeding to *hiring.*

4. Many if not most employers eliminate job-hunters on the grounds of their job-hunting *behavior,* especially their *lack of initiative* and their *lack of persistence.* Employers will often have two or more resumes at hand, from job-hunters who appear to be equally qualified. How to eliminate one or more? Many employers leap beyond the resume and proceed to compare those job-hunters' *initiative* and *persistence.* They evaluate these by looking to see which job-hunter does *all four* of the following:

Ad. Finds the employer's ad (either on the employer's own Web site, or on one of the best-known 'Internet job-boards' -- such as Monster, Headhunter, Careerbuilder, etc.)

EMailed resume. EMails their resume to that employer, either to an address given in the ad, or to the employer's own Web site.

Beautifully formatted paper copy. Mails a paper copy also, beautifully formatted, to the employer's *mailing address* that same day, so the employer can see what their resume really looks like.

Phone call. Makes a follow-up phone call within the week to see if both copies of the resume 'got there,' and to inquire about a follow-up appointment for an interview. *[N.B. You, the job-hunter, must beware of letting yourself get* interviewed *over the phone at this point. Remember, the employer is still in the screening-out mode. Just find out if the resume got there, and if a face-to-face interview can be set up. Time and date. Nothing more. "Sorry, I'm at work and can't talk right now."]*

Well, you see how it works. The job-hunter who only does a. and b. is the first to be eliminated *("lazy")*; the job-hunter who only does a., b., and c. is the next to be eliminated *("not very persistent")*. It is the job-hunter who does a., b., c., and d., who survives this elimination *round*. Let me say it again: during the first round, it isn't a hiring process to the employer's mind; it's an elimination process.

Wild Life by John Kovalic, © 1989 Shetland Productions. Reprinted with permission.

5. Many if not most employers once they've invited you in for an interview, are evaluating you on the grounds of the following seven criteria:[4]

If you would enter the employer's mind during the hiring-interview, these are the things about yourself that you want to be prepared to talk about, though in varying degree -- depending on the job. For example, "who you know" will be terribly important if you are selling yourself as a book agent or as a marketing director; but not important at all if you want to be, let us say, an IT technician.

WHEN DO WE START WITH WHAT YOU WANT?

In a traditional job-hunt, which we have been discussing in this chapter, it is assumed that your own goals are pretty well *set* before you even begin, so what you are actively looking for at this point is simply getting hired. That puts you in the employer's game, and therefore it is with the *employer's* way of doing things that you must start. Study what employers do, go where employers go, adapt your behavior to theirs. That has been the subject of this chapter.

4. This hint courtesy of Debra Angel; used with permission.

If you find all of this unfair, and you want a job-hunt that begins with what *you* want, then it is not a traditional job-hunt but a life-changing job-hunt that you want. In a life-changing job-hunt you start with what it is that *you* want out of life. You may decide you want to start your own business, you may decide you want to work for a small company instead of a large one, you may decide you want to use completely different skills than you've ever used before, in a completely different field than you've ever been in before. It's what *you* want that is the starting point. Your agenda. Your wishes. Your plans.

Yes, it is a life-changing job-hunt that begins with *you*. And, beginning with the next chapter, that is what the rest of this book is all about.

Pray, as though everything
depended on God;
then work, as though everything
depended on you.

CHAPTER FIVE

Twenty-Three Tips For A Successful Job-Hunt

"I have just come through a job-hunting escapade. A new field, career, country, culture -- the works. I resigned from the South African Navy and moved my family across the world to New Zealand. Being in the navy all my working life (18 years) I decided to move into the field of business management in New Zealand. I tried out all the normal avenues, the ads in newspapers (I applied to over 80 of these), employers' ads on the Internet (I applied to over 50 of these), and agencies (I signed up with 5 of these), without an iota of success or feedback. I then found your book and voila, I'm employed. I managed to find the exact job I wanted, by following your book's advice, in only 55 days since landing in New Zealand. I am smiling and purring like a Cheshire cat."

New Zealand Job-hunter, by eMail, 7/5/01

IT'S ALWAYS REASSURING to know that something *works.* That's why readers have begged me, over the years, to share with them successful job-hunters' stories. *"Your ideas sound intriguing, but do they work?"*

In the old days, including such stories sounded too much *(to my ears)* like 'trying to sell the book.' I declined to do it.

But as the years have worn on, I have gradually seen the merit of the idea. It cheers readers on. It inspires hope -- the most essential ingredient in a successful job-hunt. So now I include them throughout this book.

THE THREE THEMES OF JOB-HUNTERS' SUCCESS STORIES

There is something I want you to notice. Three themes run through all these stories. Think of these as the first three of our twenty-three *tips.*

1

The first theme is that no one owes you a job. If you want a job, you are going to have to go out and hunt for it -- hard. This may sound obvious, but we know from various studies that one-third of all job-hunters *give up* during the first months of their job-hunt.[1] They give up because they thought it was going to be simple, quick and easy. And somehow they expected rescue, they awaited rescue, and it did not come. They failed to learn the hard truth: no one owes you a job, no matter what your friends may have told you; if you want a job, it is you who are going to have to go out, and work hard to find it.

2

The second theme that runs through all those stories is that job-hunting success is in direct proportion to job-hunting effort. The more you try, the more hours you put into your job-hunt, the more likely it is that you will find the job you are looking for. If, that is, your effort is intelligently directed.

3

The third theme that runs through all these stories is simply this: successful job-hunting requires *a willingness to*

1. Currently as I write, July 2001, the average number of weeks an unemployed person in the U.S. has been unemployed is 13 weeks, though at least 1,540,000 have been unemployed for 15 weeks or longer.

change your tactics. If you try something, and it doesn't work, move on to another strategy. Job-expert Carol Christen defines job-hunting *insanity* as "when something doesn't work, you respond by doing more of it." In the job-hunt, the cure for this kind of insanity is obvious: if you answer ads in the newspapers, if you answer job-postings on the Internet, if you send out your resume *everywhere,* if you sign up with agencies in vain, and nothing works, don't just do more of it. *Change your tactics.*

IF YOU DON'T KNOW HOW TO FIND A JOB

Now, it may be that you don't know any other tactics. If you tried to do a traditional job-hunt -- resumes, agencies, ads, the Internet -- *and nothing worked,* you may have awakened to a sudden realization: "You know, I really don't think I know any other way to find a job." Well, not to worry. There is a simple remedy, which we'll count here as tip #4:

4

Go talk to the *successful* job-hunters among your family, friends, and acquaintances -- people who *were* out of work, and since then have found a job they really love -- and learn what *they* did. Then go imitate it. If you do that, you can probably throw away this book.

This is, after all, how you master *anything.* If you play tennis, and you want to learn how to improve your game, you go talk to, or train with, *good* tennis players, to learn how they do it. If you run, and want to improve your running, you would go talk to, or train with, *good* runners, and learn how they do it. If you paint, and want to learn how to paint better, you would go study under *master* painters, to see how they do it.

It is the same with job-hunting. If you are job-hunting, and you want to learn how to do it better, talk to people who are good at it.

Of course, it may be that you don't know that many successful job-hunters, among your circle of acquaintances.

Which is why you have this book in your hand. You are hoping that I do. Ah indeed I do! And, in the remainder of this chapter, I want to share with you a number of hints, tips, shortcuts, and strategies that I have learned from them during the last thirty years, via *letter, phone calls, eMails,* and *personal conversations*. We'll continue with the next tip, #5.

5

To speed up your search for one of the jobs that *are* out there, *you must think of yourself as having already found a job.* Your job, in this case, is that of hunting for work. Looking at your whole life, think of yourself as someone *who always has a job*. It's just that its nature varies at different times in your life. Some of your life, you have been working for someone else. That was your job. Some of your life, you may have been working for yourself. That was your job. If you are now job-hunting, that is your job. You are never without a job. Even when the *world* would think of you as 'unemployed,' *you* must think of yourself as having a full-time job (without pay) from 9 to 5 every weekday. You should 'punch in' at 9, and 'punch out' at 5, just as a worker does.

I emphasize this nine-to-five business, because studies have revealed the depressing fact that two-thirds of all job-hunters spend 5 hours or less hunting for a job, each week.[2]

You must spend 35 hours a week, at least, on your search for one of the jobs that are out there. That should cut down, dramatically, the number of weeks it takes you to find work -- more so, than any other factor.

If I'm not making myself clear, here, let me illustrate. Let us imagine a woman job-hunter devotes only 5 hours a week to her search; and it turns out, in the end, to take 30

2. According to the U.S. Census Bureau some years ago, discussed in "Job Search Assistance Programs: Implications for the School," authored by the late Robert G. Wegmann, and first appearing in *Phi Delta Kappan,* December 1979, pp. 271ff. The statistic is still true today; in fact, if anything, it has gotten worse over the intervening years, due to the influence of the Internet (Job-Hunting at Warp Speed) etc.

weeks before she finds a job. That means her job-hunt took a total of 150 hours.

Now let us suppose that same job-hunter were to be hurled back in time, but this time she knew it was going to take 150 hours. Therefore she decides to give 35 hours *a week* to the task, in order to 'eat up' the 150 hours faster. As you can figure out for yourself, her 150 hour job-hunt should now take only 4 weeks or so, before she found work, other things being equal.[3]

"I DON'T HAVE A PARACHUTE OF ANY COLOR."

3. Of course, there are some factors beyond a job-hunter's control, that may prolong the job-hunt, such as how long it takes an interviewing-committee to schedule the next round of interviews at the place that interests you (you will often be invited back two or three times before they make up their mind about you), etc. Nonetheless, the main point of our illustration still remains.

6

You must be mentally (and financially) prepared for your job-hunt to last a lot longer than you think it will. *The shortest job-hunt still lasts between two and eighteen weeks, depending on a variety of factors, even if you work full-time at it.* It depends, of course, on what kind of job you are looking for, where you are living, how old you are, how high you are aiming, and what the state is of the local economy.

But don't count on the "two weeks" minimum. Be prepared for the eighteen weeks or longer. Experienced outplacement people have long claimed that *your search for one of the jobs that* are *out there* will probably take one month for every $10,000 of salary that you are seeking. This may be pure drivel, but this statistic could only have survived because it fits what people know from their own (or their friends') experience.

7

Keep going until you find a job. **Persistence** is the name of the game. *Persistent* means sending an eMailed resume, then sending a formatted resume by mail to the same organization, then following it up one week later with a phone call. *Persistent* means being willing to go back to places that interested you, at least a couple of times in the following months, to see if by any chance their 'no vacancy' situation has changed. *Persistent* means learning to work without quotas. For, what 'does in' so many job-hunters is some *unspoken* mental quota in their head, which goes like this: *I expect I'll be able to find a job after about 50 applications online, 25 eMails, 15 calls in person, and three interviews.* They go about their job-hunt, fill or exceed those quotas, and -- finding no job -- they then give up. Without a job. At least one out of every three job-hunters do. So, don't let this happen to you.

The one thing a job-hunter needs above everything else is hope, and hope is born of *persistence*.

YOU'LL LIKE THIS JOB, EXCEPT EVERY NOW AND THEN, WHEN THEY DUMP A LOT OF PAPER WORK ON YOU.

8

In all of this, do not expect that you will necessarily be able to find exactly the same kind of work that you used to do. Oh, I know what you're thinking. If you enjoyed your last job, you're thinking: *"I would like to look for exactly the kind of work I used to do, in the past, with the same exact job-title."*

And maybe you can. *But,* be prepared for the fact that in this changing life, and changing world, jobs do vanish. You must not necessarily expect that you will be able to find exactly the same kind of work that you did in the past. So, you need to take the job-label off yourself *("I am an auto-worker," etc.)* and define yourself instead as *"I am a person who . . ."* Define some other line (or lines) of work that you could do, can do, and would enjoy doing.

9

Forget "what's available out there." Go after the job you really want the most.

10

Once you know what kind of work you are looking for, tell everyone what it is; have as many other eyes and ears out there looking on your behalf, as possible.

11

If you happen to own an answering machine, you might even consider putting the kind of work you are looking for, on that machine, in your opening message: *"Hi, this is Sandra. I'm busy right now, looking for a job in the accounting department at a hospital. Leave me a message after the beep, and if you happen to have any leads or contacts for me, be sure to mention that too, along with your phone number. Thanks a lot."*

12

To speed up your search for one of the jobs that *are* out there, find some kind of a support group, so that you don't have to face the job-hunt all by yourself. You'd be amazed how much the support of others can keep you going, when you otherwise would be discouraged, and thus speed up your job-hunt. Here are the options you can choose from:

a. Job-hunting groups that already exist in your city or town, such as "Forty Plus Clubs," "Experience Unlimited" groups, job-hunt classes at your local Federal/state employment offices, or at the local Chamber of Commerce, or at your local college or community college, or at your local Adult Education center, or at your local church, synagogue, or place of worship. The likelihood that such help is available in your community increases dramatically for you if you are from certain groups regarded as disadvantaged, such as low income, or welfare recipients, or youth, or displaced workers, etc. Ask around.

b. A job-hunting group that doesn't currently exist, but that you could help form, perhaps with the aid of your priest, minister, rabbi or religious leader, at your local church, synagogue or religious centre, or elsewhere -- including the Internet. Some enterprising job-hunters, unable to locate any group, have formed their own by running an ad in the local newspaper, near the "help wanted" listings. *"Am currently job-hunting, would like to meet weekly with other job-hunters for mutual support and encouragement. Am using* What Color Is Your Parachute? *as my guide."*

c. Your mate or partner, grandparent, brother or sister, or best friend. A loving 'taskmaster' is what you need. Someone who will make a regular weekly appointment to meet with you, check you out on what you've done that week, and be very stern with you if you've done little or nothing since you last met. You want understanding, sympathy, *and discipline.* If your mate, brother or sister, or best friend, can offer you all of these, run -- do not walk -- to enlist them immediately.

d. A local career counselor. I grant you that career counselors aren't usually thought of as a 'support group.' But many of them do have group sessions; and even by themselves they can be of inestimable support. If you can afford their services, and none of the above suggestions have worked, this is a good fall-back strategy. Before choosing such a counselor, however, *please* read Appendix C, beginning on page 393. That also tells you how to locate such counselors.

13

To speed up your search for one of the jobs that *are* out there, *go after many different organizations, instead of just one or two.* Restricting your search to just one favorite place is *job-hunting death.* No matter how much you love that place, no matter how much you would *die* to work for that person, no matter how promising the situation there looks, for you (*"We'll call you next week. Promise!"*) keep on searching every day.

If a favorite place does seem interested in you, don't let your job-hunt go on 'hold' just because you *hope* this place will now pan out. Continue searching, at other organizations, until the day you actually begin working!!! Otherwise you will lose valuable, valuable time, when something that looked like *a sure thing* falls through, at the last moment.

I repeat this warning several times in the rest of this book. Many of you will ignore this anyway; but will have good cause to remember these words, later, when you repent at leisure your decision to ignore them.

14

To speed up your search for one of the jobs that *are* out there, *determine to go after* any *place that interests you. Pay no attention to whether or not there is a known vacancy at that place.*

Underline this rule, copy it, paste it on your bathroom mirror, memorize it, repeat it to yourself every morning. I'll say it again: Pay no attention to whether or not there is a known vacancy!

If you base your job-hunt just on places where there is a known vacancy, you will prolong your search *forever!* Vacancies often develop at places *long before* any notice is put out that this vacancy exists. Moreover, when bosses or managers are thinking of creating a new position, this *intention* often lies in their mind for quite some time before they get around to doing anything about it. If you contact them during this opportune, quiescent period, you come as the answer to their prayers. And you will have no competitor for that job.

15

To speed up your search for one of the jobs that *are* out there, *concentrate on organizations with twenty or less employees.* There is a natural tendency for job-hunters to make large organizations *'the measure of all things'* going on in the job-market. So much so, that if the newspapers are filled

with the news of companies like AT&T, General Motors, and others laying off thousands of workers, most job-hunters *assume* things are bad everywhere. When they can't find a job at any of these large places, they assume that *no one* is hiring. This is a very common, and very costly, mistake.

The fact is, there are always companies that are hiring -- but they are usually small companies -- with one hundred or less employees.

So, if you would speed up your job-hunt, you need to concentrate on every *small* firm in your field that is within commuting distance, and has one hundred or less employees. Personally, I would begin with firms that have twenty or less employees. Read the business section of your newspaper daily, notice which smaller firms are hiring, also talk to everyone you can, talk to your Chamber of Commerce, to find out which small businesses they think are growing and expanding.

16

To speed up your search for one of the jobs that *are* out there, *go face-to-face with* at least *4 employers a day; or if contacting them by telephone, 40 a day, minimum; or if you're contacting them only over the Internet, there is no limit.* I emphasize this, because studies have shown that the average U.S. job-hunter goes face-to-face with only six employers a month. That adds up to little more than one employer *per week.* Logic alone will tell you that this is one of the reasons the average job-hunt takes so long. Say you were an average job-hunter, you go face-to-face with only *six employers a month,* and let us say it took you *six months* to find a job. That means, mathematically, you had to contact 36 employers, face-to-face, in order to find that job.

But were you to be flung back in time to start all over again, except that this time you knew it will take you 36 employers, face-to-face, before you got hired, you might determine to contact, say, *three* employers *per day,* each weekday, in which case you would cover the 36 employers, and subsequently get a job, in just a little over *two weeks,* instead of six months!

All of this, which we may figure by simple logic, was confirmed by an actual study a few years ago, which found that if a job-hunter went face-to-face with two employers a week, the job-search typically lasted up to a year; if ten employers a week, the search typically ended with a job within six months; *and,* at twenty employers a week, the search time typically dropped to 90 days or less.[4]

Therefore, common sense will tell you that you should determine to see *at least* three employers per weekday, one in the morning and two in the afternoon, at a minimum. And you should determine to do this for as many weeks (or months) as your job-hunt may last. For thus you should greatly shorten your job-hunt.

When you approach employers, be prepared always to tell them what makes you different from nineteen other people who can do the same thing that you do. And don't be put off by rejection, if they have nothing to offer you. Be polite, ask them if they know of anyone else who might be hiring. Keep going until you find someone who is hiring, for the job you want.

17

To speed up your search for one of the jobs that *are* out there, *use the telephone.* Some experts, of course, advise against this strategy: never, never use the telephone, they say, under *any* circumstances: it only makes it easier for the employer to screen you out over the phone.

Nonetheless, all the successful group job-search programs that I have studied over the years, from Nathan Azrin's *Job Club* to Dean Curtis's *Welfare Reform* programs *(based on the Dave Perschau/Chuck Hoffman model)* have based their programs on the *heavy* use of the telephone.

And what I have noticed is the better a group job-hunting program has worked and the faster it has succeeded in its people finding jobs, the more phone calls it has their job-hunters make. Nathan has had job-hunters make at least

4. Goodrich & Sherwood Co., reported in "How to Succeed in Rotten Times," Oct. 1992.

10 phone calls a day; Chuck has had them make 100 phone calls in the morning, and 100 in the afternoon.

So if you've tried *everything* and all else fails, telephoning is your fall-back strategy. It is almost guaranteed to turn up something, just by its sheer weight of numbers.

Of course, I know this isn't easy -- for most of us. Some job-hunters are born to it, like a duck to water. But most of us *hate* telephone solicitation, when it is directed at us; and we hate the thought of doing it to others (namely, employers).

But, if you decide to do it (because you're desperate, or *really* impatient) you can go to your local library or bookstore and find books telling you exactly how to go about this.

In essence, the ten things the experts emphasize are these:

1. Take the Yellow Pages of the phone book, and call up every single company or organization in the Yellow Pages that looks interesting to you, to ask them if they might be hiring, for the kind of work you do.
2. Before you get on the phone, *write out* what you plan to say. This is akin to some experts' advice that before you make your call, you should set down an outline of the objective of that call, and the key points you want to make during the conversation. But the best experts say, *Write out every word.* This is your *script*; don't try to *wing it.* Unabashedly read it, but try not to sound like you're reading it. Read it with enthusiasm. Rehearse it first, several times.
3. Stand up when you make your phone calls; your voice is more forceful that way.
4. Have a mirror in front of you, on the wall, at eye level, so you can watch yourself in it, to be sure you are smiling as you talk.
5. Call before 8 a.m., shortly before noon, or after 5 p.m. If it's managers you're seeking, and if they're hardworking, they're likely to be there at those times -- without a screener.

6. When you are connected, ask to speak with the manager. When she or he comes on the line, address them by name, introduce yourself by name, and then if someone suggested you call this person, use their name as a reference when you call. "Your name was given to me by . . . " Alternatively, start the call by making a connection between you and that person. If for example you saw a news item about them in the paper, or on the Internet, you might begin with "I just read that you . . . and I . . ." However, if you can't find a connection, don't try to invent one.
7. Then *briefly* (in one sentence) describe your greatest personal strength or top skill, a *brief* description of your experience, and then ask if there is a job opening for someone with your skills and background. For example, *"I am an experienced writer, with three published books, and I wonder if you have any job openings for someone with my experience?"* If *"yes,"* set up an interview time, repeat it, and repeat your name; if *"no,"* ask if they know of anyone else who might be hiring a person with your background. *(This hint courtesy of Dean Curtis.)*
8. If you've done something in the community, written articles for the local paper, or served on a volunteer committee, work that into the conversation if it goes on for more than one minute.
9. If you run into an interviewer's sharp objections about something, try responding with:
   I understand . . .
   I can appreciate your position . . .
   I see your point . . .
   Of course! However . . .
10. Some experts advise you not to try to make too many *surface* calls, but to restrict your calling to places that *really* interest you, and take the time to research each of them before you call. Other experts advise you not to call about a job, but to call only for information. All advise you to thank the employer before signing off, whether they gave you a job lead, or not.

18

To speed up your search for one of the jobs that *are* out there, *knock on doors* -- particularly if you *hate* to use the telephone.

Choose places where you would like to work. Either from the phone book, or by walking down those streets in your village, city, or town, where you would *like* to work. Then, physically go in there, at any place that looks interesting, and ask if they might be looking for someone with your skills. Generally speaking, and particularly at small organizations, it is the boss, or hiring manager -- the one who makes the actual decision to hire -- that you want to talk to, to ask if they're hiring.

The rationale for this tip is that you want to speed up your job-hunt as much as you can; hence, you need to go *face-to-face* with employers whenever possible, rather than sending paper, such as a resume. 47.7% of those job-hunters who use this approach, get a hiring-interview and then a job, thereby.

Said one job-hunter: *"The very first real job I got was by knocking door-to-door, asking if they needed a draftsman. I got a favorable response at the fifth, but not the last, place I knocked; interviewed a few days after; and was working within the week. I was incredibly lucky, as were they: their current draftsman had given notice that day I knocked. I worked there two years and then went on to a much better position at the invitation of friends I had made at that first job."*

Most of us get cold feet at the idea of doing this. But *if* nothing else is working, it's a good fall-back strategy for you to rely on.

This direct 'walk-in' approach may pay off for you, or it may not.[5] The effectiveness of the approach to employers is

5. When you knock on the doors of larger organizations, you will generally be well-advised to try to avoid the human resources department, since their primary function is often to screen out job-hunters, so as not to bother the people 'upstairs' -- though there are exceptions to this rule, where the department is helpful, kind, and capable of hiring. It's a judgment call, on your

probably in inverse proportion to the level sought: more effective for blue collar jobs than for managerial ones. In their pioneering study of the job-hunt a number of years ago, *The Job Hunt: Job-Seeking Behavior of Unemployed Workers in a Local Economy,* A. Harvey Belitsky and Harold A. Sheppard discovered that going face-to-face at a workplace, without introduction or *leads,* was *the* most effective job-hunting method *if you were a blue-collar worker.* (Blue-collar workers take note.)

---

part. (You are not likely to run into such departments unless you are knocking on the door of larger organizations, inasmuch as only 15% of all organizations, mostly large ones, even have such departments.)

At large organizations, they may decline to give you the simple answer you were looking for, until you have filled out a job application. Job applications are question-and-answer forms which have such simple questions as: Your Name, Address, Age, Places of Previous Employment, etc. Such applications vary greatly in their complexity, from ones used by fast-food chains, to those used by, say, engineering firms. *If* you decide to fill one out, use a black pen, *print* neatly, fill in every question or space, even questions that don't apply to you (write *n.a.* "not applicable" in that space), write *"Open"* for salary, and sign your name. If they ask your reasons for leaving a previous job, you can choose between: *the job ended, my family needed me at the time (no longer a problem), it was a seasonal job, it was a temporary job, I wanted to make a career change, I want more responsibility than they gave me.* (Courtesy of Dean Curtis.)

If you've never seen a job application in your life, and you plan to be approaching organizations *cold,* you should familiarize yourself with an application form ahead of time. One way to do this without jeopardizing your job chances at places you care about, is to go to visit some fast-food place or any large organization with a human relations department where you *don't* care to work, and simply *ask* for a job application, then immediately go back out the door. Take the application form home with you, where you can study it, and take a stab at filling it out, just for practice. Then throw it in the waste basket, after you've learned what you need to know. Do *not* return it to the place you got it from, unless you are seriously interested in working there. The purpose of this exercise is simply to find out what an application form looks like, not to use it -- at least at this point. Anyway, now you know what an application form looks like, and how to fill it out. But I hope you never need to.

19

To speed up your search for one of the jobs that *are* out there, be willing to look at different *kinds* of jobs: full-time jobs, part-time jobs, unlimited contract jobs *(formerly called 'permanent jobs')*, short-term contract jobs, temporary jobs, working for others, working for yourself, etc.

20

Most of us think that when we go job-hunting we have some special handicap (hidden or obvious), that's going to keep us from getting a job. *Forever.*

The handicaps that we are sure make us unemployable are such things as:

I have a physical handicap
I have a mental handicap
I never graduated from high school
I never graduated from college
I am just graduating
I just graduated a year ago
I graduated too long ago
I am a self-made man
I am a self-made woman
I am too handsome
I am too beautiful
I am too ugly
I am too thin
I am too fat
I am too young
I am too old
I am too new to the job-market
I am too near retirement
I have a prison record
I have a psychiatric history
I have never held a job before
I have held too many jobs before
I have only had one employer
I am Hispanic
I am Black
I am Asian
I am a foreigner
I have not had enough education
I have had too much education
I am too much of a generalist
I am too much of a specialist
I am a clergyperson
I am just coming out of the military
I've only worked for volunteer organizations
I have only worked for large employers
I have only worked for small employers
I am too shy
I am too assertive
I come from a very different kind of background
I come from another industry
I come from another planet

I guess the true meaning of the above comprehensive list is that there are about three weeks of your life when you're employable.

Many of us think we need a million instructions about how to job-hunt with our handicap.

Actually, all we really need to keep firmly in mind is this one simple truth: There are **two** kinds of employers out there: *those who will be put off by your handicap, and therefore won't hire you;*

AND

those who will not be put off by your handicap, and therefore will hire you, if you are able to do the job.

You are not interested in the former kind of employer, no matter how many of them there are -- except as a source of referrals.

You are only looking for those employers who are not put off by your handicap, and therefore will hire you *if you can do the job.*

So: if the employer you are talking to in a particular interview is obviously bothered by your (supposed) handicap, you want to quietly bring that interview to a conclusion, and ask them -- in parting -- if they know of anyone else who might be interested in your skills. Keep going, until you find that second kind of employer.

That kind knows that it doesn't matter what skills-you-don't-have, as long as the skills-that-you-do-have exactly match those-needed-in-the-job you are discussing.

21

Don't be wearied by rejection. As I mention elsewhere, Tom Jackson's model (from his out-of-print *Guerrilla Tactics in the Job Market*) of the typical job-hunt is:

NO NO NO NO NO NO NO NO NO NO NO NO NO NO NO NO NO NO NO NO NO NO NO NO NO NO NO NO NO NO NO NO NO NO NO NO NO NO NO NO NO NO NO NO NO NO NO NO NO NO NO **YES**.

Even if you get rejected at a lot of places, the more NOs you get out of the way, the closer you are to that YES. Ideally, of course, you want to end up with two YESES. Two, so that you'll have at least two things to choose between.

22

Every evening after an interview sit down and write (with pen, keyboard/printer, or eMail) a thank-you note to each person you saw that day. This means not only employers, but also their secretaries, receptionists, or anyone else who gave you a friendly helping hand, in any way. Don't make this *perfunctory.* Make it personal. Mention something individual about the way they treated you, or what you liked about them. Use the thank-you note to underline anything that was discussed during the interview, or to add anything you left out, that was important.

The thank-you note is *crucial.* Once upon a time, a job-hunter presented herself for a hiring-interview as public relations officer for a major-league baseball team. That evening, she wrote and mailed a thank-you note. She was eventually hired for the job, and when she asked why, they told her that out of thirty-five applicants, she was the only one who had written a thank-you note, after the interview.

If you want to stand out from the others applying for the same job, if you want to speed up your getting hired, send thank-you notes -- to *everyone* you meet there, that day.

23

Treat every employer with courtesy, even if it seems certain they can offer you no job there; they may be able to refer you to someone else next week, if you made a good impression.

What If None of This Works?

Following the strategies in this chapter, which were learned from *successful* job-hunters, you should dramatically improve your chance of finding a job. Good luck, and if you find a job, congratulations. You do not need to read the rest of this book -- *until the next time.*

But if you faithfully try everything listed in this chapter, and *none of it works* for you, what then? Well, there is a life-preserver still available to you: flee to Chapters 6–11. Read them, and painstakingly do the exercises in *The Flower Exercise* (it will take you no more than a good weekend, if you keep at it).

Above all, never abandon hope, my friend.

I close this chapter, with the story of another successful job-hunter, who wrote me as follows:

"A collegiate professor of mine told me to buy What Color is Your Parachute? *That was in December 1998. I bought the book a year later while employed in a career field I love, but with a company I hated. Nevertheless, I still didn't read your book.*

"I resigned from my employer upon coming home from military duty, August 14th, 2000. That's when I started reading. Applying Parachute *techniques to my efforts yielded tremendous results. I've always worked hard, but the theories in your book help a jobseeker work smart. The spiritual insight was awesome. For a while I was wanting to scrap my passionate desire to become an empowering, wise, public servant and go into computers. Because that's what everyone else seems to want to do.*

"I kept my faith and contacted the Media Relations Representative at the local Housing Authority. I met her in January 2000 on a school tour of the facility. She told me to give her a call when I returned home from the military. I called her on August 21st, 2000. She let me know of an opening and suggested that I call and write the hiring V.P. I called, applied and hand-delivered my resume/cover letter to them.

"I wrote the Media Relations Representative a thank-you note and interviewed for the position on September 6th at 10 a.m. I then went to have lunch where people within my desired career field eat.

"The Media Relations Representative was there along with the new CEO of the Housing Authority. I tactfully introduced myself and informed the CEO that I had interviewed for a position within her organization. I also congratulated her on becoming the new CEO. Two hours later I received a phone call. I got the career starting position. It pays seven thousand more dollars per year than my previous job. But most importantly, I love what I do. It's directly in line with my calling. I then gave the book to my girlfriend who has been on dead-end jobs for the last five years. She landed a career starting position with a local bank."

Two roads diverged in a yellow wood,
And sorry I could not travel both
And be one traveler, long I stood
And looked down one as far as I could
To where it bent in the undergrowth;

Then took the other, as just as fair,
And having perhaps the better claim,
Because it was grassy and wanted wear;
Though as for that the passing there
Had worn them really about the same,

And both the morning equally lay
In leaves no step had trodden black.
Oh, I kept the first for another day!
Yet knowing how way leads on to way,
I doubted if I should ever come back.

I shall be telling this with a sigh
Somewhere ages and ages hence:
Two roads diverged in a wood, and I—
I took the one less traveled by,
And that has made all the difference.[1]

Robert Frost (1874–1963)

CHAPTER SIX

How To Start Your Own Business

The Art of Self-employment or Working for Yourself

"ALL I DO
THE WHOLE DAY THROUGH
IS DREAM OF YOU . . ."

SURE, YOU'VE THOUGHT about it, a million times. Hasn't everyone? Everytime you're tied up in traffic going to or from work. You've toyed with the idea of not having to go to an office or other place of business, but of running your own business, maybe even out of your own home, making your own product or selling your own services, being your own boss, and keeping all the profits for yourself. It's called *self-employment*, or being *an independent contractor*, or *free-lancing* or *contracting out your services*. Great idea! *But*, nothing's ever come of all this day-dreaming. Until now. Now, you're out of work, or maybe you're still working but you're really fed up with your job, and -- dusting off those old dreams -- you're thinking to yourself: *Maybe it's now, or never. Maybe I ought to just* do *it.*

THE MANY PATHS YOU CAN TAKE
STAYING AT YOUR PRESENT ORGANIZATION
SAME CAREER BUT IN A NEW PLACE
DOING TEMP WORK
CONTINUING IN YOUR PRESENT CAREER
STARTING A NEW CAREER
YOUR NEXT STEP
STAYING WHERE YOU LIVE NOW
OR MOVING TO A NEW PLACE

A COMPOSITE CAREER (2, 3 OR MORE PART-TIME CAREERS)
PART-TIME WORK
FULL-TIME WORK
ONE CAREER
WORKING AT HOME
WORKING FOR SOMEONE ELSE
WORKING FOR YOURSELF
DOING VOLUNTARY WORK OR AN INTERNSHIP
GOING BACK TO SCHOOL FOR LEGITIMATE RETRAINING
STEVEN M. JOHNSON

HOME BUSINESSES IN GENERAL

Three hundred years ago, of course, nearly everybody did it. They worked at home or on their farm. But then the industrial revolution came; and the idea of working *away from* home became normal. In recent times, however, the idea of working at home has been finding new life, due to congestion on the highways, and the development of new technologies. If you can afford them, a telephone,[2] a fax machine, a computer with a modem, a Palm Pilot, eMail, online services, mail-order houses, and the like, all make working for yourself feasible, as never before.

THE THREE MAJOR PROBLEMS OF HOME BUSINESSES

(1) The first major problem of home businesses, according to experts, is that on average home-based workers *(in the U.S. at least)* only earn 70% of what their full-time office-based equals do. So, you must think carefully whether you could make enough money to survive -- *or prosper.*

(2) The second major problem of home businesses is that it's often difficult to maintain the balance between business and family time. Sometimes the *family* time gets short-changed, while in other cases the demands of family (particularly with small children) may become so interruptive, that the *business* gets short-changed. So, do investigate thoroughly, ahead of time, *how* you would go about doing this *well.*

(3) Lastly, a home business puts you into a perpetual job-hunt.

---

1. The title of the poem on page 92 is "The Road Not Taken," from The Poetry of Robert Frost edited by Edward Connery Lathem. Copyright 1944 by Robert Frost. Henry Holt and Company, Publisher. Used with permission. Incidentally, Scott Peck's modern classic, *The Road Less Traveled,* takes its title from this poem.

2. This *telephone family* includes cell phones, 'call-forwarding' -- the technology where people call your one fixed telephone number, and then get automatically forwarded to wherever you have told the phone company you currently are -- and voice/electronic mail.

Some of us who are unemployed *hate* job-hunting, and are attracted to the idea of a home business because this seems like an ideal way to cut short our job-hunt. The irony is, that a home business makes you in a very real sense a *perpetual* job-hunter -- because you have to be *always* seeking new clients or customers -- which is to say, new *employers*. (Well, yes, they are *employers*, because they *pay* you for the work you are doing. The only difference between this and a full-time job is that here *the contract is limited.* But if you are running your own business, you will have to *continually* beat the bushes for new clients or customers -- who are in fact *short-term employers*.)

"YES, THE BUSINESS HAS BECOME BIGGER, BUT FRED STILL LIKES TO WORK AT HOME."

Of course, the dream of most home business people is to become so well known, and so in demand, that clients or customers will be literally beating down your doors, and you will be able to stop this endless job-hunt. But that only happens to a relative minority, and your realistic self must know that.

The greater likelihood is that you will *always* have to beat the bushes for employers/clients. It may get easier as you get better at it, or it may get harder, if economic conditions take a severe downturn. In any event, it will probably be the one aspect of your work that you will *always* cordially dislike. If you're going to go this route, you must learn to make your peace with it -- however grudgingly.

If you can't manage that, if you avoid that task like the plague until there's literally no bread on the table, you're probably going to find *a home business* is just a glamorous synonym for *'starving.'* I know *many* home business people to whom this has happened, and it happened precisely because they couldn't stomach going out to beat the bushes for clients or customers. If that's true for you, you should plan to start out by *hiring, co-opting,* or *volunteering* somebody part-time, who is willing to do this for you -- one who, in fact, 'eats it up' -- or abandon the idea of having your own business.

WHEN YOU DON'T KNOW WHAT KIND OF HOME BUSINESS TO START

Okay, so basically the *idea* of working at home intrigues the life out of you, but you can't figure out what kind of business to start. *Minor little detail!*

There are fortunately seven steps you can take, to nail this down.

First, read. There are oodles of books out there that are *filled* with ideas for home businesses. The best of them is: *Working from Home: Everything You Need to Know About Living and Working Under the Same Roof* by Paul Edwards and Sarah Edwards (Paperback - June 1999), called 'the Bible on working from home.' For other titles, browse Amazon's categories[3], or your local library, or the business shelves in your local bookstore.

Secondly, dream. In evaluating any ideas that you pick up, the first thing you ought to look at are your dreams. What have you always dreamed about doing? Since childhood? Since last week? Now is the time to dust off those dreams.

And please don't pay any attention, for now, to whether those dreams represent *a step up* for you in life, or not. Who cares? Your dreams are yours. You may have been dreaming of earning *more* money. But then again, you may have been dreaming of doing work that you really love, even if it means a lesser salary or income than you have been accustomed to. Don't *judge* your dreams, and don't let anyone else judge them either.

Thirdly, look around your own community, and ask yourself what services or products people seem to need the most. Or what service or product already offered in the community could stand a lot of *improving?* There may be something there that *grabs* you.

3. http://www.amazon.com/

The underlying theme to 90% of the businesses that are *out there* these days is *things that save time.* It's what single parents, families where both parents work, and singles who have overcrowded lives, most want.

You might consider: Offering home deliveries of local restaurants' dinners, or home delivery of grocery orders from any downtown supermarket (pay no attention to the fact that delivery services such as *Webvan* went 'belly-up' on the Internet). Local delivery services may still be wanted. There is also: Evening delivery services of laundry, etc. Daytime or evening office cleaning services and/or home cleaning services. Home repairs, especially in the evening or on weekends, of TVs, radios, audio systems, laundries, dishwashers, etc. Lawn care. Care for the elderly in their own homes. Childcare in their own homes. Pick up and delivery of things (even personal stuff, like cleaning) at the office. Automobile care or repair services, with pickup and delivery. Offering short-term business consultancy in various fields. Other successful businesses these days deal with such arenas as leisure activities.

Fourth, consider mail order. If you find no needs within your own community, you may want to broaden your search, to ask what is needed in this country -- or the world. After all, mail-order businesses can be started *small* at home, and catalogs can be sent *anywhere.* If this interests you, read up on the subject. Also, for heaven's sakes, go talk to other mail-order people (for names, just look at the catalogs you're already likely receiving). There are books 'out there' about mail-order businesses, but they are of very unequal value.[4]

Fifth, consider telecommuting. Telecommuting is "working at home for others." The people who do this are called *'telecommuters'* -- a term coined by Jack Nilles in 1973. A good very elementary summary of telecommuting can be found at:

4. I personally like one written 14 years ago that is now out of print called *Mail Order Moonlighting* by Cecil Hoge, Sr. (but `http://www.amazon.com/` had some used copies available, last I looked).

http://kydvr.state.ky.us/programs_services/telecommuting.htm

One way to go about easing yourself into telecommuting, if you already have a job, is to talk your boss into letting you do at least *some* of your work at home. You can find plans for how you "sell" your employer on the idea, at such sites as:

http://www.workoptions.com/telecom.htm

Your boss, of course, may take the initiative here, before it has even occurred to you, and they may *ask* you to work at home, connected to the office by computer-network telephone lines.

If you are thinking about becoming a telecommuter, I advise you to investigate the idea thoroughly. In this case, the Internet is your best friend. There you can find surveys plus up-to-date discussions of the **advantages** and **disadvantages** of telecommuting, at such sites as:

http://www.eei.org/esg/na/tele.htm

You can find **lists** of actual companies that do telecommuting, at such sites as:

http://sybar.com/d/Telecommuting/telecommuting.html

And you can find **an association for telecommuters**, ITAC (International Telework Association and Council) with conventions and everything, at:

http://www.telecommute.org/

Sixth, consider a franchise. Franchises are for people who want their own business, but don't care if it's not *in the home*. (Though some franchises can be done from your home, the majority require an outside site.)

Franchises exist because some people want to have their own business, but don't want to go through the agony of starting it up. They want to *buy in* on an already established business, and they have the money in their savings with which to do that (or they know where they can get a bank loan). Fortunately for them, there are a lot of such franchises. In the U.S., the overall failure rate for franchises is less than 4%. You want to keep in mind that some *types* of franchises have a failure rate *far* greater than that. The ten *riskiest* small businesses, according to experts, are local laundries and dry cleaners, used car dealerships, gas stations, local trucking firms, restaurants, infant clothing stores, bakeries, machine shops, grocery or meat stores, and car washes -- though I'm sure there will be some new nominees for this list, by the time you read this. *Risky* doesn't mean you can't make them succeed. It only means the odds are greater than they would be with other small businesses.

You want to keep in mind also that some individual franchises are *terrible* -- and that includes well-known names. They charge too much for you to *get on board*, and often they don't do the advertising or other commitments that they promised they would.

There isn't a franchising book that doesn't warn you eighteen times to go talk to people who have *already* bought that same franchise, before you ever decide to go with them. And I mean *several* people, not just one. Most experts also warn you to go talk to *other* franchises in the same field, not just the kind you're thinking about signing up with. Maybe there's something better, that such research will uncover.

If you are drawn to the idea of a franchise, because you are in a hurry, and you don't want to do any homework first, *'cause it's just too much trouble*, you will deserve what you get, believe me. That way lies madness.

Seventh, if you've invented something, weigh doing something with it. If you are inclined toward invention or tinkering, you might want to start by improving on an idea that's already *out there*. Start with something you like, such as bicycles. You might experiment with making -- let us say -- a folding bicycle. Or, if you like to go to the beach, and your skills run to sewing, you might think about making and selling beach towels with weights sewn in the corners, against windy days.

If you've already invented something, and it's been sitting in your drawer, or the garage, but you've never attempted to duplicate or manufacture it before, now might be a good time to try. Think out very carefully just how you are going to get it manufactured, advertised, and marketed, etc.

There are programs, legitimate programs, that fund inventors. If you have access to the Internet, go to such a site as:

`http://www.oit.doe.gov/inventions/`

Under the right conditions, *they* will pay *you* a fee to continue development of your invention.

There are also promoters out there (on and off the Internet) who claim to specialize in promoting inventions *such as yours*, if *you* will pay *them* a fee. However, according to the Federal Trade Commission, in a study of 30,000 people who paid such promoters, *not a single inventor* ever made a profit after giving their invention to such promoters or firms. If you want to gamble some of your hard-earned money on such firms, consider whether you might better drop it at the tables in Las Vegas. I think the odds are *better* there.

You're much better off, *of course*, if on your own, on or off the Internet, you locate other inventors, and ask if they were successful in marketing their own invention. When you find those who were, pick their brains for everything they're worth. (Of course one of the first things they're going to tell you is to go get your invention copyrighted or trademarked or patented.)

WHEN YOU KNOW WHAT KIND OF HOME BUSINESS TO START

The above seven steps are, of course, if you don't know what kind of business you'd like to start. But, it may be that You already know exactly *what* business you want to start, because you've been thinking about it for *years*, and may even have been *doing* it for years -- only, in the employ of someone else.

But now, the turning point: you're about to set out on your own. You're thinking about doing this kind of work yourself, and for yourself, whether it be business services, or consultancy, or repair work, or some kind of craft, or the making of some kind of product, or teaching, or offering of home services, such as childcare or delivery by night.

Some sorts of jobs are just made for working out of one's home, as when you are already some kind of writer, artist, performer, business expert, lawyer, consultant, craftsperson, or the like. Be prepared for the fact that your present home may not be big enough for the kind of thing you're dreaming of. For example, your dream may be: *I want a horse ranch, where I can raise and sell horses.* Or *I want to run a bed-and-breakfast place.* Stuff like that.

Well, the nice thing about deciding to work out of your home is that you get to define what *home* is. Given today's technology, you could *literally* work wherever your preferred environment in the whole world is -- whether that be out in nature, or at your favorite vacation spot, or skiing chalet, or in some other country altogether.

The only rule is, if it involves a possible move, be sure to go talk to other people who have already done that. Pick their brains for everything they're worth. No need for you to step on the same *land mines* that they did.

YOU WANT TO SUCCEED!

And that brings us to the most important part of this chapter. The key to successfully starting your own business turns out to be this one *crucial* rule: *Find out what's involved, before you hurl yourself into this new world.*

This **research** has two steps to it:

1 Finding out what skills it takes to make this kind of enterprise work. *This involves figuring out what is "A minus B equals C."*

2 Finding out just exactly what is involved in setting up any home-based business. *This involves going on the Internet, or reading some books.*

Step #1:
Figure Out What Is
"A minus B equals C"

Over the past thirty years I have found it *mindboggling* to discover how many people start their own business, at home or elsewhere, without *ever* first going to talk to anybody who started the same kind of business earlier.

One job-hunter told me she started a home-based soap business, without ever talking to anyone who had started a similar endeavor before her. Not surprisingly, her business went belly-up within a year and a half. She concluded: no one should go into such a business. Ah, but there *are* successful home-based soap businesses -- Paula Gibbons' "Paula's Soap" of Seattle, Washington, for one. *Someone is already doing the work you are dreaming of. The key to your success, is that you go talk to them.*

This involves a simple series of methodical steps:

(1) You first write out *in as much detail as you can* just exactly what kind of business you are thinking about starting. Do you want to be a freelance writer, or a craftsperson, or a consultant, independent screenwriter, copy writer, digital artist, songwriter, photographer, illustrator, interior designer, video person, film person, counselor, therapist, plumber, electrician, agent, filmmaker, soap maker, bicycle repairer, public speaker, or *what?*

(2) You identify towns or cities that are at least fifty to seventy-five miles away, and you try to get their phone books, so you can look up addresses of their chambers of commerce, etc. In some cases, the Internet will also help. An index to such help can be found at my Web site, **www.JobHuntersBible.com/**

(3) By using the Internet or the Yellow Pages or the chamber of commerce, you try to identify three businesses in those towns, that are identical or similar to the business you are thinking of starting. You journey to that town or city, and talk to the founder or owner of each such business.

(4) When you talk to them, you explain that you're exploring the possibility of starting your own business, similar to theirs, but seventy-five miles away. You ask them

PEANUTS reprinted by permission of United Features Syndicate, Inc.

if they would mind sharing what pitfalls or obstacles they ran into when they started their own business. You ask them what skills or knowledges do they think are necessary to running that kind of business successfully. Will they give you such information? Yes, most likely. Most people love to help others get started in their same business, *if* they love it, although -- let's face it -- occasionally you may run into owners who are of an ungenerous nature. In such a case, thank them politely for their time, and go on to the next name on your list. When you've found three people willing to help you by reminiscing about their own history, you interview each of them in turn, and make a list of the necessary skills and knowledges they all agreed were necessary. Give this list a name. Let's call it "**A**."

(5) Back home you sit down and inventory your own skills and knowledges, with the information you will draw from the exercises in Chapter 8, or in the Flower Exercise. Give this list a name, also. Let's call it "**B**."

(6) Having done this, you then subtract "**B**" from "**A**." This gives you another new list, which you should name. Let's call it "**C**." "**C**" is by definition a list of the skills or knowledges that you *don't* have, but must find -- either by taking courses yourself, or by hiring someone with those skills, or by getting a friend or family member (who has those skills) to volunteer.

Why fifty to seventy-five miles away? Well, actually, that's a minimum. You want to interview businesses which, *if they were in the same geographical area as you,* would be your rivals. And if they were in the same geographical area with you, wouldn't likely tell you how to get started. After all, they're not going to train you just so you can then take business away from them.

But, when a guy, a gal, or a business is fifty to seventy-five miles away -- you're not as likely to be perceived as a rival, and therefore they're much more likely to tell you what you want to know about their own experience, and how *they* got started, and where the land mines are hidden.

Doubtless at this point you would like an example of this whole process. Okay. Our job-hunter is a woman who has been making harps for some employer, but now is thinking about going into business for herself, not only *making* harps at home, but also *designing* harps, with the aid of a computer. After interviewing several home-based harp makers and harp designers, and finishing her own self-assessment, her chart of **A – B = C** came out looking like the next page.

A – B = C

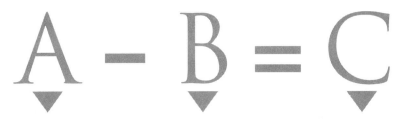

Skills and Knowledges Needed to Run This Kind of Business Successfully	Skills and Knowledges Which I Have	Skills and Knowledges Needed, Which I Have to Learn or Get Someone to Volunteer, or I Will Have to Go Out and Hire
Precision-working with tools and instruments	Precision-working with tools and instruments	
Planning and directing an entire project	Planning and directing an entire project	
Programming computers, inventing programs that solve physical problems		Programming computers, inventing programs that solve physical problems
Problem solving: evaluating why a particular design or process isn't working	Problem solving: evaluating why a particular design or process isn't working	
Being self-motivated, resourceful, patient, and persevering, accurate, methodical, and thorough	Being self-motivated, resourceful, patient, and persevering, accurate, methodical and thorough	
Thorough knowledge of: Principles of electronics	*Thorough knowledge of:*	*Thorough knowledge of:* Principles of electronics
Physics of strings	Physics of strings	
Principles of vibration	Principles of vibration	
Properties of woods	Properties of woods	
Computer programming		Computer programming
Accounting		Accounting

If she decides to try her hand at becoming an independent harp maker and harp designer, she now knows what she needs but lacks: *computer programming, knowledge of the principles of electronics, and accounting.* In other words, List **C.** These she must either go to school to acquire for herself, OR enlist from some friends of hers in those fields, on a volunteer basis, OR go out and hire, part-time. These are the essential steps for any new enterprise that you are considering: **A – B = C.**

You may also want to talk to people who have juggled two (or more) careers, at the same time. If you want to start up more than one venture, you need to interview people *in each line of work* to find out **A – B = C** for both jobs.

HOW CAN YOU DO A – B = C, WHEN NO ONE HAS DONE WHAT YOU WANT TO DO?

No matter how inventive you are, you're probably *not* going to invent a job that *no one* has ever heard of, before. You're only going to invent a job that *most* people have never heard of, before. But the likelihood is *great* that someone, somewhere, in this world of endless creativity, has already put together the kind of job you're dreaming about. Your task: to find them and interview them thoroughly. And then . . . well, you know the drill: **A – B = C.**

If there isn't someone doing *exactly* what you are dreaming of doing, there is at least someone who is *close.* This is how you find them.

1. Break down your projected business or new career into its parts.
2. If there are more than two parts, take any two of these parts to begin with. See what kind of job or person they describe.
3. Find out the names of such persons. You want three names, or more.
4. Go see, phone, or eMail them. You can learn a great deal from them, and even if they are not in the same business

as you are dreaming of, you will learn a great deal that is relevant to your dream.

5. They in turn may be able to give you a lead to someone whose business is even closer to what you are dreaming of. Ask for names. Go interview them.

Let's see how this works out, in practice. For our example, let's suppose your dream is -- here we take a ridiculous case -- to use computers to monitor the growth of plants at the South Pole. And suppose you can't find anybody who's ever done such a thing. The way to tackle this seemingly insurmountable problem, is to break the proposed business down into its parts, which -- in this case -- are: *computers, plants,* and *the Antarctic.*

Then you try combining any two parts, together, to define the person or persons you need to talk to. In this case, that would mean finding someone who's *used computers with plants here in the States,* or someone who's *used computers at the Antarctic,* or someone who has *worked with plants at the Antarctic,* etc. You go talk to them, and along the way you may discover there *is* someone who has used computers to monitor the growth of plants at the South Pole. Then again, you may not. In any event, you will learn most of the pitfalls that wait for you, by hearing the experience of those who are in *parallel* businesses or careers.

Thus, it is *always* possible -- with a little blood, sweat and imagination -- to find out what A – B = C is, for the business you're dreaming of doing.

Step #2: Going on the Internet or Reading Some Books

As I mention more than once in this book, and also on my Web site[5], the Internet offers five kinds of help to the job-hunter or career-changer:

1. **Job-posting** on the part of employers *(used to be called "classified ads," and still is, when it's not on the Internet but in newspapers).*
2. **Resume-posting** on the part of job-hunters
3. **Testing and career advice**
4. **Research** on careers, fields, companies, and salaries
5. **Contacts** with other job-hunters or resource people.

While the first two kinds of help do not work nearly as well as all the *hype* suggests, the last three kinds of help (above) work superbly. Here the Internet comes into its own, and is truly a Godsend.

So, its **career advice and research** that we're talking about here, in the arena of self-employment and/or working at home. There are some tremendously useful sites that you should visit before ever launching your own enterprise, and a list of them starts on the following page.

5. `http://www.JobHuntersBible.com/`

WEB SITES DEALING WITH HOME-BASED BUSINESSES

I and my Web consultants have combed through the various home-based business *sites*, testing them (this is all very subjective, believe me) for sensible advice, ease of use, and trustworthiness *in our judgment.*

There are probably a lot of good home-business sites that we didn't find; but among those we looked at, here is a Sampler of the ones we liked the best:

► **CCH Inc.**
SOHO Guidebook
http://www.toolkit.cch.com/scripts/sohotoc.asp

► **FreeAgent.com**
Free Agent 101
http://www.freeagent.com/resource/index.asp#

► **AHBBO -- Elena Fawkner**
Look Before You Leap: Is a Home-Based Business REALLY For You?
http://www.ahbbo.com/lookb4uleap.html
http://www.ahbbo.com/articles.html

► **U.S. Small Business Association**
How to Get Started as a Small Business
http://www.sba.gov/starting/

► **IdeaCafe**
IdeaCafe's Work at Home
http://www.ideacafe.com/workathome/workathome.html

► **Nolo Press**
Independent Contractors Legal Encyclopedia
http://www.nolo.com/category/ic_home.html?t=0030LFNAV03202000

▸ **IVillage.com**
The Basics about Self-Employment
`http://www.ivillage.com/topics/work/selfemp/`

▸ **Mompreneurs - Ten Signs It's a Scam**
Follow these guidelines to avoid getting ripped off.
`http://www.ivillage.com/work/print/0,10738,259735,00.html`

▸ **Better Business Bureau**
Tips on Work at Home Schemes *(Separating scams from real opportunities)*
`http://www.bbb.org/library/workathome.asp`

▸ **Entrepreneur Magazine**
How to Legally Establish Your Home-Based Business
`http://www.entrepreneur.com/Your_Business/YB_SegArticle/0,4621,287882,00.html`

▸ **Kauffman Center for Entrepreneurial Leadership**
Y&E: The Magazine for Teen Entrepreneurs
`http://ye.entreworld.org/`
`http://ye.entreworld.org/5-2000/7day_pricing.cfm`

▸ **Working Solo**
Working Solo: FAQs for Solo Entrepreneurs
`http://www.workingsolo.com/starting/faqs/index-2.html`

▸ **Top Ten Ways to Finance a Solo Business**
`http://www.workingsolo.com/starting/articles/topten.html`

▸ **World Wide Web Tax**
Of course they're selling something, but it has a lot of good free information about what the self-employed have to do vis-à-vis taxes, in the U.S. at least.
`http://www.wwwebtax.com/miscellaneous/self_employment_tax.htm`

▶ **Inc.com**
Articles about setting up your own business, even outside the home.
`http://www.inc.com/`

▶ **MyCounsel.com**
A site designed to sell their legal services, but which also has a number of free, helpful articles on legal issues regarding small business, employment, or hiring, intellectual property, bankruptcy, etc.
`http://www.MyCounsel.com/content/smbusiness/employmentlaw/`

FALL-BACK STRATEGIES WHEN YOU JUST CAN'T GET A BUSINESS GOING, AT FIRST

When I first started out in this field, thirty years ago, I read every book there was, on job-hunting and career-change. One thing that frustrated me was that they would offer some recommended strategies, and then act as though, *Well, of course, now you've got that job you've always wanted.*

I always wondered, as I read, *"But what if they don't?"* What if all the strategies here recommended *don't work?* So, naturally I'm concerned for my own readers who try *everything* in this chapter, and you're still out of work, and your finances are getting to the crisis stage. The advice that follows applies not only to starting your own business, but to any kind of job target.

You know about welfare, of course. It varies from country to country, but it is a safety net that most countries have constructed.

But what if you don't want to go on welfare. Then what do you do? Well, you have several choices:

- A stop-gap job
- Temp work
- Holding down two different part-time jobs
- Job-sharing

A STOP-GAP JOB

The first life-preserver is: *a stop-gap job.* This phrase, used by many experts, refers to the situation where your money is about gone, and you have exhausted all job-hunting strategies. At this point, the advice of every expert is to take *any kind of work you can get.* That fills, or stops-up, the gap between the balance in your bank account and what you need to live on -- hence, it is called a *stop-gap job.*

The mark of a stop-gap job is simple: it's a short-term job that you would *hate* if it was anything but short-term. It isn't supposed to be anything you really *like* to do. Its only requirement is that it be honest work, and that it bring in some money. It will probably be less money than you are used to making, per hour. It will probably also be hard work; or boring work. *But,* who cares? Its sole purpose is to put some honest money on the table, so you can eat. And pay the rent. And that's *it.*

The way you go about finding a stop-gap job is simple. You get your local newspaper, you look at the help-wanted ads, and you circle *any* and *every* job that you could see yourself doing *for a short time,* simply for the money. Then you go and apply for those jobs.

You also go to employment agencies, and say, "I'll do *anything*; what have you got?"

Unhappily, this spirit -- "I'll do anything" is rarer than it ought to be. Many job-hunters refuse to even consider a stop-gap job; they'd rather go on welfare, first. One reason for this financially suicidal feeling is the conviction that 'such jobs are *beneath* me.' You know: *"I wouldn't be caught* dead *washing dishes."*

I need to state the obvious here: namely, that **any honest hard work neither demeans you, nor makes you less important as a person.** The 'you' who is doing that work, remains the same. Except that it is a 'you' that *needs this money.* I should also add, while I'm at it, that there are many salutary lessons for the soul, to be learned from temporarily taking a stop-gap job. And this is especially true if that job is at a different level and in a different world than you have been accustomed to.[6]

Many of us delay in seeking a stop-gap job for a somewhat higher reason: namely, the conviction that we must have full-time to devote to our job-hunt. Well, that's important, of course; but so is eating. You may want to consider a part-time stop-gap job, in order to address both concerns, fairly. (Also you might want to keep a *time-log* for two weeks, to see just how much time you actually *are* spending on your job-hunt. The easiest person in the world to deceive is *ourselves.*)

A final reason many refuse to seek a stop-gap job is that they are receiving unemployment benefits, which of course would be cut off, if they took a job of any kind. But, needless to say, unemployment benefits do run out, and should they run out before you have found a job, then it is a very different story. Run, do not walk, to find a job, any job, apply for it and take it, once offered -- as a stop-gap measure . . . only. Keep working on Chapters 7–12. And *keep looking.*

For, as the birds say *(I overheard them just the other day)*: "A stop-gap job is like a frail branch of a tree: a lovely place to stop and catch your breath, but a lousy place to build a permanent nest."

---

6. At one point in my life, I myself took a stop-gap job which involved cutting grass, helping lay cement sidewalks, and building retaining walls. It was one of the most educational experiences of my life. It also brought in exactly the money that I so badly needed.

TEMP WORK

After stop-gap jobs, your next life-preserver is *temp work.* In these difficult times, many many employers are cutting their staff to the bone. Trouble is, as time goes on, some extra work may then come their way, work which their reduced staff can't keep up with.

At that point, employers won't usually hire back the staff they cut, but they will turn to what are called "Temporary Help" agencies, for either full- or part-time work. If you are having trouble finding a long-term full-time job, you certainly want to go register at one or more of these agencies.

In the old days, temporary agencies were solely for clerical workers and secretarial help. But the field has seen an explosion of services in recent years.

Now there are temporary agencies *(at least in the larger cities)* for many different occupations. In your city you may find temporary agencies for: accountants, industrial workers, assemblers, drivers, mechanics, construction people, engineering people, management/executives, nannies (for young and old), health care/dental/medical people, legal specialists, insurance specialists, sales/marketing people, underwriting professionals, financial services, and the like, as well as for the more obvious specialties: data processing, secretarial, and office services.

You will find the agencies listed in the Yellow Pages of your local phone book, under *Employment-Temporary.* Their listing or their ads will usually indicate what their specialities are.

They may find for you: a full-time job that lasts for a number of days or weeks or even months.

Or they may find for you: a part-time job that lasts for a number of days or weeks or even months.

Or they may not find anything for you. It is the case, as with all employment agencies, that there are often many more job-hunters who list themselves with such agencies, than there are employers who come there looking for help.

So, this cannot be your only strategy for finding work.

But it is certainly worth a try. You can increase the likelihood of the agency linking you up with a job, if you help them a little. For example, if you are in environmental engineering, and you know your field well, you can increase your chances of getting employment through a particular agency by compiling *for them* a list of the companies in your field, together with (if you know it) the name of the contact person there.[7] The temporary agency will do what it always does, initiate calls to those companies, soliciting their business; and if they uncover a vacancy, the odds are very great that it will be your name which is put forth for that job there.

HOLDING DOWN TWO DIFFERENT PART-TIME JOBS

If the temporary agencies never call, and you still can't find any full-time job, your next strategy for finding work is to look for part-time work. While there are many *involuntary* part-time workers these days[8] there are also many *voluntary* part-time workers. They don't *want* to work full-time. Period. End of story. And you of course may be among them.

But suppose you do want full-time work. Often you can put a couple of part-time jobs together, so as to make the equivalent of full-time work.

In some cases, you may even prefer this to one full-time job. Perhaps you feel yourself to be multi-talented and/or perhaps you have a couple of very different interests. You can sometimes find a part-time job in one of your fields of interest and a second part-time job in another one of your fields of interest, thus allowing you to use *all* your favorite skills and interests -- in a way that no one full-time job might be able to do.

---

7. I am indebted to one of our readers, Tathyana Pshevlozky, for this idea.

8. Involuntary part-time workers are those who want a full-time job, can't find one, so take a part-time job until a full-time job comes along.

You can put together two part-time jobs in a variety of ways. One can be a job where you work for someone else, the other can be your own business or consultancy.

One can be a job advertised in a newspaper (or agency) or *online*, and the other can be a job that you create for yourself by approaching someone you'd really like to work with (or for), and asking what kind of help they need.

One can be a job with someone you never met before, and the other can be a job with your father, mother, brother, sister, aunt, uncle, or your best friend.

One can be a job during the daytime, on weekdays, and the other can be a job you do on weekends, or on certain evenings.

How you find such jobs, will depend on the nature of the job. If it's with a family member or friend, you ask them. If one of the jobs involves starting your own business, you start it. Newspaper ads also are a way of finding part-time jobs. If they want part-time workers, they will say so. Experience usually dictates that these jobs will either be at places you like, for much less money than you want, or they will be at places you hate, for a lot more money (e.g., tollbooth collectors, check-out people at supermarkets, etc.). The general rule is: the more boring the job, the higher the pay. You decide.

JOB-SHARING

You're looking for part-time work. But one day, while you're looking through the ads or talking to some friends, you discover a full-time job that you are really interested in, and it's at just the kind of place where you would like to work. But they want someone full-time, and you only want to work part-time. There is a *possible* solution.

You can sometimes sell the organization on the idea of letting *two* of you fill that one job *(one of you from 8–12 noon, say, and the other from 1–5 p.m.)*. Of course in order to do this, you have to find someone else -- a relative, friend, or acquaintance -- who is also looking for part-time work, *and* is very competent, *and* would be willing to share that job with you. And you have to find them *first*, and talk them into it, before you approach the boss at that place that interests you. This arrangement is called *job-sharing*, and there are a number of books and places you can write to, if you need some further guidance about how to do it, and how to sell the employer on the idea.

Incidentally, don't omit larger employers, from this particular search just because they would seem to you to be too bound by their own bureaucratic rules -- *some* of them are very open to the idea of job-sharing. *On the other hand, of course, a lot of them aren't.* But it never hurts to ask.

CONCLUSION: NEW WAYS TO WORK

It takes a lot of guts to try ANYTHING new *(for you)* in today's economy. It's easier, however, if you keep three rules in mind:

1. There is always some risk, in trying something new. Your job is not to avoid risk - - there is no way to do that - - but to make sure ahead of time that the risks are *manageable.*
2. You find this out before you start, by first talking to others who have already done what you are thinking of doing; then you evaluate whether or not you still want to go ahead and try it.
3. Have a Plan B, already laid out, *before you start,* as to what you will do if it doesn't work out; i.e., know where you are going to go, next. Don't wait, *puh-leaze!* Write it out, now. *This is what I'm going to do, if this doesn't work out:*____________________

   ____________________________________.

These rules always apply, no matter where you are in your life: just starting out, already employed, unemployed, in mid-life, recovering after a crisis or accident, facing retirement, or whatever. Do take them very seriously.

If you're sharing your life with someone, sit down with that partner or spouse and ask what the implications are *for them* if you try this new thing. Will it require all your joint savings? Will they have to give up things? If so, what? Are they willing to make those sacrifices? And so on.

If you aren't out of work, you will need to debate the wisdom of quitting your job before you start up the new company, or business. And what do the experts say, here? In a word, they say, if you have a job, *don't* quit it. Better by far to move *gradually* into self-employment, doing it as a moonlighting activity first of all, while you are still holding down that regular job somewhere else. That way, you can test out your new enterprise, as you would test a floorboard in an old run-down house, stepping on it cautiously without at first putting your full weight on it, to see whether or not it will support you.

If your investigation revealed that it takes good accounting practices in order to turn a profit, and you don't know a thing about accounting, you go out and hire a part-time accountant *immediately* -- or, if you absolutely have no money, you talk an accountant friend of yours into giving you some volunteer time, for a while.

It is up to you to do your research thoroughly, weigh the risks, count the cost, get counsel from those intimately involved with you, and then if you decide you want to do **it** (whatever ***it*** is), go ahead and try -- no matter what your well-meaning but pessimistic acquaintances may say.

You only have one life here on this earth, and that life is *yours* (under God) to say how it will be spent, or not spent. Parents, well-meaning friends, etc. get no vote. Just you, and God.

CHAPTER SEVEN

The Secret To Finding Your Dream Job

What Are You In Love With?

"What happened over the last couple of years is the Valley lost its association with being the place where you were in love with technology and innovation and became the place where you are in love with getting rich."

Judith L. Estrin,
Speaking of Silicon Valley in California,
Quoted in the N.Y. Times, *7/29/01*

FOR THE PAST thirty years I have heard from thousands and thousands of readers who write each year to tell me that my book changed their life. I am always curious to know exactly *what* in my book changed their life. So, I often ask.

I remember one reader wrote back to say, "It was that sentence where you said, '*You can do anything you want to.*' "

Another reader wrote that it was the sentence where I said, *"The clearer your vision of what you seek, the closer you are to finding it."*

And yet another reader, more mystically inclined, said it was the sentence, *"What you are seeking is seeking you."*

What has always fascinated me is how often, in a book of many many pages, it is just one particular sentence *(varying from reader to reader)* that does it. It is as if our whole being is trembling on the brink of new life, sometimes, and needs only the slightest encouragement -- often a simple sentence will do -- to launch itself into a new and more satisfying orbit.

WHAT DID YOU COME INTO THE WORLD TO DO?

It may be that as you read this, *your* whole being has wanted for some time, a new, better, more satisfying, more fulfilling life.

And now -- due to your being laid off or made redundant, or due to some internal time clock ticking *within*, or some life-changing event occurring *without* (such as a death or divorce) -- you find yourself at a crossroads; and the moment to actually seek that new life and new work has arrived.

There is a name for this moment in your life; in fact, there are several names.

We call it "at last going after your dreams."
We call it "finding more purpose and meaning for your life."
We call it "making a career-change."
We call it "deciding to try something new."
We call it "setting out in a different direction in your life."
We call it "getting out of the rat race."
We call it "going after your dream job."
We call it "finding your mission in life, at last."

But what you call it doesn't really matter. It is instantly recognizable as that moment when you decide that *this time* you're not going to do just a traditional job-hunt; you're going to do a life-changing job-hunt or career-change: One that begins with **you** and what it is that *you* want out of life.

This time it's all about: *Your* agenda. *Your* wishes. *Your* dreams. *Your* mission in life, given you by the Great God, our Creator.

This is a life-changing moment, and we should celebrate its arrival, in any life.

WHY NOW?
AND, WHY YOU?

Let's face it, dear reader, neither you nor I are getting any younger. If you don't go after your dreams *now,* when will you?

Now is the time to fulfill your dreams and the vision that you once had of what your life could be. Even if it can't be done in a night and a day. Even if it takes patience. Even if it means hard work. Even if it means changing careers. Even if it means going out into the unknown, and taking risks. *(Manageable risks, please!)*

You may think that this is a selfish activity -- because this deals with You, you, you. But it is not. It is related to what *the world* most needs from you. That world currently is *filled* with workers whose weeklong question is, *When is the weekend going to be here?* And, then, *Thank God It's Friday!* Their work puts bread on the table *but*...... But they are bored out of their minds. Some of them are bored because even though they know what they'd rather be doing, they can't get out of their dead-end jobs, for one reason or another. But too many others, unfortunately, are bored simply because they have *never* given this sufficient priority in their life. They've kept busy with work and their social life, and partying, and vacation; and never taken the time to *think* -- to think out what they uniquely can do, and what they uniquely have to offer to the world. They've flopped from one job to another, letting *accident, circumstance, coincidence* and *whim* carry them wheresoever it would.

What the world most needs *from you* is not to add to their number, but to figure out, and then contribute to the world, what you came into this world to do.

It's time for you to fulfill your destiny. Dust off those dreams. Let the vision burn brightly! And let it beckon you on. Then you'll be conducting a job-hunt whose goal truly sets your heart on fire!

THE POWER OF THE BECKONING VISION

No matter what other people tell you, you won't increase your likelihood of finding your dream job by just polishing up your resume, or taking a few more tests, or memorizing a few more techniques, or reading a few better answers to an employer's interview questions.

Okay, then what is the key? It's found in the words of the reader who said that the sentence which changed her life was:

> "The clearer your vision of what you seek, the closer you are to finding it."

It is the vision, the picture of *the life you really want*, that you need to be concentrating on. It has the power to bring about the very change you desire. And the more detailed the picture, the more it is *fleshed out*, the more power it has. You make it more detailed by asking yourself such questions as: What is it that I most want to be doing with my life? What are my unfulfilled dreams? What hunches, what yearnings, do I have about why I was put here, on earth? What have I always put off for the future, that I ought to actually go after, now?

"The clearer your vision of what you seek, the closer you are to finding it." Here are four exercises to help you refine your vision:

Exercise #1:
DRAW A PICTURE OF YOUR IDEAL LIFE

Take a large piece of white paper, with some colored pencils or pens, and draw a picture of your ideal life: where you live, who's with you, what you do, what your dwelling looks like, what your ideal vacation looks like, etc. Don't let *reality* get in the way. Pretend a magic wand has been waved over your life, and it gives you everything you think your ideal life would be.

Now, *of course* you can't draw. Okay, then make symbols for things, or create little 'doodads' or symbols, with labels -- anything so that you can *see* all together on one page, your vision of your ideal life -- however haltingly expressed.

The power of this exercise is sometimes amazing. Reason? By avoiding words and using pictures or symbols as much as possible, it bypasses the left side of the brain ("the safekeeping self," as George Prince calls it) and speaks directly to the right side of your brain ("the experimental self"), whose job it is to engineer change.

Exercise #2:
PICK YOUR IDEAL JOB FROM SOME LIST

Well, sure, *words* tend to arouse your 'safekeeping self.' But not always. Sometimes words can be useful, as when they are put in the form of *lists.*

Don't think of them as *lists,* however. Think of them as a menu of options at some Vocational Restaurant.

Small problem: there is no such Restaurant, *and* the number of options is bewildering. For example, experts can name at least 12,860 different occupations or careers that you might choose from, and these have 8,000 alternative job-titles, for a total of over 20,000.[1]

Twenty thousand! There's the problem, right there. Most of us find it is impossible to choose between 20,000 of anything. In fact, we have trouble choosing between twenty items on a restaurant menu!

That's why, in the U.S. at least, people have hacked this list down, further, to just 300 options. Yes, you can find 90% of the 135 million workers in the U.S. in a mere 300 of those 20,000 job-titles. The other 19,700 job-titles are filled by just 10% of the workforce. *(Of course it's that 10% that is reading this book.)*

1. A description of all 20,000 of these occupations or careers can be found in any U.S. library, in a volume known as the U.S. *Dictionary of Occupational Titles.* It is known more familiarly as the D.O.T., and is published by the Bureau of Labor Statistics. Other countries (for example, Canada) sometimes have similar volumes. In the U.S., it has essentially been supplanted by O*Net, even though the latter has a much shorter list.

Some people have hacked the list down further still, to just 50 options. For, they say, you can find 50% of the 135 million workers in the U.S. in just 50 job-titles.

Fifty would seem to be a manageable number of careers to choose between, but in our culture we're always looking for someone who will hack the list down, further still -- books, and newspapers, publish such lists as *The Ten Hottest Fields of the New Millennium.*

On the Web, try *my* favorite list at
`http://www.review.com/career/article.cfm?id=career\car_job_top_ten&jobs=0&menuID=2&resources=1`
Or try typing "Ten Hottest Careers" into your favorite search engine, such as
`www.Metacrawler.com/` or
`www.northernlight.com/`

How useful will this exercise *(perusing lists of options)* be to you? Well, for starters, (1) all such lists are highly subjective, (2) they will differ from one magazine or book to another, (3) there is no agreement between them on which are really the 'ten hottest' careers, (4) nor will they tell you what criteria they used when compiling that list.

That's for starters. More importantly, one person's *best career* is another person's *poison*. The best career *for You* is one which uses: *Your* favorite skills, *Your* favorite subjects, *Your* primary goals, and *Your* preferred people and things to work with, plus *Your* preferred workplace, *Your* preferred objectives, and *Your* preferred level and salary.

The fact that a career is 'hot' doesn't mean a thing, unless it turns you on. *Hot* only refers to how much demand there is for a particular job or career, and how easy therefore it is to get into such a career. But that's not very relevant, if you are seeking a job that you love. For example, if some *hot* new career involves always working with computers, but you much prefer working with people, then that career is going to make you miserable, no matter how easy it may be to find that kind of job.

Hence, it doesn't matter that a career is *hot* or *easy* to get into. What matters is that you and the career should be happy with each other. Better yet, that you and your career should be in love with each other. Work that you can't wait to get up in the morning and go do. Work that you love so much, you can't believe you are being paid to do it -- since you'd be willing to do it for nothing. There are few greater joys in life, than to find such a career.

So, in the end, each individual must form his or her *own* list of 'ten best careers.' No one else can do it for you; therefore no one else's list should be taken seriously by you for even one minute -- unless you see something on that list that causes you to go, *Aha!*

As a *primer of the pump*, such a list may be useful. As *a recipe* for where you should go next, it can be a disaster.

"I'm hoping to find something in a meaningful, humanist, outreach kind of bag, with flexible hours, non-sexist bosses, and fabulous fringes."

Exercise #3: THE MIRROR METHOD OF IDENTIFYING YOUR DREAM JOB

In this method you use other people as though they were mirrors to yourself. You look at everyone you know, everyone you've ever seen on TV, or read about, and you think to yourself, "Well, whose job would I most like to have, in all the world?" Make a second and third choice. On three separate sheets of paper, write what each of these three people does. Underneath that, then, break down their job into its parts: what is it about the job that attracts you? List as many things as possible. Then look at all three sheets of paper, choose which job is actually of greatest interest to you, and figure out how you could go talk to someone actually doing such a job.[2]

One woman who changed careers this way decided that the job she most admired was that of a woman she saw on national TV, who hosted a children's program. So, she prepared a careful outline of what she thought a good children's TV program should look like, then went to her local TV station (which had no such program) and told them her ideas. They liked her proposal, hired her to host just such a program, and she became a big success. Later, she triumphantly wrote me, "I am in my ideal career . . . without ever having done any of the exercises in your book!" *Bravo,* say I.

Exercise #4: LETTING A TEST TELL YOU WHAT TO DO

When you're puzzled about what to do next with your life, the idea of taking some kind of career test may strike you as a really great idea. There are a lot of such tests out there. They are not really "tests" -- you can't flunk them. Experts call them "questionnaires" or "assessment instruments." But most people still call them "tests."

2. This assumes, of course, that you can move from one career into another without spending much time 're-tooling.'

They come in many forms and flavors -- skills tests, interests tests, values tests, psychological tests, etc. -- and their names form a veritable alphabet soup: SDS, MBTI, SII, CISS, RHETI, and the like.

In the past, if you wanted to take them, you had to get dressed and get yourself down to a community college counseling center, or career counselor's office, or State unemployment office, or one-stop career center, or a Johnson O'Connor Human Engineering Laboratory -- where the tests and the test administrators can be found. You can still do that. Ask around, in your community, to see where such tests can be found.

But since 1996, a new wrinkle has developed. If you have Internet access, career tests can now be plucked off the Internet, and taken by you in the privacy of your own home. *Our eyes light up! Now you're talking!*

Here's the best of what's available in your home, by title (most sites explain what their particular test or instrument is trying to measure). I have tried to indicate which are free, and which charge for the privilege of taking them.

JOBS AS INTERESTS AND STYLES

► **The Princeton Review Career Quiz**
`http://www.review.com/career/careerquizhome.cfm?menuID=0&careers=6`
Free. A brief 24-part questionnaire, related to the Birkman Method, with intriguing career suggestions.

► **Top Ten Jobs**
`http://www.review.com/career/article.cfm?id=career\car_job_top_ten&jobs=0&menuID=2&resources=1`
Free. Related to the Birkman Method. The article was excerpted from *Guide to Your Career, 4th Edition,* by Alan B. Bernstein and Nicholas R. Schaffzin. As I mentioned a couple of pages back, this is my favorite "Top Ten" list on the Internet. Very imaginative!

► **Analyze My Career**
`http://www.AnalyzeMyCareer.com/index.cfm?action=signup&test=expertplus`
Tests for sale: Aptitude tests, personality tests, occupation interests, entrepreneurial index ($69.95 for *everything*).

► **The RHETI Test**
`http://www.9types.com/`
Free. Related to the Enneagram.

► **Psychological Testing Tools**
`http://www.metadevelopment.com/`
$75.00 each. Eleven tests.

(More tests can be found at
`http://dir.yahoo.com/Social_Science/Psychology/Branches/Personality/Online_Tests/`)

JOBS AS PEOPLE ENVIRONMENTS

► **John Holland's Self-Directed Search**
`http://www.self-directed-search.com/`

The queen of career tests (in my opinion), it has been taken by more than 24 million people. The SDS online takes 15 minutes and costs only $8.95. Your 8–16 page personalized report will appear on your screen. This printable assessment report provides a list of the occupations and fields of study that most closely match your interests.

- **CareerPlanner.com's "Career Planning Test"**
  `http://career-planning.com/`

As the Web site says, this proprietary on-line career assessment test by Robert Reardon is based on the well-established RIASEC system developed by Dr. John Holland. Its cost is $24.95 however, so you must decide whether it is worth approximately three times the cost of John L. Holland's original (above). It does show more contemporary careers that did not exist a few years ago, including Java Programmer, Web Master, Marketing Communications Specialist, Software Alliance Manager, Network Specialist and more. The test report is approximately 8 to 11 pages long and includes listings for 30 to over 100 unique careers, related to your 'Holland Code.'

- **The Career Interests Game**
  `http://www.missouri.edu/~cppcwww/holland.shtml`

Free. Many years ago, I invented a visual short-cut to the RIASEC system called "The Party Exercise" (page 356 at the back of this book), and here is a beautiful presentation of it (here called *The Career Interests Game),* supplemented by pages of skills, suggested careers, and favorite traits. First rate.

- **The Career Key**
  `http://www.ncsu.edu/careerkey/`

Free. Related to Holland. *(Note: you have to click on "You," "Us," or "Others" in order to enter this site.)*

Now, before you reach for your modem, there are five rules to keep in mind when approaching career tests in general, on- or offline.

The Five Rules About Taking Career Tests

1. **Treat all tests as suggestive, only.**

Tests have one great mission and purpose: to give you ideas you hadn't thought of, and suggestions worth following up. But if you ask more of them -- if you ask them to absolutely tell you what to do with your life -- you're asking too much. On many online (and offline) tests, if you answer even two questions inaccurately, you will get completely wrong results and recommendations. You should therefore take all test results not with just a grain of salt, but with a barrel.

2. **Take several tests, rather than just one.**

You will get a much better picture of your preferences and profile, not to mention career ideas, from three or more tests, rather than just one.

3. **Don't let tests make you forget that you are absolutely unique.**

All tests tend to deal in categories, so they end up saying "you are an ENFP" or "you are an AES," or you are a "Blue." You are lumped with a lot of other people, as in a tribe -- and sometimes it is the wrong tribe. Just remember, you are "a unique job seeker seeking to conduct a unique job hunt, by identifying a unique career and then connecting with a unique company or organization, that you can uniquely help or serve." (Thanks, Clara Horvath.) Without some hard thinking about how you are unique, tests become just "a flytrap for the lazy," as job expert Mary Ellen Mort puts it.

4. **An online test isn't likely to be as useful as one administered by a qualified professional in your community.**

If you don't like the results you get from any of the online tests (or if you don't have access to the Internet) go out and look for tests in the kinds of places I listed above.

5. **Don't force online tests on your friends.**

If online tests do help you, don't for Heaven's sake become "A Career Test Evangelist" and try to force all your friends and family to take such tests. People are very skittish about tests. For example, some people dislike "forced choice questions," where they must pick between two choices that are equally bad, in their view. Others don't like questions about how they would behave in certain situations, because they tend to pick how they wish they behaved, rather than how in fact they actually do. And some people hate all tests. Period. End of story. So, trying to force these tests on your family or best friends could lead to your premature demise. Be gentle: the computer you save may be your own.

"Let's put it this way — if you can find a village without an idiot, you've got yourself a job."

TRY ON THE SUIT FIRST

In all of the four exercises, above, don't believe what lists, tests, experts, or well-meaning friends try to claim is an ideal job *for you.* Just as you would when buying a suit, test it, try it on, make up your own mind. *Puh-leeze.*

Go talk to at least three people who are actually *doing* this career that you find so appealing, and ask them these questions:

How did you get into this field?
What do you like best about it?
What do you like least about it?
How do I get into this career, and how much of a demand is there for people who can do this work?
Is it easy to find a job in this career, or is it hard?
Who else would you recommend or suggest I go talk to, to learn more about this career?

You *want* to know all this! Believe me, you *want* to know! Especially if, in order to prepare for this career that interests you, it's going to take some time for you to go get some schooling, or perhaps a degree.

If you fail to ask such questions *ahead of time* you may be bitterly disappointed after you get all that training, or that degree.

GETTING A JOB BY DEGREES

And do yourself a big favor: don't go get a degree because you think that will guarantee you a job! No, mon ami, it will not.

I wish you could see my mail, filled with bitter letters from people who believed such tests as you have just seen, went and got a degree in that field, thought it would be a snap to find a job, but are still unemployed after two years. You would weep! They are bitter (often), angry (always), and disappointed in a society which they feel lied to them.

They found there was no job that went with that degree. They feel lied to, by our society and by the experts, about the value of going back to school, and getting a degree in this or that 'hot' field.

Now that they have that costly worthless degree, and still can't find a job, they find a certain irony in the phrase, "*Our country believes in getting a job by degrees.*"

If you already made this costly mistake, you know what I mean.

HOW TO FIND INFORMATION, USING THE INTERNET

Besides doing *informational interviewing*, face-to-face, in the fashion I just described, there are other ways to find out helpful information, especially if you have access to the Internet. Here are tutorials *on the Internet*, about how to find information on the Internet, beginning with the tutorial that I like the best:

▸ Search The Internet *(Revised July 2001)*
A Graduated Approach In 5 Steps: Good Places to Start; Best Search Engines; Directories; Searchable Database Directories; Online Tutorial

http://www.lib.berkeley.edu/Help/search.html

http://www.lib.berkeley.edu/TeachingLib/Guides/Internet/FindInfo.html

▸ Searching the Internet *(June 2001)*
Search Engines and Subject Indexes

http://www.sldirectory.com/search.html

▸ Complete Planet Tutorial *(2001)*
Guide to Effective Searching of the Internet
The Complete Source for Search Engines and Databases Tutorial

http://www.completeplanet.com/Tutorials/Search/index.asp

▶ University at Albany Libraries *(July 2001)*
A Primer In Boolean Logic: Boolean Searching on the Internet
http://library.albany.edu/internet/boolean.html

▶ Kids Research Tools (Wordsmythe, Britannica.com, etc.)
Like faith, the Internet is best-approached with the eyes of a child.
http://www.rcls.org/ksearch.htm

▶ Rules About Finding Out About Fields, Jobs, Before You Ever Commit Yourself
http://danenet.wicip.org/jets/jet-9407-p.html

▶ Guidelines for Informational Interviews
http://www.quintcareers.com/information_guide.html

HOW TO FIND CAREER INFORMATION, USING SITE/BOOKS

Some of the very best online job-hunting experts have put up sites, that are immensely useful, and are -- in each case -- accompanied by a companion book. In other words, these are site/books. The sites are listed below. The books can be procured from Barnes and Noble, Amazon.com, Borders, or your local independent bookstore.

The Riley Guide is the best of these, by far. If you can only go to one gateway job-site on the Web, or book offsite, this should be it. Margaret Dikel is the mother of all that is intelligent about job-hunting on the Internet. *(And her on-site listings are always completely up to date.)*

▶ The Riley Guide: Employment Opportunities and Job Resources on the Internet
Compiled by Margaret F. Dikel
http://www.rileyguide.com
The companion book to this site is entitled, *The Guide to Internet Job Searching, 2000–2001 Edition,* by Margaret F. Dikel, plus Frances E. Roehm, and Joyce Lain Kennedy (great co-authors!).

▶ *WEDDLE*'s
Approaching Fields, etc. through their Associations
http://www.weddles.com/associations/index.htm
The companion book to this site is entitled, *WEDDLE's Job-Seeker's Guide to Employment Web Sites (revised annually).* Amacom, N.Y., N.Y. Pete Weddle is one of the true experts in the field of employment sites, recruiters, etc. on the Internet.

▶ CareerXRoads
This is a site which promotes the authors' book and online database.
http://www.careerxroads.com/
The companion book to this site is entitled, *CareerXRoads 2001: The Directory to Job, Resume and Career Management Sites on the Web,* by Gerry Crispin and Mark Mehler. Be aware that the title is something of a misnomer as they do not review any career management sites unless they have a job or resume database. They offer helpful information about those sites that are among the 500 they reviewed, however.

▶ Interbiznet
First Steps in the Hunt (daily newsletter for online job-seekers)
4000 Company Web Sites (current only as of January 1998)
http://www.interbiznet.com/hunt/

http://www.interbiznet.com/hunt/companies/

John Sumser, founder of this site, is one of the pioneers in the online job-hunting/recruiting business. There is a companion book to this site, for employers *(expensive!)*. However, free excerpts from either the current edition, or last year's, are available at John's site here.

HOW TO FIND CAREER INFORMATION, USING JUST BOOKS

▶ Quintessential Careers: A Career and Job-Hunting Resources Guide

One of the best *book* lists available. Forget the irony that you have to first print it from the Web (if you don't have Web access yourself, get a computer-friendly colleague to print this out for you).

http://www.quintcareers.com/career_books.html

Maintained by Randall S. Hansen, who has great taste!

HOW TO FIND CAREER INFORMATION, THROUGH INDIVIDUALS ON THE INTERNET

In spring of 2001, Google acquired the Usenet newsgroup directory and archive formerly maintained by the legendary *Deja.com* -- in this archive more than 650 million messages had been posted since 1995. A great venue for online networking.

http://groups.google.com/

▶ Verizon SuperPages (formerly *Verizon Yellow Pages*)

http://SuperPages.com

You can look up individuals, or businesses, or places. Also, they have "reverse lookup" -- start with the phone number, find out the name at that number. How accurate are these SuperPages, overall? Well, *What Color Is Your Parachute?* was listed in the right state, with the right phone number, but wrong town and wrong zip code. So, they're batting about .500, I guess.

CONCLUSION:
WHEN A DREAM JOB ISN'T ENOUGH:
THE SEARCH FOR SERENITY

The search for a 'dream job' is, on its surface, a search for happiness. We want to be happier in our work, and life, than we have been, up to now.

More specifically, we want that brand of happiness to which I give a special name, namely, *serenity*. And the pathway to serenity is found through *attitude.*

> "We who lived in concentration camps can remember the men who walked through the huts comforting others, giving away their last piece of bread. They may have been few in number, but they offer sufficient proof that everything can be taken from a man but one thing: the last of the human freedoms -- to choose one's attitude in any given set of circumstances . . ."
>
> Victor Frankl

Your attitude is the first (and last) thing everyone notices about you. It is the creator of the texture of your life. As someone has said, "What you have, is God's gift to you. How you use it, is your gift to God." Also it is your gift to all of those around you.

IN THE SEARCH FOR A DREAM JOB, ATTITUDE CAN BE YOUR GREATEST WEAKNESS

It is impossible to talk about work, and about your joy in work, and about finding a dream job, without also talking about your attitude. The job-hunt so perfectly illustrates, in its arena, what is true about all of life. For example, when asked why they didn't hire *so and so*, employers invariably reply, "He had a real *attitude* problem." *Or* "I didn't like her attitude." *Or* "I thought he had a lousy attitude." It is the first thing that every employer notices about you in your resume, or during the first telephone contact, or during a job-interview.

They notice, immediately, whether you would be a pleasant person to be around, or not. They notice, immediately, whether you are interested in other people, their interests and needs, or totally absorbed with yourself. They notice immediately whether you project energy and enthusiasm, or minimal effort and sullenness. Whether you are at

peace with yourself and the world, or seething with anger beneath your calm exterior. Whether you are outgoing, or turned in on yourself. Communicative, or monosyllabic. Interested in giving, or only in taking. Anxious to do the best job possible, going the extra mile, or anxious to 'just go through the motions.'

Your attitude shows, the minute you walk in the employer's office. If you have been unjustly let go at your previous job, your first great need is to let go of your righteous anger at how different the world of work is from what you thought it would be; otherwise, that anger will cripple your job-hunting efforts. You will reek of it to every employer you go see, even as a drunk reeks of strong drink. You may love or hate what's happened to the job market since April of the year 2000, and what it's done to your life. But you've got to make your peace with it. In this arena, as in others, your attitude is *crucial,* and every employer will notice it.

That's important because employers will hire someone with lesser skills, who has the right attitude, before they will hire a more-experienced and more-skilled person with a bad attitude. They have had enough experience with bad attitudes in the past, to know that if they were foolish enough to hire you, and you turn out to have a bad attitude, they will soon *ache* to get rid of you. That is why they are supersensitive to your attitude, from the first moment they lay eyes on you.

IN THE SEARCH FOR A DREAM JOB, ATTITUDE CAN BE YOUR GREATEST POWER

I have been speaking here of *attitude as the betrayer.* "You have a real attitude problem." But, actually, attitude can be our greatest power, as it offers us a way to *transform* all jobs into *something better.*

Maybe, we will never find our dream job, exactly, but our attitude can be a kind of *alchemy* that has the power to transform any job into something more enjoyable.

Such *alchemy*, these days, has four parts to it:

1. **The typical job in the new millennium is best viewed as a temp job.** That is, 'of uncertain length.' If you work for someone else *(and in the U.S. at least, 90% of the workforce do)* then how long your job lasts is up to the people you work for, and not just you. Your job can end at any time, and without warning. You must always be mentally prepared to go job-hunting again, at the drop of a hat.
2. **The typical job in the new millennium is best viewed as a seminar.** Almost every job today is moving and changing so fast, in its very nature, that there is a lot you will have to learn, both when you begin and throughout the time you are there. You cannot think of your job just in terms of what you accomplish. You must think of it in terms of what you learned, and are learning, and will learn, there. You must not only be ready to learn, but eager to learn. And you must emphasize to every would-be employer how much you love to learn new tasks and procedures, and how fast you learn.
3. **The typical job in the new millennium is best viewed as an adventure.** If you end up working in an organization of any size, it is very likely that the dramas which will be played out there, daily, weekly and monthly, will rival any soap opera that is on television today. Power plays! Ambition! Rumors! Poor decisions! Strange alliances! Betrayals! Rewards! Sudden twists and turns that no one could have predicted ahead of time! Sometimes you'll love the way it is turning out; sometimes you'll hate it!
4. **The typical job in the new millennium is one where the satisfaction must lie in the work itself.** In the old days, most of us hoped we would not only find work we enjoyed, but also work where we were and are appreciated. In other words, we looked for a kind of love at our place of work.

Well, there are indeed such places still out there, where you can be appreciated, saluted, singled-out and praised to the skies -- but they are not as common or as easy to find, as they used to be, particularly if the organization has over

50 employees. Despite your best research during your job-hunt, you can end up these days in a job where your bosses fail to recognize or acknowledge the fine contribution that you make, leaving you feeling unloved and unappreciated -- and finally, even after many months or years, they may let you go, and without warning, citing a business turndown, the need for 'new blood,' bankruptcy, merger, or the full-moon.

You must find work which feeds your self-esteem in the very doing of it, rather than depending on some future reward, some future raise, some future promotion.

The key to finding a dream job, is to approach all jobs with the attitude that they can be transformed.

CHAPTER EIGHT

When You Lose All Track Of Time

WHAT

ARE YOUR FAVORITE TRANSFERABLE SKILLS THAT YOU MOST LOVE TO USE?

THERE ARE BASICALLY three ways for us to identify and find the kind of work that we are dying to do -- our dream job:

1. **Drift Into It.** First of all, some of us just *drift* into it. Sheer luck, accident, coincidence, we wake up one morning and realize that we are in our *dream job.* Got there without even realizing it. We wear a big grin on our face, ever thereafter.

2. **Sort of Look for It.** Secondly, some of us *sort of* go looking for our dream job and by flying like a hawk, making lazy circles in the sky, ready to pounce on anything that looks like a dream job, we eventually find it. True, we put *some* effort into the search, but -- looking back on it -- *not that much.* It is more like a magic carpet ride, where intuition gently carries us, over the years, from something as bad as "the job from hell" to something more like "the job from heaven."

"I was a woman who majored in Humanities and then floated around after college in several jobs, which were just jobs. To be honest, I was in my early twenties (which I have nicknamed the decade of terror), and had no idea what I wanted to do. Only, I longed for self-expression and passion in my work. I purchased your book, did some informational interviews, even saw a career counselor, all to no avail.

"Five years later, now, I have come back to your book (the new edition, of course), and identified my values, skills and talents. With my values and skills in mind, I went to the library to research government and non-profit careers, and found myself much interested in the latter. I copied a list of them and began contacting the organizations whose values were closely related to mine: helping people in the community.

"One organization in particular called me back the next day, and asked if I could interview for a professional position with them. I did, explored further to be sure I understood what the job entailed, interviewed a second time, and in less than one month was offered the position of my dreams!

"Thanks to you and your advice on the most successful ways to find employment -- previously over a period of four months I had applied for at least fifty jobs from the want ads, with no hits -- I am now happily employed doing the kind of work I like best, and I did so in record time."

3. **Put In A Lot of Concentrated Hard Work, Using A Step-by-Step Process.** Thirdly, some of us go on a very determined hunt for our ideal or dream job. We buy a book, or sign up for some career counseling classes, and are willing to devote hours and days to the search, with some careful step-by-step process to guide us. It is hard work,

but the whole thing feels like a magic carpet ride: moving logically from A to B to C, and so on, and carrying us eventually to our destination, goal, and target.

How Do You Identify Your Dream Job,
Step by Step?

1. **Favorite Transferable Skills.** You do a systematic inventory of the *transferable skills* which you already possess.
2. **Fields of Fascination.** You do a systematic inventory of the fields or *bodies of knowledge* that fascinate you the most.
3. **The Flower.** From these two inventories, you fashion a description -- a picture, if you will -- of what your new career *looks like.*
4. **Names of Jobs that Fit.** Then you interview people, sharing this picture, to find out *what its name is* (or names).
5. **Informational Interviewing.** Once you know your skills, and know what kind of work you want to do, you go talk to people who are doing it. Find out how they like the work, how they found their job.
6. **Research of Organizations.** Do some research, in your chosen geographical area, on organizations which interest you, to find what they do and what kinds of problems they or their industry are wrestling with.
7. **Network.** Then identify and seek out the person who actually has the power to hire you there, for the job you want.
8. **Contacts.** Use your contacts to get in to see him or her. Show this person with the power to hire you how you can help them with their problems; and how you would stand out as 'one employee in a hundred.'
9. **Closure.** In all of this, cut no corners, take no shortcuts.

Used by permission of Johnny Hart and Creators Syndicate, Inc.

These are essentially the same steps *as the creative approach to career-change*. The creative approach to career-change has three parts to it. These parts are in the form of old familiar questions: *What, Where* and *How*:

• **WHAT?**

The full question here is *what are the skills you most enjoy using?*

To answer this question, you need to identify or inventory what **skills/gifts/talents** you have; and then you need to prioritize them, in their order of importance and enjoyment for you. Experts call these transferable skills, because they are transferable to any field/career that you choose, regardless of where you first picked them up, or how long you've had them.

• **WHERE?**

The full question here is *where do you most want to use those skills?*

This has to do *primarily* with the **fields of fascination** *you have already acquired*, which you most enjoy using. But *where* also has to do with your preferred working conditions, what kinds of data or people or things you enjoy working with, etc.

• **HOW?**

The full question here is *how do you find such jobs, that use your favorite skills and your favorite fields of knowledge?*

To answer this question, you need to do some **interviewing of various people in order to find the information you are looking for.** You begin this interviewing with the awareness that *skills* point toward job-titles; and *Fields of Fascination* point toward a career *field,* where you would use those skills. You want also to find out the names of *organizations* in your preferred geographical area which have such jobs to offer. *And,* the names of the people or person there who actually has the *power* to hire you, as well as the challenges they face. You then secure an interview with them, by using your contacts, and show them how your skills can help them with their challenges.

WHY DO WE BEGIN WITH "WHAT?"

When you first approach the job-hunt, if you are normal you will instinctively want to leap over **What** and **Where,** and go instead directly to **How.** You know: *how* do we write a resume, *how* do we find vacancies, *how* do we conduct an interview? There is, in fact, a vast industry in this country and many others, dedicated to conducting workshops that teach people only the *How* part of the job-hunt: resumes, interviews, salary negotiation.

This is a *huge* mistake.

I will explain *why.* Suppose I ask you to look around your house to see if you can find some minor object that is of interest to your cousin Ned, twice-removed, whom you don't much like. Since this assignment is of close to zero interest to you, you can imagine the listless way in which you might go hunting for that object. You'd do the search because you're a goodhearted person, but you'd give it *just a lick and a promise.*

Now, suppose there is some other object in your house, and this one is a beloved object, the only thing left to you by your dear departed grandmother, and you have been hunting for it, in vain, for years. It is *tremendously* important to you. And now I tell you that I saw it, somewhere in the house, just the other day, but can't remember exactly where. Armed with this fresh evidence that it still exists, you can imagine that you'd practically tear that house apart, to find this thing you care about so much, and have been looking for, for years.

The moral of our tale, you've already guessed: *the fervor of your hunt will be directly proportional to how much you care about* **WHAT** *you are hunting for.* That's true in life. It's true also in job-hunting.

"WHAT?" IS A MATTER OF SKILLS

You are looking here for what you may think of as the basic building-blocks of your work. So, if you're going to identify your dream job, and/or attempt a thorough career-change, you should begin by first of all identifying your functional, transferable skills. And while you may think you know what your best and favorite skills are, in most cases your self-knowledge could probably use a little work.

A weekend should do it! In a weekend, you can inventory your *past* sufficiently so that you have a good picture of the *kind* of work you would love to be doing *in the future. (You can, of course, stretch the inventory over a number of weeks, maybe doing an hour or two one night a week, if you prefer. It's up to you as to just how you do it.)*

A CRASH COURSE ON "TRANSFERABLE SKILLS"

Many people just "freeze" when they hear the word "skills."

It begins with high school job-hunters: "I haven't really got any skills," they say.

It continues with college students: "I've spent four years in college. I haven't had time to pick up any skills."

And it lasts through the middle years, especially when a person is thinking of changing his or her career: "I'll have to go back to college, and get retrained, because otherwise I won't have any skills in my new field." Or: "Well, if I claim any skills, I'll start at a very entry kind of level."

All of this fright about the word "skills" is very common, and stems from a total misunderstanding of what the word means. A misunderstanding that is shared, we might add, by altogether too many employers, or human resources departments, and other so-called "vocational experts."

By understanding the word, you will automatically put yourself way ahead of most job-hunters. And, especially if you are weighing a change of career, you can save yourself much waste of time on the folly called "I must go back to school." I've said it before, and I'll say it again: *maybe* you need some further schooling, but very often it is possible to make a dramatic career-change without any retraining. It all depends. And you won't really *know* whether or not you need further schooling, until you have finished all the exercises in this and the next chapter.

All right, then, if transferable skills are the heart of your vision and your destiny, let's see just exactly what transferable skills *are.*

Here are the most important truths you need to keep in mind about transferable, functional, skills:

1 **Your transferable** *(functional)* **skills are the most basic unit--the atoms--of whatever career you may choose.** You can see this from this diagram:

Skills as the Basic Unit of Work

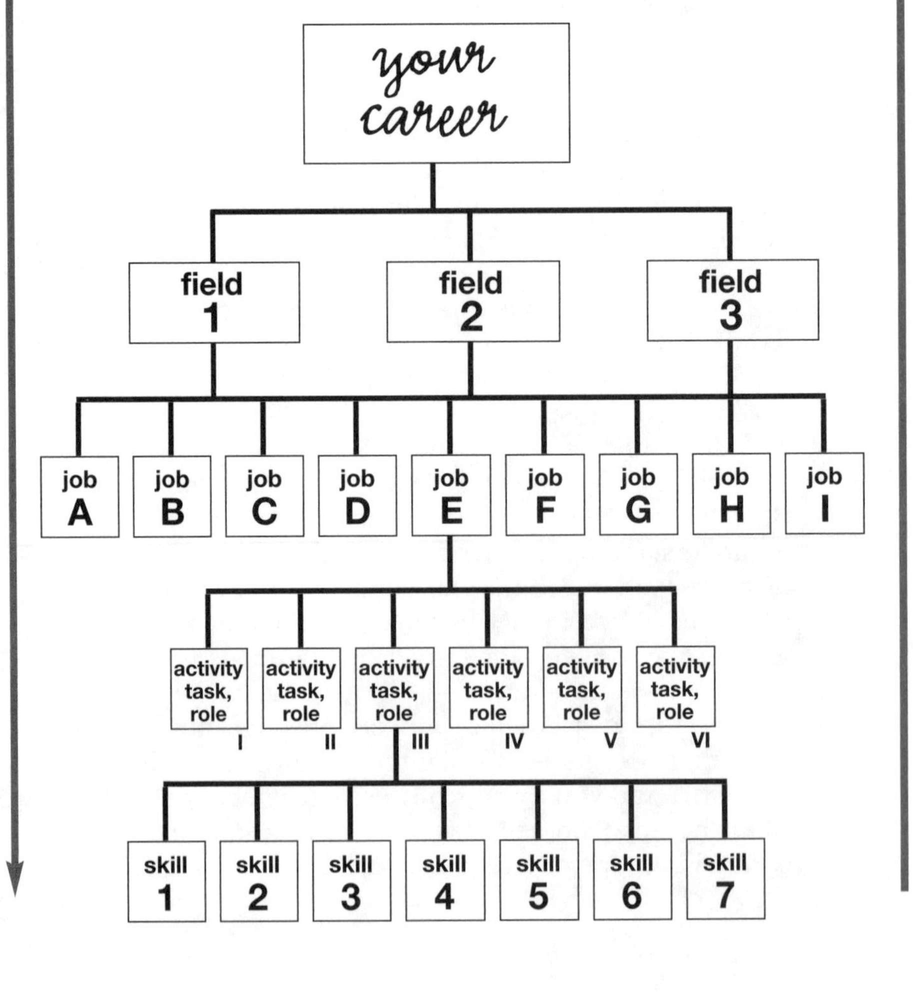

The skills you need to inventory, for yourself, are called functional or transferable skills. Here is a famous diagram of them:

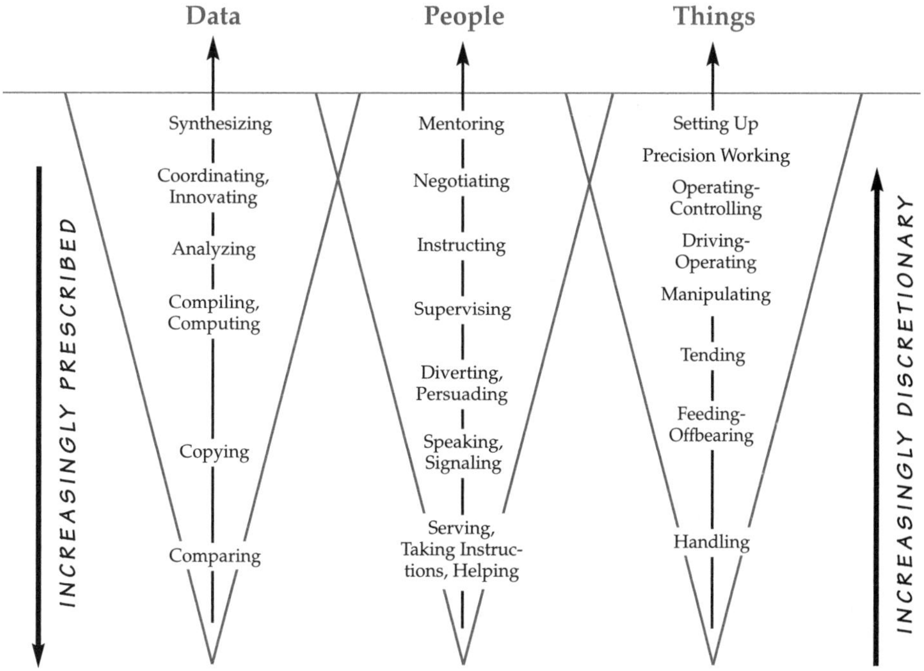

2 You should always claim the *highest* skills you legitimately can, on the basis of your past performance.

As we see in the functional/transferable skills diagram above, your skills break down into three *families,* according to whether you use them with **Data /Information,** or **People** or **Things.** And again, as this diagram makes clear, within each family there are *simple* skills, and there are higher, or *more complex* skills, so that these can be listed as inverted pyramids, with the simpler skills at the bottom, and the more complex ones in order above it, as in the diagram.

Incidentally, as a general rule -- to which there are exceptions -- each *higher* skill requires you to be able also to do all those skills listed below it, on the diagram. So of course you can usually claim *those,* as well. But you want to particularly claim the highest skill you legitimately can, on each transferable skills pyramid, based on what you have already proven you can do in the past.

3 The higher your transferable skills, the more freedom you will have on the job.

Simpler skills can be, and usually are, heavily *prescribed* (by the employer), so if you claim *only* the simpler skills, you will have to *'fit in'* -- following the instructions of your supervisor, and doing exactly what you are told to do. The *higher* the skills you can legitimately claim, the more you will be given discretion to carve out the job the way you want to -- so that it truly fits *you.*

4 The higher your transferable skills, the less competition you will face for whatever job you are seeking, because jobs which use such skills will rarely be advertised through normal channels.

Not for you the way of classified ads, resumes, and agencies, that we spoke of in earlier chapters. No, if you can legitimately claim higher skills, then to find such jobs you *must* follow what I have called "the life-changing job-hunting method" described in this and the next two chapters.

The essence of this approach to job-hunting or career-change is that once you have identified your favorite transferable skills, and your favorite Fields of Fascination, you may then approach *any organization that interests you, whether or not they have a known vacancy.* Naturally, whatever place you visit -- and particularly those which have not advertised any vacancy -- you will find far fewer job-hunters that you have to compete with.

In fact, if the employers you visit happen to like you well enough, they may be willing to create for you a job that does not presently exist. *In which case, you will be competing with no one, since you will be the sole applicant for that newly created job.* While this doesn't happen all the time, it is astounding to me how many times it *does* happen. *The reason* it does is that the employers often have been *thinking* about creating a new job within their organization, for quite some time -- but with this and that, they just have never gotten around to *doing* it. Until they saw you.

Then they decide they didn't want to let you get away, since *good employees are as hard to find as are good employers.* And they suddenly remember that job they have been thinking about creating for many weeks or months, now. So they dust off their *intention*, create the job on the spot, and offer it to you! And if that new job is not only what *they* need, but is exactly what *you* were looking for, then you have a dream job. Match-match. Win-win.

From our country's perspective, it is also interesting to note this: by this job-hunting initiative of yours, you have helped accelerate the creation of more jobs in your country, which is so much on everybody's mind here in the new millennium. How nice to help your country, as well as yourself!

5 **Don't confuse transferable skills with traits.**

Functional/transferable skills are often confused with **traits, temperaments**, or **type.** People think transferable skills are such things as: *has lots of energy, gives attention to details, gets along well with people, shows determination, works well under pressure, is sympathetic, intuitive, persistent, dynamic, dependable,* etc. Despite popular misconceptions, these are not functional/transferable skills, but traits, or the *style* with which you do your transferable skills. For example, let's take *"gives attention to details."* If one of your *transferable skills* is *"conducting research"* then *"gives attention to details"* describes the manner or style with which you do that transferable skill called *conducting research.* If you want to know what your traits are, popular tests such as the *Myers-Briggs Type Indicator,* measure that sort of thing.[1]

If you have access to the Internet, instruments there that give you some clues, at least, about your traits or 'type' can be found at such sites as:

- **The Personality Questionnaire**
  `http://meyers-briggs.com/info.html`

(Yes, "meyers" is deliberately misspelled here.)
$3.00. Related to the Myers-Briggs.

- **Keirsey Character Sorte**
  `http://www.keirsey.com/`

Free. Related to the Myers-Briggs.

If none of this works for you, and you just can't think of anything you'd really like to do, off the top of your head (or the tip of your tongue), then go to The Flower Exercise (pp. 329–369) and do the exercises there.

---

1. The Myers-Briggs Type Indicator, or 'MBTI®,' measures what is called *psychological type.* For further reading about this, see:

Paul D. Tieger & Barbara Barron-Tieger, *Do What You Are: Discover the Perfect Career for You Through the Secrets of Personality Type.* Third Edition. 2001. Little, Brown & Company, Inc., division of Time Warner Inc., 34 Beacon St., Boston MA 02108. For those who cannot obtain the MBTI®, this book includes a method for readers to identify their personality types. This is one of the most popular career books in the world. It's easy to see why. Many have found great help from the concept of Personality Type, and the Tiegers are masters in explaining this approach to career-choice. Highly recommended.

Donna Dunning, *What's Your Type of Career? Unlock the Secrets of Your Personality to Find Your Perfect Career Path.* 2001. Davies-Black Publishing, an imprint of Consulting Psychologists Press, Inc., 3803 East Bayshore Road, Palo Alto CA 94303, 1-800-624-1765. This is a dynamite new book on personality type. I found it to be the best written, most insightful, and most helpful book I have ever read about using 'Type' in the workplace. Donna Dunning's knowledge of 'Type' is encyclopedic!

David Keirsey and Marilyn Bates, *Please Understand Me: Character & Temperament Types.* 1978. Includes the Keirsey Temperament Sorter -- again, for those who cannot obtain the MBTI® (Myers-Briggs Type Indicator) -- registered trademark of Consulting Psychologists Press.

And so, the paradoxical moral of this Crash Course on Transferable Skills: The less you try to 'stay loose' and open to *anything,* the more precisely you define your skills with *Data/Information* and/or *People* and/ or *Things* in detail and at the highest level you legitimately can claim, **the more likely you are to find a job.** *Just the opposite of what the typical career-changer starts out believing.*

Steven M. Johnson

"I WOULDN'T RECOGNIZE MY SKILLS IF THEY CAME UP AND SHOOK HANDS WITH ME"

Well, now that you know what transferable skills technically *are*, the problem that awaits you now, is figuring out your own. If you are one of the few lucky people who already know what your transferable skills are, blessed are you. Write them down, and put them in the order of preference, for you.

If, however, you don't know what your skills are (and 95% of all workers *don't*), then you will need some help. That help is to be found in *The Flower Exercise* at the back of this book, on pp. 329–369.

The exercise involves the following steps:

1. Write A Story

Here is a specific example of such a story, so you can see how it is done:

"A number of years ago, I wanted to be able to take a summer trip with my wife and four children. I had a very limited budget, and could not afford to put my family up, in motels. I decided to rig our station wagon as a camper.

"First I went to the library to get some books on campers. I read those books. Next I designed a plan of what I had to build, so that I could outfit the inside of the station wagon, as well as topside. Then I went and purchased the necessary wood. On weekends, over a period of six weeks, I first constructed, in my driveway, the shell for the 'second story' on my station wagon. Then I cut doors, windows, and placed a six-drawer bureau within that shell. I mounted it on top of the wagon, and pinioned it in place by driving two-by-fours under the station wagon's rack on top. I then outfitted the inside of the station wagon, back in the wheel-well, with a table and a bench on either side, that I made.

"The result was a complete homemade camper, which I put together when we were about to start our trip, and then disassembled after we got back home. When we went on our summer trip,

we were able to be on the road for four weeks, yet stayed within our budget, since we didn't have to stay at motels.

"I estimate I saved $1900 on motel bills, during that summer's vacation."

Ideally, each story you write should have the following parts, as illustrated above:

I.) **Your goal: what you wanted to accomplish:** *"I wanted to be able to take a summer trip with my wife and four children."*

II.) **Some kind of hurdle, obstacle, or constraint that you faced** (self-imposed or otherwise): *"I had a very limited budget, and could not afford to put my family up, in motels."*

III.) **A description of what you did, step by step** (how you set about to ultimately achieve your goal, above, in spite of this hurdle or constraint): *"I decided to rig our station wagon as a camper. First I went to the library to get some books on campers. I read those books. Next I designed a plan of what I had to build, so that I could outfit the inside of* *the station wagon, as well as topside. Then I went and purchased the necessary wood. On weekends, over a period of six weeks, I . . ." etc., etc.*

IV.) **A description of the outcome or result:** *"When we went on our summer trip, we were able to be on the road for four weeks, yet stayed within our budget, since we didn't have to stay at motels."*

V.) **Any measurable/quantifiable statement of that outcome, that you can think of:** *"I estimate I saved $1900 on motel bills, during that summer's vacation."*

Once the story is written, you analyze it for transferable skills, using the "Typewriter Keys" in *The Flower Exercise* at the back of this book (pp. 336–341) And you're done with the first step of skill-identification.

2. Do This Process With Six More Stories

You now write one more story, and analyze it using the "Typewriter Keys" at the back of this book (pp. 336–341). Continue this process through seven stories, but do not write a new story until you're finished analyzing the previous one.

3. Prioritize Your Favorite Transferable Skills

Once you have identified your favorite transferable skills, you need to put them in order of priority or importance, to you. Which skill do you most enjoy using? Which next? Which next? Etc. There is a *Prioritizing Grid* in the back of this book (pp. 343–345) to help you do this task quickly and easily.

4. 'Flesh Out' the Skills You Care the Most About

Once you have identified your ten favorite transferable skills, you need to *flesh out* your skill-description for each of those ten, so that you are able to describe each of your talents or skills with more than just a one-word verb or gerund, like *organizing*.

Let's take *organizing* as our example. You tell us proudly:

"I'm good at *organizing.*" That's a fine start at defining your skills, but unfortunately it doesn't yet tell us much. Organizing WHAT? *People,* as at a party? *Nuts and bolts,* as on a workbench? Or *lots of information,* as on a computer? These are three entirely different skills. The one word *organizing* doesn't tell us which one is *yours.*

So, please *flesh out* each of your favorite transferable skills with an object -- some kind of *Data/Information,* or some kind of *People,* or some kind of *Thing,* and then add an adverb or adjective, too.

Why adjectives? Well, "I'm good at organizing information *painstakingly and logically*" and "I'm good at organizing information *in a flash, by intuition,*" are two *entirely different* skills. The difference between them is spelled out not in the verb, nor in the object, but in the adjectival or adverbial phrase there at the end. So, expand each definition of your ten favorite skills, in the fashion I have just described.

> When you are face-to-face with a person-who-has-the-power-to-hire-you, you want to be able to explain what makes you different from nineteen other people who can basically do the same thing that you can do. It is often the adjective or adverb that will save your life, during that explanation.

TRAVELS WITH FARLEY by Phil Frank © 1982. Field Enterprises, Inc. Courtesy of Field Newspaper Syndicate.

A PICTURE IS WORTH A THOUSAND WORDS

When you have your top favorite skills, in order, and *fleshed out*, it is time to put them on the central petal of the diagram, which we call *The Flower Diagram*, that you will find on pp. 330–331.

The Flower

A Picture of The Job of Your Dreams

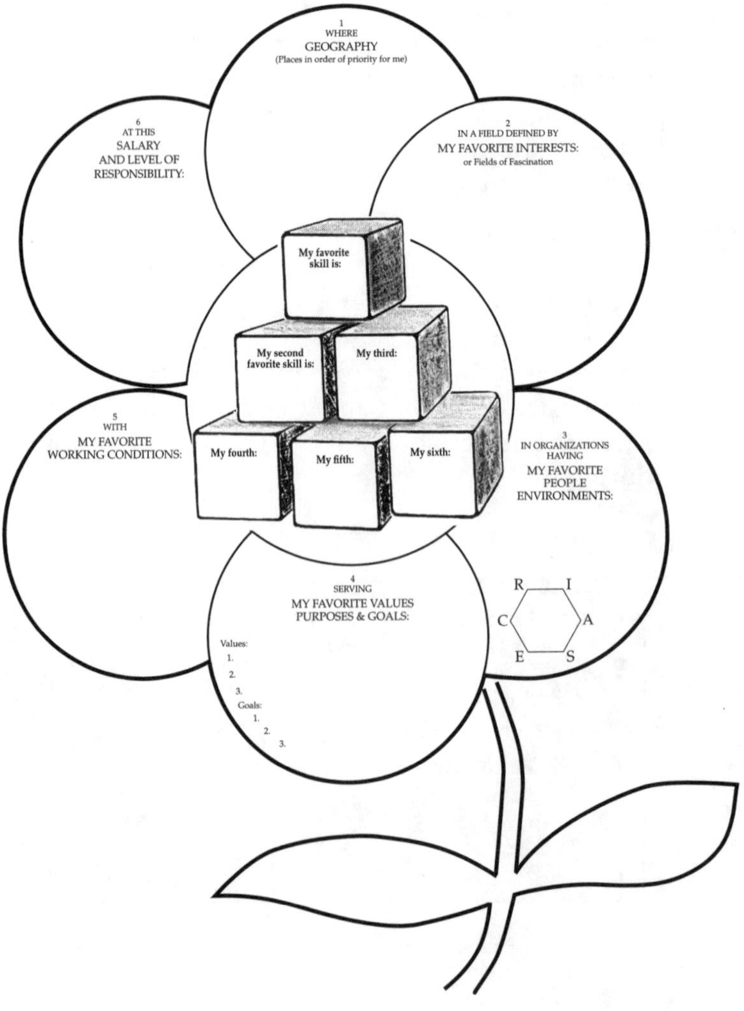

You may also, or alternatively, want to enroll them on the building-block diagram here -- which has room for you to list your top six or ten. And that's it. You are finished with **WHAT.**

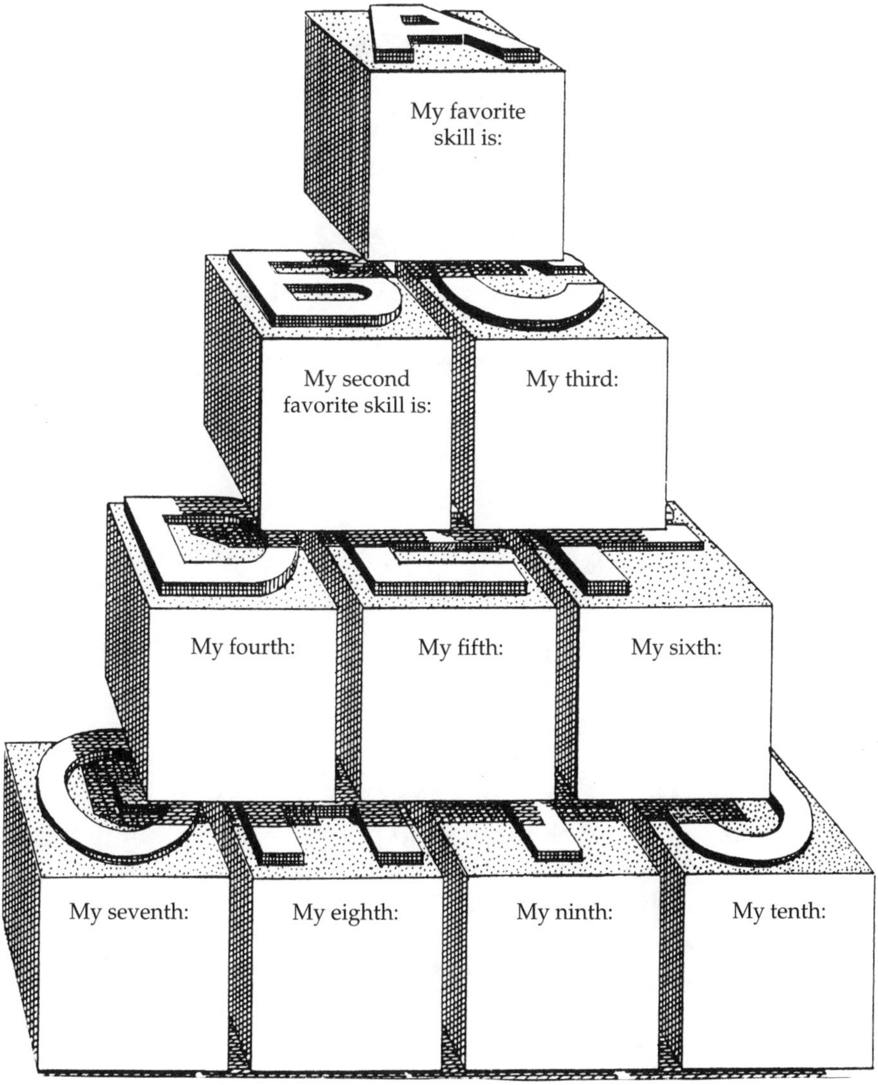

'. . . and give me good abstract-reasoning ability, interpersonal skills, cultural perspective, linguistic comprehension, and a high sociodynamic potential.'

CONCLUSION: SHORTCUTS

I know, I know, you look at this whole process overviewed in this chapter, and it just feels like too much work. You want something shorter, briefer, either on or off the Internet, that you can turn to.

Okay, here's a shortcut toward identifying your favorite transferable skills. Following is a List. It is, in fact, a *sampler* of skill-verbs, to help you quickly identify your favorite

The way in which this list is typically used by job-hunters or career-changers is to put **a check mark** in front of each skill that:

a) you believe you possess.

And **a separate check mark** in front of each skill that:

b) you also enjoy doing.

And **a separate check mark** in front of each skill that:

c) you also believe you do well.

Thus a skill could end up with three check marks -- and these, in fact, are the ones you want to look the hardest at, to see what kind of job they suggest:

A List of 246 Skills as Verbs

achieving	acting	adapting	addressing	administering
advising	analyzing	anticipating	arbitrating	arranging
ascertaining	assembling	assessing	attaining	auditing
budgeting	building	calculating	charting	checking
classifying	coaching	collecting	communicating	compiling
completing	composing	computing	conceptualizing	conducting
conserving	consolidating	constructing	controlling	coordinating
coping	counseling	creating	deciding	defining
delivering	designing	detailing	detecting	determining
developing	devising	diagnosing	digging	directing
discovering	dispensing	displaying	disproving	dissecting
distributing	diverting	dramatizing	drawing	driving
editing	eliminating	empathizing	enforcing	establishing
estimating	evaluating	examining	expanding	experimenting
explaining	expressing	extracting	filing	financing
fixing	following	formulating	founding	gathering
generating	getting	giving	guiding	handling
having responsibility	heading	helping	hypothesizing	identifying
illustrating	imagining	implementing	improving	improvising
increasing	influencing	informing	initiating	innovating
inspecting	inspiring	installing	instituting	instructing
integrating	interpreting	interviewing	intuiting	inventing
inventorying	investigating	judging	keeping	leading
learning	lecturing	lifting	listening	logging
maintaining	making	managing	manipulating	mediating
meeting	memorizing	mentoring	modeling	monitoring
motivating	navigating	negotiating	observing	obtaining
offering	operating	ordering	organizing	originating
overseeing	painting	perceiving	performing	persuading
photographing	piloting	planning	playing	predicting
preparing	prescribing	presenting	printing	problem solving
processing	producing	programming	projecting	promoting
proofreading	protecting	providing	publicizing	purchasing
questioning	raising	reading	realizing	reasoning
receiving	recommending	reconciling	recording	recruiting
reducing	referring	rehabilitating	relating	remembering
rendering	repairing	reporting	representing	researching
resolving	responding	restoring	retrieving	reviewing
risking	scheduling	selecting	selling	sensing
separating	serving	setting	setting-up	sewing
shaping	sharing	showing	singing	sketching
solving	sorting	speaking	studying	summarizing
supervising	supplying	symbolizing	synergizing	synthesizing
systematizing	taking instructions	talking	teaching	team-building
telling	tending	testing & proving	training	transcribing
translating	traveling	treating	trouble-shooting	tutoring
typing	umpiring	understanding	understudying	undertaking
unifying	uniting	upgrading	using	utilizing
verbalizing	washing	weighing	winning	working
writing				

INTERNET SHORTCUTS: TRANSFERABLE SKILLS TESTS

We saw in the last chapter that there are a number of *tests*, or *assessment instruments* that are available to help you figure out what you want to do with your life. We also saw the rules about using them (pp. 138–139).

What we want to know now is: are there tests specifically focussed on **Identifying Transferable Skills**?

And the answer is, Oh yes, indeed there are. Here's a sampler:

► **Career Storm**, and **Career Storm Compass** (Skills, Subjects, Values, Style)
`http://www.careerstorm.com/tools/skills/skills02.asp`

Probably the best skill identification instrument on the Internet, using categories similar to those in this book--interpersonal (**people**) skills; practical (**things**) skills; **information** and creative skills. A Finnish site, done by one of my former students, Heidi Viljamaa, who is quite brilliant. *Warning: I have found that in the U.S., at least, this site is sometimes slow to load; if that is the case, just come back to it later. It usually works quite well.*

▶ "Transferable Skills" and "Transferable Skills Checklist" from the State of Wisconsin's Department of Workforce Development.

http://www.dwd.state.wi.us/notespub/dwdpub/223e_28a.htm

Very thorough checklist, though it does not point to particular jobs.

▶ Internet Transferable Skills Analysis with O*NET by VocRehab

http://www.vocrehab.com/transferable_skills_analysis_onet.htm#DATA

A very well-done analysis available for U.S. job-hunters *in particular,* costing $35 U.S. (as of May 1, 2001). Points you to particular jobs, using the U.S. O*Net system.

▶ Internet Transferable Skills Analysis by VAS

http://www.vocsoft.com/transferable_skills_analysis.htm

A similar if not almost identical analysis, for Canadian job-hunters *in particular*, costing $35 Canadian. Points you to particular jobs, using the Canadian NOC Handbook.

And now, on to **WHERE?**

A realist is more correct about things in life than an optimist. But the optimist seems to have more friends and much more fun.[1]

—Megan, Age 14

1. From H. Jackson Brown, Jr.'s, *When You Lick a Slug, Your Tongue Goes Numb: Kids Share Their Wit and Wisdom.* Rutledge Hill Press, Nashville, Tennessee. 1994. Used with permission.

Chapter Nine

The Geography Of The Heart

WHERE
DO YOU MOST WANT TO USE THOSE SKILLS?

Your heart has its own geography, where it prefers to be. It may be by a mountain stream. It may be in the Alps. It may be in the hustle and bustle of the streets of London or New York. It may be on an Oregon farm. It may be in a beach town. It may be in the quiet recollection of your own backyard. Your heart knows the places that it loves.

Likewise, your mind has its own geography, where it prefers to be. It may be among books on psychology. It may be among books of art. It may be among books of romances. It may be books of travel. It may be books on business trends. It may be on computers. Your mind knows the subjects that it loves.

Your body also has its own geography, where it prefers to be. It may be walking in the hills. It may be in a Yoga class. It may be working out with weights. It may be in a marathon. It may be on a bicycle path. It may be in a physical therapy class. It may be in the local gym. It may be on a basketball court. It may be with massage. Your body knows the workout that it loves.

Your soul, too, has its own geography, where it prefers to be. It may be in a quiet place, it may be in a church, or synagogue or mosque. It may be among honest folk. It may be among those who're fixed on a kind of social change. It may be almost anywhere, where the values you prize -- community, God, compassion, generosity, faith -- are valued still by others. Your soul knows the values that it loves.

Therefore, my friend, what "a dream job" is all about (beyond skills) is identifying these favorite geographies, defining for yourself the *places* that your skills, your soul, and body, heart and mind, most often yearn to be.

If you would find your dream job, then, you must define these things.

There are two ways to approach this task -- the *intuitional "leap-to-a-conclusion"* way, and the more labored, logical, step-by-step way. This *hurry-up* culture in which we live values most the method that is quick. Intuition is quick, and sometimes can provide just the clues you're looking for. So it is there that we begin.

Intuitions

**Toward Deciding WHERE,
In A Dream Job,
Your Skills,
Your Soul and Body,
Heart and Mind,
Would Most Like
To Be**

Where you use your favorite skills, where you do your favorite tasks is largely a matter of what "field" you choose to use your skills in. Hence, these are the kind of intuitions you should be searching your heart about:

1

What are your favorite interests *(Computers? Gardening? Spanish? Law? Physics? Department stores? Hospitals? etc., etc.)*? If you just can't think of any favorite interest, ask yourself: "If I could talk about *something* with someone all day long, day after day, what would that subject or field of interest be? *Or,* if I were stuck on a desert island with a person who only had the capacity to speak on a few subjects, what would I pray those subjects were?"

If you turn out to have more than one favorite interest, take two of them at a time, and ask yourself: if you were in a conversation with someone covering two of your favorite subjects at once, toward which of the two interests would you try to steer the conversation. Repeat with another pair of favorite subjects, and keep 'sifting down.'

2

What are your favorite subjects -- the ones you're drawn to in magazines, libraries, bookstores, trade expos, and so forth? It doesn't have to be a subject you studied in school.

It can be a field that you just picked up along the way in life -- say, *antiques,* or *cars,* or *interior decorating,* or *music* or *movies* or *psychology,* or *the kind of subjects that come up on television 'game shows.'*

The only important thing is that you *like* the subject a lot, and that you picked up a working knowledge of it -- who cares where or how? As the late John Crystal used to say, it doesn't matter whether you learned it in college, or sitting at the end of a log.

Let's take *antiques* as an example. Suppose it's one of your favorite subjects, yet you never studied it in school. You picked up your knowledge of antiques by going around to antique stores, and asking lots of questions. And you supplemented this by reading a few books on the subject, and you subscribe to an antiques magazine. You've also bought a few antiques, yourself. That's enough, for you to put *antiques,* on your list of fields/interests/languages. Your degree of *mastery* of this whole field of antiques is irrelevant -- *unless you want to work at a level in the field that demands and requires* mastery.

3

What are your favorite words? Every field has its own peculiar language, vocabulary or jargon. What words or jargon do you like to use, or listen to, the most?

To illustrate this, I'll *freeze* the job-title or skills, for a moment. I'll choose "secretary." By looking then at different kinds of *secretary,* we can see how favorite *words* can give you a helpful clue about where you might like to find your dream job.

For example, if you work as a legal secretary, you have to endure a lot of talk there, all day long, about *legal procedures.* Do you like that vocabulary and *language*? If so, consider law as the field you might work in -- for your next job or career.

Again, if you work as a secretary at a gardening store, there's a lot of talk there, all day long, about gardens and such. Do you like that vocabulary and *language*? If so, consider gardening as the field you might work in -- for your next job or career.

If you work as a secretary at an airline, there's a lot of talk there, all day long, about airlines procedures and such. Do you like that vocabulary and *language*? If so, consider the airlines as the field you might work in -- for your next job or career.

If you work as a secretary at a church, there's a lot of talk there, all day long, about church procedures and matters of faith. Do you like that vocabulary and *language*? If so, consider religion as the field you might work in -- for your next job or career.

And so it continues. If you work as a secretary in a photographic laboratory, there's a lot of talk there, all day long, about photographic procedures. Do you like that vocabulary and *language*? If so, choose photography as the field you might work in -- for your next job or career.

Again, if you work as a secretary at a chemical plant, there's a lot of talk there, all day long, about chemicals manufacturing. Do you like that vocabulary and *language*? If so, consider the chemical industry as the field you might work in -- for your next job or career.

If you work as a secretary for the Federal government, there's a lot of talk there, all day long, about government procedures. Do you like that vocabulary and *language*? If so, consider government work as the field you might work in -- for your next job or career.

And so it goes. The point is not that you should be a secretary. I just *froze* the job-title and skills for a moment, so that you could see how many different fields you might use those skills in.

All of this proceeds from a simple intuition: the source of joy in your dream job derives, to a great extent, from the fact that you enjoy the *language* and vocabulary that you will be speaking or listening to all day long (provided, of course, that you also get to use your favorite skills there).

Whereas, if you don't enjoy the vocabulary or *language* that is spoken at work -- you want to talk about *gardening* but you work at a place where *law* (which has a vocabulary you hate) is what you have to listen to, and work with, all day long -- then you are not going like that job or career.

4

Once you know what subjects, fields, interests, vocabulary, etc., fascinate you the most, look back at your answers to *What skills you most enjoy*, and see if you can put skills and subjects together, in terms of a particular job. For example, if you love to work with figures *(financial, that is)*, and your favorite field is hospitals, you would want to think about working in the accounting department at a hospital.

5

Once you have some idea of what jobs interest you, go visit places where those jobs are, and talk to people doing those jobs, to see if this job or career *really* interests you, or not. This is called "informational interviewing." Fancy name for *informal research.*

6

If you have decided to try a new career or go into a new field (for you), and you are dismayed at how much preparation it looks as though it would take, go talk to people doing that work. And don't look for the rules or generalizations. Look for the exceptions to the rules. For example, everyone may tell you the rule is: *"In order to do this work you have to have a master's degree and ten years' experience at it."* So what? That's a statement about the majority of people in this field. You want to find out about the exceptions. *"Yes, but do you know of anyone in the field who hasn't gone and gotten all those credentials? And where might I find him or her? I need to find out how they did it."*

7

If you have decided to try to stay with your old career *(which you lost through downsizing or whatever)* then you need to find *"leads."* You find them by asking yourself the question: *"Who might be interested in the skills and problem-solving that I learned at my last job?"*

For example, ask yourself who you served in your last

job, or came in contact with, *who might be in a position to hire someone with your talents.*

Ask yourself who supplied training or staff development in your last company or field; *do you think any of them might be interested in hiring you?* (Ask them.)

Ask yourself what machines or technology you learned, mastered, improved on, at your last job; *and, who is interested in those machines or technology?*

Ask yourself what raw materials *(e.g., Kodak paper in a darkroom),* equipment or support services you used at your last job; *would any of those suppliers know of other places where their equipment or support services are used?*

Ask yourself who were the subcontractors, outsourcing agencies, or temp agencies that were used at your last job; *would any of them be interested in hiring you?*

Ask yourself what community or service organizations were interested in your projects at your last job; *would any of them be interested in hiring you?*[2]

2. These suggestions courtesy of Chuck Young, former Administrator for the Oregon Commission on the Blind; and Martin Kimeldorf, career counselor and author.

Step-by-Step

Ways of Deciding WHERE,
in a Dream Job,
Your Soul and Body,
Heart and Mind,
Would Most Like
to Be

Well, I said earlier that there are two ways to approach the task of finding out just where you'd love to use your skills -- the intuitional "leap to a conclusion" way, and the more labored, logical, step-by-step way. We've seen the intuitional way. Now we turn to the left-brained, step-by-step.

Step-by-step is easy.

Here you use *The Flower Exercise* (beginning on page 329). It occupies forty pages and can be done (easily) in one dedicated weekend. (If you're a slow worker, you might have to take two weekends to do this, but no more.)

It will guide you step-by-step not only through your favorite *interests, subjects, vocabulary and languages,* but through all the other parts of WHERE that I mentioned at the beginning of this chapter -- those dealing with the geography of your heart, mind, body and soul.

Step-by-step it will help you to inventory, catalog, add up all that information, and copy it on to six of the seven *petals* of the Flower Diagram there.

Those petals are called: 1. *Geography;* 2. *My Fields of Fascination;* 3. *My Favorite People Environments.* 4. *My Favorite Values, Purposes and Goals;* 5. *My Favorite Working Conditions.* 6. *Salary and Level of Responsibility.*

You already did the seventh petal, the central one, in the last chapter. Now, after a weekend of work, you will have the six *additional* petals of the *Flower Diagram* filled in. At this point, get seven sheets of large blank paper and copy all your petals on to those much larger sheets. *You can get such sheets at an office supply store or at an arts and crafts store.*

When you've copied all seven petals thus, you can then *Scotch-tape* them all together so as to form one large sheet that has your complete *Flower Diagram* on it, writ large.

Put that sheet on a wall, or on the door of your refrigerator. And there you have it: a simple picture (as it were) of Your Dream Job!

A LIGHT BULB GOES ON

But, it's not *just* a picture of your Dream Job. Just as importantly, it's a picture of *you* as well. In fact, it's both of these things at once, because you've constructed a picture of a dream job or career *that matches you.* You match it. It matches you. Bingo! Mirror images.

And when you're looking at that diagram, what should happen? Well, for some of you there will be a big *Aha!* as you look at your Flower Diagram. A light bulb will go off, over your head, and you will say, "My goodness, I see *exactly* what sort of career this points me to." This happens particularly with intuitive people.

If you are one of these extremely intuitive people, I say, "Good for you!" Just two gentle warnings, if I may:

Don't prematurely close out *other* possibilities.

And *don't* say to yourself: "Well, I see what it is that I would die to be able to do, but I *know* there is no job in the world like that, that *I* would be able to get." Dear friend, you don't know any such thing. You haven't done your research yet. Of course, it is always possible that when you've completed all that research, and conducted your search, you still may not be able to find *all* that you want -- down to the last detail. But you'd be surprised at how much of your dream you may be able to find.

Sometimes it will be found in *stages.* One retired man I know, who had been a senior executive with a publishing company, found himself bored to death in retirement, after he turned 65. He contacted a business acquaintance, who said apologetically, "We just don't have anything open that matches or requires your abilities; right now all we need is someone in our mail room." The 65-year-old executive said, "I'll take that job!" He did, and over the ensuing years steadily advanced once again, to just the job he wanted: as a senior executive in that organization, where he utilized all his prized skills, for some time. He retired as senior executive for the second time, at the age of 85. Like him, you may choose to go by stages.

Other times, it may be that you will be able to find your dream directly without having to go through stages.

The Virtue of "Passion" or Enthusiasm

Whether in stages or directly, it is amazing how often people do get their dream job or career. The more you don't *cut* the dream down, because of what you *think* you know about *the real world,* the more likely you are to find what you are looking for.

Hold on to *all* of your dream. Most people don't find their heart's desire, because they decide to pursue just half their dream -- and consequently they hunt for it with only *half a heart.*

If you decide to pursue your whole dream, your best dream, the one you die to do, I guarantee you that you will hunt for it *with all your heart.* It is this *passion* which often is the difference between successful career-changers, and unsuccessful ones.

YOU LOOK AT YOUR FLOWER DIAGRAM AND . . . A LIGHT BULB DOESN'T GO ON

In contrast to what I just said, many of you will look at your completed *Flower Diagram*, and you won't have *a clue* as to what job or career it points to. Soooo, we need a 'fall-back' strategy. Of course it involves more 'step-by-step-by-step' stuff.

Here's how it goes. Take a pad of paper, with pen or pencil, or go to your computer, with keyboard in hand, and make some notes.

1. First, look at your *Flower Diagram*, and from the center petal choose your three most *favorite* skills.
2. Then, look at your Flower Diagram and write down, from petal #2, your three *top* interests, or Fields of Fascination.
3. Now, take these notes, and show them to at least five friends, family, or professionals whom you know.

> As you will recall, skills usually point toward a **job-title** or job-level, while interests or fields of fascination usually point toward a **career field**. So, you want to ask them, in the case of your skills, *What job-title or jobs do these skills suggest to you?*

> Then ask them, in the case of your favorite Fields of Fascination, *What career fields do these suggest to you?*

4. Jot down *everything* these five people suggest or recommend to you.
5. After you have finished talking to them, you want to go home and look at all these notes. Anything helpful or valuable here? If not, if none of it looks valuable, then set

it aside, and go talk to five more of your friends, acquaintances, or people you know in the business world and non-profit sector. Repeat, as necessary.

6. When you finally have some worthwhile suggestions, sit down, look over their combined suggestions, and ask yourself some questions.

- First, you want to look at what these friends suggested about your skills: *what job or jobs came to their mind*? It will help you to know that most jobs can be classified under 19 headings or families.

JOB FAMILIES

1. Executive, Administrative, and Managerial Occupations
2. Engineers, Surveyors, and Architects
3. Natural Scientists and Mathematicians
4. Social Scientists, Social Workers, Religious Workers, and Lawyers
5. Teachers, Counselors, Librarians, and Archivists
6. Health Diagnosing and Treating Practitioners
7. Registered Nurses, Pharmacists, Dieticians, Therapists, and Physician Assistants
8. Health Technologists and Technicians
9. Technologists and Technicians in Other Fields: Computer Specialists, Programmers, Information Technicians, Information Specialists, etc.
10. Writers, Artists, Digital Artists, and Entertainers
11. Marketing and Sales Occupations
12. Administrative Support Occupations, including Clerical
13. Service Occupations
14. Agricultural, Forestry, and Fishing Occupations
15. Mechanics and Repairers
16. Construction and Extractive Occupations
17. Production Occupations
18. Transportation and Material-Moving Occupations
19. Handlers, Equipment Cleaners, Helpers, and Laborers

Which of these nineteen do your friends' suggestions predominantly point to? Which of these nineteen grabs you?

- Next, you want to look at what your friends suggested about your interests or *fields of fascination*: *what fields or careers came to their mind*? It will help you to know that most of the career fields above can be classified under four broad headings: *Agriculture, Manufacturing, Information Industries*, and *Service Industries.*

Which of these four do your friends' suggestions predominantly *point to*? Which of these four grabs you?

- The next question you want to ask yourself is: both job-titles and career-fields can be broken down further, according to whether you like to work primarily with *people* **or** primarily with *information/data* **or** primarily with *things.*

Let's take agriculture as an example. Within agriculture, you could be driving tractors and other farm machinery -- and thus working primarily with *things;* or you could be gathering statistics about crop growth for some state agency -- and thus working primarily with *information/data;* or you could be teaching agriculture in a college classroom, and thus working primarily with *people* and *ideas.* Almost all fields as well as career families offer you these three kinds of choices, though *of course* many jobs combine two or more of the three in some intricate way.

Still, you do want to tell yourself what your *preference* is, and what you *primarily* want to be working with. Otherwise your job-hunt or career-change is going to leave you very frustrated, at the end. In this matter, it is often your favorite skill that will give you the clue. If it *doesn't,* then go back and look at your skills *petal,* on your Flower Diagram. What do you think? Are your favorite skills weighted more toward working with *people,* or toward working with *information/data,* or toward working with *things*?

And, no matter what that *petal* suggests, which do you absolutely prefer?

Giving The Flower A Name

Once you have these *clues* from your friends, you need to go name your *Flower.* To do this, you need to answer four questions for yourself, in the order indicated below:

• **QUESTION #1**

What are the **names of jobs or careers** that would give me a chance to use my most enjoyable skills, in a field that is based on my favorite subjects?

• **QUESTION #2**

What **kinds of organizations** would and/or do employ people in these careers?

• **QUESTION #3**

Among the kinds of organizations uncovered in the previous question, what are the names of **particular places** that I especially like?

• **QUESTION #4**

Among the places that I particularly like, **what needs do they have** or what outcomes are they trying to produce, that my skills and knowledge could help with?

How do you find the answers to these four questions? Well, let's talk at length about the first one; because in seeing how you answer *that* question, you will understand how to answer the other three, as well.

That first question is: What are the **names of jobs or careers** that would give me a chance to use my most enjoyable skills, in a field that is based on my favorite subjects?

Where do you begin?

The Internet is one place, if you like to do research on the Internet. My Web site, **www.JobHuntersBible.com** will give you lots of research tips.

Libraries are another, if you like to do research in libraries.

The bad news, unfortunately -- for the shy -- is that the most dependable and up-to-date information on jobs and careers is *not* found in either of these two ways. It's found by going and talking to *people.* The reason for this is that last week's absolutely true certifiably guaranteed 100% accurate information about jobs and careers is this week's completely outdated information. *Things are just moving too fast.* Books can't keep up. The Internet can't keep up. In fact, I'm just astounded at how long ago some of the Internet research sites were last updated.

So, if you want to identify a new career or job that *fits* you, it is to people you must ultimately go -- with *some* reading from the Internet and/or books on the side, to *supplement* what people may tell you. The story at the end of this chapter illustrates this, abundantly.

Talk to people, that's the key! And if shyness is a problem for you, as it is for me (believe me!!) I have some helpful things to suggest about how to deal with that, at the end of this chapter.

But I reiterate: to gather the information you will need, you must go talk to people.

Well and good, you may say, but how do you decide *which people*? Well, that's not as hard as it may seem. Let me give you an actual example of how it's done. (We'll take an actual career-changer's story, here.)

After our job-hunter did his Flower Diagram, it turned out that his top/favorite skill was: diagnosing, treating or healing.

His three top/favorite *languages* or fields of fascination were: psychiatry, plants, and carpentry.

After showing five friends this information, and mulling over what they said, he concluded:

Among the 19 *Job Families,* he was most attracted to (6) Health diagnosing and treating practitioners.

Among the four *broad divisions of career-fields,* he was most attracted to Service industries.

Among the *three kinds of skills,* he most wanted to use his skills with people.

So far, so good. Now, where does he go from there?

He's going to have to go talk to people. But, how does he choose who to talk to? Easy. He takes his favorite *languages* or fields of fascination, above -- psychiatry, plants, and carpentry -- and mentally translates them into *people* with those occupations: namely, a psychiatrist, a gardener, and a carpenter.

Then he has to go find at least one of each. That's relatively easy: the Yellow Pages of the telephone directory will do, or he may know some of these among the friends or acquaintances he already has. What he wants to do, now, is go visit them and ask them: *how do you combine these three fields into one occupation?* He knows it may be a career that already exists, *or* it may be he will have to create this career for himself.

"Same career, change of career, same career . . . change of . . ."

And, how does he decide which of these three to go interview *first*? He asks himself which of these persons is most likely to have the *largest overview. (This is often, but not always, the same as asking: who took the longest to get their training?)* The particular answer here: the psychiatrist.

He would then go see two or three psychiatrists -- say, the head of the psychiatry department at the nearest colleges or universities,[3] and ask them: *Do you have any idea how to put these three subjects -- carpentry, plants, and psychiatry -- together into one job or career? And if you don't know, who do you think might?* He would keep going until he found someone who had a bright idea about how you put this all together.

3. If there were no psychiatrists at any academic institution near him, then he would do all his research with psychiatrists in private practice -- getting their names from the phone book -- and asking them for, and paying for, a half session. This, if there is no other way.

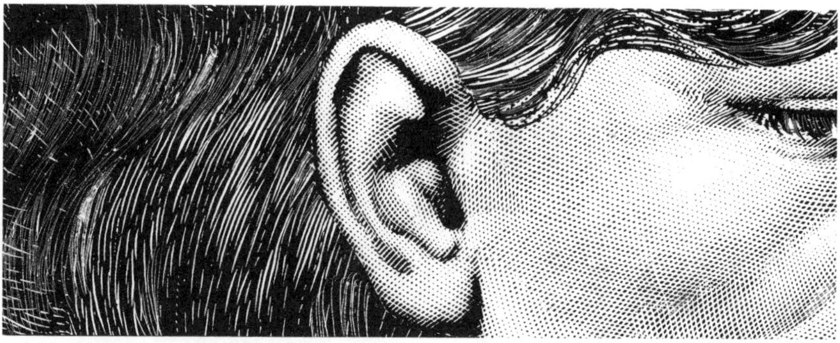

In this particular case *(as I said, this is an actual career-changer's experience)*, he was eventually told: "Yes, it can all be put together. There is a branch of psychiatry that uses plants to help heal people. That takes care of your interest in plants and psychiatry. As for your carpentry interests, I suppose you could use that to build the planters for your plants."

INFORMATIONAL INTERVIEWING

There is a name for this process I have just described. It is called *Informational Interviewing* -- a term I invented many many years ago. But it is sometimes, incorrectly, called *by other names*. Some even call this gathering of information *Networking*, which it is not.

To avoid this confusion, I have summarized in the chart on pages 196 and 197 just exactly what *Informational Interviewing* is, and how it differs from the other ways in which *people* can help and support you, during your job-hunt or career-change -- namely, *Networking, Support Groups,* and *Contacts.* I have also thrown in, at no extra charge, a *first* column in that chart, dealing with an aspect of the job-hunt that *never* gets talked about: namely, the importance before your job-hunt ever begins, of *nurturing the friendships you have let slip* -- by calling them or visiting them early on in your job-hunt -- just re-establishing relationships *before* you ever need anything from them, as you most certainly may, later on in your job-hunt. The first column in the chart explains this further.

The Job-Hunter's or Career-Changer's

The Process	1. Valuing Your *Community* Before the Job-Hunt	2. Networking
What Is Its Purpose?	To make sure that people whom you may someday need to do you a favor, or lend you a hand, know long beforehand that you value and prize them *for themselves.*	To gather a list of contacts *now* who might be able to help you with your career, or with your job-hunting, at some future date. And to go out of your way to *regularly* add to that list. *Networking is a term often reserved only for the business of adding to your list; but, obviously, this presupposes you first listed everyone you* already *know.*
Who Is It Done With?	Those who live with you, plus your family, relatives, friends, and acquaintances, however near (geographically) or far.	People in your present field, or in a field of future interest that you yourself meet; also, people whose names are given to you by others.
When You're Doing This Right How Do You Go About It? (Typical Activities)	You make time for them in your busy schedule, long before you find yourself job-hunting. You do this by: (1) Spending 'quality time' with those you live with, letting them know you really appreciate who they are, and what kind of person they are. (2) Maintaining contact (phone, lunch, a thank-you note) with those who live nearby. (3) Writing friendly notes, regularly, to those who live at a distance -- *thus letting them all know that you appreciate them* for themselves.	You deliberately attend, for this purpose, meetings or conventions in your present field, or the field/career you are thinking of switching to, someday. You talk to people at meetings and at 'socials,' exchanging calling cards after a brief conversation. Occasionally, someone may suggest a name to you as you are about to set off for some distant city or place, recommending that while you are there, you contact them. A phone call may be your best bet, with a follow-up letter after you return home, unless *they* invite *you* to lunch during the phone call. Asking *them* to lunch sometimes 'bombs.' (See below.)
When You've Really Botched This Up, What Are The Signs?	You're out of work, and you find yourself having to contact people that you haven't written or phoned in ages, suddenly asking them out of the blue for their help with your job-hunt. *The message inevitably read from this is that you don't really care about them at all, except when you can* use *them. Further, you get perceived as one who sees others only in terms of what they can do for you, rather than in a relationship that is 'a two-way street.'*	It's usually when you have approached a very busy individual and asked them to have lunch with you. If it is an aimless lunch, with no particular agenda -- they ask during lunch what you need to talk about, and you lamely say, "Well, uh, I don't know, So-and-So just thought we should get to know each other" -- you will not be practicing *Networking.* You will be practicing *antagonizing.* Try to restrict your *Networking* to the telephone.

Guide To Relationships With Others

3. Developing A Support Group	4. Informational Interviewing	5. Using Contacts
To enlist some of your family or close friends specifically to help you with your emotional, social, and spiritual needs, when you are going through a difficult transition period, such as a job-hunt or career-change -- so that you do not have to face this time all by yourself.	To screen careers *before* you change to them. To screen jobs *before* you take them, rather than afterward. To screen places *before* you decide you want to seek employment there. To find answers to *very specific questions* that occur to you during your job-hunt.	It takes, let us say, 77 pairs of eyes and ears to find a new job or career. Here you recruit those 76 other people (don't take me literally -- it can be any number you choose) to be your eyes and ears -- once you know what kind of work, what kind of place, what kind of job you are looking for, *and not before.*
You try to enlist people with one or more of the following qualifications: you feel comfortable talking to them; they will take initiative in calling you, on a regular basis; they are wiser than you are; and they can be a hard taskmaster, when you need one.	Workers, workers, workers. You *only* do informational interviewing with people actually doing the work that interests you as a potential new job or career for yourself.	Anyone and everyone who is on your 'networking list.' (See column 2.) It includes family, friends, relatives, high school alumni, college alumni, former co-workers, church/synagogue members, places where you shop, etc.
There should be three of them, at least. They may meet with you regularly, once a week, as a group, for an hour or two, to check on how you are doing. One or more of them should also be available to you on an "as needed" basis: the Listener, when you are feeling 'down,' and need to talk; the Initiator, when you are tempted to hide; the Wise One, when you are puzzled as to what to do next; and the Taskmaster, when your discipline is falling apart, and you need someone to encourage you to 'get at it.' It helps if there is also a Cheerleader among them, that you can tell your victories to.	You get names of workers from your co-workers, from departments at local community colleges, or career offices. Once you have names, you call them and ask for a chance to talk to them *for twenty minutes.* You make a list, ahead of time, of all the questions you want answers to. If nothing occurs to you, try these: (1) How did you get into this line of work? Into this particular job? (2) What kinds of things do you like the most about this job? (3) What kinds of things do you like the least about this job? (4) Who else, doing this same kind of work, would you recommend I go talk to?	Anytime you're stuck, you ask your contacts for help *with specific information.* For example: When you can't find workers who are doing the work that interests you. When you can't find the names of places which do that kind of work. When you have a place in mind, but can't figure out the name of 'the person-who-has-the-power-to-hire-you.' When you know that name, but can't get in to see that person. At such times, you call every contact you have on your Networking list, if necessary, until someone can tell you the specific answer you need.
You've 'botched it' when you have no support group, no one to turn to, no one to talk to, and you feel that you are in this, all alone. You've 'botched it' when you are waiting for your friends and family to notice how miserable you are, and to prove they love you by taking the initiative in coming after you; rather than, as is necessary with a support group, *your* choosing and recruiting them -- asking them for their help and aid.	You're trying to use this with people-who-have-the-power-to-hire-you, rather than with *workers.* You're claiming you want information when really you have some other hidden agenda, with this person. *(P.S. They usually can smell the hidden agenda, a mile away.)* You've botched it, whenever you're telling a lie to someone. The whole point of informational interviewing is that it is a search for Truth.	Approaching your 'contacts' too early in your job-hunt, and asking them for help only in the most general and vague terms: "John, I'm out of work. If you hear of anything, please let me know." *Any what thing?* You must do all your own homework *before* you approach your contacts. They will not do your homework for you.

TALKING TO WORKERS, 'TRYING ON' JOBS

When you go talk to people, you are hoping they will give you ideas, as we saw, about *what careers* will use your skills and *languages* or Fields of Fascination and interest.

That's the first step.

The second step is that you want also to get some idea of *what that work feels like, from the inside.*

In the example above, you don't just want the job-title: *psychiatrist working with plants*. You want some feel for the substance that is underneath the title. In other words, you want to find out what the day to day work is like.

For this purpose you must leave your *interviewees,* above, and talk to actual people doing the work you think you'd love to do: in the particular example we have been discussing, you would have to go talk to *psychiatrists who actually use plants, in their healing work.*

Why do you want to ask them what the work feels like, from the inside? Well, in effect, you are mentally *trying on jobs* to see if they fit you.

It is exactly analogous to your going to a clothing store and trying on different suits (or dresses) that you see in their window or on their racks. Why do you try them on? Well, the suits or dresses that look *terrific* in the window don't always look so hotsy-totsy when you see them on *you*. Lots of pins were used, on the backside of the figurine in the window. On you, without the pins, the clothes don't hang quite right, etc., etc.

Likewise, the careers that *sound* terrific in books or in your imagination don't always look so great when you see them up close and personal, in all their living glory.

You need to know that. What you're ultimately trying to find is a career that looks terrific inside or out -- in the window, *and* also on you. Essentially, you are asking what *this* job *feels* like. Here are some questions that will help *(you are talking, of course, with workers who are actually doing the career you think you might like to do)*:

- How did you get into this work?
- What do you like the most about it?
- What do you like the least about it?
- And, where else could I find people who do this kind of work? *(You should always ask them for more than one name, so that if you run into a dead end at any point, you can easily go back and visit the other names they suggested.)*

  If it becomes apparent to you, during the course of any of these Informational Interviews, that this career, occupation, or job you were exploring definitely *doesn't* fit you, then the last question (above) gets turned into a different kind of inquiry:
- Do you have any ideas as to who else I could talk to, about my skills and Fields of Fascination or interests -- so I can find out how they all might fit together, in one job or career?

Then go visit the people they suggest.

If they can't think of *anyone*, ask them if they know who *might* know. And so on. And so forth.

"THEY SAY I HAVE TO GO BACK TO SCHOOL, BUT I HAVEN'T THE TIME OR THE MONEY"

Next step: having found the names of jobs or careers that interest you, having mentally *tried them on* to see if they fit, you next want to find out *how much training, etc. it takes, to get into that field or career*. You ask the same people you have been talking to, previously.

More times than not, you will hear *bad news*. They will tell you something like: "In order to be hired for this job, you have to have a master's degree and ten years' experience at it."

If you're willing to do that, if you have the time, and the money, fine! But what if you don't? Then you search for *the exception:*

> *"Yes, but do you know of anyone in this field who got into it without that master's degree, and ten years' experience?*
> *And where might I find him or her?*
> *And if you don't know of any such person, who might know such information?"*

Throughout this Informational Interviewing, don't assume anything ("But I just assumed that . . ."). Question *all* assumptions, no matter how many people tell you that 'this is the way things are.'

Keep clearly in mind that there are people *out there* who will tell you something that absolutely *isn't* so, with every conviction in their being -- because they *think* it's true. Sincerity they have, one hundred percent. Accuracy is something else again. You will need to check and cross-check any information that people tell you or that you read in books (even this one).

No matter how many people tell you that such-and-so are the rules about getting into a particular occupation, and there are no exceptions -- believe me there *are* exceptions, to almost *every* rule, except where a profession has rigid entrance examinations, as in, say, medicine or law.

Rules are rules. But what you are counting on is that somewhere in this vast country, somewhere in this vast world, *somebody* found a way to get into this career you dream of, without going through all the hoops that everyone else is telling you are *absolutely essential.*

You want to find out who these people are, and go talk to them, to find out *how they did it.*

Okay, but suppose you are determined to go into a career that takes *years* to prepare for; and you can't find *anyone* who took a shortcut? What then?

Even here, you can get *close* to the profession *without* such long preparation. Every professional speciality has one or more *shadow* professions, which require much less training. For example, instead of becoming a doctor, you can go into paramedical work; instead of becoming a lawyer, you can go into paralegal work, instead of becoming a licensed career counselor, you can become a career coach.

HAVE A 'PLAN B'

Sooner or later, as you interview one person after another, you'll begin to get some definite ideas about a career that is of interest to you. It uses your favorite skills. It employs your favorite Fields of Fascination or fields of interest. You've interviewed people *actually doing that work,* and it all sounds fine. This part of your Informational Interviewing is over.

Just be sure that you get the names of at least *two* careers, or jobs, that you think you could be happy doing. Never, ever, put all your eggs in one basket. The secret of surviving out there in the jungle is *having alternatives.*

Be careful. Be thorough. Be persistent. This is your life you're working on, and your future. Make it glorious. Whatever it takes, find out the name of your ideal career, your ideal occupation, your ideal job -- *or jobs.*

• QUESTION #2

What **kinds of organizations** would and/or do employ people in these careers?

Now we dwelled overly long on Question #1, because -- as I said -- in seeing how you explore *that* question, you swiftly understand how to explore the other three, in turn. We can now dispatch the other three in short order:

Before you think of individual places where you might like to work, it is necessary to step back a little, as it were, and think of all the *kinds* of places where one might get hired.

Let's take an example. Suppose in your new career you want to be a teacher. You must then ask yourself: *what kinds of places hire teachers?* You might answer, *"just schools,"* -- and finding that schools in your geographical area have no openings, you might say, *"Well, there are no jobs for people in this career."*

But that is not true. There are countless other *kinds* of organizations and agencies out there, besides schools, which employ *teachers*. For example, corporate training and educational departments, workshop sponsors, foundations, private research firms, educational consultants, teachers' associations, professional and trade societies, military bases, state and local councils on higher education, fire and police training academies, and so on and so forth.

'*Kinds* of places' also means places with different *hiring modes*, besides full-time hiring, such as:

- places that would employ you part-time (maybe you'll end up deciding to hold down two or even three part-time jobs, which altogether would add up to one full-time job, in order to give yourself more variety);
- places that take temporary workers, on assignment for one project at a time;
- places that take consultants, one project at a time;
- places that operate with volunteers, etc.

- places that are nonprofit;
- places that are for profit;
- and, don't forget, places which you yourself would start up, should you decide to be your own boss. *(See Chapter 6.)*

Don't forget that as you talk to workers about their jobs or careers (in the previous section), they will accidentally volunteer information about the *kinds* of organizations. Listen keenly, and keep notes.

> • **QUESTION #3**
>
> Among the kinds of organizations uncovered in the previous question, what are the names of **particular places** that I especially like?

As you interview workers about their jobs or careers, they will along the way volunteer actual names of organizations that have such jobs -- including what's good or bad about the place where *they* work or used to work. This is important information for you. Jot it all down. Keep notes *as though it were part of your religion.*

Now when this name-gathering is all done, what do you have? Well, either you'll have *too few names* of places to work, or you'll end up with *too much information* -- too many names of places which hire people in the career that interests you. There are ways of dealing with either of these eventualities. We'll take this last scenario, first.

CUTTING DOWN THE TERRITORY

If you end up with the names of too many places, you will want to **cut the territory down**, so that you are left with *a manageable number* of 'targets' for your job-hunt.[4]

Let's take an example. Suppose you discovered that the career which interests you the most is *welding*. You want to be a welder. Well, that's a beginning. You've cut the 16 million U.S. job-markets down to:

- I want to work in a place
  that hires welders.

But the territory is still too large. There might be thousands of places in the country, that use welders. You can't go visit them all. So, you've got to cut the territory down, further. Suppose that on your geography *petal* you said that you really want to live and work in the San Jose area of California. That's helpful: that cuts the territory down further. Now your goal is:

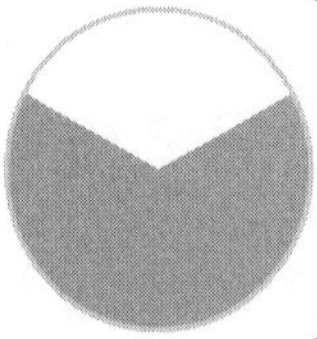

- I want to work in a place
  that hires welders,
  within the San Jose area.

But, the territory is still too large. There could be 100, 200, 300 organizations which fit that description. So you look at your Flower Diagram for further help, and you notice that under *preferred working conditions* you said you wanted to work for an organization with fifty or less employees. Good, now your goal is:

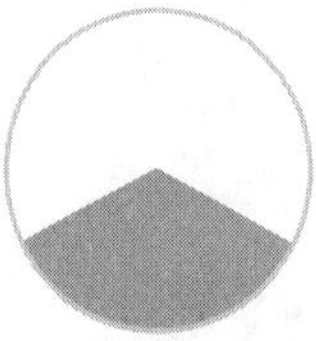

- I want to work in a place that hires welders,
  within the San Jose area,
  and has fifty or less employees.

This territory may still be too large. So you look again at your Flower Diagram for further guidance, and you see that on the Things *petal* you said you wanted to work for an organization which works with, or produces, *wheels.* So now your statement of what you're looking for, becomes:

- I want to work in a place that hires welders,
  within the San Jose area,
  has fifty or less employees,
  and makes wheels.

Using your Flower Diagram, you can thus keep cutting the territory down, until the *'targets'* of your job-hunt are no more than 10 places. That's a manageable number of places for you to *start with.* You can always expand the list later, if none of these 10 turn out to be very promising or interesting.

4. If you resist this idea of *cutting the territory down* -- if you feel you could be happy anywhere just as long as you were using your favorite skills -- then almost no organization in the country can be ruled out. So if you aren't willing to take some steps to cut the territory down, then you'll have to go visit them all. Good luck! We'll see you in about 43 years.

5,708,000 POSSIBLE TARGETS (EMPLOYERS)
57,000 POSSIBLE TARGETS
5,700 POSSIBLE TARGETS
1,000 POSSIBLE TARGETS
500 POSSIBLE TARGETS
300 POSSIBLE TARGETS
60 POSSIBLE TARGETS

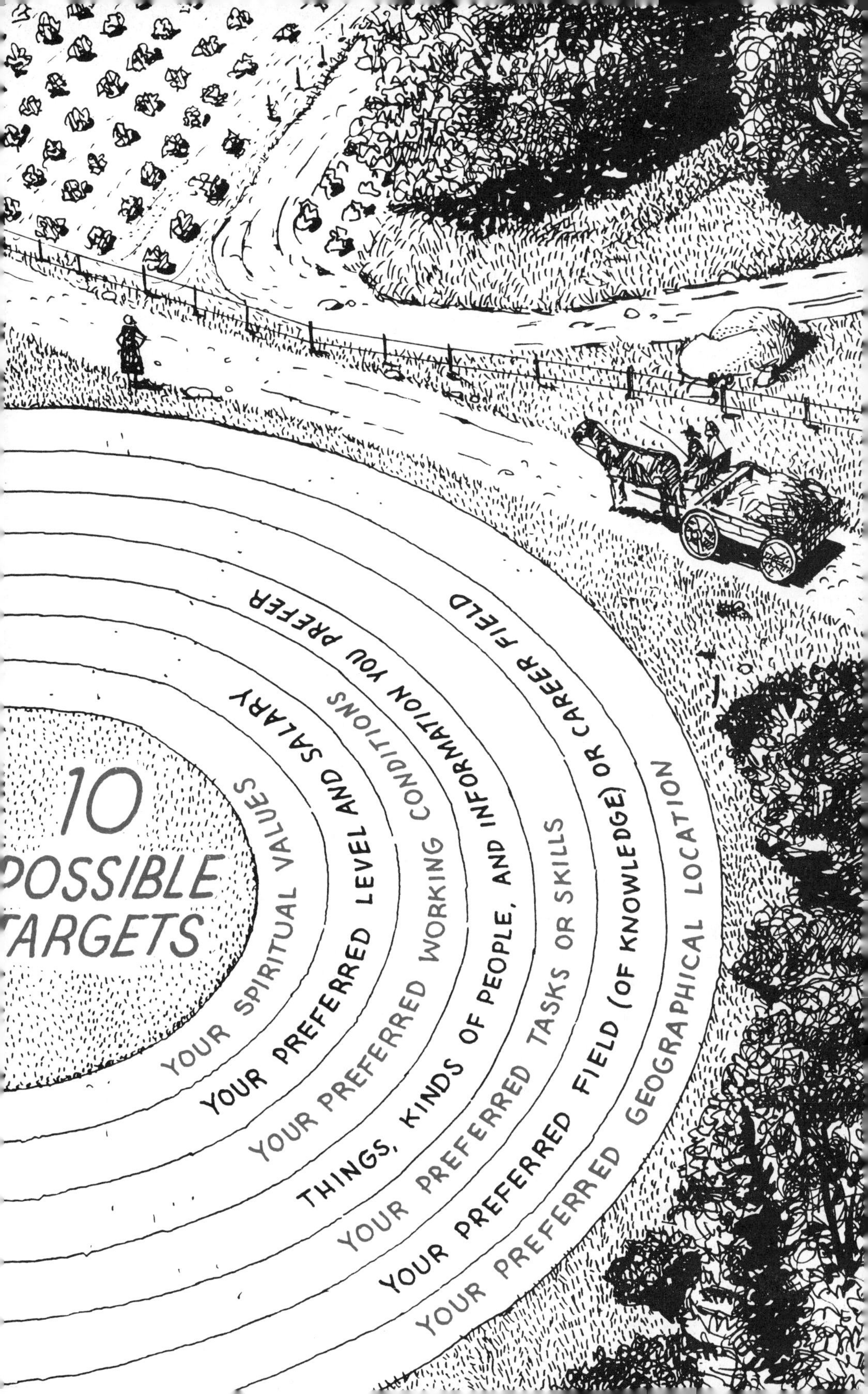
10 POSSIBLE TARGETS
YOUR SPIRITUAL VALUES
YOUR PREFERRED LEVEL AND SALARY
YOUR PREFERRED WORKING CONDITIONS
THINGS, KINDS OF PEOPLE, AND INFORMATION YOU PREFER
YOUR PREFERRED TASKS OR SKILLS
YOUR PREFERRED FIELD (OF KNOWLEDGE) OR CAREER FIELD
YOUR PREFERRED GEOGRAPHICAL LOCATION

EXPANDING THE TERRITORY

Sometimes your problem will be just the opposite. We come here to the second scenario: if your Informational Interviewing doesn't turn up enough names of places where you could get hired in your new career, then you're going to have to expand your list. You're going to have to consult some directories.

Your salvation is going to be the Yellow Pages of your local phone book. Look under every heading that is of any interest to you. Also, see if the local Chamber of Commerce publishes a business directory; often it will list not only small companies but also local divisions of larger companies, with names of department heads; and sometimes will even include the (SIC) industry codes, should you care. If you are diligent here, you won't lack for names, believe me -- unless it's a very small town you live in, in which case you'll need to cast your net a little wider, to include other towns or villages that are within commuting distance.

Once you have about *10 names* of organizations or businesses that might hire you for the kind of work you are dying to do, you proceed to our fourth and last question involved in naming your Flower:

> • **QUESTION #4**
>
> Among the places that I particularly like, **what needs do they have** or what outcomes are they trying to produce, that my skills and knowledge could help with?

RESEARCHING PLACES BEFORE YOU APPROACH THEM

Why should you research places, before you approach them for a hiring-interview? Well, first of all, you want to know something about the organization from the inside: what kind of work they do there. And what their needs or problems or challenges are. And what kind of goals are they trying to achieve, what obstacles are they running into, and how can your skills and knowledges help them? *(When you do at last go in for a hiring-interview, you want above all else to be able to show them that you have something to offer, that they need.)*

Secondly, you want to find out if you would enjoy working there. You want to take the measure of that organization or organizations. Everybody takes the measure of an organization, but the problem with most job-hunters or career-changers is they take the measure of an organization *after* they are hired there.

In the U.S., for example, a survey of the Federal/State employment service once found that 57% of those who found jobs through that service were not working at that job just 30 days later.

They were not working at that job just 30 days later, *because* they used the first ten or twenty days *on the job* to screen out that job.

By doing this research of a place ahead of time, you are choosing a better path, by far. Essentially, you are *screening out* careers, jobs, places *before* you commit to them. How sensible! How smart!

So, what you do is try to think of every way in the world that you could find out more about those organizations *(plural, not singular)* that interest you, *before you go to see if you can get hired there.* There are several ways you can do this research ahead of time:

- **Friends and Neighbors.** Ask *everybody* you know, if they know anyone who works at the place that interests you. And, if they do, ask them if they could arrange for you and that person to get together, for lunch, coffee or tea. At that time, tell them why the place interests you, and indicate you'd like to know more about it. *(It helps if your mutual friend is sitting there with the two of you, so the purpose of this little chat won't be misconstrued.)* This is the vastly preferred way to find out about a place. However, obviously you need a couple of additional alternatives up your sleeve, in case you run into a dead end here:

- **What's In Print.** The organization itself may have stuff in print, or on its Web site, about its business, purpose, etc. The CEO or head of the organization may have given talks. The organization may have copies of those talks. In addition, there may be brochures, annual reports, etc., that the organization has put out, about itself. How do you get a hold of these? The person that answers the phone is the person to check with, in small organizations. In larger organizations, the publicity office, or human relations office, are the places to check. Also, if it's a decent-sized organization that you are interested in, public libraries may have files on the organization -- newspaper clippings, articles, etc. You never know; and it never hurts to ask your friendly neighborhood research librarian.
- **People at the Organizations in Question, or at Similar Organizations.** You can also go directly to organizations and ask questions about the place, but here I must caution you about several *dangers.*

First, you must make sure you're not asking them questions that are in print somewhere, which you could easily have read for yourself instead of bothering *them.*

Secondly, you must make sure that you approach the people at that organization *whose business it is to give out information* -- receptionists, public relations people, 'the personnel office,' etc. -- *before* you ever approach other people higher up in that organization.

Thirdly, you must make sure that you approach *subordinates* rather than the top person in the place, if the subordinates would know the answer to your questions. Bothering the boss there with some simple questions that someone else could have answered is committing *job-hunting suicide.*

Fourth, you must make sure you're not using this approach simply as a sneaky way to get in to see the boss, and make a pitch for them hiring you. This is supposed to be just information gathering. Keep it at that. Keep it honest.

- **Temporary Agencies.** Many job-hunters and career-changers have found that a useful way to explore organizations is to go and work at a temporary agency. Employers turn to these agencies in order to find: a) job-hunters who can work part-time for a limited number of days; and b) job-hunters who can work full-time for a limited number of days. The advantage to you of temporary work is that if there is an agency which loans out people with your particular skills and expertise, you get a chance to be sent to a number of different employers over a period of several weeks, and see each one from the inside. Maybe the temp agency won't send you to exactly the place you hoped for; but sometimes you can develop contacts in the place you love, even while you're temporarily working somewhere else - - if both organizations are in the same field.

As I said earlier, some of you may balk at the idea of enrolling with a temporary agency, because you remember the old days when such agencies were solely for clerical workers and secretarial help. But the field has seen an explosion of services in the last decade, and there are temporary agencies these days *(at least in the larger cities)* for many different occupations. In your city you may find temporary agencies for: accountants, industrial workers, assemblers, drivers, mechanics, construction people, engineering people, software engineers, programmers, computer technicians, production workers, management/ executives, nannies (for young and old), health care/dental/medical people, legal specialists, insurance specialists, sales/marketing people, underwriting professionals, financial services, and the like, as well as for the more obvious specialties: data processing, secretarial, and office services. See your local phone book, under 'Temporary Agencies.'

- **Volunteer Work.** Another useful way to research a place before you ever ask them to hire you there, is to volunteer your services at that place that interests you. Of course, some places will turn your offer down, cold. But others will be interested. If they are, it will be relatively easy for you to talk them into letting you work there for a while, because you offer your services *without pay,* and for a brief, limited period of time. In other words, from their point of view, if you turn out to be a *pain*, they won't have to endure you for long.

In this fashion, you get a chance to learn about organizations from the inside. Not so coincidentally, if you do decide you would really like to work there, and permanently, they've had a chance to see you in action, and when you are about to end your volunteer time there, *may* want to hire you permanently. I say *may.* Don't be mad if they simply say, "Thanks very much for helping us out. Goodbye. Farewell." (That's what *usually* happens.) Even so, you've learned a lot, and this will stand you in good stead, in the future -- as you approach other organizations.

SEND A THANK-YOU NOTE

After *any one* has done you a favor, during this Informational Interviewing phase of your job-hunt, you must *be sure* to send them a thank-you note by the very next day, at the latest. Such a note goes to *everyone* who helps you, or who talks with you. That means friends, people at the organization in question, temporary agency people, secretaries, receptionists, librarians, workers, or whoever.

Ask them, at the time you are face-to-face with them, for their calling card (if they have one), or ask them to write out their name and work address, on a piece of paper, for you. You *don't* want to misspell their name. It is difficult to figure out how to spell people's names, these days, simply from the sound of it. What sounds like "Laura" may actually be "Lara." What sounds like "Smith" may actually be "Smythe," and so on. Get that name and address, *but get it right*, please. And let me reiterate: write or eMail the thank-you note that same night, or the very next day at the latest. A thank-you note that arrives a week later, completely misses the point.

Ideally it should be eMailed immediately, followed by a lovely printed copy, nicely formatted, and sent through the mails. Most employers these days prefer a printed letter to a handwritten one.

It can be just two or three sentences. Something like: *"I wanted to thank you for talking with me yesterday. It was very helpful to me. I much appreciated your taking the time out of your busy schedule, to do this. Best wishes to you,"* and then your signature. *Do* sign it, particularly if the thank-you note is printed. Printed letters sent through the mails without any signature seem to be multiplying like rabbits in the world of work, these days; the absence of a signature on anything other than an eMailed thank-you note is usually perceived as making your letter *real* impersonal. You don't want to leave that impression.

WHAT IF I GET OFFERED A JOB ALONG THE WAY, WHILE I'M JUST GATHERING INFORMATION?

You probably won't. Let me remind you that during this information gathering, you are *not* talking primarily to employers. You're talking to workers.

Nonetheless, an occasional employer *may* stray across your path during all this Informational Interviewing. And that employer *may* be so impressed with the carefulness you're showing, in going about your career-change and job-search, that they want to hire you, on the spot. So, it's *possible* that you might get offered a job while you're still doing your information gathering. Not *likely,* but *possible.* And if that happens, what should you say?

Well, if you're desperate, you will of course say *yes.* I remember one wintertime when I had just gone through the knee of my last pair of pants, we were burning old pieces of furniture in our fireplace to stay warm, the legs on our bed had just broken, and we were eating spaghetti until it was coming out our ears. In such a situation, *of course* you say yes.

But if you're not *desperate,* if you have a little time to be more careful, then you respond to the job-offer in a way that will buy you some time. You tell them what you're doing: that the average job-hunter tries to screen a job *after* they take it. But you are doing what you are *sure* this employer would do if they were in your shoes: you are examining careers, fields, industries, jobs, organizations *before* you decide where you can do your best and most effective work.

And you tell them that since your Informational Interviewing isn't finished yet, it would be premature for you to accept their job offer, until you're *sure* that this is the place where you could be most effective, and do your best work.

But, you add: "Of course, I'm tickled pink that you would want me to be working here. And when I've finished my personal survey, I'll be glad to get back to you about this, as my preliminary impression is that this is the kind of place I'd like to work in, and the kind of people I'd like to work for, and the kind of people I'd like to work with."

In other words, *if you're not desperate yet,* you don't walk immediately through any opened doors; but neither do you allow them to shut.

A Closing Word to Those Who Are Shy

The late John Crystal often had to counsel the shy. They were often *frightened* at the whole idea of going to talk to people for information, never mind for hiring. So John developed a system to help the shy. He suggested that before you even begin doing any Informational Interviewing, you first go out and talk to people about *anything* just to get good at *talking to people.* Thousands of job-hunters and career-changers have followed his advice, over the past thirty years, and found it really helps. Indeed, people who have followed John's advice in this regard have had a success rate of 86% in finding a job -- and not just any job, but *the* job or new career that they were looking for.

Daniel Porot, the job-hunting expert in Europe, has taken John's system, and brought some organization to it. He observed that John was really recommending three types of interviews: this interview we are talking about, just for practice. Then Informational Interviewing. And finally, of course, the hiring-interview. Daniel decided to call these three the *'The PIE Method,'* which has helped thousands of job-hunters and career-changers in both the U.S. and in Europe.[5]

Why is it called *'PIE'?*

P is for the *warmup* phase. John Crystal named this warmup 'The Practice Field Survey.'[6] Daniel Porot calls it **P** for *pleasure.*

I is for 'Informational Interviewing.'

E is for the employment interview with the-person-who-has-the-power-to-hire-you.

How do you use this **P** for *practice* to get comfortable about going out and talking to people *one-on-one?*

This is achieved by choosing a topic -- *any* topic, however silly or trivial -- that is a pleasure for you to talk about with your friends, or family. To avoid anxiety, it should not be connected to any present or future careers that you are considering. Rather, the kinds of topics that work best, for this exercise, are:

- **a hobby** you *love,* such as skiing, bridge playing, exercise, computers, etc.

5. Daniel has summarized his system in a book published here in the U.S. in 1996: it is called *The Pie Method for Career Success: A Unique Way to Find Your Ideal Job,* 1996, and is available still from its publisher, JIST Works, Inc., 720 North Park Avenue, Indianapolis IN 46202-3431. Phone 317-264-3720. Fax 317 264 3709. It is a fantastic book, and I give it my highest recommendation.
6. If you want further instructions about this whole process, I refer you to "The Practice Field Survey," pp. 187–196 in *Where Do I Go From Here With My Life?* by John Crystal and friend. Ten Speed Press, Box 7123, Berkeley, CA 94707.

	Pleasure	Information	Employment
Initial:	P	I	E
Kind of Interview	Practice Field Survey	Informational Interviewing or Researching	Employment Interview or Hiring Interview
Purpose	To Get Used to Talking with People to Enjoy It; To "Penetrate" Networks	To Find Out If You'd Like a Job, Before You Go Trying to Get It	To Get Hired for the Work You Have Decided You Would Most Like to Do
How You Go to the Interview	You Can Take Somebody with You	By Yourself or You Can Take Somebody with You	By Yourself
Who You Talk To	Anyone Who Shares Your Enthusiasm About a (for You) Non-Job-Related Subject	A Worker Who Is Doing the Actual Work You Are Thinking About Doing	An Employer Who Has the Power to Hire You for the Job You Have Decided You Would Most Like to Do
How Long a Time You Ask for	10 Minutes (and DON'T run over -- asking to see them at 11:50 may help keep you honest, since most employers have lunch appointments at noon)	Ditto	
What You Ask Them	Any Curiosity You Have About Your Shared Interest or Enthusiasm	Any Questions You Have About This Job or This Kind of Work	You Tell Them What It Is You Like About Their Organization and What Kind of Work You Are Looking For

	Pleasure	Information	Employment
Initial:	**P**	**I**	**E**
What You Ask Them *(continued)*	If Nothing Occurs to You, Ask: 1. How did you start, with this hobby, interest, etc.? 2. What excites or interests you the most about it? 3. What do you find is the thing you like the least about it? 4. Who else do you know of who shares this interest, hobby or enthusiasm, or could tell me more about my curiosity? a. Can I go and see them? b. May I mention that it was you who suggested I see them? c. May I say that you recommended them? ***Get their name and address***	If Nothing Occurs to You Ask: 1. How did you get interested in this work and how did you get hired? 2. What excites or interests you the most about it? 3. What do you find is the thing you like the least about it? 4. Who else do you know of who does this kind of work, or similar work but with this difference: ____________? 5. What kinds of challenges or problems do you have to deal with in this job? 6. What skills do you need in order to meet those challenges or problems? ***Get their name and address***	 You tell them the kinds of challenges you like to deal with. What skills you have to deal with those challenges. What experience you have had in dealing with those challenges in the past.
AFTERWARD: That Same Night	SEND A THANK-YOU NOTE	SEND A THANK-YOU NOTE	SEND A THANK-YOU NOTE

- **any leisure-time enthusiasm** of yours, such as a movie you just saw, that you liked a lot
- **a long-time curiosity,** such as how do they predict the weather, or what do policemen do
- **an aspect of the town or city you live in,** such as a new shopping mall that just opened
- **an issue** you feel strongly about, such as the homeless, AIDS sufferers, ecology, peace, health, etc.

There is only one condition about choosing a topic: it should be something you *love* to talk about with other people: a subject you know nothing about, but you feel a great deal of enthusiasm for it, is far preferable to something you know an awful lot about, but it puts you to sleep.

Passion or Enthusiasm

Well, I said it before, but I'm going to say it again. Throughout the job-hunt and career-change, the key to informational 'interviewing' for shy people is not found in memorizing a dozen questions about what you're supposed to say.

No, the key is just this one thing: now and always, be *sure* you are talking about something you feel *passionate about.*[7]

Enthusiasm is the key -- to *enjoying* 'interviewing,' and conducting *effective* interviews, at any level. What this exercise teaches us is that shyness always loses its power and its painful self-consciousness -- *if* and *when* you are talking about something *you love.*

For example, if you love gardens you will forget all about your shyness when you're talking to someone else about gardens and flowers. *"You ever been to Butchart Gardens?"*

If you love movies, you'll forget all about your shyness when you're talking to someone else about movies. *"I just hated that scene where they. . . ."*

If you love computers, then you will forget all about your shyness when you're talking to someone else about computers. *"Do you work on a Mac or a Windows machine?*

That's why it is important that it be your enthusiasms that you are exploring and pursuing in these conversations with others.

Having identified your enthusiasm, you then need to go talk to someone who is as enthusiastic about this thing, as you are. *For best results with your later job-hunt, this should be someone you don't already know.* Use the

Yellow Pages, ask around among your friends and family, *who do you know that* loves *to talk about this?* It's relatively easy to find the kind of person you're looking for.

You love to talk about skiing? *Try a ski-clothes store, or a skiing instructor.* You love to talk about writing? *Try a professor on a nearby college campus, who teaches English.* You love to talk about physical exercise? *Try a trainer, or someone who teaches physical therapy.*

Once you've identified someone you think shares your enthusiasm, you then go talk with them. When you are face-to-face with your *fellow enthusiast*, the first thing you must do is relieve their understandable anxiety. *Everyone* has had someone visit them who has stayed too long, who has worn out their welcome. If your *fellow enthusiast* is worried about you staying too long, they'll be so preoccupied with this that they won't hear a word you are saying.

So, when you first meet them, ask for *ten minutes of their time, only.* Period. Stop. Exclamation point. And watch your wrist-watch *like a hawk,* to be sure you stay no longer. *Never* stay longer, unless they *beg* you to. And I mean, *beg, beg, beg.*[8]

Once they've agreed to give you ten minutes, you tell them why you're there -- that you're trying to get comfortable about talking with people, for information -- and you understand that you two share a mutual interest, which is . . .

Then what? Well, a topic may have its own unique set of questions. For example, I love movies, so if I met someone who shared this interest, my first question would be, "What movies have you seen lately?" And so on. If it's a topic you love, and often talk about, you'll *know* what kinds of questions you begin with. But, if no such questions come to mind, no matter how hard you try, the following ones have proved to be good conversation starters for thousands of job-hunters and career-changers before you, no matter what their topic or interest.

So, look these over, memorize them *(or copy them on a little card that fits in the palm of your hand),* and give them a try:

Questions Shy People Can Practice With

Addressed to the person you're doing the Practice Interviewing with:

- How did you get involved with/become interested in this?

7. This is what the late Joseph Campbell used to call 'your bliss.'

8. A polite, "Oh do you have to go?" should be understood for what it is: politeness. Your response should be, "Yes, I promised to only take ten minutes of your time, and I want to keep to my word." This will almost always leave a *very* favorable impression behind you.

("*This*" is the hobby, curiosity, aspect, issue, or enthusiasm, that you are so interested in.)

- What do you like the most about it?
- What do you like the least about it?
- Who else would you suggest I go talk to that shares this interest?
- Can I use your name?
- May I tell them it was you who recommended that I talk with them?
- *Then, choosing one person off the list of several names they may have given you, you say,* Well, I think I will begin by going to talk to this person. Would you be willing to call ahead for me, so they will know who I am, when I go over there?

Incidentally, during *this* Practice Interviewing, it's perfectly okay for you to take someone with you -- preferably someone who is more outgoing than you feel you are. And on the first few interviews, let them take the lead in the conversation, while you watch to see how they do it.

Once it is *your turn* to conduct the interview, it will by that time usually be easy for you to figure out what to talk about.

Alone or with someone, keep at this Practice Interviewing until you feel very much at ease in talking with people and asking them questions about things you are curious about.

In all of this, *fun* is the key. If you're having fun, you're doing it right. If you're not having fun, you need to keep at it, until you are. It may take your seeing four people. It may take ten. Or twenty. You'll know.

Summary of This Chapter

There is no limit to what you can find out about WHERE you'd like to work -- careers, and places which hire for those careers -- if you go out and talk to people. When you find places that interest you, it is irrelevant whether they happen to have a vacancy, or not. In this dance of life, called the job-hunt, you get to decide first of all whether or not *you* want *them*, through your research. Only after you have decided that, is it appropriate to ask, as in the next chapter, if they also want you.

Forget "what's available out there."
Go after the job you really want the most.
David Maister

CHAPTER TEN

Getting In To Impossible Places

HOW

DO YOU OBTAIN AN INTERVIEW IN PLACES THAT ARE REALLY DIFFICULT TO GET IN TO?

OKAY, SO YOU don't want to work for yourself. You want to work for someone else -- like nine out of every ten workers (in the U.S.). So you've identified a job you love, you've found a place -- better yet, *places* -- where you'd *love* to work. But . . .

But, the person you'd have to see, in order to get hired there, is in an office with a ring of fire around it, three knights in full-armor guarding it, in a castle with fifty-foot walls, surrounded by a wide moat whose deep waters are filled with hungry alligators.

And you want to know how to get a hiring-interview with this person. Right? Well, it isn't as difficult as it might at first seem . . . if you are *determined*. And if you know a few simple principles.

THE FIRST CRUCIAL QUESTION: HOW LARGE IS THE ORGANIZATION?

To begin with, most discussions of job-interviewing proceed from a false assumption. They *assume* you are going to be approaching a large organization -- you know, the ones where you need a floor-plan of the building, and an alphabetical directory of the staff. There are admittedly *huge* problems in approaching such giants for a hiring-interview, not the least of which is that in troubled times, many do more downsizing than hiring.

But many job-hunters don't want to work for large corporations, anyway. They want to go after the so-called 'small organizations' -- those with 50 or less employees -- which, in the U.S. for example, represent 80% of all private businesses, and one-fourth of all workers in the private sector.

THE VIRTUES OF SMALL ORGANIZATIONS

Experts have claimed for years that small organizations create up to two-thirds of all new jobs.[1] If that makes you prefer going after a small organization, I have good news: they are *much* easier to get into than large ones, believe me.

---

1. This statistic, first popularized by David Birch of M.I.T., and widely quoted for years, was challenged during the '90s by economists such as Nobel laureate Milton Friedman and Harvard economist James Medoff. The debate was fueled by a study conducted jointly by Steven J. Davis, a labor economist at the University of Chicago, John Haltiwanger at the University of Maryland, and Scott Schuh at the Federal Reserve. Their study, however, was of U.S. *manufacturing,* not of the economy as a whole. Anyway, what these researchers discovered at that time is that small *manufacturing* companies with 50 or fewer employees created only *one-fifth* of all new manufacturing jobs (*New York Times,* 3/25/94). Other researchers, notably Birch, claim that if you include all small companies, they create as many as two-thirds of all new jobs. Has this changed in the new millennium? Hard to tell. Certainly, the U.S. dot.com - dot-bomb melt-down that began in April of 2000 has made many people afraid to work for small companies -- in the Internet field, at least, and in the so-called "New Economy" for sure.

With a small organization, you don't need to wait until there's a *known* vacancy, because they rarely advertise vacancies even when there is one. You just go there and ask if they need someone.

With a small organization, there is no Personnel or Human Resources Department to screen you out.

With a small organization, there's no problem in identifying the person-who-has-the-power-to-hire-you. It's *the boss.* Everyone there knows who it is. They can point to his or her office door, easily.

With a small organization, you do not need to approach them through the mail; if you use your personal contacts, you can get in to see the boss. And if, by chance, he or she is well-protected from intruders, it is relatively easy to figure out how to get around *that.* Contacts are the answer, as I just indicated.

With a small organization, if it is growing, there is a greater likelihood that they will be willing to create a new position for you, *if you quietly convince them that you are too good to let slip out of their grasp.*

For all of these reasons and more, small organizations must be kept in mind, as much as, or more than, large organizations, when we begin talking about techniques or strategies for securing a hiring-interview. But let's take each separately, as they involve two different techniques:

APPROACHING LARGE ORGANIZATIONS FOR AN INTERVIEW

In securing hiring-interviews, it's the large organizations that are the problem -- the ones, as I mentioned above, where you need a floor-plan of the building, and an alphabetical directory of the staff.

But you can simplify your task, if you keep certain things in mind. To begin with, you don't want to just get into the building. You want to get in in order to see *a particular person* in that building, and only that person: namely, the person-who-has-the-power-to-hire-you for the job you are interested in.

Most job-hunters *don't* even *try* to find out *who* that person is, before approaching a large organization. Rather, they approach each large organization in what can only be described as a haphazard, scatter-shot fashion -- sending them their resume or c.v.[2], with or without some covering letter, or posting their resume on that organization's Web site -- hoping that their resume or covering letter will function as a kind of extended calling card, arousing employers' interest, who will then ask the job-hunter to come in and see them.

This blanket, depersonalized approach is many job-hunters' favorite way of approaching an organization, particularly a large organization, for a hiring-interview. It's their favorite because you don't have to *go* somewhere needlessly, you don't have to look into the employers' eyes when they reject you, and -- let's admit it, sometimes it actually works: you do get invited in for a possible hiring-interview.

Also, to be truthful, *some* employers love this 'mail approach,' but for all the wrong reasons (from your point of view). They love it, because it enables them to screen you out *in about eight seconds,* without ever 'wasting their time' on your coming in for an interview.

It is not uncommon for job-hunters to approach eight hundred organizations or more in this fashion and not get *one* single invitation to come in for a hiring-interview.

But fortunately, there is a far far more effective way to approach employers -- and that is to identify *who* at that organization has the power to hire you for the position you have in mind, and then to discover what mutual friend the two of you might have in common, who could help you get an appointment. **The person-who-has-the-power-to-hire-you** will see you because that mutual friend got the appointment for you.

2. C.v. stands for *curriculum vitae,* a term for *resume* that is favored in academic circles in the U.S. and in other countries.

HOW DO I FIND OUT EXACTLY WHO HAS THE POWER TO HIRE ME?

In a small organization with 50 or less employees, this is a relatively easy problem. Calling the place and asking for the name of the boss, should do it. It's what we call *The One-Minute Research Project.*

But if the place where you are dying to work is a much larger organization, then the answer is: "Through the *research* you already learned how to do in Chapter 9; *and* by asking every *contact* you have."

Let's say that one of the places you are interested in is an organization which we will call *Mythical Corporation.*

You know the kind of job you'd like to get there, but first you know you need to find out the name of the **person-who-has-the-power-to-hire-you** there. What do you do?

If it's a large organization, you go on the Internet or you go to your local public library, and search the directories there. Hopefully that search will yield the name of the person you want.

But if it doesn't, which will particularly be the case with smaller organizations, *then you turn to your contacts.*

THE VIRTUE OF CONTACTS

Who or What Is a "Contact"?

Since this subject of *contacts* is widely misunderstood by job-hunters and career-changers, let's be very specific, here.

Every person you know, is a contact.

Every member of your family.

Every friend of yours.

Every person in your address book.

Every person on your Christmas-card list.

Every person you met at any party you attended in the last year or two.

Every co-worker from your last five jobs.

Every person you know at your gym or athletic place.

Every person you know on any athletic team.

Every merchant or salesperson you ever deal with.

Every person who comes to your apartment or house to do any kind of repairs or maintenance work.

Every person you meet in line at the supermarket or bank.

Every check-out clerk you know.

Every gas station attendant you know.

Everyone who does personal work on you: your barber, hairdresser, manicuress, physical trainer, body worker, and the like.

The waiters, waitresses, and manager of your favorite restaurants.

All the people you meet on the Internet. All the people whose eMail addresses you have.

Every leisure partner you have, as for walking, exercising, swimming, or whatever.

Every doctor, or medical professional you know.

Every professor, teacher, etc. you once knew or maybe still know how to get a hold of.

Every person in your church, synagogue, mosque, or religious assembly.

Everyone you know in Rotary, Kiwanis, Lions, or other service organizations.

Every person you know at any group you belong to.

Every person you are newly introduced to.

Every person you meet, stumble across, or blunder into, during your job-hunt, whose name, address, and phone number you have the grace to ask for. (*Always* have the grace to ask for it.)

Got the picture?

So now, to our task. You want to approach, let us say, *Mythical Corporation* and you know that to get in there, you will need to use your contacts. So, what do you do? Well, you approach as many people from the above list as necessary and you ask each of them, "Do you know anyone who works, or used to work, at *Mythical Corporation*?"

You ask that question again and again of *everyone* you know, or meet, until you find someone who says, *"Yes, I do."*

Then you ask them:

"What is the name of the person you know who works, or used to work, at *Mythical Corporation*? Do you have their phone number and/or address?"

"Would you be willing to call ahead, to tell them who I am?"

You then either phone them yourself or make an appointment to go see them (*"I won't need more than 20 minutes of your time."*). Once you are talking to them, after the usual polite chit-chat, you ask them the question you are dying to know. Because they are *inside* the organization that interests you, they are usually able to give you the exact answer to the question that has been puzzling you: "Who would have the power to hire me at *Mythical Corporation*, for this kind of position *(which you then describe)*?" If they answer that they do not know, ask if they know *who* might know. If it turns out that they do know, then you ask them not only for that hiring person's name, address, phone, and eMail address, but also what they can tell you about that person's job, that person's interests, and their style of interviewing.

Then, you ask them if they could help you get an appointment with that person. You repeat once again the familiar refrain:

"Given my background, would you recommend I go see them?"

"Do you know them, personally? If not, could you give me the name of someone who does?"

"If you know them personally, may I tell them it was you who recommended that I talk with them?"

"If you know them personally, would you be willing to call ahead, to tell them who I am, and to help set up an appointment?"

Also, before leaving, you can ask them about the organization, in general.

Then you thank them, and leave; and you *never never* let the day end, without sitting down to write them a thank-you note. *Always* do it. *Never* forget to.

GETTING IN

If the contact you talked to, doesn't know the **person-who-has-the-power-to-hire-you** well enough to get you an interview, then you go back to your other contacts -- now armed with the name of the person you are trying to get in to see -- and pose a new question. Approaching as many of your contacts as necessary, you ask each of them, "Do you know Ms. or Mr. See, at *Mythical Corporation* or do you know someone who does?"

You ask that question again and again of *everyone* who is on your file cards, until you find someone who says, *"Yes, I do."*

Then of course, over the phone or -- better -- in person, you ask them the same familiar questions, carefully, and in this exact order:

- "What can you tell me about him -- or her?"
- "Given the kind of job I am looking for *(which you here describe)*, do you think it would be worth my while to go see them?"
- "Do you have their phone number and/or address?"
- "May I tell them it was you who recommended that I talk with them?"
- "Would you be willing to call ahead, to set up an appointment for me, and tell them who I am?"

MAY-DAY, MAY-DAY!

Whenever a job-hunter writes me and tells me they've run into a brick wall, and just can't find out the name of the **person-who-has-the-power-to-hire-them**, the problem *always* turns out to be: they aren't making *sufficient* use of their contacts. They're making a *pass* at using their contacts, but they aren't putting their whole heart and soul into it.

My favorite (true) story in this regard, concerns a job-hunter I know, in Virginia. He decided he wanted to work for a particular health-care organization in that State, and not knowing any better, he approached them by visiting their Human Resources Department. After dutifully filling out a job application, and talking to someone there in that department, he was told there were no jobs available. Stop. Period. End of story.

Approximately three months later he learned about this technique of approaching your favorite organization by using contacts. He explored his contacts *diligently*, and succeeded in getting an interview with the person-who-had-the-power-to-hire-him for the position he was interested in. The two of them hit it off, immediately. The appointment went swimmingly. "You're hired," said the person-who-had-the-power-to-hire-him. "I'll call Human Resources and tell them you're hired, and that you'll be down to fill out the necessary stuff."

Our job-hunter never once mentioned that he had previously approached that same organization through that same Human Resources Department, and been turned down cold.

Just remember: contacts are the key. It takes about eighty pairs of eyes, and ears, to help find the career, the workplace, the job that you are looking for.

Your contacts *are* those eyes and ears.

They are what will help you get the ideal job you are looking for, and they are key to finding out the name of the person-who-has-the-power-to-hire-you.

The more people you know, the more people you meet, the more people you talk to, the more people you enlist as part of your own personal job-hunting network, the better your job-finding success is likely to be. Therefore, you must try to grow your contacts wherever you go.

Here's how some people have gone about doing that. If they go to hear a speaker on some subject that interests them, they make it a point to join the crowd that gathers 'round the speaker at the end of the talk, and -- with notepad poised -- ask such questions as: "Is there anything special that people with my expertise can do?" And here they mention their *generalized* job-title: computer scientist, health professional, chemist, writer, or whatever. Very useful information has thus been turned up. You can also go up to the speaker afterwards, and ask if you can contact him or her for further information -- "and at what address?"

Conventions, likewise, afford rich opportunities to make contacts. Says one college graduate: "I snuck into the Cable Advertisers Convention at the Waldorf in N.Y.C. That's how I got my job."

Another way people have cultivated contacts, as I mentioned on page 76, is to leave a message on their telephone answering machine which tells everyone who calls, what information they are looking for. One job-hunter used the following message: "This is the recently laid off John Smith. I'm not home right now because I'm out looking for a good job as a computer trouble-shooter in the telecommunications field; if you have any leads or just want to leave a message, please leave it after the tone."

You may also cultivate contacts by studying the *things* that you like to work with, and then writing to the manufacturer of that *thing* to ask them for a list of organizations in your geographical area which use that *thing.* For example, if you like to work on a particular machine, you would write to the manufacturer of that machine, and ask for names of organizations in your geographical area which use that machine. Or if you like to work in a particular environment, think of the supplies used in that environment. For example, let's say you love darkrooms. You think of what brand equipment or supplies is usually used in darkrooms, and then you contact the sales manager of the company that makes those supplies, to ask where his (or her) customers are. Some sales managers will not be at all responsive to such an inquiry; but others graciously will, and thus you may gain some very helpful leads.

Because your memory is going to be overloaded during your job-hunt or career-change, it is useful to set up a filing system, where you put the name of each contact of yours on a 3×5 card, with addresses, phone numbers, and anything about where they work or who they know that may be of use at a later date. Go back over those cards frequently.

That does add up to *a lot* of file cards, just because you've got *a lot* of contacts. But that's the whole point.

You may need *every one* of them, *when push comes to shove.*

RESCUING THE EMPLOYER

As you can see, getting in to see someone, even for a hiring-interview, is not as difficult as people will tell you.

It just takes some *know-how,* some *determination,* some *perseverance,* some *going the extra mile.* It works because everyone has friends, including this **person-who-has-the-power-to-hire-you**. You are simply approaching them through *their* friends. And you are doing this, not *wimpishly,* as one who is coming to ask a favor. You are doing it *helpfully,* as one who is asking to help rescue them.

Rescue? Yes, rescue! I cannot tell you the number of employers I have known over the years, who can't figure out how to find the right employee. It is absolutely mind-boggling, particularly in these hard times when job-hunters would seem to be gathered on every street corner.

You're having trouble finding the employer. The employer is having trouble finding you. *What a great country!*

So, if you now present yourself directly to the **person-who-has-the-power-to-hire-you**, you are not only answering your own prayers. You are hopefully answering the employer's, as well. You will be *just* what the employer is looking for, but didn't know how to find, if . . .

if you took the trouble to do Chapters 8 and 9, and

if you therefore figured out what are your favorite and best skills, and

if you therefore figured out what are your favorite Fields of Fascination or *languages*, and

if you took the trouble to figure out what places *might* need such skills and such *languages*, and

if you researched this place with the intent of finding out what their tasks, challenges and problems are, and

if you took the trouble to figure out who there has the power to hire you.

Of course, you don't for sure *know* they need you; that remains for the hiring-interview to uncover. But at least by this thorough preparation you have *increased* the chances that you are at the right place -- whether they have an announced vacancy or not. And, if you are, you are not imposing on this employer. You are coming not as 'job-beggar,' but as 'resource person.' You may well be absolutely rescuing him or her, believe me!

And yourself. *"The hiring-interview! I'm actually there."*

Yes, and so, it's time for the next chapter.

CONCLUSION

It is astonishing how often this approach (using contacts) works -- it has, in fact, an 86% effectiveness rate for getting a hiring-interview and, subsequently, a job. Of course, there is that 14% of the time when it *doesn't* work. There are places where it is absolutely *impossible* to get in to see 'the boss' -- i.e., the one who has the power to hire you -- in spite of *contacts,* mutual friends, or whatever. As mentioned earlier, he or she may be isolated in a castle surrounded by a moat, with eight large over-sized hungry alligators in that moat. You of course will hurl yourself against the ramparts of that castle a half-dozen times, anyway, furious that you can't get in to see that person, despite all the techniques recommended in this book.

But, could I ask you a question: "*Why* do you want to work for *a place like that*?" I mean, never mind that you're understandably taking this very personally. *Rejection, rejection, rejection,* is flashing on and off in your brain. But, haven't they *(by these actions)* told you something about *the way they work* that is important information for you to have? And having gained that information, isn't it time for you to reassess *whether you really want to work at a place so guarded, so impenetrable, so 'un-user-friendly'?*

> They've just taught you something really important about that place, which you would do well to take very seriously. Look elsewhere.

THE TEN GREATEST MISTAKES MADE IN JOB INTERVIEWS

Whereby Your Chances of Finding a Job Are Greatly Decreased

I. **Going after large organizations only (such as the Fortune 500).**

II. **Hunting all by yourself for places to visit, using ads and resumes.**

III. **Doing no homework on an organization before going there.**

IV. **Allowing the Personnel Department (or Human Resources) to interview you -- *their primary function is to screen you OUT.***

V. **Setting no time limit when you make the appointment with an organization.**

VI. **Letting your resume be used as the agenda for the job interview.**

VII. **Talking primarily about yourself, and what benefit the job will be for you.**

VIII. **When answering a question of theirs, talking anywhere from 2 to 15 minutes, at a time.**

IX. **Basically approaching them as if you were a job-beggar, hoping they will offer you a job, however humble.**

X. **Not sending a thank-you note right after the interview.**

THE TEN COMMANDMENTS FOR JOB INTERVIEWS

Whereby Your Chances of Finding a Job Are Vastly Increased

I. **Go after small organizations with twenty or less employees, since they create 2/3 of all new jobs.**

II. **Hunt for interviews using the aid of friends and acquaintances, because a job-hunt requires eighty eyes and ears.**

III. **Do thorough homework on an organization before going there, using Informational Interviews plus the library.**

IV. **At any organization, identify who has the power to hire you there, for the position you want, and use your friends and acquaintances' contacts, to get in to see that person.**

V. **Ask for just 20 minutes of their time, when asking for the appointment; and keep to your word.**

VI. **Go to the interview with your own agenda, your own questions and curiosities about whether or not this job fits you.**

VII. **Talk about yourself only if what you say offers some benefit to that organization, and their 'problems.'**

VIII. **When answering a question of theirs, talk only between 20 seconds and 2 minutes, at any one time.**

IX. **Basically approach them as if you were a resource person, able to produce better work for that organization than any predecessor.**

X. **Always write a thank-you note the same evening of the interview, and mail it at the latest by the next morning.**

You're a bunch of jackasses. You work your rear ends off in a trivial course that no one will ever care about again. You're not willing to spend time researching a company that you're interested in working for. Why don't you decide who you want to work for and go after them?

Professor Albert Shapiro
The late William H. Davis Professor of the American Free Enterprise System at Ohio State University

CHAPTER ELEVEN

Interviewing Tips For Smarties

HOW

DO YOU LAND THE JOB?

ON: DUMMIES, SMARTIES, AND OTHER PHENOMENA

FUTURISTS AND OTHER people who study Mankind[1] are always telling us what the trends are with respect to, oh, the aging of the population, or the size of 'Gen X', or the influence of the 'baby-boomers' or the movement of minorities to or from the major cities, etc. But there has been a deafening silence about one of the most important trends of the last decade or two. I speak of the tremendous, explosive growth rate in the number of people who are willing to identify themselves as "dummies" or "idiots."

Many years ago when I saw the first volume in the series "So-and-So for Dummies," and "So-and-So for Idiots," I

1. And 'Womankind' of course. (I'd rather die than be politically incorrect.)

couldn't believe my eyes. How many people, I asked myself, are going to be willing to buy a book that blatantly proclaimed they were either a Dummy or an Idiot? None, I thought.

Was I ever wrong! The two series have become huge runaway hits.

Golly, it's nice to know the world still has a sense of humor. And so, as matter of fact, do I. I grew up in a house filled with laughter, where the word "idiot" was used as a kind of cool way of saying, "I love you." I had one brother, one sister. My Dad was always clowning around, particularly at the dinner table. After he played out some particularly outrageous little skit, my Mom would always reach over, and -- touching him affectionately on the cheek -- say, "Oh Don, you idiot!" It was admiring, affectionate, a salute to someone who didn't follow the beaten path but went wherever laughter was to be found, even at the expense of making a bit of a fool out of himself so that we would laugh. He was a grand man. *(Jack Benny, a boyhood hero of mine, had the same kind of humor -- always making himself the butt of his own humor, rather than -- as has become the fashion in more recent times -- putting someone else down.)* Early on, I always heard 'idiot' only as a term of endearment at our dinner table, spoken with a big, affectionate twinkle.

Against this background, books for 'Dummies' and 'Idiots' of course amuse me whenever I see them on bookstore shelves. They bring back memories of my childhood family's loving, laughing, dinner table.

But let me point out, in this same spirit, that I think I detect a slight injustice going on here: I'm sure you've noticed it, too. 'Smarties' are being subjected to a lot of neglect. Look in your local bookstore. Lots of books for 'Dummies,' sure. But, seen any book for 'Smarties' lately? Me neither. I think it's time to address this imbalance. Hence, this chapter: "Interviewing Tips for Smarties." You know who I'm talking about, here. I'm talking about You.

FIRST INTERVIEWING TIP FOR SMARTIES: FRAME VS. CONTENT

To begin with, successful job-hunters have found it very useful to think of a job-interview as a picture, within a frame. The frame is how you mentally structure and prepare for the interview *ahead of time*. The picture inside is the content of what you say *during* the interview.

Interviewing books and articles often focus only on the *picture* -- what you say once you're in the room with the interviewer. But, of equal importance is *the frame:* how you set up the whole interview, first of all in your mind, and secondly in the arrangements you make before going in.

Therefore, let us begin here with some tips about the *frame*.

Ask for Twenty Minutes, No More, When You First Set Up the Interview

If you are the one who asks for the job-interview, only ask for twenty minutes; and keep to this, religiously. Once you're into the interview, stay aware of the time and determine that you will not stay *one minute longer* than the twenty minutes you requested -- unless the employer begs you to. And I mean *begs*. Keep to your original agreement. ("I said I would only require twenty minutes of your time, and I like to honor agreements.") This will always impress an employer!

Research the Organization, Before You Go In

Wherever possible, you *must* research the organization ahead of time, before going in for an interview. This will put you ahead (in the employer's mind) of the other people they talk to.

Toward this end, when the appointment is first set up, ask them right then and there if they have anything *in writing* about their organization; if so, request they mail it to you, so you'll have time to read it before the interview. Or, if the interview is the next day, offer to come down that very day and pick it up, yourself.

Also go to their Web site *(if they have one)* and read everything they have there "About Us."

Also, go to your local library, and ask the librarian for help in locating any newspaper articles or other information about that organization.

Finally, ask all your friends if they know anyone who is working there, or used to work there; if they do, ask them to put you in contact with them, *please*. Tell them you have a job-interview there, and you'd like to know anything they can tell you about the place.

This is a matter of becoming familiar with their history, their purposes and their goals. All organizations, be they large or small, profit or nonprofit, love to be loved. If you have gone to all this trouble, to learn so much about them -- before you ever walk in their doors -- they will be impressed, believe me, because most job-hunters never go to this trouble. *They* walk in knowing little or nothing about the organization. This drives employers *nuts.*

One time, the first question an IBM college recruiter asked a graduating senior was, "What do the initials IBM stand for?" The senior didn't know, and the interview was over.

Another time, an employer said to me, "I'm so tired of job-hunters who come in, and say, *'Uh, what do you do here?'* that the next time someone walks in who already knows something about us, I'm going to hire him or her, on the spot." And he did, within the week.

Thus, if *you* come in, and have done your homework on the organization, this immediately makes you stand out from other job-hunters, and dramatically speeds up your chances of being offered a job there.

During the Interview, Determine to Observe the 50-50 Rule

Studies have revealed that generally speaking the people who get hired are those who mix speaking and listening fifty-fifty in the interview. That is, half the time they let the employer do the talking, half the time in the interview they do the talking. People who didn't follow that mix, were the ones who didn't get hired, according to the study.[2] My hunch as to the *reason* why this is so, is that if you talk too much about yourself, you come across as one who would ignore the needs of the organization; while if you talk too little, you come across as trying to hide something about your background.

In Answering the Employer's Questions, Observe the Twenty Second to Two-Minute Rule

Studies[3] have revealed that when it is your turn to speak or answer a question, you should plan ahead of time not to speak any longer than two minutes at a time, if you want to make the best impression. In fact, a good answer to an employer's question sometimes only takes twenty seconds to give. This is useful information for you to know, in conducting a successful interview -- as you certainly want to do.

2. This one was done by a researcher at Massachusetts Institute of Technology, whose name has been lost in the mists of time.
3. This one was conducted by my friend and colleague, Daniel Porot, of Geneva, Switzerland.

Determine to Be Seen In the Interview As A Resource Person, Not A Job Beggar

Determine that during the interview you will stay focussed on what you can do for the employer, rather than on what the employer can do for you. You want the employer to see you as a potential *Resource Person* for that organization, rather than as simply *A Job Beggar* (to quote Daniel Porot). You want to come across as *a problem solver*, rather than as *one who simply keeps busy.* You need to make it clear during the job-interview that you are there in order to make an oral proposal of what *you can do for them*, to help them with *their* problems. And determine that once the interview is over, you will follow this up with a carefully-worded written proposal on the same theme. You will see immediately what a switch this is from the way most job-hunters approach an employer! *("How much do you pay, and how much time off will I have?")* Will he or she be glad to see you, with this different emphasis? In most cases, you bet they will. They *want* a resource person, and a problem-solver.

Determine to be Seen As A Part of the Solution, Not As A Part of the Problem

Every organization has two main preoccupations for its day-by-day work: the problems they are facing, and what solutions to those problems people are coming up with, there. Therefore, the main thing the employer is going to be trying to figure out during the hiring-interview with you, is: will you be part of the *solution* there, or just another part of the *problem*.

In trying to answer this concern, figure out prior to the interview how a *bad* employee would 'screw up,' in the position you are asking for -- such things as *come in late, take too much time off, follow his or her own agenda instead of the employers, etc.* Then plan to emphasize to the employer during the interview how much you are the very opposite: your sole goal is to increase the organization's effectiveness and service and bottom line.

Be aware of the skills employers are looking for, these days, regardless of the position you are seeking. Overall, they are looking for employees: *who are punctual, arriving at work on time or early; who stay until quitting time, or even leave late; who are dependable; who have a good attitude; who have drive, energy, and enthusiasm; who want more than a paycheck; who are self-disciplined, well-organized, highly motivated, and good at managing their time; who can handle people well; who can use language effectively; who can work on a computer; who are committed to team work; who are flexible, and can respond to novel situations, or adapt when circumstances at work change; who are trainable, and love to learn; who are project-oriented, and goal-oriented; who have creativity and are good at problem solving; who have integrity; who are loyal to the organization; who are able to identify opportunities, markets, coming trends.* They also want to hire people who can bring in more money than they are paid. *Plan on claiming all of these that you* legitimately *can, during the hiring-interview.*

Realize that The Employer Thinks The Way You Are Doing Your Job-Hunt Is The Way You Will Do the Job

Plan on illustrating by the way you conduct your job-hunt whatever it is you claim will be true of you, once hired. For example, if you plan on claiming during the interview that you are very *thorough* in all your work, be sure to be thorough in the way you have researched the organization ahead of time. For, the manner in which you do your job-hunt and the manner in which you would do the job you are seeking, are not assumed by most employers to be two unrelated subjects, but one and the same. They can tell when you are doing a slipshod, half-hearted job-hunt (*"Uh, what do you guys do here?"*) and this is taken as a clear warning that you might do a slipshod, half-hearted job, were they foolish enough to ever hire you. Employers know this simple truth: Most people job-hunt the same way they live their lives, and the way they do their work.

Bring Evidence If You Can

Try to think of some way to bring evidence of your skills, to the hiring-interview. For example, if you are an artist, craftsperson or anyone who produces a product, try to bring a sample of what you have made or produced -- either in person, or through photos, or even videotapes.

Determine Ahead of Time Not to Bad Mouth Your Previous Employer(s) During the Interview

During the hiring-interview, plan on never speaking badly of your previous employer(s). Employers often feel as though they are a fraternity or sorority. During the interview you want to come across as one who displays courtesy toward *all* members of that fraternity or sorority. Bad-mouthing a previous employer only makes this employer worry about what you would say about *them,* after they hire you.

I learned this in my own experience. I once spoke graciously about a previous employer, to my (then) present employer. Unbeknownst to me, my present employer already *knew* that my previous employer had badly mistreated me. He therefore thought very highly of me because I didn't drag it up. In fact, he never forgot this incident; talked about it for years afterward. Believe me, it always makes a *big* impression when you don't bad mouth a previous employer.

Plan on saying something nice about your previous employer, or if you are afraid that the previous employer is going to give you a very bad recommendation, seize the bull by the horns. Say something simple like, "I usually get along with everybody; but for some reason, my past employer and I just didn't get along. Don't know why. It's never happened to me before. Hope it never happens again."

Determine That The Interview Will Be Part of Your Ongoing Research, And Not Just A Sales Pitch

Your natural question, as you approach any job-interview, will tend to be, "How do I convince this employer to hire me?" Wrong question. It implies that you have already made up your mind that this would be a grand place to work at, and he or she a grand person to work for, so that all that remains is for you to sell yourself. But, in most cases, despite your best attempts to research the place thoroughly, you don't know enough about it yet, to say that. You have *got* to use the hiring-interview as a chance to gather further information about this organization, and this boss.

If you understand *this* about an interview, you will be ahead of 98% of all other job-hunters -- who all too often go to the hiring-interview as a lamb goes to the slaughter, or as a criminal goes on trial before a judge.

You *are* on trial, of course, in the employer's eyes.

But, good news -- so is that employer and that organization, in *your* eyes.

This is what makes the job-interview tolerable or even enjoyable: you are studying everything about this employer, at the same time that they are studying everything about you.

Two people, both sizing each other up. You know what that reminds you of, of course. *Dating.*

Well, the job-interview is every bit like the 'dating game.' Both of you have to like each other, before you can even discuss the question of *'going steady,'* i.e., a job. So, you're sitting there, sizing each other up.

The importance of your not just leaving the evaluation to the employer, but of doing your own weighing of this person, this organization, and this job, *during* the hiring-interview, cannot be overstated. The tradition in the U.S., and throughout the world for that matter, is to find a job, take it, and *then* after you're in it trying to figure out in the next three months whether it is a good job or not -- and quitting if you decide it isn't.

You are going against this stupid custom, as any smartie should, by using the hiring-interview to screen the organization *before you decide to go to work there.* And if you decide you don't like what you're hearing during the job-interview, then you in effect, *quit before you're offered the job*, rather than *quitting after you've taken the job*. Believe me, if you show that kind of smartness, the employer will thank you, your Mother will thank you, your spouse or partner will thank you, and of course you will thank yourself.

SECOND INTERVIEWING TIP FOR SMARTIES:

So much for the frame of the interview. Now for the picture within that frame, the actual content of what you say during the interview. We begin with this simple thought:

Many Employers Are as Scared as You Are During the Hiring Interview

As you go in to the interview, keep in mind that **the person-who-has-the-power-to-hire-you** is sweating too. Why? Because, the hiring-interview is not a very reliable way to choose an employee. In a survey conducted some years ago among a dozen top United Kingdom employers,[4] it was discovered that the chances of an employer finding a good employee through the hiring interview was only ***3% better*** than if they had picked a name out of a hat. In a further ironic finding, it was discovered that if the interview were conducted by someone who would be working directly with the candidate, the success rate dropped to ***2% below*** that of picking a name out of a hat. And if the interview were conducted by a so-called personnel expert, the success rate dropped to ***10% below*** that of picking a name out of a hat.

No, I don't know how they came up with these figures. But they sure are a hoot! And, more importantly, they are totally consistent with what I have learned about the world of hiring during the past thirty years. I have watched so-called personnel or human resources experts make *wretchedly* bad choices about hiring *in their own office,* and when they would morosely confess this to me some months later, over lunch, I would playfully tease them with, "If you don't even know how to hire well for your own office, how do you keep a straight face when you're called in as a hiring consultant by another organization?" And they would ruefully reply, "We act *as though it were* a science." Well, let me tell you, dear reader, the hiring-interview is *not* a science. It is a very very hazy art, done badly by most of its employer-practitioners, in spite of their own past experience, their very best intentions and their carloads of goodwill.

4. Reported in the *Financial Times Career Guide 1989* for the United Kingdom.

The hiring interview is not what it seems to be. It seems to be one individual (*you*) sitting there, scared to death while the other individual *(the employer)* is sitting there, blasé and confident.

But what it really is, is two individuals *(you* and *the employer)* sitting there scared to death. It's just that the employer has learned to *hide* his or her fears better than you have, because they've had more practice.

But this employer is, after all, a human being just like you. They were *never* hired to do *this.* It got thrown in with all their other duties. And they may *know* they're not very good at it. So, they're afraid.

THIRD INTERVIEWING TIP FOR SMARTIES:

It Will Help If You Mentally Catalog, Ahead of Time, Not Your Fears, But the Employer's

The employer's fears include *any or all* of the following:

A. That you won't be able to do the job: that you lack the necessary skills or experience, and the hiring-interview didn't uncover this.

B. That if hired, you won't put in a full working day, regularly.

C. That if hired, you'll be frequently "out sick," or otherwise absent whole days.

D. That if hired, you'll only stay around for a few weeks or at most a few months, and then quit without advance warning.

E. That it will take you too long to master the job, and thus it will be too long before you're profitable to that organization.

F. That you won't get along with the other workers there, or that you will develop a personality conflict with the boss himself (or herself).

G. That you will do only the minimum that you can get away with, rather than the maximum that they hired you for.
H. That you will always have to be told what to do next, rather than displaying initiative -- always in a responding mode, rather than an initiating mode (and mood).
I. That you will have a work-disrupting character flaw, and turn out to be: dishonest, or totally irresponsible, a spreader of dissention at work, lazy, an embezzler, a gossip, a sexual harasser, a drug-user or substance abuser, a drunk, a liar, incompetent, or -- in a word -- *bad news.*
J. *If this is a large organization, and your would-be boss is not the top person:* that you will bring discredit upon them, and upon their department/section/division, etc., for ever hiring you in the first place -- making them lose face, possibly also costing them a raise or a promotion.
K. That you will cost a lot of money, if they make a mistake by hiring you. Currently, in the U.S. the cost to an employer of a bad hire can far exceed $50,000 including relocation costs, lost pay for the period for work not done or aborted, and severance pay -- if *they* are the ones who decide to let you go.

No wonder the employer is *sweating.*

In the old days, the employer had help in making this decision. They could get useful information by talking to your previous employers. No more. Employers have gotten badly burned since the 1980s by job-hunters filing lawsuits alleging 'unlawful discharge,' or 'being deprived of an ability to make a living.' Most employers have consequently adopted the policy of refusing to volunteer *any* information about Past Employees, except name, rank and serial number -- i.e., the person's job-title and dates of employment.

So now, during the hiring interview, the employer is completely on his or her own in trying to figure out whether or not to hire you. Their fears have moved to the front burner. The hiring-interview these days has become *everything.*

FOURTH INTERVIEWING TIP FOR SMARTIES:

You Don't Have to Spend Hours Memorizing A Lot of 'Good Answers' to Potential Questions from The Employer; There Are Only Five Questions That Matter

Of course, the employer is going to be asking you some questions, as a way of helping them to figure out whether or not they want to hire you. Books on *interviewing*, of which there are many, often publish lists of these questions -- or at least some *typical* ones that employers often ask. They include such questions as:

- What do you know about this company?
- Tell me about yourself.
- Why are you applying for this job?
- How would you describe yourself?
- What are your major strengths?
- What is your greatest weakness?
- What type of work do you like to do best?
- What are your interests outside of work?
- What accomplishment gave you the greatest satisfaction?
- What is your greatest weakness?
- Why did you leave your last job?
- Why were you fired (if you were)?
- Where do you see yourself five years from now?
- What are your goals in life?
- How much did you make at your last job?

Well, the list goes on and on. In some books, you'll find eighty-nine questions, or more.

You are then told that you should prepare for the hiring-interview by writing out, practicing, and memorizing some devilishly clever answers to *all* these questions -- answers which those books of course furnish you.

All of this is well-intentioned, and has been *the state of the art* for decades. But, dear friend, Good news! We are in the new millennium, and things are getting simpler.

Beneath the dozens and dozens of possible questions that the employer could ask you, we now know that there are only *five basic questions,* that you really need to pay attention to.

Five. Just five. The people-who-have-the-power-to-hire-you usually want to know the answers to these five questions, which they may ask directly or try to find out obliquely:

1. **"Why are you here?"** *They mean by this, "Why are you knocking on my door, rather than someone else's door?"*
2. **"What can you do for us?"** *They mean by this, "If I were to hire you would you be part of the problems I already have, or would you be a part of the solution to those problems? What are your skills, and how much do you know about some subject or field that is of interest to us?"*
3. **"What kind of person are you?"** *They mean by this, "Do you have the kind of personality that makes it easy for people to work with you, and do you share the values which we have at this place?"*
4. **"What distinguishes you from nineteen other people who can do the same tasks that you can?"** *They mean by this, "Do you have better work habits than the nineteen others, do you show up earlier, stay later, work more thoroughly, work faster, maintain higher standards, go the extra mile, or... what?"*
5. **"Can I afford you?"** *They mean by this, "If we decide we want you here, how much will it take to get you, and are we willing and able to pay that amount -- governed, as we are, by our budget, and by our inability to pay you as much as the person who would be above you, on the organizational chart?"*

These are the five principal questions that most employers are dying to know the answers to. *This is the case, even if the interview begins and ends with these five questions never once being mentioned overtly by the employer.* The questions are still *floating in the air* there, beneath the surface of the conversation, beneath all the other things that are being discussed. Anything you can do, during the interview, to help the employer find the answers to these five questions, will make the interview very satisfying to the employer.

Nothing for you to go memorize. If you just do the homework in this book, you will know the five answers. Period. End of story.

FIFTH INTERVIEWING TIP FOR SMARTIES:

You Need To Find Out The Answers To The Very Same Questions That The Employer Would Like to Ask You

During the hiring-interview you have the right -- nay, the duty -- to find out the answers to the very same five questions *as the employer's*, only in a slightly different form. Your questions will come out looking like this:

1. **"What does this job involve?"** *You want to understand exactly what tasks will be asked of you, so that you can determine if these are the kinds of tasks you would really like to do.*
2. **"What are the skills a top employee in this job would have to have?"** *You want to know if your skills match those which the employer thinks a top employee in this job would have to have, in order to do this job well.*
3. **"Are these the kinds of people I would like to work with, or not?"** *Do not ignore your intuition if it tells you that you would not be comfortable working with these people!! You want to know if they have the kind of personality that would make it easy for you to accomplish your work, and if they share the values which are important to you."*
4. **"If we like each other, and both want to work together, can I persuade them there is something unique about me, that makes me different from nineteen other people who can do the same tasks?"** *You need to think out, way*

ahead of time, what does make you different from nineteen other people who can do the same job. For example, if you are good at analyzing problems, how do you do that? Painstakingly? Intuitively, in a flash? By consulting with greater authorities in the field? You see the point. You are trying to put your finger on the 'style' or 'manner' in which you do your work, that is distinctive and hopefully appealing, to this *employer.*

5. **"Can I persuade them to hire me at the salary I need or want?"** *This requires some knowledge on your part of how to conduct salary negotiation. See the next chapter.*

You will probably want to ask questions one and two out loud. You will *observe* quietly the answer to question three. You will be prepared to make the case for questions four and five, when the *appropriate* time in the interview arises (again, see the next chapter).

How do you get into these questions? You might begin by reporting to them just exactly how you've been conducting your job-hunt, and what impressed you so much about *their* organization during your research, that you decided to come in and talk to them about a job. Then you can fix your attention, during the remainder of the interview, on finding out the answers to the five questions above -- in your own way.[5]

Yes, there are only *five* questions that really count in a job-interview; but how these five questions keep popping up! They pop up in a slightly different form (yet again), if you're there to talk *not* about a job that already exists but rather, one that you want them to *create* for you. In that kind of interview, or approach to an organization, these five

5. Additional questions you may want to ask, to elaborate upon these five:
What significant changes has this company gone through in the last five years?
What values are sacred to this company?
What characterizes the most successful employees this company has?
What future changes do you see in the work here?
Who do you see as your allies, colleagues or competitors in this business?

questions get changed into five *statements*, that you make to this person-who-has-the-power-to-hire-you:

1. What you **like** about this organization.
2. What sorts of **needs** you find intriguing in this field and in this organization (unless you first hear the word *'problems'* coming out of their mouth don't ever use the word *'problems,'* inasmuch as most employers prefer synonyms such as *'challenges'* or *'needs'*).
3. What **skills** seem to you to be needed in order to meet such needs.
4. **Evidence** from your past experience that demonstrates you have the very skills in question, and that you perform them in the manner or style you claim.
5. What is **unique** about the way *you* perform those skills. As I said before: every prospective employer wants to know *what makes you different* from nineteen other people who can do the same kind of work as you do. You *have* to know what that is. And then not merely talk about it, but actually demonstrate it by the way you conduct your part of the hiring-interview. *For example, "I am very thorough in the way I would do the job for you"* translates into the imperative that you be thorough in the way you have researched the place before you go in for the hiring-interview. That's *evidence* the employer can see with their own eyes.

SIXTH INTERVIEWING TIP FOR SMARTIES:

Employers Don't Really Care About Your Past;
They Only Ask About It,
in Order to Try to Predict Your Future (Behavior)

In the U.S. employers may only ask you questions that are related to the requirements and expectations of the job. They cannot ask about such things as your creed, religion,

The latest self-help book for pessimists.

race, age, sex or marital status. Any other questions about your past are *fair game.* But don't be fooled by any employer's absorption with your past. You must realize that the only thing any employer can possibly care about is your future . . . with *them.* Since that future is impossible to uncover, they usually try to gauge what it would be by asking about your past (behavior).

Therefore, during the hiring-interview before you answer any question the employer asks you about your past, you should pause to think out what fear about the *future* lies underneath that question -- and then address that fear, obliquely or directly.

In most cases, as I have been emphasizing, the person-who-has-the-power-to-hire-you is *scared.* If you think that is too strong a word, let's settle for *anxious,* or *afraid,* or *worried.* And this worry lies beneath all the questions they may ask.

Here are some *examples*:

Employer's Question	The Fear Behind The Question	The Point You Try To Get Across	Phrases You Might Use To Get This Across
"Tell me about yourself"	The employer is afraid he/she isn't going to conduct a very good interview, by failing to ask the right questions. Or is afraid there is something wrong with you, and is hoping you will blurt it out.	You are a good employee, as you have proved in the past at your other jobs. (Give the briefest history of who you are, where born, raised, interests, hobbies, and kind of work you have enjoyed the most to date.) *Keep it to two minutes, max.*	In describing your past work history, use any *honest* phrases you can about your work history, that are self-complimentary: "Hard worker." "Came in early, left late." "Always did more than was expected of me." Etc.
"What kind of work are you looking for?"	The employer is afraid that you are looking for a different job than that which the employer is trying to fill. E.g., he/she wants a secretary, but you want to be an office manager, etc.	You are looking for precisely the kind of work the employer is offering (but don't say that, if it isn't true). Repeat back to the employer, in your own words, what he/she has said about the job, and emphasize the skills you have to do *that.*	If the employer hasn't described the job at all, say, "I'd be happy to answer that, but first I need to understand exactly what kind of work this job involves." *Then* answer, as at left.
"Have you ever done this kind of work before?"	The employer is afraid you don't possess the necessary skills and experience to do this job.	You have skills that are transferable, from whatever you used to do; and you did it well.	"I pick up stuff very quickly." "I have quickly mastered any job I have ever done."

Employer's Question	The Fear Behind The Question	The Point You Try To Get Across	Phrases You Might Use To Get This Across
"Why did you leave your last job?" -- *or* "How did you get along with your former boss and co-workers?"	The employer is afraid you don't get along well with people, especially bosses, and is just waiting for you to 'bad-mouth' your previous boss or co-workers, as proof of that.	Say whatever positive things you possibly can about your former boss and co-workers (*without telling lies*). Emphasize you usually get along very well with people -- and then let your gracious attitude toward your previous boss(es) and co-workers prove it, right before this employer's very eyes (and ears).	If you left voluntarily: "*My boss and I* both felt I would be happier and more effective in a job where [here describe your strong points, such as] I would have more room to use my initiative and creativity." If you were fired: "Usually, I get along well with everyone, but in this particular case the boss and I just didn't get along with each other. Difficult to say why." *You don't need to say any more than that.* If you were laid off and your job wasn't filled after you left: "My *job* was terminated."
"How is your health?" -- *or* "How much were you absent from work during your last job?"	The employer is afraid you will be absent from work a lot, if they hire you.	You will not be absent. If you have a health problem, you want to emphasize that it is one which will not keep you from being at work, daily. Your productivity, compared to other workers', is excellent.	If you were *not* absent a lot at your last job: "I believe it's an employee's job to show up every work day. Period." If you *were* absent a lot, say why, and stress that it was due to a difficulty that is now *past.*

Employer's Question	The Fear Behind The Question	The Point You Try To Get Across	Phrases You Might Use To Get This Across
"Can you explain why you've been out of work so long?" -- *or* **"Can you tell me why there are these gaps in your work history?"** ***(Usually said after studying your resume.)***	The employer is afraid that you are the kind of person who quits a job the minute he/she doesn't like something at it; in other words, that you have no 'stick-to-it-iveness.'	You love to work, and you regard times when things aren't going well as challenges, which you enjoy learning how to conquer.	"During the gaps in my work record, I was studying/doing volunteer work/doing some hard thinking about my mission in life/finding redirection." (Choose one.)
"Wouldn't this job represent a step down for you?" -- *or* **"I think this job would be way beneath your talents and experience."** -- *or* **"Don't you think you would be underemployed if you took this job?"**	The employer is afraid you could command a bigger salary, somewhere else, and will therefore leave him/her as soon as something better turns up.	You will stick with this job as long as you and the employer agree this is where you should be.	"This job isn't a step down for me. It's a step up -- from welfare." "We have mutual fears: every employer is afraid a good employee will leave too soon, and every employee is afraid the employer might fire him/her, for no good reason." "I like to work, and I give my best to every job I've ever had."
And, lastly: **"Tell me, what is your greatest weakness?"**	The employer is afraid you have some character flaw, and hopes you will now rashly blurt it out, or confess it.	You have limitations just like anyone else but you work constantly to improve yourself and be a more and more effective worker.	Mention a weakness and then stress its positive aspect, e.g., "I don't like to be oversupervised, because I have a great deal of initiative, and I like to anticipate problems before they even arise."

SEVENTH INTERVIEWING TIP FOR SMARTIES:

As The Interview Proceeds, You Want to Quietly Notice The Time-Frame of the Questions The Employer is Asking

When the interview is going favorably for you, the time-frame of the employer's questions will often move -- *however slowly* -- through the following stages.

1. Distant past: *e.g., "Where did you attend high school?"*
2. Immediate past: *e.g., "Tell me about your most recent job."*
3. Present: *e.g., "What kind of a job are you looking for?"*
4. Immediate future: *e.g., "Would you be able to come back for another interview next week?"*
5. Distant future: *e.g., "Where would you like to be five years from now?"*

The more the time-frame of the interviewer's questions moves from the past to the future, the more favorably you may assume the interview is going for you. On the other hand, if the interviewer's questions stay firmly in the past, the outlook is not so good. *Ah well, y' can't win them all!*

When the time-frame of the interviewer's questions moves firmly into the future, *then* is the time for you to get more specific about the job in question. Experts suggest you ask, at that point, these kinds of questions:

What is the job, specifically, that I am being considered for?

If I were hired, what duties would I be performing?

What responsibilities would I have?

What would you be hiring me to accomplish?

Would I be working with a team, or group? To whom would I report?

Whose responsibility is it to see that I get the training I need, here, to get up to speed?

How would I be evaluated, how often, and by whom?

What were the strengths and weaknesses of previous people in this position?

Why did *you* yourself decide to work here?

What do you wish you had known about this company before you started here? What particular characteristics do you think have made you successful in your job here?

May I meet the persons I would be working with and for (if it isn't you)?

Remember, throughout this *weighing of each other*, we're not talking scientific measurement here. As Nathan Azrin has said for many years, *The hiring process is more like choosing a mate, than it is like deciding whether or not to buy a new house.* 'Choosing a mate' here is a metaphor. To elaborate upon the metaphor a little bit, it means that *the mechanisms* by which human nature decides to hire someone, are *similar to* the mechanisms by which human nature decides whether or not to marry someone. Those mechanisms, of course, are impulsive, intuitional, non-rational, unfathomable and often made on the spur of the moment.

EIGHTH INTERVIEWING TIP FOR SMARTIES:

Interviews Are Often Lost to Mosquitoes Rather Than To Dragons, and Lost Within the First Two Minutes

Think about this: you can have all the skills in the world, have researched this organization to death, have practiced *interviewing* until you are a master at giving 'right answers,' be absolutely the perfect person for this job, and yet lose the hiring-interview because . . . *your breath smells terrible.* Or some other small personal reason. It's akin to your being ready to fight dragons, and then being killed by a mosquito.

It's the reason why interviews are most often lost, when they are lost, *during the first two minutes.* Believe it or not.

Let us look at *what* interview-mosquitoes *(as it were)* can fly in, during the first 30 seconds to two minutes of your interview so that *the person-who-has-the-power-to-hire-you* starts muttering to themselves, *"I sure hope we have some other candidates besides this person"*:

1. Your appearance and personal habits: interview after interview has revealed that if you are a male, *you are much more likely to get the job if:*

- you have obviously freshly bathed, have your face freshly shaved or your hair and beard freshly trimmed, have clean fingernails, and are using a deodorant; *or*
- you have on freshly laundered clothes, pants with a sharp crease, and shoes freshly polished; *or*
- you do not have bad breath, do not dispense gallons of garlic, onion, stale tobacco, or the odor of strong drink, into the enclosed office air, but have brushed and flossed your teeth; *or*
- you are not wafting tons of after-shave cologne fifteen feet ahead of you, as you enter the room.

Remember, since the hiring process is more like choosing a mate, than deciding whether or not to buy a new house, the employer is simply trying to determine if they like you. If you 'bomb' in one of these areas just listed, the person-who-has-the-power-to-hire-you may decide they really don't like you, in which case you're not going to get hired there, no matter how qualified you otherwise may be. The same thing happens on dates, incidentally.

If you are a female, interview after interview has revealed that *you are much more likely to get the job if:*

- you have obviously freshly bathed; have not got tons of makeup on your face; have had your hair newly 'permed' or 'coiffed'; have clean or nicely manicured fingernails, that don't stick out ten inches from your fingers; and are using a deodorant; *or*
- you wear a bra, have on freshly cleaned clothes, a suit or sophisticated-looking dress, shoes not sandals, and are not wearing clothes so daring that they call *a lot* of attention to themselves. In these days of sexual harassment lawsuits, this tends to make many employers, male and female, *very* nervous. I grant you there are some employers who might like this kind of outfit, but -- trust me -- in most cases you don't want to work for *them* (as with all items here, I am only reporting what can affect your chances of getting hired -- not whether or not I think this employer preoccupation with just outward appearance is asinine); *or*
- you do not have bad breath; do not dispense gallons of garlic, onion, stale tobacco, or the odor of strong drink, into the enclosed office air; but have brushed and flossed your teeth; *or*
- you are not wafting tons of perfume fifteen feet ahead of you, as you enter the room.

Remember, since the hiring process is more like choosing a mate, than deciding whether or not to buy a new house, the employer is simply trying to determine if they like you. If you 'bomb' in one of these areas just listed, the person-who-has-the-power-to-

hire-you may decide they really don't like you, in which case you're not going to get hired there, no matter how qualified you otherwise may be.

2. Nervous mannerisms: *it is a turn-off for employers if:*

- you continually avoid eye contact with the employer (that's a *big, big* no-no), *or*
- you give a limp handshake, *or*
- you slouch in your chair, or endlessly fidget with your hands, or crack your knuckles, *or* constantly play with your hair during the interview.

Remember, since the hiring process is more like choosing a mate, than deciding whether or not to buy a new house, the employer is simply trying to determine if they like you. If you 'bomb' in one of these areas just listed, the person-who-has-the-power-to-hire-you may decide they really don't like you, in which case you're not going to get hired there, no matter how qualified you otherwise may be.

3. Lack of self-confidence: *it is a turn-off for employers if:*

- you are speaking so softly you cannot be heard, or so loudly you can be heard two rooms away, *or*
- you are giving answers in an extremely hesitant fashion, *or*
- you are giving one-word answers to all the employer's questions, *or*
- you are constantly interrupting the employer, *or*
- you are downplaying your achievements or abilities, or are continuously being self-critical in comments you make about yourself during the interview.

Remember, since the hiring process is more like choosing a mate, than deciding whether or not to buy a new house, the employer is simply trying to determine if they like you. If you 'bomb' in one of these areas just listed, the person-who-has-the-power-to-hire-you may decide they really don't like you, in which case you're not going to get hired there, no matter how qualified you otherwise may be.

4. Your considerateness toward other people: *it is a turn-off for employers if:*

- you show a lack of courtesy to the receptionist, secretary, and (at lunch) to the waiter or waitress, *or*
- you display extreme criticalness toward your previous employers and places of work, *or*
- you drink strong stuff (ordering a drink if and when the employer takes you to lunch is always an extremely bad idea, as it raises the question in the employer's mind, *Do they normally stop with one, or do they normally keep on going?* Don't . . . ever . . . do . . . it! Even if they do.), *or*
- you forget to thank the interviewer as you're leaving, or forget to send a thank-you note afterward. Says one human resources manager:

> "A prompt, brief, faxed business letter thanking me for my time along with a (brief!) synopsis of his/her unique qualities communicates to me that this person is an assertive, motivated, customer-service-oriented salesperson who utilizes technology and knows the rules of the 'game.' These are qualities I am looking for . . . At the moment I receive approximately one such letter . . . for every fifteen candidates interviewed."

Remember, since the hiring process is more like choosing a mate, than deciding whether or not to buy a new house, the employer is simply trying to determine if they like you. If you 'bomb' in one of these areas just listed, the person-who-has-the-power-to-hire-you may decide they really don't like you, in which case you're not going to get hired there, no matter how qualified you otherwise may be.

• Incidentally, *many* an employer watches to see if you smoke, either in the office or at lunch. *In a race between two equally qualified people, the nonsmoker will win out over the smoker 94% of the time, according to a study done by a professor of business at Seattle University. If you hunt hard enough on the Internet or elsewhere you can find some experts giving detailed instructions on how to hide the fact that you smoke (if you do). Their advice runs along these lines: "If you are a smoker, do not*

think it will be easy to hide it. It will take a lot of work, on your part. The more that smoke has been hovering around you and your clothes, the more your clothes, hair, and breath will reek of smoke when you go in for the interview. You are so inured to it, that you will not be able to detect this; but the employer will know it, instantly, *as you move forward to greet them. Breath mints and perfume/cologne will NOT cover it up; it will take much more formidable measures than that. Like what? Like this: don't smoke for at least four hours prior to the interview, bathe completely, including your hair, immediately before leaving for the interview, keep a set of smoke-free interview clothes, underwear, and shoes (at home) in a tight plastic bag in a room far-removed from anyplace you smoke in the house, and wear those smoke-free clothes to the interview." That's the advice of the You-Can-Hide-It school of thinking.*

Personally, I think none of this really works, in the end. So what if you do pull it off? It will *come out that you smoke, after you are hired, and the employer who hates smoking can always manage to get you out of there after you are hired, on one pretext or another, without ever mentioning the word 'smoke.' So, my advice is: don't try to hide it.*

On the other hand, it is legitimate, I think, to postpone *revealing it, if you can. But once a job-offer has been made, then I think it is important for you to tell the employer you smoke, and to offer an easy way out: "If this is a truly offensive habit to you, and one you don't want in any of your employees, I'd rather bow out gracefully now, than have it become an issue between us down the road."* Such consideration, thoughtfulness, and graciousness on your part may go a long way to soften the employer's resistance to the fact that you are a smoker. Many places, as you probably know, do allow their employees to go outside for a 'smoke break' at stated intervals.

5. Your values: *it is a complete turn-off for most employers, if they see in you:*

- any sign of arrogance or excessive aggressiveness; any sign of tardiness or failure to keep appointments and commitments on time, including the hiring-interview; *or*
- any sign of laziness or lack of motivation; *or*
- any sign of constant complaining or blaming things on others; *or*
- any signs of dishonesty or lying -- on your resume or in the interview; *or*
- any signs of irresponsibility or tendency to goof off; *or*
- any sign of not following instructions or obeying rules; *or*
- any sign of a lack of enthusiasm for this organization and what it is trying to do; *or*
- any sign of instability, inappropriate response, and the like; *or*
- the other ways in which you evidence your *values*, such as: what things impress you or don't impress you in the office; *or* what you are willing to sacrifice in order to get this job *and* what you are *not* willing to sacrifice in order to get this job; *or* your enthusiasm for work; *or* the carefulness with which you did or didn't research this company before you came in; and blah, blah, blah.

Remember, since the hiring process is more like choosing a mate, than deciding whether or not to buy a new house, the employer is simply trying to determine if they like you. If you 'bomb' in one of these areas just listed, the person-who-has-the-power-to-hire-you may decide they really don't like you, in which case you're not going to get hired there, no matter how qualified you otherwise may be.

Well, dear reader, there you have it: the *mosquitoes* that can kill you, when you're only on the watch for dragons, during the hiring-interview.

One favor I ask of you: do not write me, telling me how picayune or asinine some of this is. Believe me, I already *know* that. I'm not reporting the world as it *should* be, and certainly not as I would like it to be. I'm only reporting what study after study has revealed about the hiring world as it *is*.

You may take all this to heart, or just ignore it. However, if you decide to ignore these points, and then -- despite interview after interview -- you never get hired, you might want to rethink your position on all of this. It may be *mosquitoes*, not dragons, that are killing you.

And, good news: you can *fix* all these mosquitoes. Yes, you control *every one* of these factors.

Read them all over again. There isn't a one of them that you don't have the power to determine, or the power to change. You can decide to bathe before going to the interview, you can decide to shine your shoes, you can decide not to smoke, etc., etc. All the little things which could torpedo your interview are within your control, and *you can fix* them, if they are keeping you from getting hired.

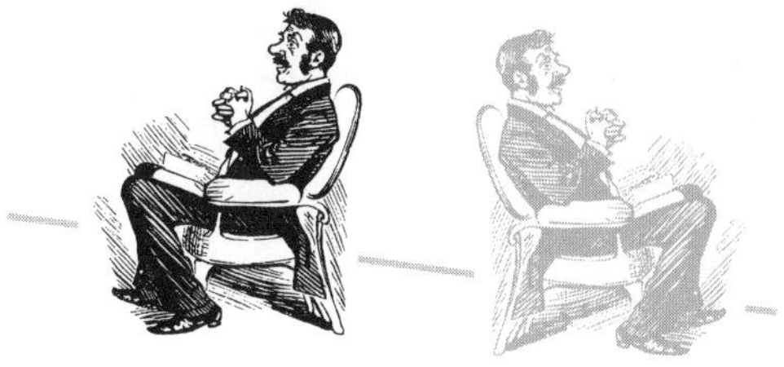

NINTH INTERVIEWING TIP FOR SMARTIES:

There are Some Questions You Must Ask Before You Let the Interview Close

Before you let the interview end, there are six questions you should *always* ask:

#1. *"Given my skills and experience, is there work here that you would consider me for?"* This is if you haven't come after a specific job, from the beginning.

#2. *"Can you offer me this job?"* **I know this seems stupid, but it is astonishing (at least to me) how many job-hunters have secured a job simply by being bold enough to ask for it, at the end of the interview, either with the words *May I have this job,* or something similar to it, in language they feel comfortable with.** I don't know *why* this is. I only know *that* it is. Maybe it has something to do with employers not liking to say "No," to someone who directly asks them for something. Anyway, if after hearing all about this job at this place, you decide you'd really like to have it, you must *ask for it.* The worse thing the employer can say is "No," or "We need some time to think about all the interviews we're conducting."

#3. *"Do you want me to come back for another interview, perhaps with some of the other decision-makers here?"* If you are a serious candidate in this employer's mind for this job, there usually *is* a second round of interviews. And, often, a third, and fourth. You, of course, want to make it to that second round. Indeed, many experts say the *only* purpose you should have in the first interview, at a particular place, is *to be invited back* for a second interview. If you've secured *that,* say they, it has been a successful first interview.

#4. *"When may I expect to hear from you?"* You *never* want to leave control of the ensuing steps in this process in the hands of the employer. You want it in your own hands. If the employer says, *"We need time to think about this,"* or *"We will be calling you for a second interview,"* you don't want to leave this as an undated good intention on the employer's part. You want to nail it down.

#5. *"Might I ask what would be* the latest *I can expect to hear from you?"* The employer has probably given you their *best* guess, in answer to your previous question. Now you want to know *what is the worst-case* scenario? Incidentally, one employer, when I asked him for the *worst-case* scenario, replied, *"Never!"* I thought he had a great sense of humor. Turned out he was dead serious. I never did hear from him, despite repeated attempts at contact, on my part.

#6. *"May I contact you after that date, if for any reason you haven't gotten back to me by that time?"* Some employers resent this question. You'll know that is the case if they snap at you, *"Don't you trust me?"* But most employers appreciate your offering them what is in essence a safety-net. They know they can get busy, become overwhelmed with other things, forget their promise to you. It's reassuring, in such a case, for you to offer to rescue them.

[Optional: #7. *"Can you think of anyone else who* might *be interested in hiring me?"* This question is invoked *only* if they replied *"No,"* to your first question, above.]

Jot down any answers they give you to the questions above, then stand up, thank them sincerely for their time, give a firm handshake, and leave. Write a thank-you note *that night,* to them, and mail it without fail the next morning.

TENTH INTERVIEWING TIP FOR SMARTIES:

Always, Always Send A Thank-You Note the Same Night, At the Latest

Every expert on interviewing will tell you two things: (1) Thank-you notes *must* be sent after *every* interview, by every job-hunter; and (2) Most job-hunters ignore this advice. Indeed, it is safe to say that it is the most overlooked step in the entire job-hunting process.

If you want to stand out from the others applying for the same job, send thank-you notes -- to *everyone* you met there, that day. If you need any additional encouragement *(besides the fact that it may get you the job)*, here are six reasons for sending a thank-you note, most particularly to the employer who interviewed you:

First, you were presenting yourself as one who has good skills with people. Your actions with respect to the job-interview must back this claim up. Sending a thank-you note does that. The employer can see you *are* good with people; you remember to thank them.

Secondly, it helps the employer to remember you.

Thirdly, if a committee is involved in the hiring process, the one man or woman who interviewed you has something to show the rest of the committee.

Fourth, if the interview went rather well, and the employer seemed to show an interest in further talks, the thank-you letter can reiterate *your* interest in further talks.

Fifth, the thank-you note gives you an opportunity to correct any wrong impression you left behind you. You can add anything you forgot to tell them, that you want them to know. And from among all the things you two discussed, you can underline the main two or three points that you want to stand out in their minds.

Lastly, if the interview did not go well, and you lost all interest in working there, they may still hear of other openings, elsewhere, that might be of interest to you. In the thank-you note, you can mention this, and ask them to keep you in mind. Thus, from kindly interviewers, you may gain additional leads.

In the following days, rigorously keep to all that you said, and don't contact them except with that mandatory thank-you note, until after the *latest* deadline you two agreed upon, in answer to question #4, above. If you do have to contact them after that date, and if they tell you things are still up in the air, you must ask questions #3, #4, and #5, all over again. And so on, and so forth.

Incidentally, it is entirely appropriate for you to insert a thank-you note into the running stream, after *each* interview or telephone contact. Just keep it brief.

WHEN NONE OF THIS WORKS, AND YOU NEVER GET INVITED BACK

There is no magic in job-hunting. No techniques that always work, and work for everyone. Anyone who tells you there is magic, is delusional. I hear regularly from job-hunters who report that they paid attention to all the matters I have mentioned in this chapter and this book, and are quite successful at getting interviews -- but they still don't get hired. And they want to know what they're doing wrong.

Well, unfortunately, the answer *sometimes* is: "Maybe nothing." I don't know *how often* this happens, but I know it does happen -- because more than one employer has confessed it to me, and in fact at one point in my life it actually happened to *moi*: namely, *some* employers play wicked, despicable tricks on job-hunters, whereby they invite you in for an interview despite the fact that they have already hired someone for the position in question, and they know from the beginning that they have absolutely no intention of hiring you -- not in a million years!

You are cheered, of course, by the ease with which you get these interviews. But unbeknownst to you, the manager who is interviewing you (we'll say it's a *he*) has a personal friend he already agreed to give the job to. Of course, one small problem remains: the State or the Federal government gives funds to this organization, and has mandated that this position be opened to all. So this manager must comply. He therefore *pretends* to choose ten candidates, including his favorite, and pretends to interview them all *as though* the job opening were still available. But, he intended, from the beginning, to reject the first nine and choose his favorite, and since you were selected for the honor of being among those nine, you automatically get rejected -- even if you are a much better candidate. This tenth person is, after all, his *friend*. But you have been very helpful, even without intending to be: you have helped the manager establish his claim that he followed the mandated hiring procedures to the letter.

You will of course be baffled as to *why* you got turned down. Trouble is, you will never know if it was because you met an employer who was playing this little trick, *or* not. All you know is: you're very depressed.

If you *never* get invited back for a second interview, there is always, of course, the chance that no games are being played. You are getting rejected, at place after place, because there is something really wrong with the way you are coming across, during these hiring-interviews.

Employers will rarely ever tell you this. You will never hear them say something like, "You come across as just too cocky and arrogant during the interview." You will almost always be left completely in the dark as to *what* it is you're doing wrong.

If you've been through a whole bunch of employers, one way around this deadly silence, is to ask for *generalized* feedback from whoever was the *friendliest* employer that you saw in your whole job-hunt. You can always try phoning the friendliest one, reminding them of who you are, and then asking the following question -- deliberately kept generalized, vague, unrelated to just *that* place, and above all, *future-directed*: Something like: "*You know, I've been on several interviews at several different places now, where I've gotten turned down. From what you've seen, is there something about me in an interview, that you think might be causing me not to get hired at those places? If so, I'd really appreciate your giving me some pointers so I can do better in my future hiring-interviews."*

Most of the time they'll *still* duck saying anything hurtful or helpful. First of all, they're afraid of lawsuits. Secondly, they don't know how you will use what they might have to say. (Said an old veteran to me once, "I used to think it was my duty to hit everyone with the truth. Now I only give it to those who can use it.")

'I'll tell you why I want this job. I thrive on challenges. I like being stretched to my full capacity. I like solving problems. Also, my car is about to be repossessed.'

But *occasionally* you will run into an employer who is willing to risk giving you the truth, because they think you will know how to use it wisely. If so, thank them from the bottom of your heart, no matter how painful their feedback is. Such advice, seriously heeded, can bring about just the changes in your interviewing strategy that you most need, in order to win the interview.

In the absence of any such help from employers who interviewed you, you might want to get a good business friend of yours to role-play a mock hiring-interview with you, in case they immediately see something glaringly wrong with how you're 'coming across.'

When all else fails, I would recommend you go to a career counselor that charges by the hour, and put yourself in their tender knowledgeable hands. Role-play an interview with them, and take their advice seriously (you've just paid for it, after all).

CONCLUSION

I have left out the subject of salary negotiation, in this chapter. It requires a chapter of its own (next!).

Hopefully, however, with that advice plus these ten tips for smarties, you will do well in your interviews. And if you do get hired, make one resolution to yourself right there on the spot. Plan to keep track of your accomplishments at this new job, on a weekly basis--jotting them down, every weekend, in your own private diary. Career experts, such as Bernard Haldane, recommend you do this without fail. You can then summarize these accomplishments annually on a one-page sheet, for your boss's eyes, when the question of a raise or promotion comes up.[6]

6. In any good-sized organization, you will often be amazed at how little attention your superiors pay to your noteworthy accomplishments, and how little they are aware at the end of the year that you really are entitled to a raise. Noteworthy your accomplishments may be, but no one is taking notes... unless you do. You may even need to be the one who brings up the subject of a raise or promotion. Waiting for the employer to bring this up may never happen.

Work is Love made visible.
And if you can't work with love but only with distaste,
It is better that you should leave your work
and sit at the gate of the temple and
take alms of the people who work with joy.
Kahlil Gibran, *The Prophet*

CHAPTER TWELVE

The Seven Secrets Of Salary Negotiation

HOW

DO YOU NEGOTIATE FOR THE SALARY YOU WANT?

I REMEMBER ONCE TALKING to a breathless college graduate, who was elated at having just landed her first job. "How much are they going to pay you?" I asked. She looked startled. "I don't know," she said, "I never asked. I just assume they will pay me a fair wage." *Boy*! did she get a rude awakening when she received her first paycheck. It was so miserably *low*, she couldn't believe her eyes. And thus did she learn, painfully, what you must learn too: *Before accepting a job, always ask about salary*. Indeed, *ask and negotiate.*

It's the *negotiate* that throws fear into our hearts. We feel ill-prepared to do this. Well, it's not all that difficult. While whole books can be (and have been) written on this subject, there are basically just seven secrets to keep in mind.

THE FIRST SECRET OF SUCCESSFUL SALARY NEGOTIATION:

Never Discuss Salary Until The End Of The Interviewing Process, When They Have Definitely Said They Want You

"The end of the interviewing process" is difficult to define. It's the point at which the employer says, or thinks, "We've got to get this person!" That may be at the end of the first (and therefore the last) interview; or it may be at the end of a whole series of interviews, often with different people within the same company or organization. But assuming things are going favorably for you, whether after the first, or second, or third, or fourth interview, if *you* like them and *they* increasingly like you, a job offer *will* be made. Then, and only then, it is time to deal with the question that is inevitably on any employer's mind: *how much is this person going to cost me?* And the question that is on *your* mind: *how much does this job pay?*

If the employer raises the salary question earlier, in some form like "What kind of salary are you looking for?", you should have three responses at your fingertips.

Response #1: If the employer seems like a kindly man or woman, your best and most tactful reply might be: "Until you've decided you definitely want me, and I've decided I definitely could help you with your tasks here, I feel any discussion of salary is premature." That will work, in most cases.

Response #2: There are instances however, where that doesn't work. You may be face-to-face with an employer

YOU CAN NAME YOUR OWN SALARY HERE.
...I CALL MINE "FRED"!
tom wilson

who will not so easily be put off, and demands within the first two minutes that you're in the interview room to know what salary you are looking for. At this point, you use your second response: "I'll gladly come to that, but could you first help me to understand what this job involves?"

Response #3: That is a good response, *in most cases.* But what if it doesn't work? The employer with rising voice says, "Come, come, don't play games with me. I want to know what salary you're looking for." You have response #3 prepared for *this* very eventuality. It's an answer in terms of a *range.* For example, "I'm looking for a salary in the range of $35–45,000 a year."

If the employer still won't let it go until later, then consider what this means. Clearly, you are being interviewed by an employer who has no range in mind. Their beginning figure is their ending figure. No negotiation is possible.[1]

This happens, when it happens, because many employers are making salary their major criterion for deciding who to hire, and who not to hire, out of -- say -- nineteen possible candidates.

1. One job-hunter said his interviews always began with the salary question, and no matter what he answered, that ended the interview. Turned out, this job-hunter was doing all the interviewing over the phone. That was the problem. Once he went face-to-face, salary was no longer the first thing discussed in the interview.

> *It's an old game, played with new determination by many employers these days, called* "among two equally qualified candidates, the one who is willing to work for the lower salary *wins."*

If you run into this situation, and you want that job badly enough, you will have no choice but to capitulate. Ask what salary they have in mind, and make your decision. (Of course you should always say, *"I need a little time, to think about this."*)

However, all the foregoing is merely the *worst-case scenario.* Usually, things don't go this way. Not by a long shot. In most interviews, these days, the employer will be willing to save salary negotiation until they've finally decided they want you (and you've decided you want them). And at that point, salary will be negotiable.

> When To Discuss Salary
>
> *Not until all of the following conditions have been fulfilled--*
>
> - *Not until they've gotten to know you, at your best, so they can see how you stand out above the other applicants.*
> - *Not until you've gotten to know them, as completely as you can, so you can tell when they're being firm, or when they're flexible.*
> - *Not until you've found out exactly what the job entails.*
> - *Not until they've had a chance to find out how well you match the job-requirements.*
> - *Not until you're in the final interview at that place, for that job.*
> - *Not until you've decided, "I'd really like to work here."*
> - *Not until they've said, "We want you."*
> - *Not until they've said, "We've got to have you."*
>
> *--should you get into salary discussion with this employer.*

If you'd prefer this to be put in the form of a diagram, here it is:[2]

When To Negotiate Salary

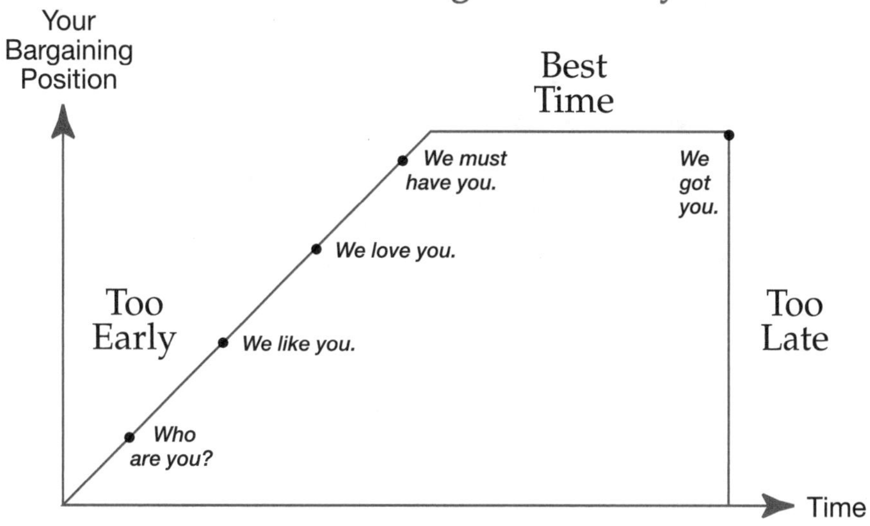

Why is it to your advantage to delay salary discussion? Because, if you really *shine* during the hiring-interview, they may -- at the end -- mention a higher salary than they originally had in mind, when the interview started -- and this is particularly the case when the interview has gone so well, that they're *determined* to obtain your services.

2. Reprinted, by permission of the publisher, from *Ready, Aim, You're Hired,* by Paul Hellman, © 1986 Paul Hellman. Published by AMACOM, a division of American Management Association, New York. All rights reserved.

THE SECOND SECRET OF SUCCESSFUL SALARY NEGOTIATION:

The Purpose of Salary Negotiation Is To Uncover The Most That An Employer Is Willing To Pay To Get You

Salary negotiation would never happen if *every* employer in *every* hiring-interview were to mention, right from the start, the top figure they are willing to pay for that position. *Some* employers do, as I was mentioning, above. And that's the end of any salary negotiation. But, of course, most employers don't. Hoping they'll be able to get you for less, they start *lower* than they're ultimately willing to go. This creates *a range*. And that range is what salary negotiation is all about.

For example, if the employer wants to hire somebody for no more than $12 an hour, they may start *the bidding* at $8 an hour. In which case, their *range* runs between $8 and $12 an hour. Or if they want to pay no more than $20 an hour, they may start the bidding at $16 an hour. In which case their range runs between $16 and $20 an hour.

So, why do you want to negotiate? Because, if a range *is* thus involved, you have every right to try to discover the highest salary that employer is willing to pay *within that range*.

The employer's goal, is to save money, if possible. Your goal is to bring home to your family, your partner, or your own household, the best salary that you can, for the work you will be doing. Nothing's wrong with the goals of either of you. But it does mean that, where the employer starts lower, salary negotiation is proper, and expected.

"WHILE YOU'RE WAITING FOR YOUR SHIP TO COME IN, WHY DON'T YOU DO SOME MAINTENANCE WORK ON THE PIER ?"

THE THIRD SECRET OF SUCCESSFUL SALARY NEGOTIATION:

During the Salary Discussion, Try Never to Be The First One To Mention A Salary Figure

Where salary negotiation has been kept *off stage* for much of the interview process, when it finally does come *on stage* you want the employer to be the first one to mention *a figure*, if you can.

Nobody knows why, but it has been observed over the years -- where the goals are opposite, as in this case, you are trying to get the employer to pay the most that they can, and the employer is trying to pay the least that they can -- in this back-and-forth negotiation, *whoever mentions a salary figure first, generally loses.* You can speculate from now until the cows come home, as to *why* this is; all we know is *that* it is.

Inexperienced employer/interviewers often don't know this quirky rule. But experienced ones are very aware of it; that's why they will *always* toss the ball to you, with some innocent-sounding question, such as: "What kind of salary are you looking for?" *Well, how kind of them to ask me what I want*--you may be thinking. No, no, no. Kindness has nothing to do with it. They are hoping *you* will be the first to mention a figure, because they know this odd experiential truth: that *whoever mentions a salary figure first, generally loses salary negotiation, at the last.*

Accordingly, if they ask you to name a figure, the *countermove* on your part should be: "Well, you created this position, so you must have some figure in mind, and I'd be interested in knowing what that figure is."

THE FOURTH SECRET OF SUCCESSFUL SALARY NEGOTIATION:

Before You Go to the Interview, Do Some Careful Homework on How Much You Will Need, if You Are Offered This Job

Suppose they offer you $12 an hour, you think this pay is just dandy. But you discover, one month into the job, that you can't possibly survive on that salary because *you just realized* you need $18 an hour, if you are even to barely survive. Well, you see the problem. The problem is that you didn't sit down, ahead of time, to figure out what your minimal survival salary would be.

Important homework, indeed! And how do you go about figuring this out?

You can determine this in one of two ways: a) take a wild guess -- and risk finding out after you take the job that it's simply impossible for you to live on that salary *(the favorite strategy in this country, and many others)*; or, b) make out a detailed outline of your estimated expenses *now*, listing what you think you will need *monthly* in the following categories:[3]

3. If this kind of financial figuring is not your cup of tea, find a buddy, friend, relative, family member, or anyone, who can help you do this. If you don't know anyone who could do this, go to your local church, synagogue, religious centre, social club, gym, or wherever you hang out, and ask the leader or manager there, to help you find someone. If there's a bulletin board, put up a notice on the bulletin board.

My Monthly Budget

Housing	
Rent or mortgage payments	$________
Electricity/gas	$________
Water	$________
Telephone	$________
Garbage removal	$________
Cleaning, maintenance, repairs[4]	$________
Food	
What you spend at the supermarket and/or meat market, etc.	$________
Eating out	$________
Clothing	
Purchase of new or used clothing	$________
Cleaning, drycleaning, laundry	$________
Automobile/transportation[5]	
Car payments	$________
Gas	$________
Repairs	$________
Public transportation *(bus, train, plane)*	$________
Insurance	
Car	$________
Medical or health-care	$________
Possessions *(house, personal)*	$________
Life Insurance	$________
Medical expenses	
Doctors' visits	$________
Prescriptions	$________
Fitness costs	$________
Support for other family members	
Child-care costs *(if you have children)*	$________
Child-support *(if you're paying that)*	$________
Support for your parents *(if you're helping out)*	$________
Charity giving/tithe *(to help others)*	$________
School/learning	
Children's costs *(if you have children in school)*	$________

Your learning costs *(adult education, job-hunting classes, etc.)*	$________
Pet care *(if you have pets)*	$________
Bills and debts *(Usual monthly payments)*	
Credit cards	$________
Local stores	$________
Other obligations you pay off monthly	$________
Taxes	
Federal[6] *(next April's due, divided by months remaining until then)*	$________
State *(likewise)*	$________
Local/property *(next amount due, divided by months remaining until then)*	$________
Tax-help *(if you ever use an accountant, pay a friend to help you with taxes, etc.)*	$________
Savings	$________
Retirement fund *(Keogh, IRA, SEP, etc.)*	$________
Charity	$________
Amusement/discretionary spending	
Movies, video rentals, etc.	$________
Other kinds of entertainment	$________
Reading *(newspapers, magazines, books)*	$________
Gifts *(birthday, Christmas, etc.)*	$________
Summer or winter vacation	$________
Total Amount You Need Each Month	$________

---

4. If you have extra household expenses, such as a security system for example, be sure and include the quarterly (or whatever) expenses here, divided by three (months).

5. Your checkbook stubs will tell you a lot of this stuff. But you may be vague about your cash or credit card expenditures. For example, you may not know how much you spend at the supermarket, or how much you spend on gas, etc. But there is a simple way to find out. Just carry a little notepad and pen around with you for two weeks or more, and jot down everything you pay cash (or use credit cards) for - - on the spot, right after you pay it. At the end of those two weeks, you'll be able to take that notepad and make a realistic guess of what should be put down in these categories that now puzzle you. (Multiply the two-weeks figure by two, and you'll have the monthly figure.)

Multiply the total amount you need each month by 12, to get the yearly figure. Then divide the yearly figure by 2000, and you will be reasonably near the *minimum* hourly wage that you need. Thus, if you need $3333 per month, multiplied by 12 that's $40,000 a year, and then divided by 2,000, that's $20 an hour.

Incidentally, you may want to prepare two different versions of the above budget: one with the expenses you'd ideally *like* to make, *the ceiling;* and the other a minimum budget, which will give you what you are looking for, here: *the floor*, below which you simply cannot afford to go.

P.S. If you're planning to move to another part of the country (U.S.), The Salary Calculator offered by Homefair.com (**`http://www2.homefair.com/calc/salcalc.html?NETSCAPE_LIVEWIRE.src=Espan`**) will translate your present standard of living into what it would cost in the place you are moving to.

6. Incidentally, looking ahead to next April 15th if you live in the U.S., be sure and check with your local IRS office or a reputable accountant to find out if you can deduct the expenses of your job-hunt on your Federal (and State) income tax returns. At this writing, some job-hunters can, if - - big IF - - this is not your first job that you're looking for, if you haven't been unemployed too long, and if you aren't making a career-change. Go find out what the latest "ifs" are. If IRS tells you you are eligible to deduct your job-hunting expenses, then keep careful receipts of everything related to your job-hunt, as you go along: telephone calls, stationery, printing, postage, travel, etc.

THE FIFTH SECRET OF SUCCESSFUL SALARY NEGOTIATION:

Before You Go to the Interview, Do Some Careful Research on Typical Salaries For Your Field and/or That Organization

As I said earlier, salary negotiation is possible *anytime* the employer does not open their discussion of salary by naming the top figure they have in mind, but starts instead with a lower figure.

Okay, so here is our $64,000 question: how do you tell whether the figure the employer first offers you is only their *starting bid*, or is their *final final offer*? The answer is: by doing some research on the field *and* that organization, first.

Oh, come on! I can hear you say. *Isn't this all more trouble than it's worth?* No, not if you're determined.

If you're determined, this is one step you don't want to overlook. Trust me, salary research pays off *handsomely.*

Let's say it takes you from one to three days to run down this sort of information on the three or four organizations that interest you the most. And let us say that because you've done this research, when you finally go in for the hiring-interview you are able to ask for and obtain a salary that is $4,000 a year higher in range, than you would otherwise have gotten. In just the next three years, you will be earning $12,000 extra, because of your salary research. *Not bad pay, for one to three days' work!* And it can be even more. I know *many* job-hunters and career-changers to whom this has happened. Thus you can see that there is a financial penalty exacted from those who are too lazy, or in too much of a hurry, to go gather this information. In plainer language: *you don't do this research, it'll cost ya!*

Okay then, how do you do this research? There are two ways to go: on the Internet, and off the Internet. Let's look at each, in turn:

Salary Research on the Internet

If you have access to the Internet, and you want to research salaries for particular geographical regions, positions, occupations, or industries, here are some free sites that may give you just what you're looking for:

► The Bureau of Labor Statistics' survey of salaries in individual occupations, *The Occupational Outlook Handbook 2000–2001.*

http://stats.bls.gov/ocohome.htm

► The Bureau of Labor Statistics' survey of salaries in individual industries *(it's a companion piece to The Occupational Outlook Handbook 2000–2001).*

http://stats.bls.gov/oco/cg/cgindex.htm

► "High Earning Workers Who Don't Have a College Degree," by Matthew Mariani, appearing first in the Fall 1999 issue of the *Occupational Outlook Quarterly.* For those who want to know how to earn *a lot* without having to go to college first.

http://stats.bls.gov/opub/ooq/1999/fall/art02.pdf

► JobOptions.com gives a nice index to the best salary sites on the Web, including a splendid list of salary guides and surveys by industry; plus some useful hints on how to do salary negotiation successfully.

http://ww1.joboptions.com/careertools/salary_info.jsp?session_id=0&app_id=0

► The oldest of the salary-specific job-sites. One of the largest and most complete lists of salary reviews on the Web, and run by a genius (Mary Ellen Mort).

http://www.jobstar.org/

► The most visited of all the salary-specific job-sites. Over two million visitors per month (as of 7/01), with 50 online partners that use their "Salary Wizard," such as AOL and Yahoo.

http://www.salary.com/

► We'll let John Sumser's great Interbiznet site have the final word here: "One key to successful job-hunting is estimating how much your labor is worth. Salary surveys are the most widely used method for doing this, and they are readily available on the Net. Unfortunately most of the data for these surveys originates from phone or print surveys, and takes a long time to compile and format. Therefore the data always runs months to years out of date. You may have to adjust the salary ranges by adding 5% (more or less, depending on your profession) for every year the survey data is out of date."

http://www.interbiznet.com/hunt/archives/010114.html

Incidentally, if these free sites don't give you what you want, you can always *pay* for the info, and hopefully get more-up-to-date surveys. Salary Source (**http://www.salarysource.com/**) offers up-to-date salary information at $29.95 a pop, for each position you request data about. (To be sure, they only have 350+ benchmark positions in their databank, but it may be worth a try.)

If you 'strike out' on all the above sites, then you're going to have to get a little more clever, and work a little harder, and pound the pavements, as I describe below.

Salary Research off the Internet

Off the Internet, how do you go about doing salary research? Well, there's a simple rule: generally speaking, abandon books, and go talk to people. Use books and libraries only as a *second*, or *last*, resort. (Their information is often just way too outdated.)

You can get much more complete and up to date information from people who are in the same job *at another com-*

pany or organization. Or, people at the nearby university or college who *train* such people, whatever that department may be. Teachers and professors will usually know what their graduates are making.

Now, exactly how do you go about getting this information, by talking to people? Let's look at some concrete examples:

First Example: Working at your first entry-level job, say at a fast-food place.

You may not need to do any salary research. They pay what they pay. You can walk in, ask for a job application, and interview with the manager. He or she will usually tell you the pay, outright. It's usually *inflexible.* But at least you'll find that it's easy to discover what the pay is. (Incidentally, filling out an application, or having an interview there, doesn't commit you to take the job -- but you probably already know that. You can always decline an offer from *any place.* That's what makes this approach harmless.)

Second Example: Working at a place where you can't discover what the pay is, say *at a construction company.*

If that construction company where you would *hope* to get a job is difficult to research, go visit a *different* construction company in the same town -- one that isn't of much interest to you -- and ask what they make *there.* Or, if you don't know who to talk to there, fill out one of their applications, and talk to the hiring person about what kinds of jobs they have (or might have in the future), at which time prospective wages is a legitimate subject of discussion. Then, having done this research on a place you don't care about, go back to the place that *really* interests you, and apply. You still don't know *exactly* what they pay, but you do know what their competitor pays -- which will usually be *close*.

> *Third Example:* Working in a one-person office, say *as a secretary.*

Here you can often find useful salary information by perusing the *Help Wanted* ads in the local paper for a week or two. Most of the ads probably won't mention a salary figure, but a few *may*. Among those that do, note what the lowest salary offering is, and what the highest is, and see if the ad reveals some reasons for the difference. It's interesting how much you can learn about salaries, with this approach. I know, because I was a secretary myself, once upon a time (dinosaurs were still roaming the earth).

Another way to do salary research is to find a *Temporary Work Agency* that places secretaries, and let yourself be farmed out to various offices: the more, the merrier. It's relatively easy to do salary research when you're *inside* the place. (Study what that place pays *the agency*, not what the agency then pays you.) If it's an office where the other workers *like* you, you'll be able to ask questions about a lot of things, including salary. It's like *summertime,* where the research is easy.

THE SIXTH SECRET OF SUCCESSFUL SALARY NEGOTIATION:

Define a Range that the Employer Has in Mind, and Then Define an Inter-related Range for Yourself

The Employer's Range

Before you finish your research, before you go in to that organization for your final interview, you want more than just *one* figure. You want *a range:* what's the *least* the employer may be willing to offer you, and what's the *most* the employer may be willing to offer you. In any organization which has more than five employees, that range is relatively easy to figure out. It will be less than what the person *who would be above you* makes, and more than what the person *who would be below you* makes.

If The Person Who Would Be Below You *Makes*	*And the Person* Who Would Be Above You *Makes*	*The Range for Your Job Would Be*
$45,000	*$55,000*	*$47,000–$53,000*
$30,000	*$35,500*	*$31,500–$33,500*
$15,240	*$18,000*	*$16,500–$17,200*

One teensy-tiny little problem: *how* do you find out the salary of those who would be above and below you? Well, first you have to find out their *names* or the names of their *positions*. If it is a small organization you are going after -- one with twenty or less employees -- finding this information out should be *duck soup*. Any employee who works there is likely to know the answer, and you can usually get in touch with one of those employees, or even an ex-employee, through your own personal contacts. Since up to two-thirds of all new jobs are created by companies that size, that's the size organization you are likely to be researching, anyway.

If you are going after a larger organization, then you fall back to our familiar life-preserver, namely, every contact you have (family, friend, relative, business, or church acquaintance) who might know the company, and therefore, the information you seek. In other words, you are looking for Someone Who Knows Someone who either is working, or has worked, at the particular place or places that interest you, and who therefore has or can get this information for you.

If you absolutely run into a blank wall on a particular organization (everyone who works there is pledged to secrecy, and they have shipped all their ex-employees to Siberia), then seek out information on their nearest *competitor* in the same geographic area. *For example,* let us say you were researching Bank X, and they were proving to be inscrutable about what they pay their managers. You would then try Bank Y as your research base, to see if the information were easier to come by, there. And if it were, you would then assume the two were similar in their pay scales, and that what you learned about Bank Y was applicable also to Bank X.

Also experts say that in researching salaries, you should take note of the fact that most governmental agencies have civil service positions matching those in private industry, and their job descriptions and pay ranges are available to the public. Go to the nearest City, County, Regional, State or Federal Civil Service office, find the job description nearest what you are seeking in private industry, and then ask for the starting salary.

Your Own Range

Once you've made a guess at what the employer's range might be, for the job you have in mind, you then define your own range *accordingly*. Let me give an example. Suppose you guess that the employer's range is one of those stated in the chart above, viz., $16,500 to $17,200. Accordingly, you now *invent* an 'asking' range for yourself, where your *minimum* 'hooks in' just below that employer's *maximum.*

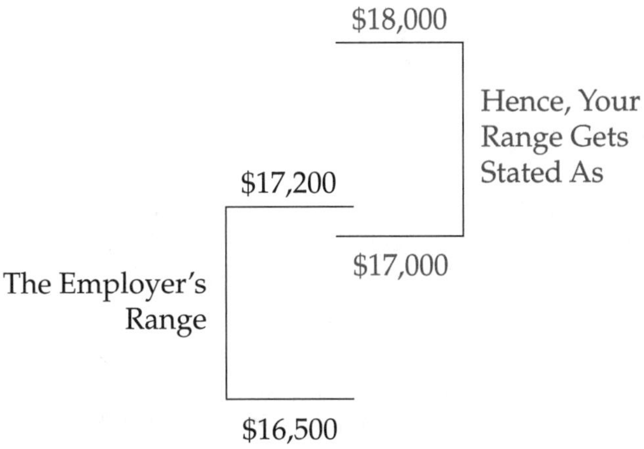

And so, when the employer has stated a figure (probably around his or her *lowest* -- i.e., $16,500), you will be ready to respond something like: "I understand of course the constraints under which all organizations are operating during this downturn in the economy, but I believe my productivity is such that it would *justify* a salary" -- *and here you mention a* range *whose bottom hooks in just below the top of their*

range, and goes up from there, accordingly, as shown on the diagram above -- " in the range of $17,000 to $18,000."

It will help a lot if during this discussion, you are prepared to show in what ways you will *make money* or in what ways you will *save money* for that organization, such as will justify the higher salary you are seeking. Hopefully, this will succeed in getting you the salary you want.

Daniel Porot, the job-expert in Europe, suggests that if you and an employer really hit it off, and you're *dying* to work there, but they cannot afford the salary you need, consider offering them part of your time. If you need, and believe you deserve, say $25,000, but they can only afford $15,000, you might consider offering them three days a week of your time for that $15,000 (15/25 = 3/5). This leaves you free to take work elsewhere during those other two days. You will *of course* produce so much work during those three days per week, that they will be ecstatic that they got you for even those three days.

THE SEVENTH SECRET OF SUCCESSFUL SALARY NEGOTIATION:

Know How to Bring The Salary Negotiation to a Close; Don't Leave It 'Just Hanging'

Your salary negotiation with this particular employer is not finished until you've addressed the issue of so-called fringe benefits. 'Fringes' such as life insurance, health benefits or health plans, vacation or holiday plans, and retirement programs typically add anywhere from 15 to 28 percent to many workers' salaries. That is to say, if an employee receives $3000 salary per month, the fringe benefits are worth another $450 to $840 per month.

If your job is *at a high level,* benefits may include but not be limited to: health, life, dental, disability, malpractice insurance; insurance for dependents; sick leave; vacation; personal leave/personal days; educational leave; educational cost reimbursement for coursework related to the job; maternity and or parental leave; health leave to care for dependents; bonus system or profit sharing; stock options; expense accounts for entertaining clients; dues to professional associations; travel reimbursement; fee sharing arrangements for clients that the employee generates; organizational memberships; parking; automobile allowance; relocation costs; sabbaticals; professional conference costs; time for community service; flextime work schedules; fitness center memberships.

You should therefore, before you walk into the interview, know what benefits are particularly important to you, then at the end of salary negotiation remember to ask what benefits are offered -- and negotiate if necessary for the benefits you particularly care about. Thinking this out ahead of time, of course, makes your negotiating easier, by far.

You also want to achieve some understanding about what their policy is about future raises. You can prepare the ground at the end of salary negotiation, by saying: *"If I accomplish this job to your satisfaction, as I fully expect to -- and more -- when could I expect to be in line for a raise?"*

Finally, you want to get *all of this* summarized, in writing. Always request a letter of agreement -- or employment contract -- that they give to you. If you can't get it in writing, now's a good time to start wondering *why.* The Road to Hell is paved with oral promises that went unwritten, and -- later -- unfulfilled.

Many executives unfortunately 'forget' what they told you during the hiring-interview, or even deny they ever said such a thing.

Also, many executives leave the company for another position and place, and their successor or the top boss may disown any *unwritten* promises: *"I don't know what caused them to say that to you, but they clearly exceeded their authority, and of course we can't be held to that."*

CONCLUSION: THE GREATEST SECRET

All of this, of course, presumes that your interview, and salary negotiation, goes well. There are times, however, when it looks like it's going well, and then all of a sudden and without warning it comes totally unravelled. You're hired, told to report next Monday, and then get a phone call on Friday telling you that all hiring has been put, mysteriously, 'on hold.' You're therefore back out 'on the pavements.' Having seen this happen so many times, over the years, and having studied successful and unsuccessful job-hunters for over a quarter of a century, now, I have discovered that the single greatest secret of *successful* job-hunters is *that they always have alternatives.*

Alternative ideas of what they could do with their life.

Alternative ways of describing what they want to do right now.

Alternative ways of going about the job-hunt (not just the Internet, not just resumes, agencies, and ads).

Alternative job prospects.

Alternative 'target' organizations that they go after.

Alternative ways of approaching employers.

And so on, and so forth.

What all this means for you, the seeker of secrets, is: be sure you are pursuing more than just one employer, right up until after you start your new job. That organization, that office, that group, that church, that factory, that government agency, that volunteer organization that you've targeted may be *the ideal place* where you would like to work. But no matter how appetizing this *first choice* looks to you, no matter how much it makes your mouth water at the thought of working there, *you are committing job-hunting suicide* if you don't have some alternative places in mind. Sure, maybe you'll get that dream-come-true. But -- *big question* -- what are your plans if you don't? You've *got* to have other plans **now** -- not when that first target runs out of gas three months from now. You must go after more than one organization. I recommend five 'targets', at least.

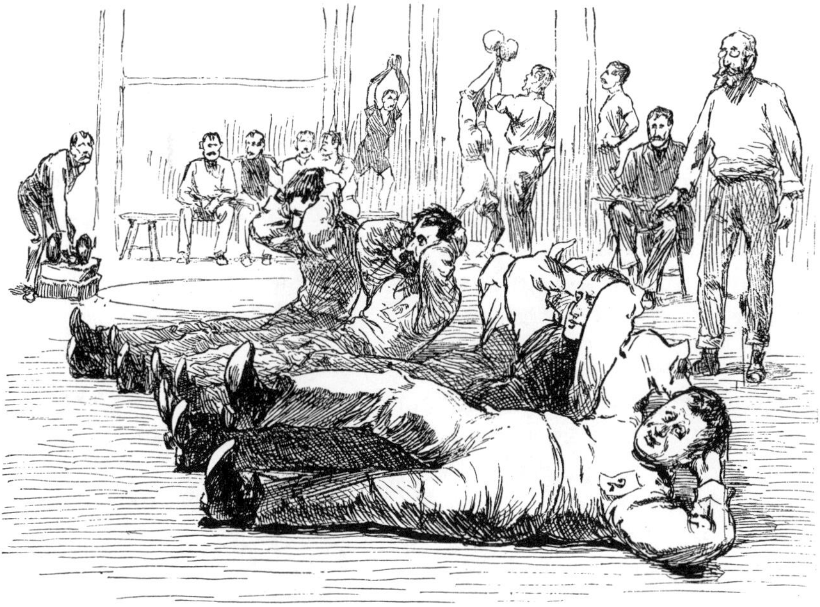

Target Small Organizations

Were I myself looking for a job tomorrow, this is what I would do. After I had figured out, as in the previous chapters, what my ideal job looked like, and after I had collected a list of those workplaces that have such jobs, in my chosen geographical area, I would then circle the names and addresses of those which are *small* organizations (personally I would restrict my *first draft* to those with 25 or less employees) -- and then go after them, in the manner I have described in previous chapters. However, as the dot.com *downturn* of *April 2000 and following* taught us, small organizations can sometimes be fraught with danger *(a nova-like birth, a sudden black hole death),* I would look particularly for small organizations that are ***established*** or ***growing***. And if *'organizations with 25 or less employees'* eventually didn't turn up enough *leads* for me, then I would broaden my search to *'organizations with 50 or less employees,'* and finally -- if that turned up nothing -- to *'organizations with 100 or less employees.'* But I would *start* small. Very small.

Remember, job-hunting always involves luck, to some degree. But with a little bit of luck, and a lot of hard work, plus determination, these instructions about how to get hired, should work for you, even as they have worked for so many hundreds of thousands before you.

Take heart from those who have gone before you, such as this determined job-hunter, who wrote me this heartfelt letter, with which I close:

"Before I read this book, I was depressed and lost in the futile job-hunt using Want Ads Only. I did not receive even one phone call from any ad I answered, over a total of 4 months. I felt that I was the most useless person on earth. I am female, with a 2½ year old daughter, former professor in China, with no working experience at all in the U.S. We came here seven months ago because my husband had a job offer here.

"Then, on June 11th of last year, I saw your book in a local bookstore. Subsequently, I spent 3 weeks, 10 hours a day except Sunday, reading every single word of your book and doing all of the flower petals in the Flower Exercise. After getting to know myself much better, I felt I was ready to try the job-hunt again. I used Parachute *throughout as my guide, from the very beginning to the very end, namely, salary negotiation.*

"In just two weeks I secured (you guessed it) two job offers, one of which I am taking, as it is an excellent job, with very good pay. It is (you guessed it again) a small company, with 20 or so employees. It is also a career-change: I was a professor of English; now I am to be a controller!

"I am so glad I believed your advice: there are jobs out there, and there are two types of employers out there, and truly there are!

"I hope you will be happy to hear my story."

Epilogue

How To Find Your Mission In Life

God and One's Vocation

Foreword

As I started writing this section, I toyed at first with the idea of following what might be described as an "all-paths approach" to religion. But, after much thought, I decided not to try that. This, because I have read many other writers who tried, and I felt the approach failed miserably. An "all-paths" approach to religion ends up being a "no-paths" approach, even as a woman or man who tries to please everyone ends up pleasing no one. It is the old story of the "universal" vs. the "particular."

Those of us who do career counseling could predict, ahead of time, that trying to stay universal is not likely to be helpful, in writing about religion. We know well from our own field that truly helpful career counseling depends upon defining the **particularity** or uniqueness of each person we try to help. No employer wants to know only what you have in common with everyone else. He or she wants to know what makes you unique and individual. As I have argued throughout this book, the identification and inventory of your uniqueness or *particularity* is crucial if you are ever to find meaningful work.

This particularity invades and carries over to *everything* a person does; it is not suddenly "jettisonable" when he or she turns to religion. Therefore, when I or anyone else writes about religion I believe we **must** write out of our own particularity -- which *starts,* in my case, with the fact that I write, and think, and breathe as a Christian -- as you might expect from the fact that I have been an ordained Episcopalian minister for the last forty-five years. Understandably, then, this article speaks from a Christian perspective. I want you to be aware of that, at the outset.

Balanced against this is the fact that I have always been acutely sensitive to the fact that this is a pluralistic society in which we live, and that I owe a great deal to my readers who may have religious convictions quite different from my own. It has turned out that the people who work or have worked here in my office with me, over the years, have been predominantly of other faiths, mainly Jewish. Furthermore, **Parachute's** more than 7 million readers have not only included Christians of every variety and persuasion, Christian Scientists, Jews, members of the Baha'i faith, Hindus, Buddhists, adherents of Islam, but also believers in 'new age' religions, secularists, humanists, agnostics, atheists, and many others. I have therefore tried to be very courteous toward the feelings of all my readers, *while at the same time* counting on them to translate my Christian thought forms into their own thought forms. This ability to thus translate is the indispensable *sine qua non* of anyone who wants to communicate helpfully with others, these days.

In the Judeo-Christian tradition from which I come, one of the indignant Biblical questions is, "Has God forgotten to be gracious?" The answer was a clear No. I think it is important *for all of us* also to seek the same goal. I have therefore labored to make this section gracious as well as helpful.

R.N.B

TURNING POINT

For many of us, the job-hunt offers a chance to make some fundamental changes in our whole life. It marks a turning point in how we live our life.

It gives us a chance to ponder and reflect, to extend our mental horizons, to go deeper into the sub-soil of our soul.

It gives us a chance to wrestle with the question, "Why am I here on Earth?" We don't want to feel that we are just another grain of sand lying on the beach called humanity, unnumbered and lost in the 5 billion other human beings.

We want to do more than plod through life, going to work, coming home from work. We want to find that special joy, "that no one can take from us," which comes from having a sense of Mission in our life.

We want to feel we were put here on Earth for some special purpose, to do some unique work that only we can accomplish.

We want to know what our Mission is.

THE MEANING OF THE WORD 'MISSION'

When used with respect to our life and work *Mission* has always been a religious concept, from beginning to end. It is defined by Webster's as "a continuing task or responsibility that one is destined or fitted to do or specially called upon to undertake," and historically has had two major synonyms: *Calling* and *Vocation*. These, of course, are the same word in two different languages, English and Latin. Both imply God. To be given a Vocation or Calling implies *Someone who* calls. To have a Destiny implies *Someone who determined the destination for us*. Thus, the concept of Mission lands us inevitably in the lap of God, before we have hardly begun.

I emphasize this, because there is an increasing trend in our culture to try to speak about religious subjects without reference to God. This is true of "spirituality," "soul," and "Mission," in particular. More and more books talk about Mission as though it were simply "a purpose you choose for your own life, by identifying your enthusiasms."

This attempt to obliterate all reference to God from the originally religious concept of Mission, is particularly ironic because the proposed substitute word -- enthusiasms -- is derived from two Greek words, 'en theos,' and means "God in us."

In the midst of this "redefining culture" we find an oasis called the "job-hunting field." It is a field that was raised on a firm concept of "God." That's because most of its inventors, most of its leaders over the years -- the late John Crystal, Arthur Miller, Ralph Mattson, Tom and Ellie Jackson, Bernard Haldane, Arthur and Marie Kirn, myself and many others -- have been people who believe firmly in God, and came into this field because we think about Him a lot, in connection with meaningful work.

Nor are we alone. Many many job-hunters also think about God a lot. In the U.S., 94% of us believe in God, 90% of us pray, 88% of us believe God loves us, and 33% of us report we have had a life-changing religious experience - - and these figures have remained virtually unchanged for the past fifty years, according to opinion polls conducted by the Gallup Organization. (*The People's Religion: American Faith in the 90s*. Macmillan & Co. 1989).

What is not so clear is whether we think about God in connection with our work. Often these two subjects -- spiritual beliefs and Work -- live in separate mental ghettos within the same person's head.

But unemployment offers us a chance to fix all that: to marry our work and our religious beliefs together, to talk about Calling, and Vocation, and Mission in life -- to think out why we are here, and what plans God has for us.

That's why a period of unemployment can absolutely change our life.

THE SECRET OF FINDING YOUR MISSION IN LIFE: TAKING IT IN STAGES

> I will explain the steps toward finding your Mission in life that I have learned in my seventy-four years on Earth. Just remember two things. First, I speak from a Christian perspective, and trust you to translate this into your own thought-forms.
>
> Secondly, I know that these steps are not the only Way -- by any means. Many people have discovered their Mission by taking other paths. And you may, too. But hopefully what I have to say may shed some light upon whatever path you take.

I have learned that if you want to figure out what your Mission in life is, it will likely take some time. It is not a *problem* to be solved in a day and a night. It is a *learning process* which has steps to it, much like the process by which we all learned to eat. As a baby we did not tackle adult food right off. As we all recall, there were three stages: first there had to be the mother's milk or bottle, then strained baby foods, and finally -- after teeth and time -- the stuff that grown-ups chew. Three stages -- and the two earlier stages were not to be disparaged. It was all Eating, just different forms of Eating -- appropriate to our development at the time. But each stage had to be mastered, in turn, before the next could be approached.

There are usually three stages also to learning what your Mission in life is, and the two earlier stages are likewise not to be disparaged. It is all "Mission" -- just different forms of Mission, appropriate to your development at the time. But each stage has to be mastered, in turn, before the next can be approached.

Of course, there is a sense in which you never master any of these stages, but are always growing in understanding and mastery of them, throughout your whole life here on Earth.

As it has been impressed on me by observing many people over the years (admittedly through *Christian spectacles*), it appears that the three parts to your Mission here on Earth can be defined generally as follows:

(1) *Your first Mission here on Earth* is one which you share with the rest of the human race, but it is no less your individual Mission for the fact that it is shared: and it is, **to seek to stand hour by hour in the conscious presence of God, the One from whom your Mission is derived**. *The Missioner before the Mission,* is the rule. In religious language, your Mission here is: *to know God, and enjoy Him forever, and to see His hand in all His works.*

(2) Secondly, once you have begun doing that in an earnest way, *your second Mission here on Earth* is also one which you share with the rest of the human race, but it is no less your individual mission for the fact that it is shared: and that is, **to do what you can, moment by moment, day by day, step by step, to make this world a better place, following the leading and guidance of God's Spirit within you and around you**.

(3) Thirdly, once you have begun doing that in a serious way, *your third Mission here on Earth* is one which is uniquely yours, and that is:

a) **to exercise that Talent which you particularly came to Earth to use -- your greatest gift, which you most delight to use,**

b) **in the place(s) or setting(s) which God has caused to appeal to you the most,**

c) **and for those purposes which God most needs to have done in the world.**

When fleshed out, and spelled out, I think you will find that there you have the definition of your Mission in life. Or, to put it another way, these are the three Missions which you have in life.

The Two Rhythms of the Dance of Mission: Unlearning, Learning, Unlearning, Learning

The distinctive characteristic of these three stages is that in each we are forced to *let go* of some fundamental assumptions which the world has *falsely* taught us, about the nature of our Mission. In other words, throughout this quest and at each stage we find ourselves engaged not merely in a process of *Learning.* We are also engaged in a process of *Un*learning. Thus, we can restate the above three Learnings, in terms of what we also need to *un*learn at each stage:

• We need in the first Stage to *un*learn the idea that our Mission is primarily to keep busy *doing* something (here on Earth), and learn instead that our Mission is first of all to keep busy *being* something (here on Earth). In Christian language (and others as well), we might say that we were sent here to learn how *to be* sons of God, and daughters of God, before anything else. "*Our Father, who art in heaven . . .*"

• In the second stage, "Being" issues into "Doing." At this stage, we need to *un*learn the idea that everything about our Mission must be *unique* to us, and learn instead that some parts of our Mission here on Earth are *shared* by all human beings: e.g., we were all sent here to bring more gratitude, more kindness, more forgiveness, and more love, into the world. We share this Mission because the task is too large to be accomplished by just one individual.

• We need in the third stage to *un*learn the idea that that part of our Mission which is truly unique, and most truly ours, is something Our Creator just *orders* us to do, without any agreement from our spirit, mind, and heart. (On the other hand, neither is it something that each of us chooses and then merely asks God to bless.) We need to learn that God so honors our free will, that He has ordained our unique Mission be something which we have some part in choosing.

• In this third stage we need also to *un*learn the idea that our unique Mission must consist of some achievement which all the world will see -- and learn instead that as the stone does not always know what ripples it has caused in the pond whose surface it impacts, so neither we nor those who watch our life will always know *what we have achieved* by our life and by our Mission. *It may be* that by the grace of God we helped bring about a profound change for the better in the lives of other souls around us, but it also may be that this takes place beyond our sight, or after we have gone on. And we may never know what we have accomplished, until we see Him face-to-face after this life is past.

• Most finally, we need to *un*learn the idea that what we have accomplished is our doing, and ours alone. It is God's Spirit breathing in us and through us which helps us to do whatever we do, and so the singular first person pronoun is never appropriate, but only the plural. Not "*I* accomplished this" but "*We* accomplished this, God and I, working together . . ."

That should give you a general overview. But I would like to add some random comments on my part about each of these three Missions of ours here on Earth.

Some Random Comments About Your First Mission in Life

Your first Mission here on Earth is one which you share with the rest of the human race, but it is no less your individual Mission for the fact that it is shared: and that is, **to seek to stand hour by hour in the conscious presence of God, the One from whom your Mission is derived**. The Missioner before the Mission, is the rule. In religious language, your Mission is: to know God, and enjoy Him forever, and to see His hand in all His works.

Comment 1: How We Might Think of God

Each of us has to go about this primary Mission according to the tenets of his or her own particular religion. But I will speak what I know out of the context of my own particular faith, and you may perhaps translate and apply it to yours. I will speak as a Christian, who believes (passionately) that Christ is the Way and the Truth and the Life. But I also believe, with St. Peter, "that God shows no partiality, but in every nation any one who fears him and does what is right is acceptable to him." (Acts 10:34-35)

Now, Jesus claimed many unique things about Himself and His Mission; but He also spoke of Himself as the great prototype for us all. He called Himself "the Son of Man," and He said, "I assure you that the man who believes in me will do the same things that I have done, yes, and he will do even greater things than these . . ." (John 14:12)

Emboldened by His identification of us with His Life and His Mission, we might want to remember how He spoke about His Life here on Earth. He put it in this context: **"I came from the Father and have come into the world; again, I am leaving the world and going to the Father."** (John 16:28)

If there is a sense in which this is, in even the faintest way, true also of our lives (and I shall say in a moment in what sense I think it is true), then instead of calling our great Creator "God" or "Father" right off, we might begin our approach to the subject of religion by referring to the One Who gave us our Mission and sent us to this planet not as "God" or "Father" but -- *just to help our thinking* -- as: **"The One From Whom We Came and The One To Whom We Shall Return,"** when this life is done.

If our life here on Earth be at all like Christ's, then this is a true way to think about the One Who gave us our Mission. We are not some kind of eternal, pre-existent *being*. We are **creatures**, who once did not exist, and then came into Being, and continue to have our Being, only at the will of our great Creator. But as creatures we are both body and soul; and although we know our body was created in our mother's womb, our soul's origin is a great mystery. Where it came from, at what moment the Lord created it, is something we cannot know. It is not unreasonable to suppose, however, that the great God created our *soul* before it entered our body, and in that sense we did indeed stand before God before we were born; and He is indeed **"The One From Whom We Came and The One To Whom We Shall Return."**

Therefore, before we go searching for "what work was I sent here to do?" we need to establish or in a truer sense *reestablish* -- contact with this **"One From Whom We Came and The One To Whom We Shall Return."** Without this reaching out of the creature to the great Creator, without this reaching out of *the creature with a Mission* to *the One Who Gave Us That Mission*, the question ***what** is my Mission in life?* is void and null. The *what* is rooted in the *Who;* absent the Personal, one cannot meaningfully discuss The Thing. It is like the adult who cries, "I want to get married," without giving any consideration to *who* it is they want to marry.

Comment 2: How We Might Think of Religion or Faith

In light of this larger view of our creatureliness, we can see that *religion* or *faith* is not a question of whether or not we choose to (*as it is so commonly put*) "have a relationship with God." Looking at our life in a larger context than just our life here on Earth, it becomes apparent that some sort of relationship with God is a given for us, about which we have absolutely no choice. God and we **were** and **are** related, during the time of our soul's existence before our birth and in the time of our soul's continued existence after our death. The only choice we have is what to do about **The Time In Between**, i.e., what we want the nature of our relationship with God to be during our time here on Earth and how that will affect the *nature* of the relationship, then, after death.

One of the corollaries of all this is that by the very act of being born into a human body, it is an inevitable that we undergo a kind of *amnesia* -- an amnesia which typically embraces not only our nine months in the womb, our baby years, and almost one-third of each day (sleeping), but more importantly any memory of our origin or our destiny. We wander on Earth as an amnesia victim. To seek after Faith, therefore, is to seek to climb back out of that amnesia. Religion or faith is **the hard reclaiming of knowledge we once knew as a certainty**.

Comment 3: The First Obstacle to Executing This Mission

This first Mission of ours here on Earth is not the easiest of Missions, simply because it is the first. Indeed, in many ways, it is the most difficult. All can see that our life here on Earth is a very physical life. We eat, we drink, we sleep, we long to be held, and to hold. We inherit a physical body, with very physical appetites, we walk on the physical earth, and we acquire physical possessions. It is the most alluring of temptations, *in our amnesia*, to come up with just a *Physical* interpretation of this life: to think that the Universe is merely interested in the survival of species. Given this interpretation, the story of our individual life could be simply told: we are born, grow up, procreate, and die.

But we are ever recalled to do what we came here to do: that without rejecting the joy of the Physicalness of this life, such as the love of the blue sky and the green grass, we are to reach out beyond all this to **recall** and recover a *Spiritual* interpretation of our life. *Beyond* the physical and *within* the physicalness of this life, to detect a Spirit and a Person from beyond this Earth who is with us and in us -- the very real and loving and awesome Presence of the great Creator from whom we came -- and the One to whom we once again shall go.

Comment 4: The Second Obstacle to Executing This Mission

It is one of the conditions of our earthly amnesia and our creatureliness that, sadly enough, some very *human* and very *rebellious* part of us *likes* the idea of living in a world where we can be our own god -- and therefore loves the purely Physical interpretation of life, and finds it *anguish* to relinquish it. Traditional Christian vocabulary calls this "**sin**" and has a lot to say about the difficulty it poses for this first part of our Mission. All who live a thoughtful life know that it is true: our greatest enemy in carrying out this first Mission of ours is indeed *our own* heart and our own rebellion.

Comment 5: Further Thoughts About What Makes Us Special and Unique

As I said earlier, many of us come to this issue of our Mission in life, because we want to feel that we are unique. And what we mean by that, is that we hope to discover some "specialness" intrinsic to us, which is our birthright, and which no one can take from us. What we, however, discover from a thorough exploration of this topic, is that we are indeed special -- but only because God thinks us so. Our specialness and uniqueness reside in Him, and His love, rather than in anything intrinsic to our own *being*. The proper appreciation of this distinction causes our feet to carry us in the end not to the City called Pride, but to the Temple called Gratitude.

> What is religion? Religion is the service of God out of grateful love for what God has done for us. The Christian religion, more particularly, is the service of God out of grateful love for what God has done for us in Christ.
>
> Phillips Brooks, author of
> *O Little Town of Bethlehem*

Comment 6: The Unconscious Doing of The Work We Came To Do

You may have *already* wrestled with this first part of your Mission here on Earth. You may not have called it that. You may have called it simply "learning to believe in God." But if you ask what your Mission is in life, this one was and is the precondition of all else that you came here to do. Absent this Mission, and it is folly to talk about the rest. So, if you have been seeking faith, or seeking to strengthen your faith, you have -- willy nilly -- already been about *the doing of the Mission you were given*. Born into **This Time In Between**, you have found His hand again, and reclasped it. You are therefore ready to go on with His Spirit to tackle together what you came here to do -- the other parts of your Mission.

Some Random Comments About Your Second Mission in Life

Your second Mission here on Earth is also one which you share with the rest of the human race, but it is no less your individual Mission for the fact that it is shared: and that is, **to do what you can moment by moment, day by day, step by step, to make this world a better place -- following the leading and guidance of God's Spirit within you and around you**.

Comment 1: The Uncomfortableness of One Step at a Time

Imagine yourself out walking in your neighborhood one night, and suddenly you find yourself surrounded by such a dense fog, that you have lost your bearings and cannot find your way. Suddenly, a friend appears out of the fog, and asks you to put your hand in theirs, and they will lead you home. And you, not being able to tell where you are going, trustingly follow them, even though you can only see one step at a time. Eventually you arrive safely home, filled with gratitude. But as you reflect upon the experience the next day, you realize how unsettling it was to have to keep walking when you could see only one step at a time, even though you had guidance in which you knew you could trust.

Now I have asked you to imagine all of this, because this is the essence of the second Mission to which *you* are called -- and *I* am called -- in this life. It is all very different than we had imagined. When the question, *"What is your Mission in life?"* is first broached, and we have put our hand in God's, as it were, we imagine that we will be taken up to *some mountaintop*, from which we can see far into the distance. And that we will hear a voice in our ear, saying, "Look, look, see that distant city? That is the goal of your Mission; that is where everything is leading, every step of your way."

But instead of the mountaintop, we find ourself in *the valley* -- wandering often in a fog. And the voice in our ear says something quite different from what we thought we would hear. It says, **"Your Mission is to take one step at a time, even when you don't yet see where it all is leading, or what the Grand Plan is, or what your overall Mission in life is. Trust Me; I will lead you."**

Comment 2: The Nature of This Step-by-Step Mission

As I said, in every situation you find yourself, you have been sent here to do whatever you can -- moment by moment -- that will bring more gratitude, more kindness, more forgiveness, more honesty, and more love into this world.

There are dozens of such moments every day. Moments when you stand -- as it were -- at a spiritual crossroads, with two ways lying before you. Such moments are typically called **"moments of decision."** It does not matter what the frame or content of each particular decision is. It all devolves, in the end, into just two roads before you, *every time*. **The one** will lead to *less* gratitude, *less* kindness, *less* forgiveness, *less* honesty, or *less* love in the world. **The other** will lead to *more* gratitude, *more* kindness, *more* forgiveness, *more* honesty, or *more* love in the world. Your Mission, each moment, is to seek to choose the latter spiritual road, rather than the former, *every time*.

Comment 3: Some Examples of This Step-by-Step Mission

I will give a few examples, so that the nature of this part of your Mission may be unmistakably clear.

You are out on the freeway, in your car. Someone has gotten into the wrong lane, to the right of *your* lane, and needs to move over into the lane you are in. You *see* their need to cut in, ahead of you. **Decision time.** In your mind's eye you see two spiritual roads lying before you: the one leading to less kindness in the world (you speed up, to shut this driver out, and don't let them move over), the other leading to more kindness in the world (you let the driver cut in). **Since you know this is part of your Mission, part of the reason why you came to Earth, your calling is clear. You know which road to take, which decision to make.**

You are hard at work at your desk, when suddenly an interruption comes. The phone rings, or someone is at the door. They need something from you, a question of some of your time and attention. **Decision time**. In your mind's eye you see two spiritual roads lying before you: the one leading to less love in the world (you tell them you're just too busy to be bothered), the other leading to more love in the world (you put aside your work, decide that God may have sent this person to you, and say, "Yes, what can I do to help you?"). **Since you know this is part of your Mission, part of the reason why you came to Earth, your calling is clear. You know which road to take, which decision to make.**

Your mate does something that hurts your feelings. **Decision time.** In your mind's eye you see two spiritual roads lying before you: the one leading to less forgiveness in the world (you institute an icy silence between the two of you, and think of how you can punish them or otherwise get even), the other leading to more forgiveness in the

world (you go over and take them in your arms, speak the truth about your hurt feelings, and assure them of your love). **Since you know this is part of your Mission, part of the reason why you came to Earth, your calling is clear. You know which road to take, which decision to make.**

You have not behaved at your most noble, recently. And now you are face-to-face with someone who asks you a question about what happened. **Decision time.** In your mind's eye you see two spiritual roads lying before you: the one leading to less honesty in the world (you lie about what happened, or what you were feeling, because you fear losing their respect or their love), the other leading to more honesty in the world (you tell the truth, together with how you feel about it, in retrospect). **Since you know this is part of your Mission, part of the reason why you came to Earth, your calling is clear. You know which road to take, which decision to make.**

Comment 4: The Spectacle Which Makes the Angels Laugh

It is necessary to explain this part of our Mission in some detail, because so many times you will see people wringing their hands, and saying, *"I want to know what my Mission in life is,"* all the while they are cutting people off on the highway, refusing to give time to people, punishing their mate for having hurt their feelings, and lying about what they did. And it will seem to you that the angels must laugh to see this spectacle. *For these people wringing their hands,* their Mission was right there, on the freeway, in the interruption, in the hurt, and at the confrontation.

Comment 5: The Valley vs. The Mountaintop

At some point in your life your Mission may involve some grand *mountaintop experience,* where you say to yourself, "This, this, is why I came into the world. I know it. I know it." *But until then,* your Mission is here in *the valley,* and the fog, and the little callings moment by moment, day by day. More to the point, it is likely you cannot ever get to your mountaintop Mission unless you have first exercised your stewardship faithfully in the valley.

It is an ancient principle, to which Jesus alluded often, that if you don't use the information the Universe has already given you, you cannot expect it will give you any more. If you aren't being faithful in small things, how can you expect to be given charge over larger things? (Luke 16:10–12; 19:11–24) If you aren't trying to bring more gratitude, kindness, forgiveness, honesty, and love into the world each day, you can hardly expect that you will be entrusted with the Mission to help bring peace into the world or anything else large and important. If we do not live out our day-by-day Mission in the valley, we cannot expect we are yet ready for a larger *mountaintop* Mission.

Comment 6: The Importance of Not Thinking of This Mission As 'Just A Training Camp'

The valley is not just a kind of "training camp." There is in your imagination even now an invisible *spiritual* mountaintop to which you may go, if you wish to see where all this is leading. And what will you see there, in the imagination of your heart, but the goal toward which all this is pointed: **that Earth might be more like heaven. That human's life might be more like God's**. That is the large achievement toward which all our day-by-day Missions *in the valley* are moving. This is a *large* order, but it is accomplished by faithful attention to the doing of our great Creator's **will** in little things as well as in large. It is much like the building of the pyramids in Egypt, which was accomplished by the dragging of a lot of individual pieces of stone by a lot of individual men.

The valley, the fog, the going step-by-step, is no mere training camp. The goal is real, however large. **"Thy Kingdom come, Thy will be done, on Earth, as it is in heaven."**

Some Random Comments About Your Third Mission in Life

Your third Mission here on Earth is one which is uniquely yours, and that is:

a) **to exercise that Talent which you particularly came to Earth to use -- your greatest gift which you most delight to use,**

b) **in those place(s) or setting(s) which God has caused to appeal to you the most,**

c) **and for those purposes which God most needs to have done in the world.**

Comment 1: Our Mission Is Already Written, "in Our Members"

It is customary in trying to identify this part of our Mission, to advise that we should ask God, in prayer, to speak to us -- and **tell us** plainly what our Mission is. We look for a voice in the air, a thought in our head, a dream in the night, a sign in the events of the day, to reveal this thing which is otherwise *(it is said)* completely hidden. Sometimes, from just such answered prayer, people do indeed discover what their Mission is, beyond all doubt and uncertainty.

But having to wait for the voice of God to reveal what our Mission is, is not the truest picture of our situation. St. Paul, in Romans, speaks of a law "written in our members" -- and this phrase has a telling application to the question of **how** God reveals to each of us our unique

Mission in life. Read again the definition of our third Mission (above) and you will see: the clear implication of the definition is that God has **already** revealed His will to us concerning our vocation and Mission, by causing it to be "**written in our members**." We are to begin deciphering our unique Mission by studying our talents and skills, and more particularly which ones (or One) we most rejoice to use.

God actually has written His will *twice* in our members: *first in the talents* which He lodged there, and secondly *in His guidance of our heart*, as to which talent gives us the greatest pleasure from its exercise (**it is usually the one which, when we use it, causes us to lose all sense of time**).

Even as the anthropologist can examine ancient inscriptions, and divine from them the daily life of a long lost people, so we by examining **our talents** and **our heart** can *more often than we dream* divine the Will of the Living God. For true it is, our Mission is not something He **will** reveal; it is something He **has already** revealed. It is not to be found written in the sky; it is to be found written in our members.

Comment 2: Career Counseling: We Need You

Arguably, our first two Missions in life could be learned from religion alone -- without any reference whatsoever to career counseling, the subject of this book. Why then should career counseling claim that this question about our Mission in life is its proper concern, *in any way?*

It is when we come to this third Mission, which hinges so crucially on the question of our Talents, skills, and gifts, that we see the answer. If you've read the body of this book, before turning to this Epilogue, you know without my even saying it, how much the identification of Talents, gifts, or skills is the province of career counseling. Its expertise, indeed its *raison d'etre*, lies precisely in the identification, classification, and (forgive me) "prioritization" of Talents, skills, and gifts. To put the matter quite simply, career counseling knows how to do this better than any other discipline -- **including** traditional religion. This is not a defect of religion, but the fulfillment of something Jesus promised: "When the Spirit of truth comes, He will guide you into all truth." (John 16:12) Career counseling is part (we may hope) of that promised late-coming truth. It can therefore be of inestimable help to the pilgrim who is trying to figure out what their greatest, and most enjoyable, talent is, as a step toward identifying their unique Mission in life.

If career counseling needs religion as its helpmate in the first two stages of identifying our Mission in life, religion repays the compliment by clearly needing career counseling as **its** helpmate here in the third stage.

And this place where you are in your life right now -- facing the job-hunt and all its anxiety -- is the perfect time to seek the union within your own mind and heart of both career counseling (as in the pages of this book) and your faith in God.

Comment 3: How Our Mission Got Chosen: A Scenario for the Romantic

It is a mystery which we cannot fathom, in this life at least, as to why one of us has this talent, and the other one has that; why God chose to give one gift -- and Mission -- to one person, and a different gift -- and Mission -- to another. Since we do not know, and in some degree cannot know, we are certainly left free to speculate, and imagine.

We may imagine that before we came to Earth, our souls, *our Breath, our Light,* stood before the great Creator and volunteered for this Mission. And God and we, together, chose what that Mission would be and what particular gifts would be needed, which He then agreed to give us, after our birth. Thus, our Mission was not a command given preemptorily by an unloving Creator to a reluctant slave without a vote, but was a task jointly designed by us both, in which as fast as the great Creator said, "**I wish**" our hearts responded, "**Oh, yes**." As mentioned in an earlier Comment, it may be helpful to think of the condition of our becoming human as that we became amnesiac about any consciousness our soul had before birth -- and therefore amnesiac about the nature or manner in which our Mission was designed.

Our searching for our Mission now is therefore a searching to recover the memory of something we ourselves had a part in designing.

I am admittedly a hopeless romantic, so of course I like this picture. If you also are a hopeless romantic, you may like it too. There's also the chance that it just may be true. We will not know until we see Him face-to-face.

Comment 4: Mission As Intersection

> There are all different kinds of voices calling you to all different kinds of work, and the problem is to find out which is the voice of God rather than that of society, say, or the superego, or self-interest. By and large a good rule for finding out is this: the kind of work God usually calls you to is the kind of work (a) that you need most to do and (b) the world most needs to have done. If you really get a kick out of your work, you've presumably met requirement (a), but if your work is writing TV deodorant commercials, the chances are you've missed requirement (b). On the other hand, if your work is being a doctor in a leper colony, you have probably met (b), but if most of the time you're bored and depressed by it, the chances are you haven't only bypassed (a) but probably aren't helping your patients much either. Neither the hair shirt nor the soft birth will do. **The place God calls you to is the place where your deep gladness and the world's deep hunger meet.**
>
> Fred Buechner
> *Wishful Thinking -- A Theological ABC*
>
>

Comment 5: Examples of Mission As Intersection

Your unique and individual Mission will most likely turn out to be a mission of Love, acted out in one or all of three arenas: either in the Kingdom of the Mind, whose goal is to bring more Truth into the world; or in the Kingdom of the Heart, whose goal is to bring more Beauty into the world; or in the Kingdom of the Will, whose goal is to bring more Perfection into the world, through Service.

Here are some examples:

"My mission is, out of the rich reservoir of love which God seems to have given me, to nurture and show love to others -- most particularly to those who are suffering from incurable diseases."

"My mission is to draw maps for people to show them how to get to God."

"My mission is to create the purest foods I can, to help people's bodies not get in the way of their spiritual growth."

"My mission is to make the finest harps I can so that people can hear the voice of God in the wind."

"My mission is to make people laugh, so that the travail of this earthly life doesn't seem quite so hard to them."

"My mission is to help people know the truth, in love, about what is happening out in the world, so that there will be more honesty in the world."

"My mission is to weep with those who weep, so that in my arms they may feel themselves in the arms of that Eternal Love which sent me and which created them."

"My mission is to create beautiful gardens, so that in the lilies of the field people may behold the Beauty of God and be reminded of the Beauty of Holiness."

Comment 6: Life As Long As Your Mission Requires

Knowing that you came to Earth for a reason, and knowing what that Mission is, throws an entirely different light upon your life from now on. You are, generally speaking, delivered from any further fear about how long you have to live. You may settle it in your heart that you are here until God chooses to think that you have accomplished your Mission, or until God has a greater Mission for you in another Realm. You need to be a good steward of what He has given you, while you are here; but you do not need to be an anxious steward or stewardess.

You need to attend to your health, *but you do not need to constantly worry about it*. You need to meditate on your death, *but you do not need to be constantly preoccupied with it*. To paraphrase the glorious words of G. K. Chesterton: "**We now have a strong desire for living combined with a strange carelessness about dying. We desire life like water and yet are ready to drink death like wine**." We know that we are here to do what we came to do, and we need not worry about anything else.

Final Comment: A Job-Hunt Done Well

If you approach your job-hunt as an opportunity to work on this issue as well as the issue of how you will keep body and soul together, then hopefully your job-hunt will end with your being able to say: "Life has deep meaning to me, now. I have discovered more than my ideal job; I have found my Mission, and the reason why I am here on Earth."

APPENDIX A

The Flower Exercise

A PICTURE OF THE JOB OF YOUR DREAMS

YOUR FLOWER

IN ORDER TO HUNT FOR YOUR IDEAL JOB, or even something close to your ideal job, you must have a picture of it, in your head. The clearer the picture, the easier it will be to hunt for it. The purpose of this exercise is to guide you as you draw that picture.

We have chosen a "Flower" as the model for that picture. While such expressions as "plugging in," "turning on," and other common phrases portray you (implicitly) as a machine, you are actually much more like a Flower than a machine. That is to say, you flourish in some job-environments, but wither in others. Therefore, the purpose of putting together this Flower Picture of yourself is to help you identify what kind of a work climate you will flourish in, and thus do your very best work. Your twin goals should be to be as happy as you can be at your job, while at the same time you do your most effective work.

There is a picture of the Flower on pages 330–331, that you can use as your worksheet.

As you can see, skills are at the center of the Flower, even as they are at the center of your mission, career, or job. They are listed in order of priority.

Surrounding them are six petals. Listed in the order in which you will work on them, they are:

1. Geography
2. Interests (Fields of Fascination)
3. People Environments
4. Values, Purposes, and Goals
5. Working Conditions
6. Salary & Level of Responsibility

When you are done filling in these skills and petals, you will have the complete Flower picture of your Ideal Job. Okay? Then, get out your pen or pencil and let's get started.

The Flower

A Picture of The Job of Your Dreams

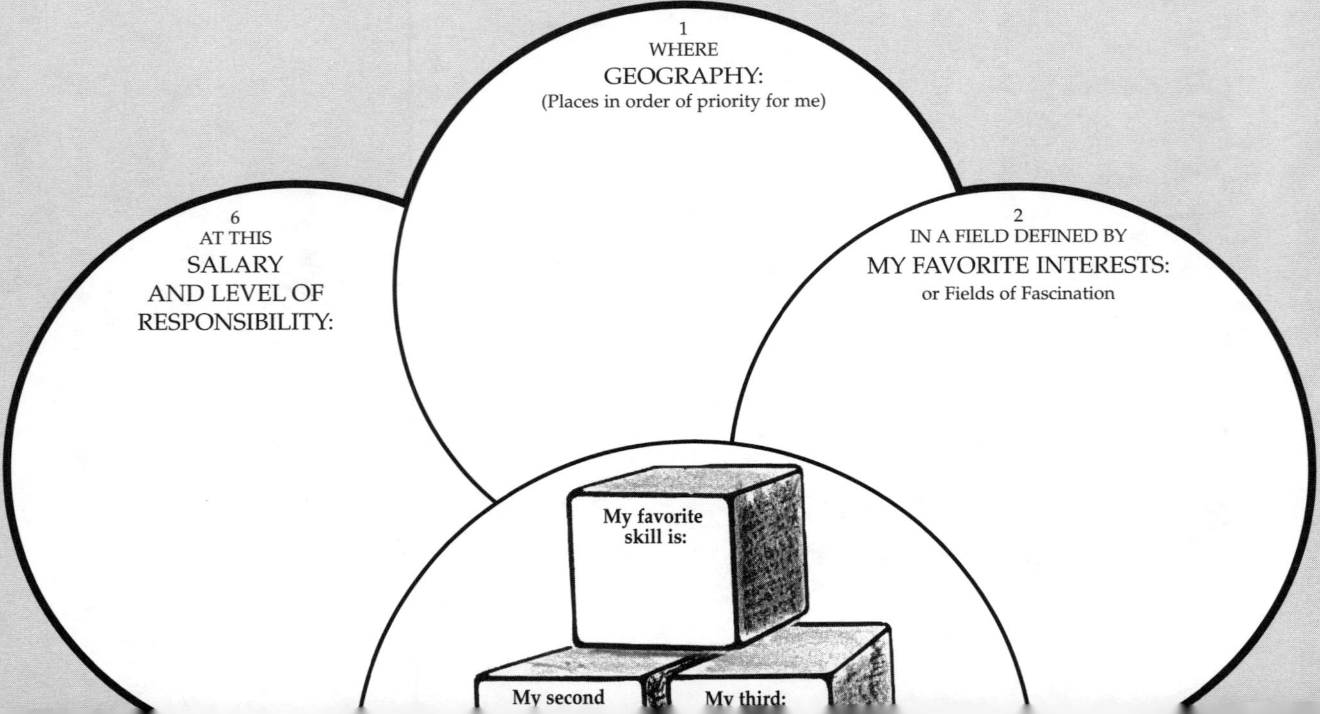

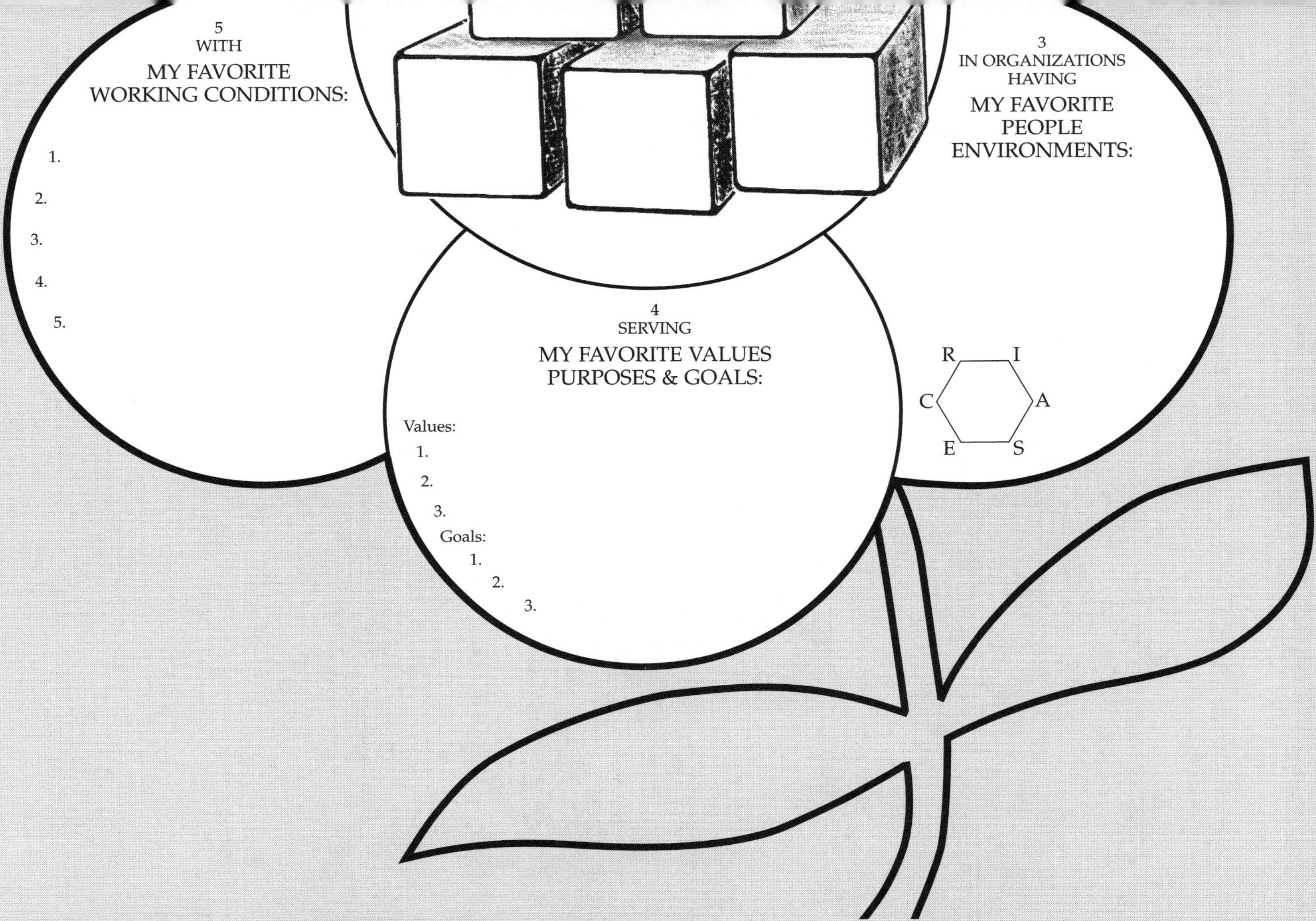
5
WITH
MY FAVORITE
WORKING CONDITIONS:
1.
2.
3.
4.
5.
4
SERVING
MY FAVORITE VALUES
PURPOSES & GOALS:
Values:
1.
2.
3.
Goals:
1.
2.
3.
3
IN ORGANIZATIONS
HAVING
MY FAVORITE
PEOPLE
ENVIRONMENTS:
R
I
C
A
E
S

Example (Six Favorite Skills)

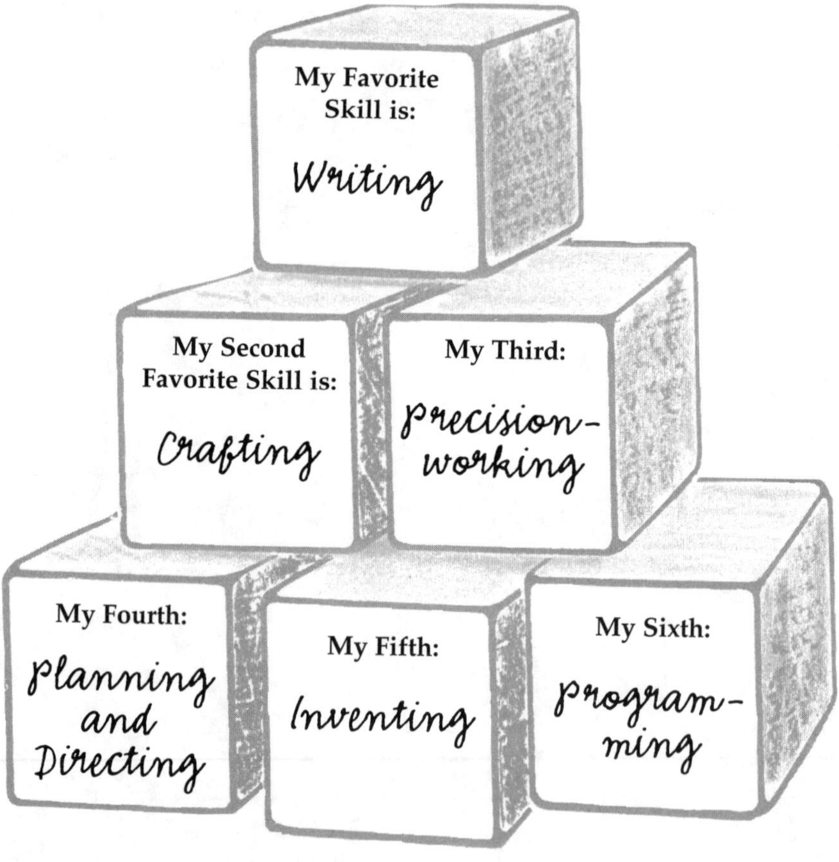

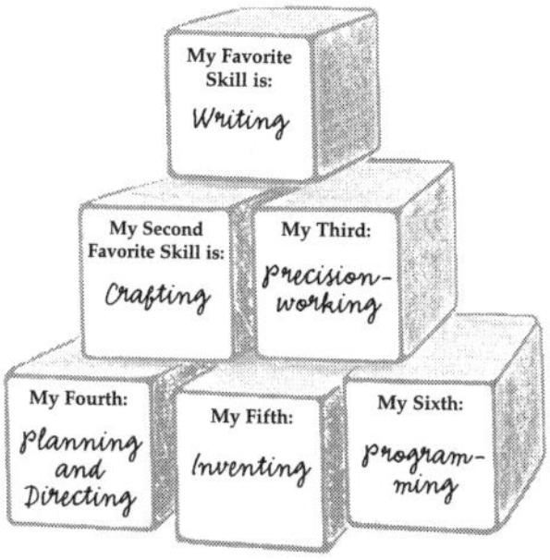

Your Favorite Transferable Skills

We begin with skills. You must, first of all, identify your favorite transferable skills that you most enjoy using, *in order of priority or importance to you.* Here are the five steps to accomplishing that.

1. Write Your First Story

To do this, you will need to write **seven stories** about things you did just because they were fun, or because they gave you a sense of adventure, or gave you a sense of accomplishment. It does not matter whether anyone else ever knew about this accomplishment, or not. Each story can be about something you did at work, or in school, or at play -- and can be from any time period of your life. It should not be more than two or three paragraphs, in length.

> Below is a form to help you write each of your Seven Stories. *(You will obviously want to go down to Kinko's or your local copy shop and make seven copies of this form* before *you begin filling it out, for the first time. The copies work best if you make them on seven pieces of* $8\frac{1}{2}'' \times 11''$ *paper,* turned sideways.*)*

If you need an example of what to put in each of the five columns, turn back to page 167ff here in *Parachute.* After you have written your first story, we will show you how to analyze it for the transferable skills that you used therein.

My Seven Life Stories

Column 1 Your Goal: What You Want to Accomplish	Column 2 Some Kind of Obstacle (or limit, hurdle or restraint you had to overcome before it could be accomplished)	Column 3 What You Did Step-by-Step (It may help if you pretend you are telling this story to a whining 4-year-old child, who keeps asking, after each of your sentences, "An' then whadja do? An' then whadja do?")	Column 4 Description of the Result (What you accomplished)	Column 5 Any Measure or Quantities To Prove Your Achievement

2. Analyze The Story for Transferable Skills

Once you have written Story #1 (and before you write the other six), you will want to analyze it for the transferable skills you *used.* (You can decide later if you loved those skills or not. For now, just do an inventory.)

To do this inventory, go to the list of Skills Keys found on pages 336–341, which resemble a series of typewriter keys. Transferable skills divide into:

1. Physical Skills: the transferable skills you enjoy, using primarily *your hands or body* -- with things, or nature;
2. Mental Skills: the transferable skills you enjoy, using primarily *your mind* -- with data/information, ideas, or subjects;
3. Interpersonal Skills: the transferable skills you enjoy, involving primarily *personal relationships* -- as you serve or help people or animals, and their needs or problems.[1]

Therefore you will find three sets of Skills Keys, labeled accordingly.

As you look at each key in the three sets, the question you need to ask yourself, is: "Did I use this transferable skill *in this Story* (#1)?"

That is the *only* question you ask yourself (at the moment). Then you go to the little box named #1 (under each Skill Key), and this is what you do:

If the answer is "Yes", fill in the little box, as shown below:

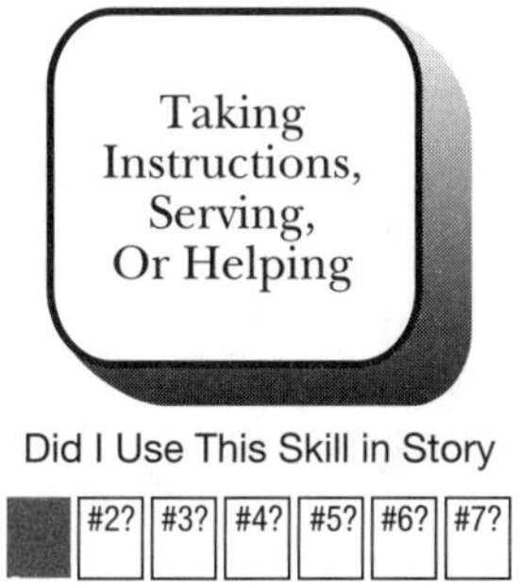

Yes

Ignore the other little boxes for the time being; they belong to your other stories (all the little boxes named #2 belong to Story #2, all the little boxes named #3 belong to Story #3, etc.).

My Physical Skills

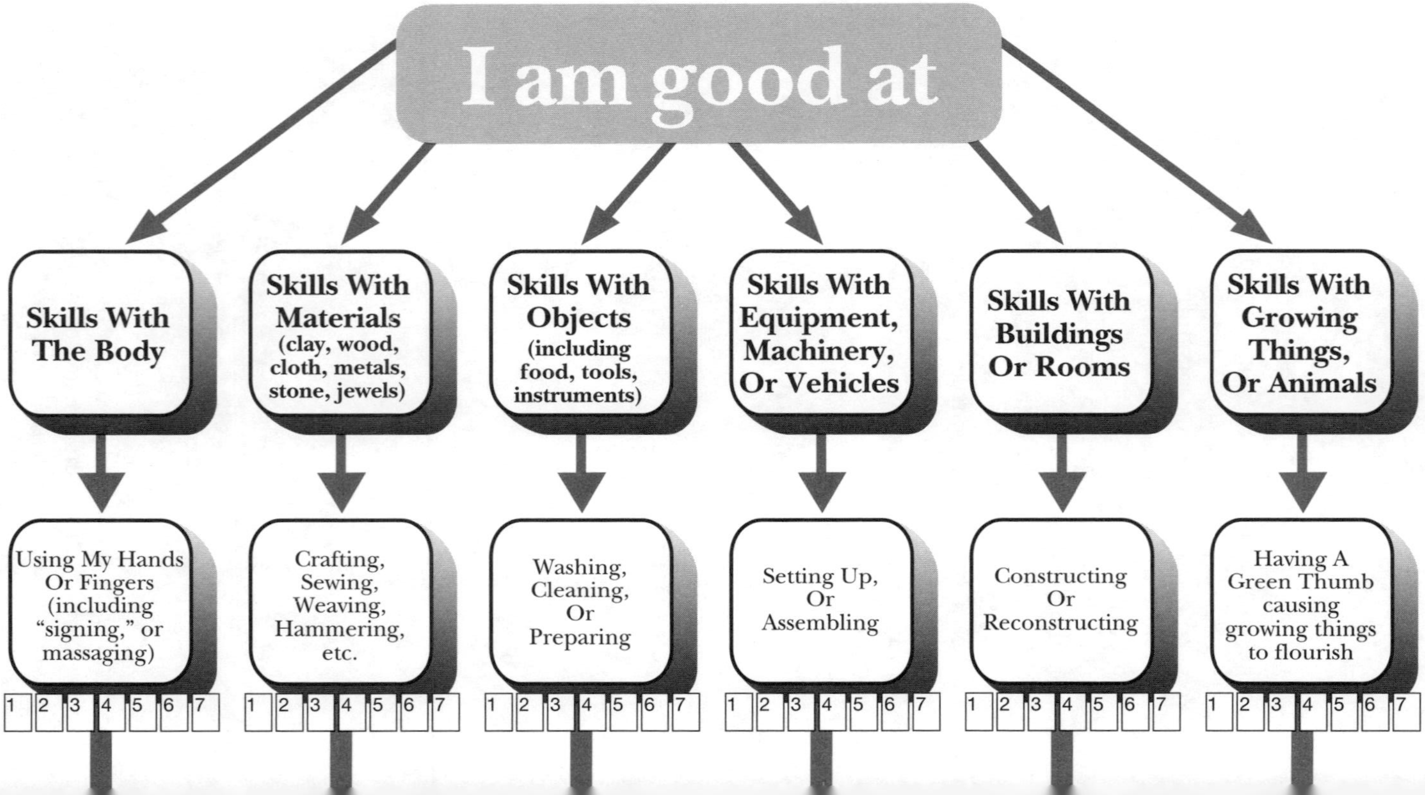

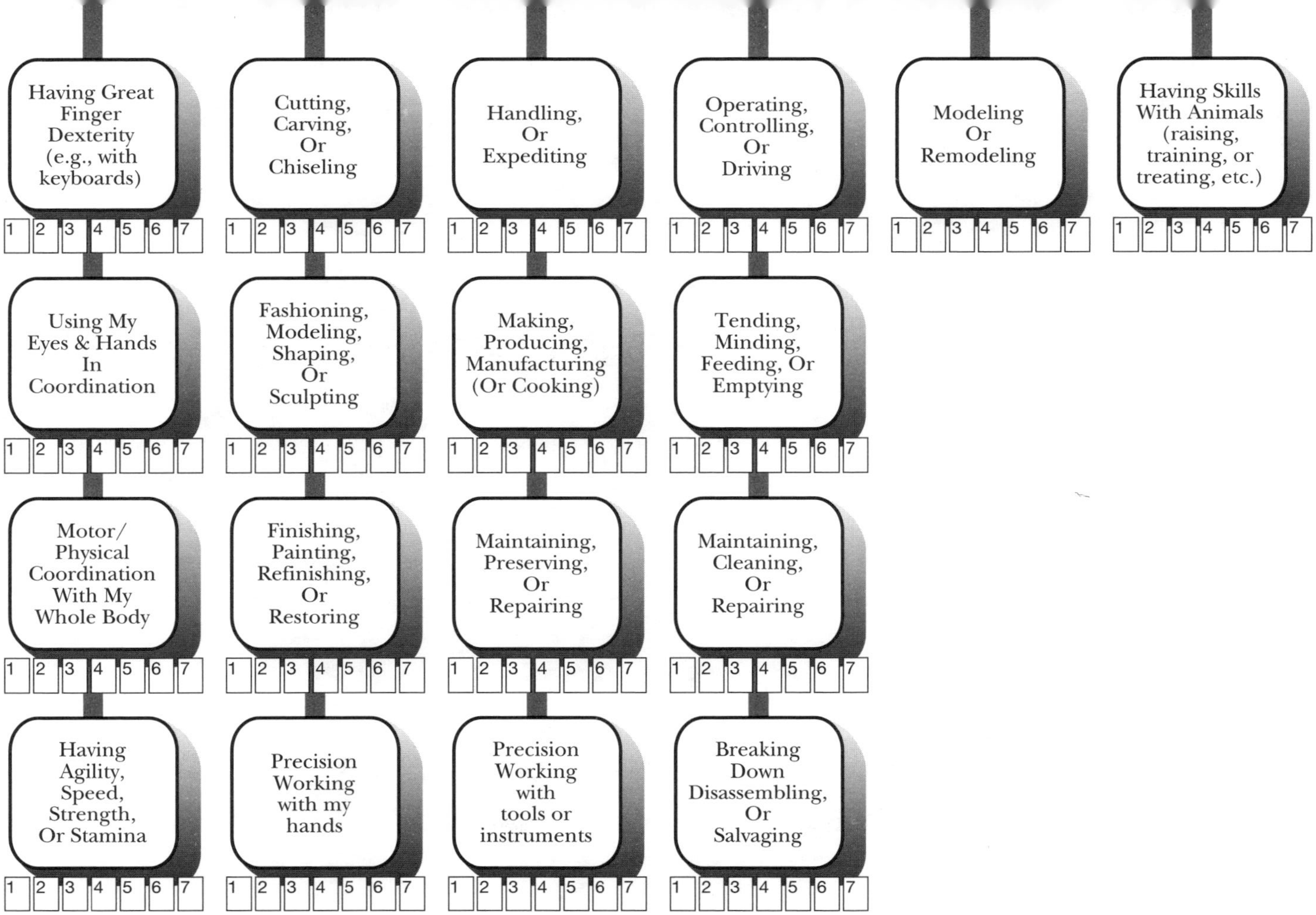
Having Great Finger Dexterity (e.g., with keyboards)
Cutting, Carving, Or Chiseling
Handling, Or Expediting
Operating, Controlling, Or Driving
Modeling Or Remodeling
Having Skills With Animals (raising, training, or treating, etc.)
Using My Eyes & Hands In Coordination
Fashioning, Modeling, Shaping, Or Sculpting
Making, Producing, Manufacturing (Or Cooking)
Tending, Minding, Feeding, Or Emptying
Motor/ Physical Coordination With My Whole Body
Finishing, Painting, Refinishing, Or Restoring
Maintaining, Preserving, Or Repairing
Maintaining, Cleaning, Or Repairing
Having Agility, Speed, Strength, Or Stamina
Precision Working with my hands
Precision Working with tools or instruments
Breaking Down Disassembling, Or Salvaging
1 2 3 4 5 6 7

My Mental Skills

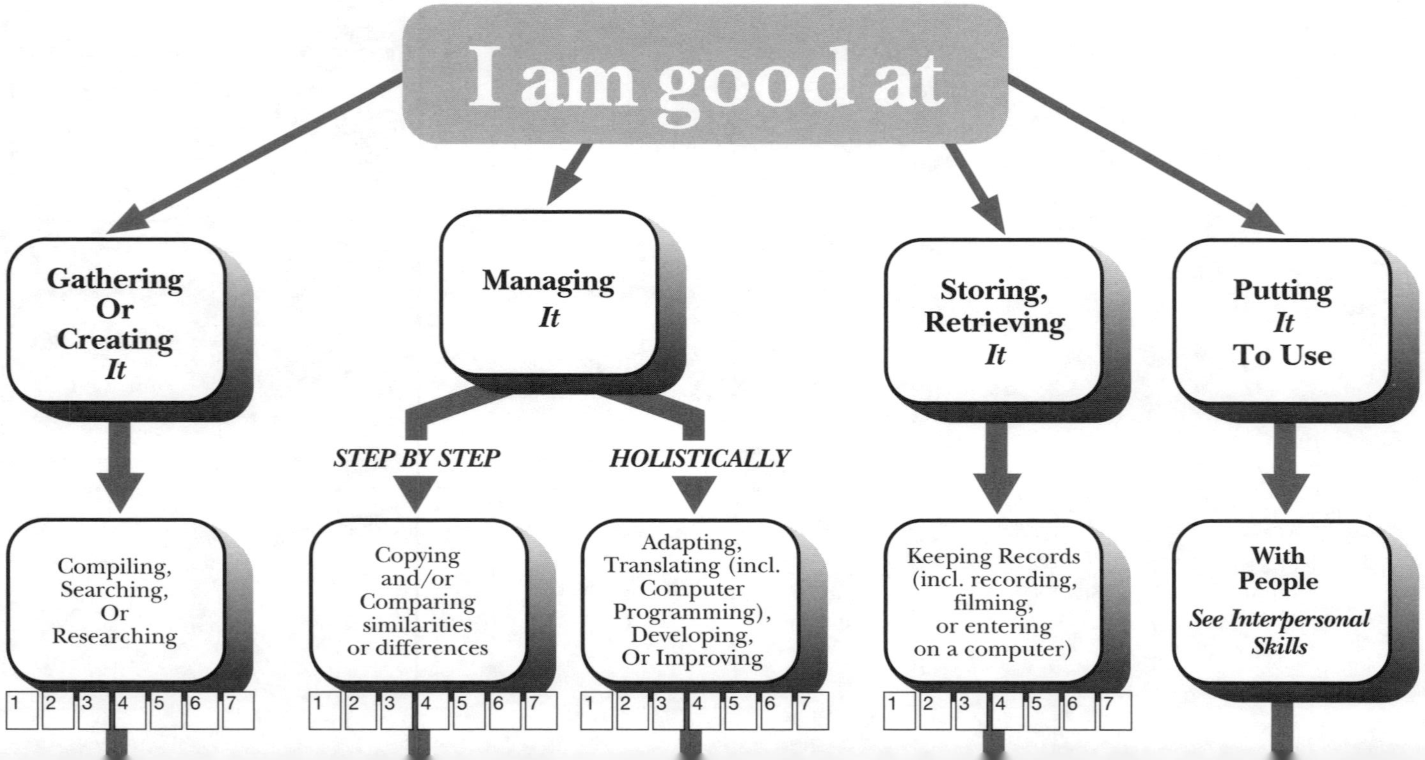
I am good at
Gathering Or Creating It
Managing It
Storing, Retrieving It
Putting It To Use
STEP BY STEP
HOLISTICALLY
Compiling, Searching, Or Researching
Copying and/or Comparing similarities or differences
Adapting, Translating (incl. Computer Programming), Developing, Or Improving
Keeping Records (incl. recording, filming, or entering on a computer)
With People
See Interpersonal Skills
1 2 3 4 5 6 7
1 2 3 4 5 6 7
1 2 3 4 5 6 7
1 2 3 4 5 6 7

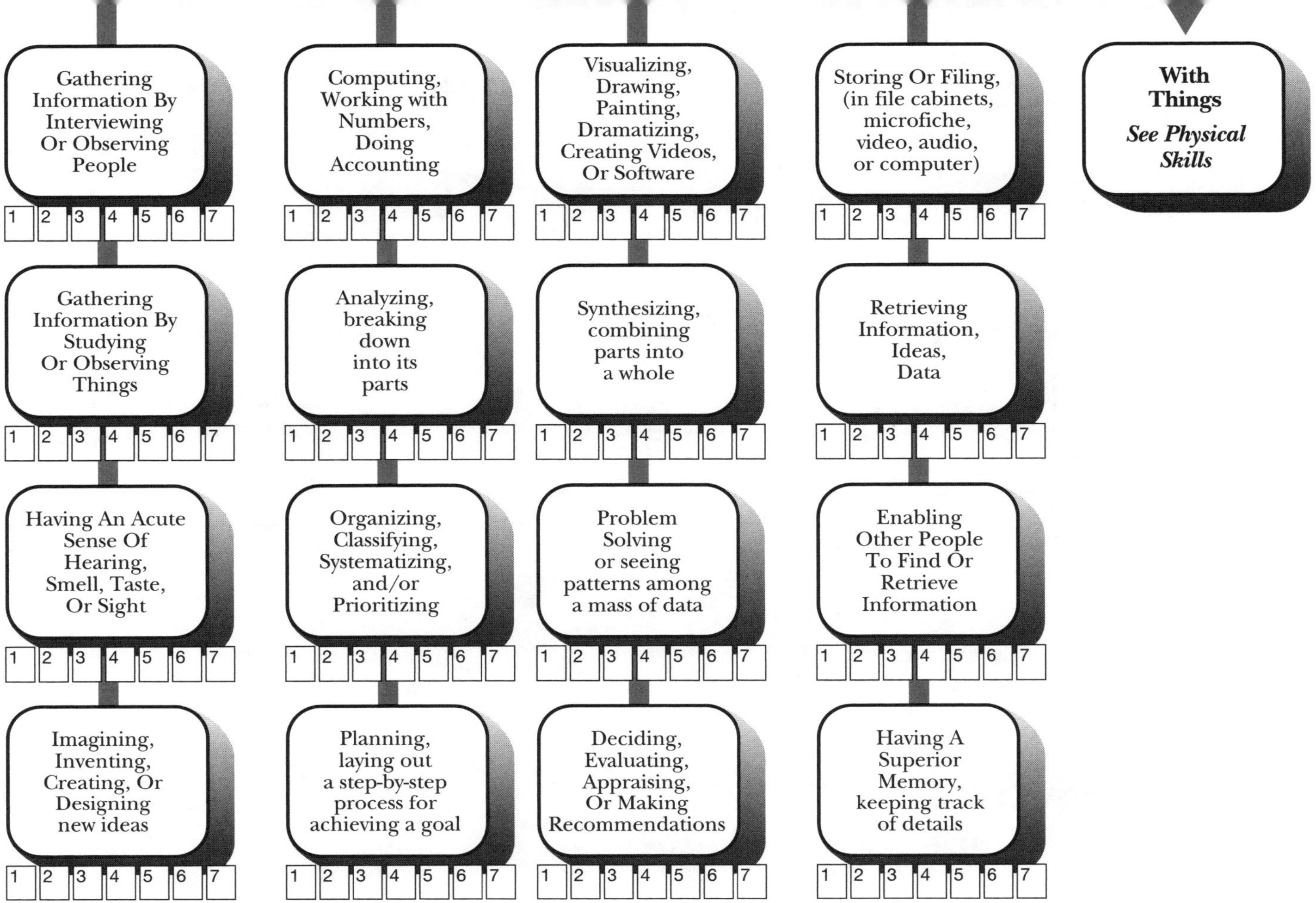
Gathering Information By Interviewing Or Observing People
1 2 3 4 5 6 7
Computing, Working with Numbers, Doing Accounting
1 2 3 4 5 6 7
Visualizing, Drawing, Painting, Dramatizing, Creating Videos, Or Software
1 2 3 4 5 6 7
Storing Or Filing, (in file cabinets, microfiche, video, audio, or computer)
1 2 3 4 5 6 7
With Things
See Physical Skills
Gathering Information By Studying Or Observing Things
1 2 3 4 5 6 7
Analyzing, breaking down into its parts
1 2 3 4 5 6 7
Synthesizing, combining parts into a whole
1 2 3 4 5 6 7
Retrieving Information, Ideas, Data
1 2 3 4 5 6 7
Having An Acute Sense Of Hearing, Smell, Taste, Or Sight
1 2 3 4 5 6 7
Organizing, Classifying, Systematizing, and/or Prioritizing
1 2 3 4 5 6 7
Problem Solving or seeing patterns among a mass of data
1 2 3 4 5 6 7
Enabling Other People To Find Or Retrieve Information
1 2 3 4 5 6 7
Imagining, Inventing, Creating, Or Designing new ideas
1 2 3 4 5 6 7
Planning, laying out a step-by-step process for achieving a goal
1 2 3 4 5 6 7
Deciding, Evaluating, Appraising, Or Making Recommendations
1 2 3 4 5 6 7
Having A Superior Memory, keeping track of details
1 2 3 4 5 6 7

My Interpersonal Skills

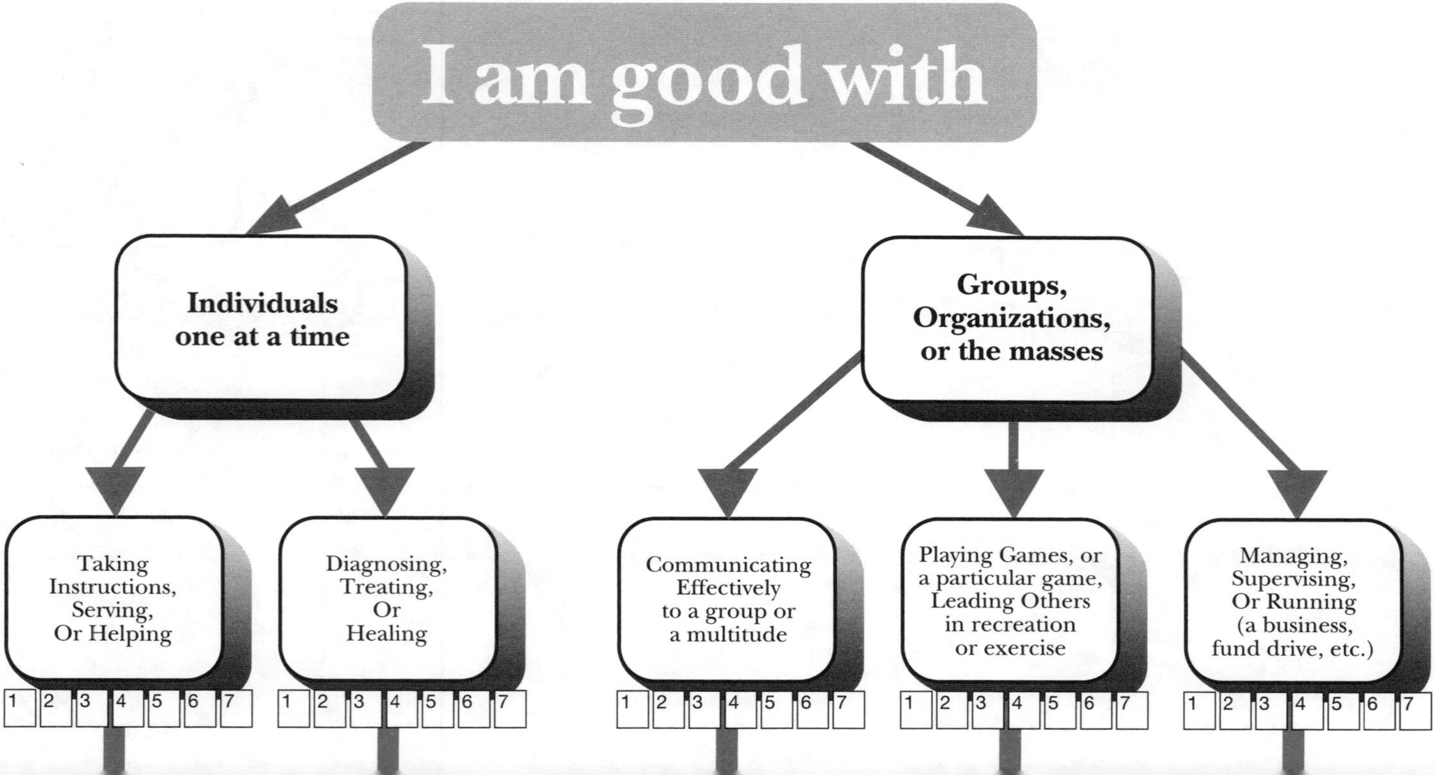
I am good with
Individuals one at a time
Groups, Organizations, or the masses
Taking Instructions, Serving, Or Helping
Diagnosing, Treating, Or Healing
Communicating Effectively to a group or a multitude
Playing Games, or a particular game, Leading Others in recreation or exercise
Managing, Supervising, Or Running (a business, fund drive, etc.)
1 2 3 4 5 6 7

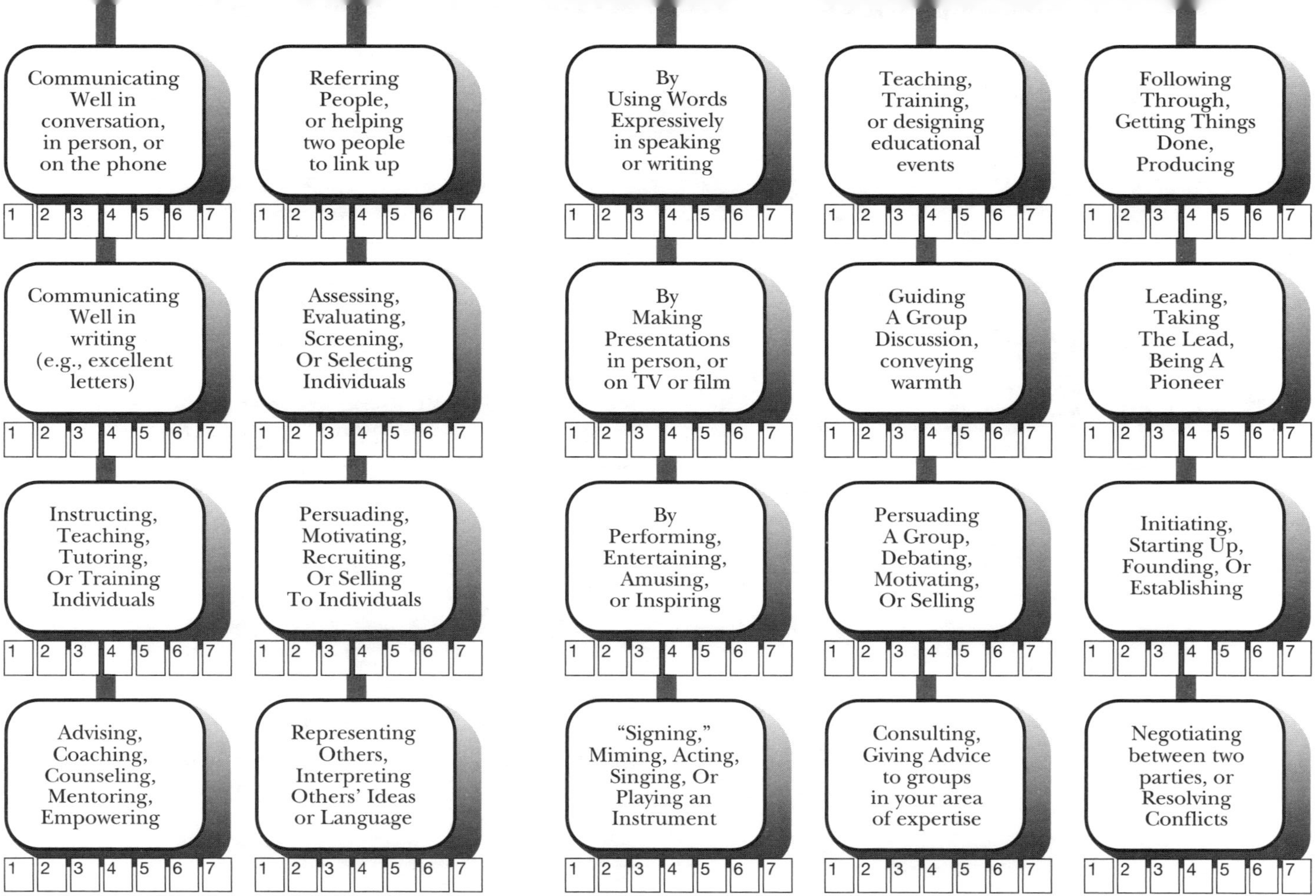
Communicating Well in conversation, in person, or on the phone
1 2 3 4 5 6 7
Communicating Well in writing (e.g., excellent letters)
1 2 3 4 5 6 7
Instructing, Teaching, Tutoring, Or Training Individuals
1 2 3 4 5 6 7
Advising, Coaching, Counseling, Mentoring, Empowering
1 2 3 4 5 6 7
Referring People, or helping two people to link up
1 2 3 4 5 6 7
Assessing, Evaluating, Screening, Or Selecting Individuals
1 2 3 4 5 6 7
Persuading, Motivating, Recruiting, Or Selling To Individuals
1 2 3 4 5 6 7
Representing Others, Interpreting Others' Ideas or Language
1 2 3 4 5 6 7
By Using Words Expressively in speaking or writing
1 2 3 4 5 6 7
By Making Presentations in person, or on TV or film
1 2 3 4 5 6 7
By Performing, Entertaining, Amusing, or Inspiring
1 2 3 4 5 6 7
"Signing," Miming, Acting, Singing, Or Playing an Instrument
1 2 3 4 5 6 7
Teaching, Training, or designing educational events
1 2 3 4 5 6 7
Guiding A Group Discussion, conveying warmth
1 2 3 4 5 6 7
Persuading A Group, Debating, Motivating, Or Selling
1 2 3 4 5 6 7
Consulting, Giving Advice to groups in your area of expertise
1 2 3 4 5 6 7
Following Through, Getting Things Done, Producing
1 2 3 4 5 6 7
Leading, Taking The Lead, Being A Pioneer
1 2 3 4 5 6 7
Initiating, Starting Up, Founding, Or Establishing
1 2 3 4 5 6 7
Negotiating between two parties, or Resolving Conflicts
1 2 3 4 5 6 7

If the answer is "No", leave the box labeled #1 blank, as shown below:

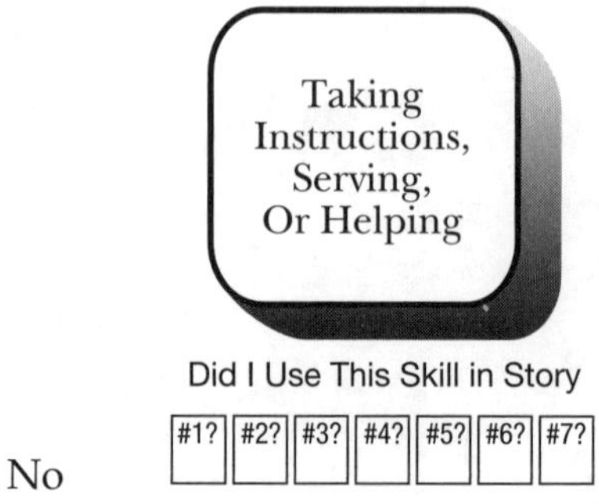

3. Write Six Other Stories, and Analyze Them for Transferable Skills

Voila! You are done with Story #1. However, 'one swallow doth not a summer make,' so the fact that you used certain skills in this first Story doesn't tell you much. What you are looking for is **patterns** -- transferable skills that keep reappearing in story after story. They keep reappearing because they are your favorites (assuming you chose stories where you were *really* enjoying yourself).

So, now, write Story #2, from any period in your life, analyze it using the keys, etc., etc. And keep this process up, until you have written, and analyzed, seven stories.

4. Decide Which Skills Are Your Favorites, and Prioritize Them

When you're done writing and analyzing all Seven Stories, you should now go back and look over the six pages of "Skills Keys" to see which skills got used the most often. Make a list.

Cross out any that you don't enjoy using.

Prioritize the remainder, using the Prioritizing Grids on the next two pages.

The Prioritizing Grid

How to Prioritize Your Lists of Anything

Here is a method for taking (say) ten items, and figuring out which one is most important to you, which is next most important, etc.

• Insert the items to be prioritized, in any order, in Section A. Then compare two items at a time, circling the one you prefer -- between the two -- in Section B. Which one is more important to you? State the question any way you want to: In the case of geographical factors, you might ask. "If I were being offered two jobs, one in an area that had factor #1, but not factor #2; the other in an area that had factor #2, but not factor #1, all other things being equal, which job would I take? Circle it. Then go on to the next pair, etc.

• When you are all done, count up the number of times each number got circled, all told. Enter these totals on the TIMES line in Section C. Then notice the number of times each item was circled ("Times" = "Times Circled"). This determines the item's ranking. Most circled = #1, next most circled = #2, etc. Enter this ranking on the RANK line in Section C. If two items are circled the same number of times, look back in Section B to see -- when those two were compared there -- which one you preferred. Give that one an extra half point. List the items, now in their proper rank, in Section D.

> *Since you will be using this Prioritizing Grid more than once in these exercises you will want to go down to Kinko's or your local copy shop and make a number of copies of this form* before *you begin filling it in, for the first time.*

The question to ask yourself, on the Grid, as you confront each 'pair' is: "If I were offered two jobs, and in one job I could use the first skill, but not the second; while in the other job, I could use the second skill, but not the first, which job would I choose?" When you've got your ten favorite transferable skills, in order, copy the top six onto the Flower Diagram on pages 330–331.

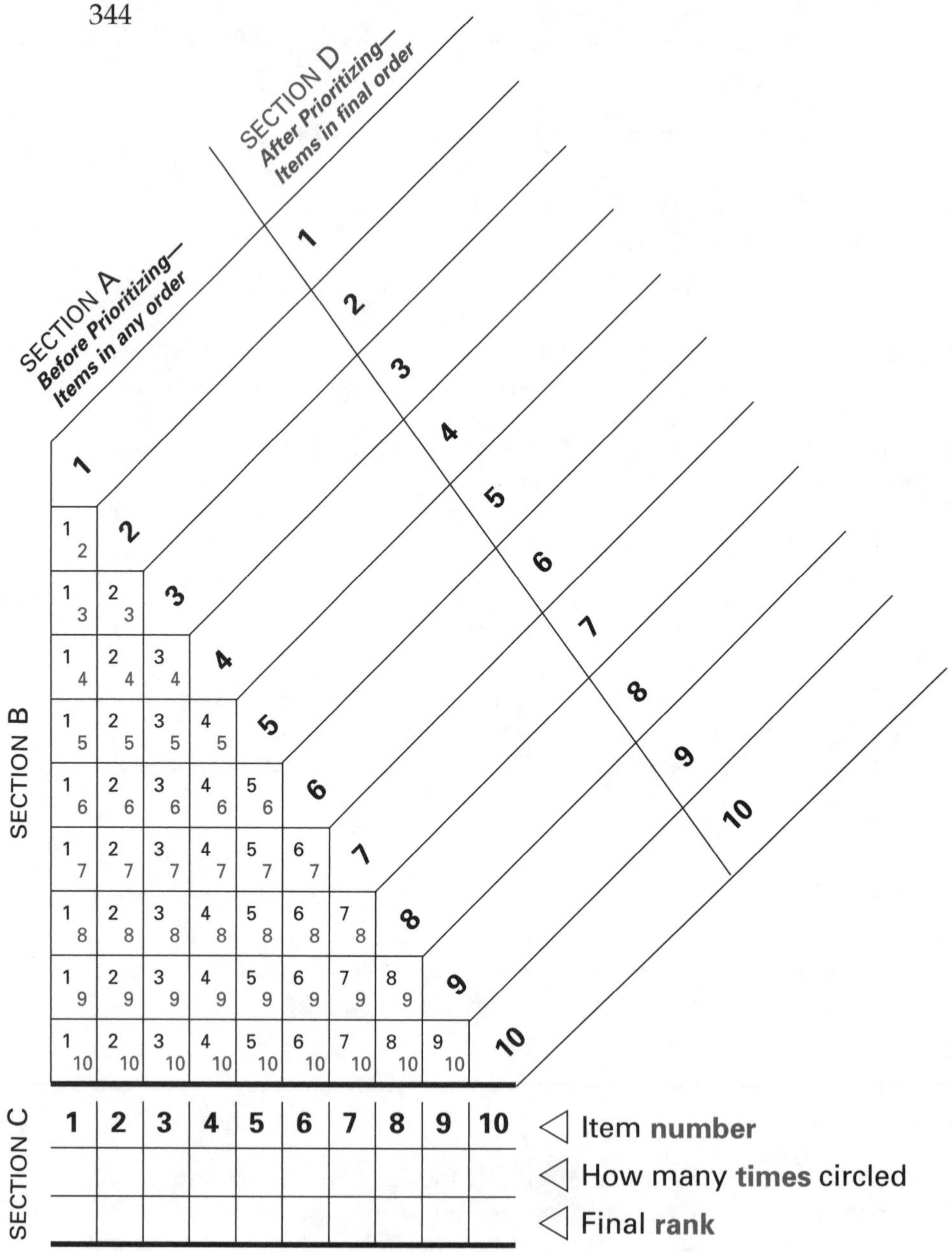

Prioritzing Grid
for 10 Items

1 1 1 1 1 1 1 1 1 1 1 1 1 1 1 1 1 1 1 1 1 1 1
2 3 4 5 6 7 8 9 10 11 12 13 14 15 16 17 18 19 20 21 22 23 24

2 2 2 2 2 2 2 2 2 2 2 2 2 2 2 2 2 2 2 2 2 2
3 4 5 6 7 8 9 10 11 12 13 14 15 16 17 18 19 20 21 22 23 24

3 3 3 3 3 3 3 3 3 3 3 3 3 3 3 3 3 3 3 3 3
4 5 6 7 8 9 10 11 12 13 14 15 16 17 18 19 20 21 22 23 24

4 4 4 4 4 4 4 4 4 4 4 4 4 4 4 4 4 4 4 4
5 6 7 8 9 10 11 12 13 14 15 16 17 18 19 20 21 22 23 24

5 5 5 5 5 5 5 5 5 5 5 5 5 5 5 5 5 5 5
6 7 8 9 10 11 12 13 14 15 16 17 18 19 20 21 22 23 24

6 6 6 6 6 6 6 6 6 6 6 6 6 6 6 6 6 6
7 8 9 10 11 12 13 14 15 16 17 18 19 20 21 22 23 24

7 7 7 7 7 7 7 7 7 7 7 7 7 7 7 7 7
8 9 10 11 12 13 14 15 16 17 18 19 20 21 22 23 24

8 8 8 8 8 8 8 8 8 8 8 8 8 8 8 8
9 10 11 12 13 14 15 16 17 18 19 20 21 22 23 24

9 9 9 9 9 9 9 9 9 9 9 9 9 9 9
10 11 12 13 14 15 16 17 18 19 20 21 22 23 24

10 10 10 10 10 10 10 10 10 10 10 10 10 10
11 12 13 14 15 16 17 18 19 20 21 22 23 24

11 11 11 11 11 11 11 11 11 11 11 11 11
12 13 14 15 16 17 18 19 20 21 22 23 24

12 12 12 12 12 12 12 12 12 12 12 12
13 14 15 16 17 18 19 20 21 22 23 24

13 13 13 13 13 13 13 13 13 13 13
14 15 16 17 18 19 20 21 22 23 24

14 14 14 14 14 14 14 14 14 14
15 16 17 18 19 20 21 22 23 24

15 15 15 15 15 15 15 15 15
16 17 18 19 20 21 22 23 24

16 16 16 16 16 16 16 16
17 18 19 20 21 22 23 24

17 17 17 17 17 17 17
18 19 20 21 22 23 24

18 18 18 18 18 18
19 20 21 22 23 24

19 19 19 19 19
20 21 22 23 24

20 20 20 20
21 22 23 24

21 21 21
22 23 24

22 22
23 24

23
24

Total times each number got circled

1	2	3	4	5	6
7	8	9	10	11	12
13	14	15	16	17	18
19	20	21	22	23	24

Prioritizing Grid for 24 Items

5. 'Flesh Out' Your Favorite Transferable Skills With Your Traits

In general, traits describe:
How you deal with time, and promptness.
How you deal with people and emotions.
How you deal with authority, and being told what to do at your job.
How you deal with supervision, and being told how to do your job.
How you deal with impulse vs. self-discipline, within yourself.
How you deal with initiative vs. response, within yourself.
How you deal with crises or problems.

A Check-List of My Strongest Traits

I am very. . .

- ❑ Accurate
- ❑ Achievement-oriented
- ❑ Adaptable
- ❑ Adept
- ❑ Adept at having fun
- ❑ Adventuresome
- ❑ Alert
- ❑ Appreciative
- ❑ Assertive
- ❑ Astute
- ❑ Authoritative
- ❑ Calm
- ❑ Cautious
- ❑ Charismatic
- ❑ Competent
- ❑ Consistent
- ❑ Contagious in my enthusiasm
- ❑ Cooperative
- ❑ Courageous
- ❑ Creative
- ❑ Decisive
- ❑ Deliberate
- ❑ Dependable/have dependability
- ❑ Diligent
- ❑ Diplomatic
- ❑ Discreet
- ❑ Driving
- ❑ Dynamic
- ❑ Extremely economical
- ❑ Effective
- ❑ Energetic
- ❑ Enthusiastic
- ❑ Exceptional
- ❑ Exhaustive
- ❑ Experienced
- ❑ Expert
- ❑ Firm
- ❑ Flexible
- ❑ Humanly oriented
- ❑ Impulsive
- ❑ Independent
- ❑ Innovative
- ❑ Knowledgeable
- ❑ Loyal
- ❑ Methodical
- ❑ Objective
- ❑ Open-minded
- ❑ Outgoing
- ❑ Outstanding
- ❑ Patient
- ❑ Penetrating
- ❑ Perceptive
- ❑ Persevering
- ❑ Persistent
- ❑ Pioneering
- ❑ Practical
- ❑ Professional
- ❑ Protective
- ❑ Punctual
- ❑ Quick/work quickly
- ❑ Rational
- ❑ Realistic
- ❑ Reliable
- ❑ Resourceful
- ❑ Responsible
- ❑ Responsive
- ❑ Safeguarding
- ❑ Self-motivated
- ❑ Self-reliant
- ❑ Sensitive
- ❑ Sophisticated, very sophisticated
- ❑ Strong
- ❑ Supportive
- ❑ Tactful
- ❑ Thorough
- ❑ Unique
- ❑ Unusual
- ❑ Versatile
- ❑ Vigorous

Once you've checked off your favorites, prioritize them (using another copy of the Prioritizing Grid if necessary), and then integrate your favorites into the building blocks of transferable skills, as described on page 333.

SOME PROBLEMS YOU MAY RUN INTO, WHILE DOING YOUR SKILL-IDENTIFICATION

In trying to identify your skills, it will not be surprising if you run into some problems. Let us look at the five most common ones that have arisen for job-hunters in the past:

1. *"When I write my skill stories, I don't know exactly what is an achievement."*

When you're looking for a story/achievement to illustrate one of your skills, you're *not* looking for something that only you have done, in the history of the world. What you're looking for is a lot simpler than that. You're looking for *any* time in your life when you did something that was, at that time of your life, a source of pride and accomplishment *for you.* It might have been learning to ride a bike. It might be achieving your first quota, at work. It might be a particularly significant project that you designed, in mid-life. It doesn't matter whether or not it pleased anybody else; it only matters that it pleased you.

I like Bernard Haldane's definition of an achievement. He says it is: something you yourself feel you have done well, that you also enjoyed doing and felt proud of. In other words you are looking for an accomplishment which gave you two pleasures: enjoyment while doing it, and satisfaction from the outcome. That doesn't mean you may not have sweated as you did it, or hated *some parts* of the process, but it does mean that basically you enjoyed *most of* the process. The pleasure was not simply in the outcome, but along the way as well. Generally speaking, an achievement will have all the parts outlined on page 167ff.

2. *"I don't see why I should look for skills I enjoy; it seems to me that employers will only want to know what skills I do well. They will not care whether I enjoy using the skill or not."*

Well, sure, it is important for you to find the skills you do well, above all else. But, generally speaking, that is hard for you to evaluate about yourself. *Do I do this well, or not? Compared to whom?* Even aptitude tests can't resolve this dilemma for you. So it's better to take the following circular equation, which experience has shown to be true:

If it is a skill you do well, you will generally enjoy it.

If it is a skill you enjoy, it is generally because you do it well.

With these equations in hand, you will see that -- since they are equal anyway -- it is much more useful to ask yourself, "Do I enjoy doing it?" instead of hunting for the elusive "Do I do it well?" I repeat: listing the skills you most *enjoy* is -- in most cases -- just another way of listing the skills you do *best.*

The reason why this idea -- of making *enjoyment* the key -- causes such feelings of uncomfortableness in so many of us is that we have an old historical tradition in this country which insinuates you shouldn't really enjoy yourself in life. To suffer is virtuous.

Sample: Two girls do babysitting. One hates it. One enjoys it thoroughly. Which is more virtuous in God's sight? According to that old tradition, the one who hates it is more virtuous. Some of us feel this instinctively, even if more logical thought says, Whoa!

We have this subconscious fear that if we are caught enjoying life, punishment looms. Thus, the story of two Scotsmen who met on the street one day: "Isn't this a beautiful day?" said one. "Aye," said the other, "but we'll pay for it."

We feel it is okay to talk about our failures, but not about our successes. To talk about our successes appears to be boasting, and that is manifestly a sin. Or so we think. We shouldn't be enjoying so much about ourselves.

But look at the birds of the air, or watch your pets at play. You will notice one distinctive fact about that part of God's creation: when a bird or a pet does what it is meant to do, by God and nature, it manifests true joy.

Joy is so clearly a part of God's plan for us. God wants us to eat; therefore He made eating enjoyable. God wants us to sleep; therefore He made sleeping enjoyable. God wants us to procreate, love, and make love; therefore He made sex enjoyable, and love even more so.

Likewise, God gives to each of us unique combinations of skills and talents which He wants us to contribute to His general plan -- to the symphony of the world, and the music of the spheres. Therefore, **when we use the talents He most wants each of us to use, He attends it with a feeling of great joy.** Everywhere in God's plan for His creation, joy rewards right action.

Bad employers will not care whether you enjoy a particular task, or not. But good employers will care greatly. They know that unless a would-be employee has **enthusiasm** for his or her work, the quality of that work will always suffer.

3. *"I have no difficulty finding stories to write up, from my life, that I consider to be enjoyable achievements; but once these are written, I have great difficulty in seeing what the skills are -- even if I stare at the skills keys in the Exercises* for hours. *I need somebody else's insight."*

You may want to consider getting two friends or two other members of your family to sit down with you, and do skill identification through the practice of 'Trioing' which I invented some twenty years ago to help with this very problem. This practice is fully described in my book, *Where Do I Go From Here With My Life?* But to save you the trouble of reading it, here is -- in general -- how it goes:

a. Each of the three of you quietly writes up some story of an accomplishment in their life that was enjoyable.

b. Each of the three of you quietly analyzes just your own story to see what skills you see there; you jot these down.

c. One of you then volunteers to go first. You read your story aloud. The other two jot down on a piece of paper whatever skills they hear you using. They ask you to pause if they're having trouble keeping up. You finish your story. You read aloud the skills *you* picked out in that story.

d. Then the second person tells you what's on their list: what skills *they* heard you use in your story. You copy them down, below your own list, even if you don't agree with every one of them.

e. Then the third person tells you what's on their list; what skills *they* heard you use in your story. You copy them down, below your own list, even if you don't agree with every one of them.

f. When they're both done, you ask them any questions for further elaboration that you may have. *"What did you mean by this skill? Where did you think you heard me using it?"*

g. Now it is the next person's turn, and you repeat steps 'c' through 'f' with them. Then it is the third person's turn, and you repeat steps 'c' through 'f' with them.

h. Now it is time to move on to a second story for each of you, so you begin with steps 'a' through 'g' all over again, except that each of you writes a new story. And so on, through seven stories.

4. *"I don't like the skill words you offer in the Exercises. Can't I use my own words, the ones I'm familiar with from my past profession?"*

It's okay to invent your own words for your skills, but it is not useful to state your transferable skills in the jargon of your old profession, such as (in the case of ex-clergy), *"I am good at preaching."* If you are going to choose a new career, out there in what people call the secular world, you must not use language that locks you into the past -- or suggests that you were good in one profession but in one profession only. Therefore, it is important to take jargon words such as *preaching* and ask yourself what is its larger form? *"Teaching?"* Perhaps. *"Motivating people?"* Perhaps. *"Inspiring people to the depths of their being?"* Perhaps. Only you can say what is true, for you. But in one way or another be sure to get your skills out of any jargon that locks you into your past career.

5. *"Once I've listed my favorite transferable skills, I see immediately a job-title that they point to. Is that okay?"*

Nope. Once you've finished your skill-identification, steer clear of prematurely putting a job-title on the skills you see. Skills can point to *many* different jobs, which have a multitude of titles. Therefore, don't lock yourself in, prematurely. *"I'm looking for a job where I can **use** the following skills,"* is fine. But, *"I'm looking for a job where I can **be** a (job-title)"* is a no-no, at this point in your job-hunt. Always define **WHAT** you want to do with your life and **WHAT** you have, to offer to the world, in terms of your favorite talents/gifts/skills -- not in terms of a job-title. That way, you can stay mobile in the midst of this constantly changing economy, where you never know what's going to happen next.

Petal #1
Geography

Even if you *love* where you are now, or even if you're *stuck* where you are now, you never know when an opportunity may suddenly open up for you, down the road. You want to be ready. Don't wait until then to do this exercise; do it now!

The question you need to answer is: Where would you most like to live and work, if you had a choice (besides where you are now)? In answering this question, it is important -- before you come to names -- to list the geographical *factors* that are important to you.

To help you do this, fill out the accompanying chart. *(You may copy it on to a larger piece of paper if you wish, before you begin working on it. And, if you are doing this exercise with a partner, make a copy of the chart, for them also, before you start filling it out, so that each of you may have a 'clean' copy of your own.)*

My Geographical Preferences

Decision Making for Just You

Column 1 Names of Places I Have Lived	*Column 2* From the Past: Negatives	*Column 3* Translating the Negatives into Positives	*Column 4* Ranking of My Positives
	Factors I Disliked and Still Dislike about That Place	Factors I Liked and Still Like about That Place	1. 2. 3. 4. 5. 6. 7. 8. 9. 10. 11. 12. 13. 14. 15.

Column 5 Places Which Fit These Criteria

Our Geographical Preferences

Decision Making for You and A Partner

Column 6 Ranking of His/Her Preferences	*Column 7* Combining Our Two Lists (Columns 4 & 6)	*Column 8* Places Which Fit These Criteria
a.	a.	
	1.	
b.	b.	
	2.	
c.	c.	
	3.	
d.	d.	
	4.	
e.	e.	
	5.	
f.	f.	
	6.	
g.	g.	
	7.	
h.	h.	
	8.	
i.	i.	
	9.	
j.	j.	
	10.	
k.	k.	
	11.	
l.	l.	
	12.	
m.	m.	
	13.	
n.	n.	
	14.	
o.	o.	
	15.	

Then, this is how you use the chart. There are seven easy steps:

1. List all the places (towns, cities, etc.) where you have ever lived. These go in Column 1.

2. List the factors you *disliked* and still dislike about each place. Naturally, there will be some repetition. In which case, just put an extra check mark in front of any factor you already have written down, when it comes up again. All of these negative factors go in Column 2.

3. Then take each of those negative factors and translate the negatives into positives.

This will not *necessarily* be the opposite. For example, "rains all the time" does not necessarily translate into "sunny all the time." It might be more like: "sunny at least 200 days a year." *It's your call.* All these positive factors go in Column 3. Feel free to add at the bottom of the column here, any positive factors you remember, off the top of your head, about the places in Column 1.

4. Now, rank your positive factors list (Column 3) in their order of importance, to you.

They will be things like: "has cultural opportunities," "skiing in the winter," "good newspaper," etc. List your top 10 positive factors, in exact order, in Column 4.

If you are baffled as to how to prioritize these factors in exact order, use the Prioritizing Grid on page 344. In using that grid, the question to ask yourself as you confront each 'pair' is: "If I could live in a place that had this first 'factor', but not the second; or if I could live in another place that had the second 'factor,' but not the first, in which place would I choose to live?"

5. When you are done, show this list of ten prioritized, positive factors to everyone you know, and ask them what cities, towns, or places they know of that have all or most of these factors.

You want to particularly emphasize the top factors, the ones that are the most important to you. If there is only a partial overlap between your factors and the places your friends suggest, be sure the overlap is in the factors you placed first on your list.

6. From all the names your friends suggest to you, choose the three that look most intriguing to you, in order of your personal preference, based on what you now know.

This goes in Column 5. These are the places you will want to find out more about, until you are sure which is your absolute first preference, second, and third.

> N.B. If you are doing this with a partner, you will not use Column 5. Instead, copy *their* Column 4 into your Column 6. Then alternately combine *their* first five factors and *your* first five factors, until you wind up with a list of ten altogether. (First you list their top one, then your top one, then their second preference, then your second preference, etc.) *This goes in Column 7.* It is *this* list of ten positive factors which you both then show to *everyone* you know, to ask them what cities, towns, or places they know of that have all or most of these factors, *beginning with the top ones*. From all the names those friends suggest to you, you then choose the three places that look the most intriguing to both of you, and rank them in order. This goes in Column 8.

7. Now, go back to the Flower Diagram on page 330, and copy Column 5 (or 8) onto the Geography petal.

You may also, if you wish, copy the first three to five Positives, from column 4 or 7. Voila! You are done with Geography. You now know the place(s) to find out more about, through their Chamber of Commerce, the Internet, a summer visit, etc.

Petal #2
Your Favorite Interests

You will find the instructions for inventorying these in chapter 9. You may have already done the exercises there.

When you have, come back to the Flower Diagram on page 330, and copy the Field(s) you selected, plus your strongest interests (favorite knowledges) on to the Interests petal, in order of priority for you.

Petal #3
Your Favorite People

With the great emphasis upon the importance of the environment, in recent years, it has become increasingly realized that jobs are environments too. The most important environmental factor always turns out to be people, since every job, except possibly that of a full-fledged hermit, surrounds us with people to one degree or another.

Indeed, many a good job has been ruined by the people one is surrounded by. Many a mundane job has been made delightful, by the people one is surrounded by. Therefore, it is important to think out what kinds of people you want to be surrounded by.

Dr. John L. Holland offers the best description of people environments. He says there are six principal ones:

1. The **Realistic** People-Environment: filled with people who prefer activities involving "the explicit, ordered, or systematic manipulation of objects, tools, machines, and animals." 'Realistic,' incidentally, refers to Plato's conception of "the real" as that which one can apprehend through the senses.

I summarize this as: **R** = people who like nature, or athletics, or tools & machinery.

2. The **Investigative** People-Environment: filled with people who prefer activities involving "the observation and symbolic, systematic, creative investigation of physical, biological or cultural phenomena."

I summarize this as: **I** = people who are very curious, liking to investigate or analyze things.

3. The **Artistic** People-Environment: filled with people who prefer activities involving "ambiguous, free, unsystematized activities and competencies to create art forms or products."

I summarize this as: **A** = people who are very artistic, imaginative and innovative.

4. The **Social** People-Environment: filled with people who prefer activities involving "the manipulation of others to inform, train, develop, cure or enlighten."

I summarize this as: **S** = people who are bent on trying to help, teach, or serve people.

5. The **Enterprising** People-Environment: filled with people who prefer activities involving "the manipulation of others to attain organizational or self-interest goals."

I summarize this as: E = people who like to start up projects or organizations, and/or influence or persuade people.

6. The **Conventional** People-Environment: filled with people who prefer activities involving "the explicit, ordered, systematic manipulation of data, such as keeping records, filing materials, reproducing materials, organizing written and numerical data according to a prescribed plan, operating business and data processing machines." 'Conventional,' incidentally, refers to the "values" which people in this environment usually hold -- representing the broad mainstream of the culture.

I summarize this as: C = people who like detailed work, and like to complete tasks or projects.

According to John's theory and findings everyone has three preferred people-environments, from among these six. The letters for your three preferred people-environments gives you what is called your "Holland Code."

> There is, incidentally, a relationship between the people you like to be surrounded by *and* your skills *and* your values. See John Holland's book, *Making Vocational Choices* (3rd. ed., 1997). You can procure it by writing to Psychological Assessment Resources, Inc., Box 998, Odessa, FL 33556. Phone: 1-800-331-8378. *The book is $29.95 at this writing.* PAR also has John Holland's instrument, called *The Self-Directed Search* (or SDS, for short) for discovering what your Holland Code is. PAR says you can take the test online for a small fee (if you have Internet access) at `http://www.self-directed-search.com/`.

For those who don't have Internet access (or are in a hurry) I invented (many years ago) a quick and easy way to get an *approximation* of your 'Holland Code,' as it's called. I call it "The Party Exercise." Here is how the exercise goes (do it!):

On the next page is an aerial view of a room in which a two-day (!) party is taking place. At this party, people with the same or similar interests have (for some reason) all gathered in the same corner of the room.

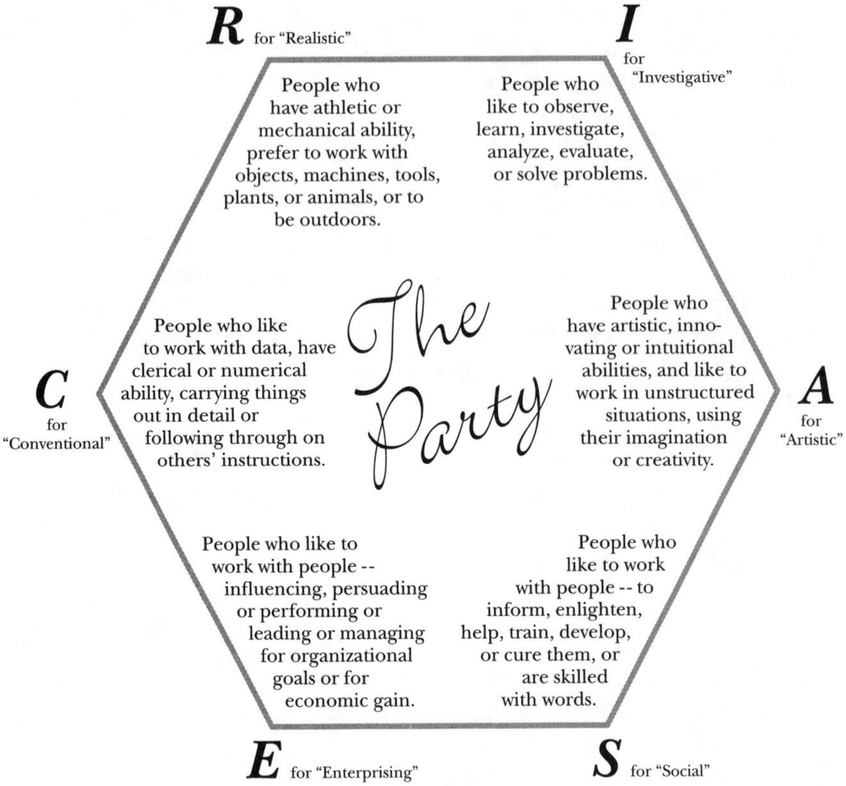
R for "Realistic"
I for "Investigative"
People who have athletic or mechanical ability, prefer to work with objects, machines, tools, plants, or animals, or to be outdoors.
People who like to observe, learn, investigate, analyze, evaluate, or solve problems.
The Party
People who like to work with data, have clerical or numerical ability, carrying things out in detail or following through on others' instructions.
People who have artistic, innovating or intuitional abilities, and like to work in unstructured situations, using their imagination or creativity.
C for "Conventional"
A for "Artistic"
People who like to work with people -- influencing, persuading or performing or leading or managing for organizational goals or for economic gain.
People who like to work with people -- to inform, enlighten, help, train, develop, or cure them, or are skilled with words.
E for "Enterprising"
S for "Social"

(1) Which corner of the room would you instinctively be drawn to, as the group of people you would most enjoy being with for the longest time? (Leave aside any question of shyness, or whether you would have to talk to them.) Write the letter for that corner here:

(2) After fifteen minutes, everyone in the corner you have chosen leaves for another party crosstown, except you. Of the groups that still remain now, which corner or group would you be drawn to the most, as the people you would most enjoy being with for the longest time? Write the letter for that corner here:

(3) After fifteen minutes, this group too leaves for another party, except you. Of the corners, and groups, which remain now, which one would you most enjoy being with for the longest time? Write the letter for that corner here:

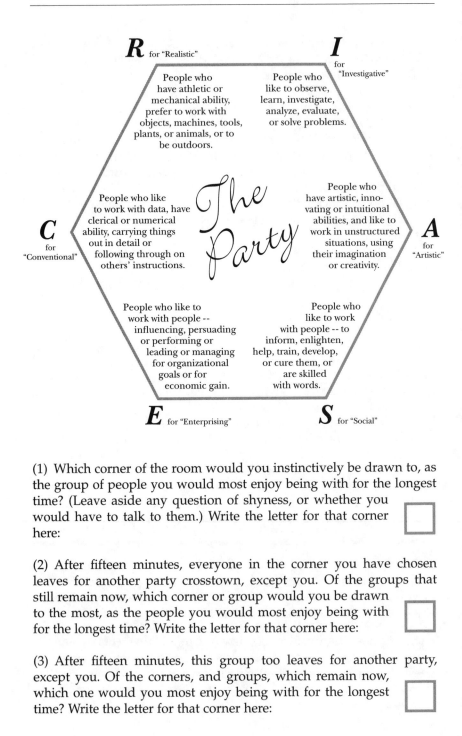

The three letters you just chose, in the three steps, are called your "Holland Code." Here is what you should now do:

1. Circle them on the People petal, on page 331.

Put three circles around your favorite corner; two circles around your next favorite; and one circle around your third favorite.

2. Once the corners are circled, you may wish to write up (for yourself and your eyes only) a temporary statement about your future job or career, using the descriptors above.

If your "Code" turned out to be IAS, for example, you might write: *"I would like a job or career best if I was surrounded by people who are very curious, and like to investigate or analyze things (I); who are also very innovative (A); and who are bent on trying to help or serve people (S)."*

3. Finally, here, look over the skills you have just described *in others*, and see how much of this is also true of *you*.

What I call "The Mirror Theory" holds that we often see *ourselves* best by looking into the faces of others. Hence, once we have described the people we would most like to be surrounded by, in many cases we have also described ourselves. ("Birds of a feather flock together.") So, look over the circled items on your People petal. Are these, perchance, *your* favorite proclivities, skills, tasks, etc.? Or not?

Petal #4
Your Favorite Values & Goals

1. Values are a matter of what guides you through every day, every task, every encounter with another human being. Yet, we are often unaware of what our values are.

One way to bring values to your consciousness is to imagine that shortly before the end of your life you are invited to dinner -- and to your great surprise people have secretly come in from all over the country and all over the world, to attend a surprise testimonial dinner for You.

At the dinner, to your great embarrassment, there is one testimonial after another about the good things you did, or the good person that you were, in your lifetime. No mention of any parts of your life that you don't want to have remembered. Just the good stuff.

So, this brings us to some questions. If you get the life you really want between now and then, what would you hope you would hear at that dinner, as they looked back on your life?

If you do achieve what you want with your life, what about you would you like to have remembered, after you are gone from this earth? Here is a checklist to help you[2]:

It would be a good life, if at its end here, people remembered me as one who (check as many items as are important to you):

- ❑ Served or helped those who were in need.
- ❑ Impressed people with my going the second mile, in meeting their needs.
- ❑ Was always a great listener.
- ❑ Was always good at carrying out orders, or bringing projects to a successful conclusion.
- ❑ Mastered some technique, or field.
- ❑ Did something that everyone said couldn't be done.
- ❑ Did something that no one had ever done before.
- ❑ Excelled and was the best at whatever it is I did.
- ❑ Pioneered or explored some new technology.
- ❑ Fixed something that was broken.

- ❑ Made something work, when everyone else had failed or given up.
- ❑ Improved something, made it better, or perfected it.
- ❑ Combatted some bad idea/philosophy/force/influence/pervasive trend -- and I persevered and/or prevailed.
- ❑ Influenced people and gained a tremendous response from them.
- ❑ Had an impact, and caused change.
- ❑ Did work which brought more information/truth into the world.
- ❑ Did work which brought more beauty into the world, through gardens, or painting, or decorating, or designing, or whatever.
- ❑ Did work which brought more justice, truth, and ethical behavior into the world.
- ❑ Brought people closer to God.
- ❑ Growing in wisdom and compassion was my great goal all my life.
- ❑ Had a vision of what something could be, and helped that vision to come true.
- ❑ Developed or built something, where there was nothing.
- ❑ Began a new business, or did some project from start to finish.
- ❑ Exploited, shaped and influenced some situation, market, before others saw the potential.
- ❑ Put together a great team, which made a huge difference in its field, industry, or community.
- ❑ Was a good decision-maker.
- ❑ Was acknowledged by everyone as a leader, and was in charge of whatever it was that I was doing.
- ❑ Had status in my field, industry, or community.
- ❑ Was in the spotlight, gained recognition, and was well-known.
- ❑ Made it into a higher echelon than I was, in terms of reputation, and/or prestige, and/or membership, and/or salary.
- ❑ Was able to acquire possessions, things or money.

- ❑ Other goals which occur to me:______________________________

  ____

When you're done checking off all the values that are important to you, go back, and pick out the ten that you care the most about, and then prioritize them in exact order of importance to you. As always, if you just can't prioritize them by guess and by gosh, then use the Prioritizing Grid on page 344.

The question to ask yourself, there, as you confront each 'pair' on the Grid is: "If I could only have this true about me, at the end of my life, but not the other, which would I prefer?" *Try not to pay attention to what others might or might not think of you, if they knew this was your heart's desire. This is just between you and God.*

Put your top three values on the Values & Goals petal, in the Flower Diagram on page 331.

We turn, now from values to goals.

2. Goals are a matter of what you hope to accomplish before you die. Figuring out now, what we'd like to achieve before our life is over, gives us greater direction in our present career choices. Here are some questions, in the form of a check-list, that may prove helpful in surfacing what your goals in life are:

My goal, before I die, is to be able to help people with their need for:

❑ **Clothing** (people's need to find and choose appropriate and affordable clothing); *and in my case what interests me particularly is*__________________________.

❑ **Food** (people's need to be fed, to be saved from starvation or poor nutrition) *and in my case what interests me particularly is*__________________________.

❑ **Housing** and **real estate** (people's need to find appropriate and affordable housing, office or land); *and in my case what interests me particularly is*__________________________.

❑ **Language** (people's need for literacy, to be able to read, or to learn a new language); *and in my case what interests me particularly is*__________________________.

❑ **Personal services** (people's need to have someone do tasks they can't do, or haven't time to do, or don't want to do, for themselves -- ranging from childcare to helping run a farm); *and in my case what interests me particularly is*__________________________.

❑ **Finances** (people's need to have help with budgeting, taxes, financial planning, money management, etc.); *and in my case what interests me particularly is*__________________________.

❑ **Acquisition** (people's need for help in buying something); *and in my case what interests me particularly is*__________________________.

❑ **Transportation** (people's need for travel locally or elsewise); *and in my case what interests me particularly is*__________________________.

❑ **Legal services** (people's need for expert counseling concerning the legal implications of things they are doing, or things that have been done to them); *and in my case what interests me particularly is*________________________.

❑ **Child development** (people's need for help with various problems as their children are moving from infancy through childhood, including behavioral disabilities); *and in my case what interests me particularly is*________________________.

❑ **Physical fitness** (people's need to get their body in tune through physical or occupational therapy, 'body-work,' exercise or diet); *and in my case what interests me particularly is*________________________.

❑ **Health services** (people's need to have preventative medicine or help with ailments, allergies and disease); *and in my case what interests me particularly is*____________________ .

❑ **Healing** including **Alternative medicine** and **Holistic health** (people's need to have various injuries, ailments, maladies or diseases healed); *and in my case what interests me particularly is*________________________.

❑ **Medicine** (people's need to have help with diagnosing, treating various diseases, or removing diseased or badly injured parts of their body, etc.); *and in my case what interests me particularly is*________________________.

❑ **Mental health** (people's need for help with stress, depression, insomnia or other forms of emotional or mental disturbance); *and in my case what interests me particularly is*________________________.

❑ **Personal counseling and guidance** (people's need for help with family relations, dysfunctions, or various crises in their life, including a lack of balance in their use of time); *and in my case what interests me particularly is*________________________.

❑ **Job-hunting, job-placement or vocational rehabilitation** (people's need to have help in finding the work they have chosen, particularly when handicapped, or unemployed, or enrolling for welfare under the new regulations); *and in my case what interests me particularly is*________________________.

❑ **Life/work planning** (people's need for help in choosing a career or planning a holistic life); *and in my case what interests me particularly is*________________________.

❑ **Learning or training** (people's need to learn more about something, at work or outside of work); *and in my case what interests me particularly is*____________________.

❑ **Entertainment** (people's need to be entertained, by laughter, wit, intelligence, or beauty); *and in my case what interests me particularly is*________________________.

❑ **Spirituality** or **religion** (people's need to learn as much as they can about God, character, and their own soul, including their values and principles); *and in my case what interests me particularly is*_________________________.

❑ **The needs of animals or plants** (their need for nurturing, growth, health and other life cycles which require the kinds of sensitivities often referred to as 'interpersonal skills'); *and in my case what interests me particularly is*_________________________.

❑ **The creating, making, marketing, handling of things**, such as: airplanes, antiques, bicycles, blueprints, books, bridges, buildings, bushes, cameras, campers, cars, catalogs, chemicals, cooking utensils, clothing, computers, crops, diagrams, electricity, electronics, drugs, farms, farm machinery, fish, flowers, gardens, groceries, guidebooks, houses, kitchens appliances, lawns, machines, magazines, makeup, manuals, medicines, minerals, money, music, musical instruments, newspapers, office machines, paints, paper, plants, radios, rivers, rooms, sailboats, security systems, sewing machines, skiing equipment, soil, telephones, toiletries, tools, toys, trains, trees, valuable objects, videotapes, wine, wood, etc.; *and in my case what interests me particularly is*____________________.

❑ **Other goals** not listed above, that fascinate me are:____.

When you're done checking off all the goals that are important to you, go back, and pick out the ten that you care the most about, and then prioritize them in exact order of importance to you. As always, if you just can't prioritize them by guess and by gosh, then use the Prioritizing Grid on page 344.

Put your top three Goals on the Values & Goals petal, in the Flower Diagram on page 331.

Petal #5

Your Favorite Working Conditions

Plants that grow beautifully at sea level, often perish if they're taken ten thousand feet up the mountain. Likewise, we do our best work under certain conditions, but not under others. Thus, the question: What are your favorite 'working conditions'? actually is a question about "Under what circumstances do you do your most effective work?"

The best way to approach this is by starting with the things you *disliked* about all your previous jobs, using the following chart to list these. The chart, as you can see, has three columns, and you fill them out in the same order, and manner, that you filled out the geography chart earlier. Here too, you may copy this chart on to a larger piece of paper if you wish, before you begin filling it out. *Column A may begin with such factors as: "too noisy," "too much supervision," "no windows in my workplace," "having to be at work by 6 a.m.," etc.*

Of course, when you get to Column B, you must rank these factors that are in Column A, in their exact order of importance, to you.

As always, if you are baffled as to how to prioritize these factors in exact order, use the Prioritizing Grid on page 344 or 345.

The question to ask yourself, there, as you confront each 'pair' is: "If I were offered two jobs, and in the first job I would be rid of this first distasteful working condition, but not the second; while in the second job, I would be rid of the second distasteful working condition, but not the first, which distasteful working condition would I choose to get rid of?"

Note that when you later come to Column C, the factors will be already prioritized. Your only job, there, is to think of the "positive" form of that factor that you hated so much (in Column B). (It is not always "the exact opposite." For example, *too much supervision,* listed in Column B, does not always mean *no supervision,* in Column C. It *might* mean: *a moderate amount of supervision, once or twice a day.*)

Once you've finished Column C, enter the top five factors from there on the Working Conditions petal of the Flower Diagram, on page 331.

DISTASTEFUL WORKING CONDITIONS

	Column A − Distasteful Working Conditions	Column B − Distasteful Working Conditions Ranked	Column C + The Keys to My Effectiveness At Worl
Places I Have Worked Thus Far In My Life	*I Have Learned From the Past that My Effectiveness at Work is Decreased When I Have To Work Under These Conditions:*	*Among the Factors or Qualities Listed in Column A, These Are The Ones I Dislike Absolutely The Most (in order of Decreasing Dislike):*	*The Opposite of These Qualities, in order:* *I Believe My Effectivenes Would Be at an Absolute Maximum, if I Could Work Under These Conditions:*

Petal #6
Level & Salary

As you saw in chapter 12, salary is something you must think out ahead of time, when you're contemplating your ideal job or career. Level goes hand-in-hand with salary, of course.

1. The first question here is at what level would you like to work, in your ideal job?

Level is a matter of how much responsibility you want, in an organization:

- ❑ Boss or CEO (this may mean you'll have to form your own business)
- ❑ Manager or someone under the boss who carries out orders, but also gives them
- ❑ The head of a team
- ❑ A member of a team of equals
- ❑ One who works in tandem with one other partner
- ❑ One who works alone, either as an employee or as a consultant to an organization, or as a one-person business.

Enter a two- or three-word summary of your answer, on the Salary and Level petal of your Flower Diagram, on page 330.

2. The second question here is what salary would you like to be aiming at?

Here you have to think in terms of minimum or maximum. Minimum is what you would need to make, if you were just barely 'getting by.' And you need to know this *before* you go in for a job interview with anyone *(or before you form your own business, and need to know how much profit you must make, just to survive).*

Maximum could be any astronomical figure you can think of, but it is more useful here to put down the salary you realistically think you could make, with your present competency and experience, were you working for a real, *but generous,* boss. (If this maximum figure is still depressingly low, then put down the salary you would like to be making five years from now.)

Make out a detailed outline of your estimated expenses *now,* listing what you need *monthly* in the following categories:[3]

Housing
- Rent or mortgage payments . . . . $ ________
- Electricity/gas. . . . . $ ________
- Water . . . . $ ________
- Telephone . . . . $ ________
- Garbage removal . . . . $ ________
- Cleaning, maintenance, repairs[4] . . . . $ ________

Food
- What you spend at the supermarket and/or meat market, etc. . . . . $ ________
- Eating out . . . . $ ________

Clothing
- Purchase of new or used clothing . . . . $ ________
- Cleaning, dry cleaning, laundry . . . . $ ________

Automobile/transportation[5]
- Car payments . . . . $ ________
- Gas . . . . $ ________
- Repairs . . . . $ ________
- Public transportation *(bus, train, plane)*. . . . . $ ________

Insurance
- Car . . . . $ ________
- Medical or health-care . . . . $ ________
- House and personal possessions . . . . $ ________
- Life . . . . $ ________

Medical expenses
- Doctors' visits . . . . $ ________
- Prescriptions. . . . . $ ________
- Fitness costs . . . . $ ________

Support for Other Family Members
- Child-care costs *(if you have children)* . . . . $ ________
- Child-support *(if you're paying that)* . . . . $ ________
- Support for your parents *(if you're helping out)* . . . . $ ________

Charity giving/tithe *(to help others)* . . . . $ ________

School/learning
- Children's costs *(if you have children in school)* . . . . . $ ________
- Your learning costs *(adult education, job-hunting classes, etc.)* . . . . $ ________

Pet care *(if you have pets)*. . . . . $ ________

Bills and debts *(Usual monthly payments)*

Credit cards . . . . $ ________

Local stores . . . . $ ________

Other obligations you pay off monthly . . . . $ ________

Taxes

Federal[6] *(next April's due, divided by months remaining until then)* . . . . $ ________

State *(likewise)* . . . . $ ________

Local/property *(next amount due, divided by months remaining until then)* . . . . $ ________

Tax-help *(if you ever use an accountant, pay a friend to help you with taxes, etc.)*. . . . . $ ________

Savings . . . . $ ________

Retirement (Keogh, IRA, Sep, etc.). . . . . $ ________

Amusement/discretionary spending

Movies, video rentals, etc. . . . . $ ________

Other kinds of entertainment . . . . $ ________

Reading, newspapers, magazines, books . . . . $ ________

Gifts *(birthday, Christmas, etc.)* . . . . $ ________

Total Amount You Need Each Month . . . . $ ________

Multiply the total amount you need each month by 12, to get the yearly figure. Divide the yearly figure by 2000, and you will be reasonably near the *minimum* hourly wage that you need. Thus, if you need $3333 per month, multiplied by 12 that's $40,000 a year, and then divided by 2,000, that's $20 an hour.

Parenthetically, you may want to prepare two different versions of the above budget: one with the expenses you'd ideally *like* to make, and the other a minimum budget, which will give you what you are looking for, here: the floor, below which you simply cannot afford to go.

Enter the maximum, and minimum, on your Salary & Level petal on the Flower Diagram on page 330.

Optional Exercise: You may wish to put down other rewards, besides money, that you would hope for, from your next job or career. These might be:

❑ Adventure
❑ Challenge
❑ Respect
❑ Influence
❑ Popularity
❑ Fame
❑ Power
❑ Intellectual stimulation from the other workers there
❑ A chance to exercise leadership
❑ A chance to be creative
❑ A chance to make decisions
❑ A chance to use my expertise
❑ A chance to help others
❑ A chance to bring others closer to God
❑ Other:

If you do check off things on this list, arrange your answers in order of importance to you, and then add them to the Salary & Level petal on page 330.

Done!

Voila! Your Flower Diagram should now be complete. At this point, take a hard look at it, and see how this new knowledge of yourself and your ideal job helps you to narrow down what it is you are looking for.

Footnotes to the Flower Exercise

1. For the curious, "animals" are placed in this category with "people," because **the skills** required to deal with animals are more like those used with people, than like those used with "things."

2. I am indebted to Arthur Miller, of People Management, Inc., for many of these ideas.

3. If this kind of financial figuring is not your cup of tea, find a buddy, friend, relative, family member, or *anyone,* who can help you do this. If you don't know anyone who could do this, go to your local church, synagogue, religious centre, social club, gym, or wherever you hang out, and ask the leader or manager there, to help you find someone. If there's a bulletin board, put up a notice on the bulletin board.

4. If you have extra household expenses, such as a security system for example, be sure and include the quarterly (or whatever) expenses here, divided by three.

5. Your checkbook stubs will tell you a lot of this stuff. But you may be vague about your cash or credit card expenditures. For example, you may not know how much you spend at the supermarket, or how much you spend on gas, etc. But there is a simple way to find out. Just carry a little notepad and pen around with you for two weeks or more, and jot down *everything* you pay cash *(or use credit cards)* for -- *on the spot, right after you pay it.* At the end of those two weeks, you'll be able to take that notepad and make a realistic guess of what should be put down in these categories that now puzzle you. *(Multiply the two-weeks figure by two, and you'll have the monthly figure.)*

6. Incidentally, for U.S. citizens, looking ahead to next April 15th, be sure and check with your local IRS office or a reputable accountant to find out if you can deduct the expenses of your job-hunt on your Federal (and State) income tax returns. At this writing, some job-hunters can, if -- big IF -- this is not your first job that you're looking for, if you haven't been unemployed too long, and if you aren't making a career-change. Do go find out what the latest "ifs" are. If IRS tells you you are eligible, keep careful receipts of everything related to your job-hunt, as you go along: telephone calls, stationery, printing, postage, travel, etc.

Two are better than one;
for if they fall,
the one will lift up his fellow;

but woe to him that is alone when he falleth,
and hath not another to lift him up.
Ecclesiastes

APPENDIX B

Finding Help: A Sampler

THIS IS NOT a complete directory of anything. It is exactly what its name implies: a *Sampler*. Were I to list all the career counselors out there, we would end up with an encyclopedia. Some states, in fact, have encyclopedic lists of counselors and businesses, in various books or directories, and your local bookstore or library should have these, in their Job-Hunting Section, under such titles as "How to Get A Job in . . ." or "Job-Hunting in . . ."

The places listed in this Sampler are listed at their own request, and I offer them to you simply as places for you to begin your investigation with -- nothing more.

Many truly helpful places are not listed here. If you discover such a place, which is very good at helping people with *Parachute* and creative job-hunting or career-change, do send us the pertinent information. We will ask them, as we do all the listings here, a few intelligent questions and if they sound okay, we will add that place to next year's edition.

We do ask a few questions because our readers want counselors and places which claim some expertise in helping them finish their job-hunt, using this book. So, if they've never even heard of *Parachute,* we don't list them. On the other hand, we can't measure a place's expertise at this long distance, no matter how many questions we ask.

Even if listed here, you must do your own sharp questioning before you decide to go with anyone. If you don't take time to research two or three places, before choosing a counselor, you will deserve whatever you get (or, more to the point, don't get). So, please, do your research. The purse or wallet you save, will be your own.

Yearly readers of this book will notice that we do remove people from this Sampler, without warning. Specifically, we remove (without further notice or comment) places we didn't mean to remove, but a typographical error was made, somehow (it happens). We also remove places which have moved, and don't bother to send us their new address. If you are listed here, we expect you to be a professional at communication. When you move, your first priority should be to let us know, immediately. As one exemplary counselor just wrote: "You are the first person I am contacting on my updated letterhead . . . hot off the press just today!" So it should always be. A number of places get removed every year, precisely because of their poor communication skills, and their sloppiness in letting us know where they've gone to. Other causes for removal:

- Places which have disconnected their telephone, or otherwise suggest that they have gone out of business.
- Places which our readers lodge complaints against, with us, as being either unhelpful or obnoxious. The complaints may be falsified, but we can't take that chance.
- Places which change their personnel, and the new person has never even heard of *Parachute,* or creative job-search techniques.
- Places which misuse their listing here, claiming in their brochures, ads or interviews, that they have some kind of '*Parachute* Seal of Approval,'-- that we feature them in *Parachute,* or recommend them or endorse them. This is a big 'no-no.' A listing here is no more of a recommendation than is a listing in the phone book.
- College services that we discover (belatedly) serve only 'Their Own.'

- Counseling firms which employ salespeople as the initial 'in-take' person that a job-hunter meets.

If you discover that any of the places listed in this Sampler falls into any of the above categories, you would be doing a great service to our other readers by dropping us a line and telling us so. (P.O. Box 379, Walnut Creek, CA 94597.)

The listings which follow are alphabetical within each state, and counselors listed by their name are in alphabetical order according to their last name.

What do the letters after their name mean? Well, B.A., M.A. and Ph.D. you know. However, don't assume the degree is in career counseling. Ask. NCC means "Nationally Certified Counselor." There are about 20,000 such in the U.S. This can mean general counseling expertise, not necessarily career counseling. On the other hand, NCCC does mean "Nationally Certified Career Counselor." There are currently about 850 in the U.S. Other initials, such as LPC -- "Licensed Professional Counselor" -- and the like, often refer to State licensing. There are a number of States, now, that have some sort of regulation of career counselors. In some States it is mandatory, in others it is optional. But, mostly, this field is unregulated.

Some offer group career counseling, some offer testing, some offer access to job-banks, etc.

One final note: generally speaking, these places counsel anybody. A few, however, may turn out to have restrictions unknown to us ("we counsel only women," etc.). If that's the case, your time isn't wasted. They may be able to help you with a referral. So, don't be afraid to ask them "who else in the area can you tell me about, who helps with job-searches, and are there any (among them) that you think are particularly effective?"

AREA CODES

Throughout the U.S. now, area codes are sub-dividing constantly, sometimes more than once during a short time-span. If you're calling a local counselor, you probably don't need the area code anyway. But if you call a phone number below that is any distance away from you, and they tell you "this number cannot be completed as dialed," the most likely explanation is that the area code got changed -- maybe some time ago. (We ask counselors listed here to notify us when the area code changes, but some do and some don't.) Anyway, call Information and check.

* *Throughout this Sampler, an asterisk before their name, in red, means they offer not only regular job-search help, but also (when you wish) counseling from a spiritual point of view; i.e., they're not afraid to talk about God if you're looking for some help, in finding your Mission in life.*

ALABAMA

*__Career Decisions__, 638 Winwood Dr., Birmingham, AL 35226
Phone: 205-822-8662 or 205-870-2639
Contact: Carrie Pearce Hild, M.S.Ed., Career Counselor and Consultant

Chemsak, Maureen J., NCC, NCCC, LPC, Director of Counseling and Career Services, Athens State University, 300 North Beaty St., Athens, AL 35611
Phone: 256-233-8285 or 256-830-4610
eMail: mchemsak@athens.edu

Vantage Associates, 2100-A Southbridge Pkwy., Suite 480, Birmingham, AL 35209
Phone: 205-879-0501 or 205-631-5544
Contact: Michael A. Tate

Work Matters Career Coaching, P.O. Box 130756, Birmingham, AL 35213
Phone: 205-879-8494
Contact: Gayle H. Lantz

ALASKA

Career Transitions, 2600 Denali St., Suite 430, Anchorage, AK 99503
Phone: 907-274-4510
Contact: Deeta Lonergan,Director
eMail: deeta@alaska.net

ARIZONA

The Orion Institute, 1220 S. Alma School Rd., Mesa, AZ 85277
Phone: 480-380-6885 or toll-free 888-313-6749
Contact: Debra B. Danvenport, M.A., L.C.C., Ph.D.(c)
eMail: davenportinc@prodigy.net

West Valley Career Services, 10720 W. Indian School, #19-141, Phoenix, AZ 85037
Phone: 623-872-7303
Contact: Shell Mendelson Herman, M.S., CRC

ARKANSAS

McKinney, Donald, Ed.D., Career Counselor, Rt. 1, Box 351-A, DeQueen, AR 71832
Phone: 870-642-5628
eMail: eaglnest@ipa.net

CALIFORNIA

BC Career Strategy Associates, 508 E. Chapman Ave., Fullerton, CA 92832
Phone: 714-871-2380
Contact: Brent Wood, Cassandra Clark
eMail: bccareer@pacbell.net

Berrett & Associates, 1551 E. Shaw, Suite 103, Fresno, CA 93710
Phone: 559-221-6543 Fax: 559-221-6540
Contact: Dwayne Berrett, M.A., RPCC
eMail: dberrett3@fresno.com

Brown, Beverly, M.A., NCCC, NCC 809 So. Bundy Dr., #105, Los Angeles, CA 90049
Phone: 310-447-7093
eMail: bbcareers@aol.com

California Career Services, 6024 Wilshire Blvd., Los Angeles, CA 90036
Phone: 323-933-2900 Fax: 323-933-9929
Contact: Susan W. Miller, M.A.
eMail: swmcareer@aol.com

Career Action Center, 10420 Bubb Rd., Suite 100, Cupertino, CA 95014
Phone: 408-253-3200
Contact: Betsy Collard, Director; Linda Surrell, Counseling Services Manager
eMail: info@careeraction.org

Career Balance, 215 Witham Road, Encinitas, CA 92024
Phone: 760-436-3994
Contact: Virginia Byrd, M.Ed., Work/Life Specialist, Career Management.

*__Career Choices__, Castro Valley, CA
Phone: 510-733-6644
Contact: Dana E. Ogden, M.S.Ed., CCDV, Counselor and Trainer
eMail: deogden@pacbell.net

Career Counseling and Assessment Associates, 9229 West Sunset Blvd., Suite 502, Los Angeles, CA 90069
Phone: 310-274-3423
Contact: Dianne Y. Sundby, Ph.D., Director and Psychologist

(A) Career Counseling and Psychotherapy Service, 1623 Fifth Ave., Bldg. D, Suite 8, San Rafael, CA 94901-1860
Phone: 415-789-9113
Contact: Suzanne Penney Lindenbaum LCSW, NCC, Registered Career Counselor
eMail: LindenCCS@aol.com

Career Development Center, John F. Kennedy University, 1250 Arroyo Way, Walnut Creek, CA 94596
Phone: 925-295-0610
Contact: Susan Geifman, Director

Career Development Life Planning, 3585 Maple St., Suite 237, Ventura, CA 93003
Phone: 805-656-6220
Contact: Norma Zuber, NCCC, M.S.C., & Associates

*__Career Development and Vocational Testing Services__, 2515 Park Marina, Suite 203-B, Redding, CA 96001
Phone: 916-246-2871

Career Dimensions, P.O. Box 7402, Stockton, CA 95267
Phone: 209-957-6465
Contact: Fran Abbott

Career Options, 1855 San Miguel Drive #11, Walnut Creek, CA 94596
Phone: 925-945-0376
Contact: Joan Schippman, M.A., NCCC
Email: joangoforth@cs.com

Career and Personal Development Institute, 690 Market St., Suite 402, San Francisco, CA 94104
Phone: 415-982-2636
Contact: Bob Chope

Career Planning Center/Business Action Center, 1623 S. La Cienega Blvd., Los Angeles, CA 90035
Phone: 310-273-6633

Center for Career Growth and Development, P.O. Box 283, Los Gatos, CA 95031
Phone: 408-354-7150
Contact: Steven E. Beasley
eMail: careergrowth@juno.com

Center for Creative Change, 3130 West Fox Run Way, San Diego, CA 92111
Phone: 619-268-9340
Contact: Nancy Helgeson, M.A., MFCC.

*__Center for Life & Work Planning,__ 1133 Second St., Encinitas, CA 92024
Phone: 760-943-0747 Fax: 760-436-7158
Contact: Mary C. McIsaac, Executive Director

*__The Center for Ministry__ (an Interdenominational Church Career Development Center) 8393 Capwell Dr., Suite 220, Oakland, CA 94621-2123
Phone: 510-635-4246
Contact: Robert L. Charpentier, Director.

Cheney-Rice, Stephen, M.S., 2113 Westboro Ave., Alhambra, CA 91803-3720
Phone: 625-281-6066 or 909-607-7388
eMail: stephen.cheney-rice@claremontmckenna.edu

Christen, Carol, Atascadero, CA.
Phone: 805-462-8795.
eMail: gardencc@hotmail.com

*__Christian Career Center__, 448 S. Marengo Ave., Pasadena, CA 91101
Phone: 626-577-2705
Contact: Kevin Brennfleck, M.A., NCCC, and Kay Marie Brennfleck, M.A., NCCC, Directors
eMail: cocareer@aol.com

The Clarity Group Inc., 388 Market Street, Suite 500, San Francisco, CA 94111
Phone: 415-292-4814
Contact: George Schofield, Ph.D

Cricket Consultants, 502 Natoma St., Folsom, CA 95630
Phone: 916-985-3211
Contact: Bruce Parrish, M.S., CDMS
eMail: cricketcnsul@cs.com

Cypress College, Career Planning Center, 9200 Valley View St., Cypress, CA 90630
Phone: 714-484-7000

Dream Job Coaching, 14895 E. 14th St., Suite 450, San Leandro, CA 94578
Phone: 510-357-2522
Contact: Joel Garfinkle
eMail: joel@dreamjobcoach.com

Eadie, Margaret L., M.A., A.M.Ed. Career Consultant, 1000 Sage Place, Pacific Grove, CA 93950
Phone: 831-373-7400

Experience Unlimited Job Club. There are 35 Experience Unlimited Job Clubs in California, found at the Employment Development Department in the following locations: Anaheim, Corona, El Cajon, Escondido, Fremont, Fresno, Hemet, Hollywood, Lancaster, Monterey, North Hollywood, Oakland, Ontario, Pasadena, Pleasant Hill, Redlands, Ridgecrest, Riverside, Sacramento (Midtown and South), San Bernardino, San Diego (also East and South), San Francisco, San Mateo, San Rafael, Santa Ana, Santa Cruz, Santa Maria, Simi Valley, Sunnyvale, Torrance, Victorville, and West Covina. Contact the club nearest you through your local Employment Development Department (E.D.D.)

Floyd, Mary Alice, M.A., NCCC, Career Counselor/Consultant, 3233 Lucinda Lane, Santa Barbara, CA 93105
Phone: 805-687-5462 Fax: 805-898-1066
eMail: glfloyd@sbceo.org

Frangquest, Deborah Gavrin, M.S., Life Purpose & Career Consultant, 1501 20th St., San Francisco, CA 94107
Phone: 415-642-0225 Fax: 415-642-0232
eMail: workpath@ix.netcom.com

Fritsen, Jan, Career Counseling and Coaching, 23181 La Cadena Drive, Suite 103, Laguna Hills, CA 92653
Phone: 949-497-4869
eMail: janfritsen@home.com

Geary & Associates, Inc., 1100 Coddingtown Ctr., Ste. A, P.O. Box 3774, Santa Rosa, CA 95402
Phone: 707-525-8085 Fax: 707-528-8088
Contact: Jack Geary, M.A., C.R.C.; Edelweiss Geary, M.Ed.
eMail: geary@gearyassociates.com
(Career Transition Programs, Outplacement and Spouse Re-employment Assistance)

G/S Consultants, P.O. Box 7855, South Lake Tahoe, CA 96158
Phone: 530-541-8587 Fax: 530-541-3773
Contact: Judith Grutter, M.S., NCCC
eMail: gstahoe@sierra.net

The Guidance Center, 1150 Yale St., Suite One, Santa Monica, CA 90403
Phone: 310-829-4429
Contact: Anne Salzman, Career Counselor and Psychologist

H.R. Solutions, Human Resources Consulting, 390 South Sepulveda Blvd., Suite 104, Los Angeles, CA 90049
Phone: 310-471-2536
Contact: Nancy Mann, M.B.A, President/Career Consultant

Jewish Vocational Service, 5700 Wilshire Blvd., 2nd Floor, Suite 2303, Los Angeles, CA 90036
Phone: 323-761-8888

The Job Forum, 235 Montgomery St., 12th Floor, San Francisco, CA 94104
Phone: 415-392-4520

Judy Kaplan Baron Associates, 6046 Cornerstone Ct. West, Suite 208, San Diego, CA 92121
Phone: 858-558-7400
Contact: Judy Kaplan Baron, Director

Kerwin & Associates, 926 W. Kenneth Road, Glendale, CA 91202
Phone: 808-246-5621
Contact: Patrick Kerwin, M.B.A., NCCC

LifePrint, 120 Montgomery St., Suite 600, San Francisco, CA 94104
Phone: 415-274-4700
eMail: info@lifeprint.org

Lindenbaum Career and Counseling Services, 1623 Fifth Ave., Bldg. D, Suite 8, San Rafael, CA 94901-1860
Phone: 415-789-9113
Contact: Suzanne Lindenbaum, MSW, LCSW, BCD
eMail: lindenccs@aol.com

*__Miller, Lizbeth__, M.S., 3880 S. Bascom Ave., Suite 202, San Jose, CA 95124
Phone: 408-559-1115
(Affiliated with the Christian Counseling Center)

Montgomery & Associates, Career Development Services, 2515 Park Marina Dr., Suite 203B, Redding, CA 96001-2831
Phone: 530-246-2871
Contact: Gale Montgomery, Director

Networking Grace Career Counseling, Napa, CA 94558
Phone: 707-226-3438
Contact: Lauralyn Bauer, M.S.

Peller, Marion, 388 Market St., Suite 500, San Francisco, CA 94111
Phone: 415-296-2559

Slaughter, Olivia Keith, LEP, Sunshine Plaza, 71301 Highway 111, Suite 1, Rancho Mirage, CA 92270
Phone: 760-568-1544

Turning Point Career Center, University YMCA, 2600 Bancroft Way, Berkeley, CA 94704
Phone: 510-848-6370
Contact: Winnie Froehlich, M.S., Director

Wilson, Patti, P.O. Box 35633, Los Gatos, CA 95030
Phone: 408-354-1964

COLORADO

Accelerated Job Search, 4490 Squires Circle, Boulder, CO 80303
Phone: 303-494-2467
Contact: Leigh Olsen, Counselor

Arapahoe Community College Resource Center, 2500 West College Dr., P.O. Box 9002, Littleton, CO 80160-9002
Phone: 303-797-5805

CRS Consulting, 425 W. Mulberry, Suite 205, Fort Collins, CO 80521
Phone: 970-484-9810
Contact: Marilyn Pultz

Helmstaedter, Sherry, 5040 South El Camino, Englewood, CO 80111-1122
Phone: 303-794-5122

Life Work Planning, P.O. Box 1738, Berthoud, CO 80513
Phone: 970-532-5351
Contact: Lauren T. Murphy, Career Development Counselor

The McGee Group, 2485 W. Main, Suite 202, Old Littleton, CO 80120
Phone: 303-794-4749
Contact: Betsy C. McGee

The Oakes Review, 9129 W. Phillips Dr., Littletown, CO 80128
Phone: 303-282-0715
Contact: Janna L. Oakes, M.A.
eMail: janna@oakesreview.com

O'Keefe, Patricia, M.A., 1550 S. Monroe St., Denver, CO 80210
Phone: 303-759-9325

Peterson, April, M.A., NCC, Career Counselor, P.O. Box 17896, Boulder, CO 80308
Phone: 303-442-1023
eMail: aprilncc@netscape.net

Strategic Career Moves,
2329 N. Glenisle Ave., Durango, CO 81301
Phone: 970-385-9597
Contact: Mary Jane Ward, M.Ed., NCC, NCCC

Women's Resource Agency, 31 N. Farragut, Colorado Springs, CO 80909
Phone: 719-471-3170

YWCA of Boulder County Career Center,
2222 14th St., Boulder, CO 80302
Phone: 303-443-0419
Contact: Rosemary Arp, NCCC, Career Services Manager

CONNECTICUT

Accord Career Services, The Exchange, Suite 305, 270 Farmington Ave., Farmington, CT 06032
Phone: 800-922-1480 or 860-674-9654
Contact: Tod Gerardo, M.S., Director

Career Choices/RFP Associates,
141 Durham Rd., Suite 24, Madison, CT 06443
Phone: 203-245-4123

Career Transformations,
761 Valley Road, Fairfield, CT 06432
Phone: 203-374-7649
Contact: Robert N. Olsen, M.A., NCC

Cohen, James S., Ph.D., Career & Voc. Rehab. Services, 8 Barbara's Way, Ellington, CT
Phone: 860-871-7832

Crossroads, 30 Tower Lane, Avon, CT 06001
Phone: 860-677-2558
Contact: Carolyn A. Stigler, Psy.D
eMail: Cstigler@msn.com

Fairfield Academic and Career Center, Fairfield University, Dolan House, Fairfield, CT 06430
Phone: 203-254-4220

Jamieson Associates, 61 South Main St., Suite 101, West Hartford, CT 06107-2403
Phone: 860-521-2373
Contact: Lee Jamieson

The Offerjost-Westcott Group,
263 Main St., Old Saybrook, CT 06475
Phone: 860-388-6094
Contact: Russ Westcott

Pannone, Bob, M.A., NCCC, Career Specialist, 768 Saw Mill Road, West Haven, CT 06516
Phone: 203-933-6383

People Management International Ltd.,
8B North Shore Rd., New Preston, CT 06777
Phone: 203-868-0317
Contact: Arthur Miller

Preis, Roger J., RPE Career Dynamics, P.O. Box 16722, Stamford, CT 06905
Phone: 203-322-7225

Vocational and Academic Counseling for Adults (VOCA), 115 Berrian Rd., Stamford, CT 06905
Phone: 203-322-8353
Contact: Ruth A. Polster

J. Whitney Associates, 11092 Elm St., Rocky Hill, CT 06067
Phone: 860-721-0842
Contact: Jean Whitney, Career Manager

DELAWARE

The Brandywine Center, LLC,
2500 Grubb Road, Suite 240, Wilmington, DE 19810. Phone: 302-475-1880 Ext. 7
Contact: Kris Bronson, Ph.D
eMail: info@brandywinecenter.com

YWCA of New Castle County,
Women's Center for Economic Options, 233 King St., Wilmington, DE 19801
Phone: 302-658-7161

DISTRICT OF COLUMBIA

Blackwell Career Management of Capitol Hill, 626 A St. SE, Washington, D.C. 20003
Phone: 202-546-6835
eMail: mablack@citizen.infi.net

Community Vocational Counseling Service, 718 21st St. NW, Washington, D.C. 20052
Phone: 202-994-4860
Contact: Robert J. Wilson, M.S., Asst. Director for Educational Services

George Washington University, Center for Career Education, 2020 K St., Washington, D.C. 20052
Phone: 202-994-5299
Contact: Abigail Pereira, Director

Horizons Unlimited, Inc., 1050 17th St. NW, Suite 600, Washington, D.C. 20036
Phone: 202-296-7224 or 301-258-9338
Contact: Marilyn Goldman

FLORIDA

Adler, Barbara, Ed.D., Career Consulting, 203 North Shadow Bay Dr., Orlando, FL 32825-3766
Phone: 407-249-2189

Career Moves, Inc.,
4331 N. Federal Highway, Suite 305, Ft. Lauderdale, FL 33308
Phone: 954-772-6875
Contact: Diane Alford, M.Ed, NCC
eMail: cmoves@prodigy.net

The Centre for Women,
305 S. Hyde Park Ave., Tampa, FL 33606
Phone: 813-251-8437
Contact: Dae C. Sheridan, M.A., CRC, Employment Counselor

Chabon & Associates,
1665 Palm Beach Lakes Blvd., Suite 402, West Palm Beach, FL 33401
Phone: 407-640-8443
Contact: Toby G. Chabon, M.Ed., NCC, President

The Challenge Program for Displaced Homemakers, Florida Community College at Jacksonville,
101 W. State St., Jacksonville, FL 32202
Phone: 904-633-8316
Contact: Harriet Courtney, Project Coordinator
eMail: hcourtney@fccj.org

Crossroads, Palm Beach Community College, 4200 Congress Ave.,
Lake Worth, FL 33461-4796
Phone: 407-433-5995
Contact: Pat Jablonski, Program Manager

Focus on the Future: Displaced Homemaker Program,
Santa Fe Community College,
3000 N.W. 83rd St., Gainesville, FL 32606
Phone: 904-395-5047
Contact: Nancy Griffin, Program Coordinator
(Classes are free)

Harmon, Larry, Ph.D.,
Career Counseling Center, Inc.,
2000 South Dixie Highway,
Suite 103, Miami, FL 33133
Phone: 305-858-8557

Jonassen, Ellen O., Ph.D.,
10785 Ulmerton Rd., Largo, FL 34648
Phone: 813-581-8526

Life Designs, Inc.,
19526 East Lake Drive, Miami, FL 33015
Phone: 305-829-9008 (Sept.–May)
Contact: Dulce Muccio Weisenborn
eMail: dmw@qsrhelp.com

New Beginnings,
Polk Community College,
Station 71, 999 Avenue H- NE,
Winter Haven, FL 33881-4299
(Lakeland Campus)
Phone: 813-297-1029

WINGS Program,
Broward Community College,
1000 Coconut Creek Blvd.,
Coconut Creek, FL 33066
Phone: 305-973-2398

The Women's Center,
Valencia Community College,.
1010 N. Orlando Ave.,
Winter Park, FL 32789
Phone: 407-628-1976

GEORGIA

Albea, Emmette H., Jr., M.S., LPC, NCCC,
2706 Melrose Dr., Valdosta, GA 31602
Phone: 912-241-0908

Ashkin, Janis, M.Ed., NCC, NCCC,
219 Quail Run, Roswell, GA 30076
Phone: 678-319-0297
eMail: jashkin@mindspring.com

***Career Development Center of the Southeast** (an Interdenominational Church Career Development Center),
531 Kirk Rd., Decatur, GA 30030
Phone: 404-371-0336
Contact: Earl B. Stewart, D.Min., Director

***Career Pathways**,
601 Broad St., Gainesville, GA 30501
Phone: 800-722-1976
Contact: Lee Ellis, Director

Career Quest/Job Search Workshop,
St. Ann, 4905 Roswell Rd. N.E.,
Marietta, GA 30062-6240
Phone: 770-552-6402
Contact: Tom Chernetsky
(Focus on Internet job-hunting)

***Center for Growth & Change, Inc.**,
6991 Peachtree Ind. Blvd., Suite 310,
Norcross, GA 30092
Phone: 404-441-9580
Contact: James P. Hicks, Ph.D., LPC, Director

D & B Consulting,
3390 Peachtree Road N.E.,
Suite 900, Atlanta, GA 30326
Phone: 404-240-8063
Contact: Deborah R. Brown, MSM, MSW, Career Consultant

DeLorenzo, R., Ph.D., LPC, NCCC, NCC,
431 Asbury Commons Dr., Suite E,
Dunwoody, GA 30338
Phone: 770-457-6535
Email: ddeloren@mindspring.com

Jewish Vocational Service, Inc.,
4549 Chamblee Dunwoody Road,
Dunwoody, GA 30338-6120
Phone: 770-677-9440

***St. Jude's Job Network**,
St. Jude's Catholic Church,
7171 Glenridge Dr.,
Sandy Springs, GA 30328
Phone: 404-393-4578

Satterfield, Mark,
720 Rio Grand Dr., Alpharetta, GA 30202
Phone: 770-640-8393

IDAHO

***The Job Search Advisor**,
915 W. Iowa Ave., Boise, ID 83686
Phone: 208-463-2375
Contact: Christopher G. Gilliam, PHR, Job Search Advisor

OCM Organizational Consultants to Management, 720 Park Blvd.,
Suite 265, Boise, ID 83712-7714
Phone: 208-338-6584
eMail: ocm-id@rmci.net

Transitions, 1970 Parkside Dr.,
Boise, ID 83712
Phone: 208-368-0499
Contact: Elaine Simmons, M.E.

ILLINOIS

Alumni Career Center,
University of Illinois Alumni Association,
200 South Wacker Dr., Chicago, IL 60606
Phone: 312-996-6350
Contact: Barbara S. Hundley, Director;
Claudia M. Delestowicz, Associate Director;
Julie L. Hays, Staff

Beddoe, Marti, Career/Life Counselor
Phone: 312-281-7274

Career Path, 1240 Iroquois Ave.,
Suite 510, Naperville, IL 60563
Phone: 630-369-3390
Contact: Donna Sandberg, M.S., NCC,
Owner/Counselor

Career Workshops, 5431 W. Roscoe St.,
Chicago, IL 60641
Phone: 773-282-6859
Contact: Patricia Dietze

Davis, Jean, Adult Career Transitions,
1405 Elmwood Ave., Evanston, IL 60201
Phone: 847-492-1002

Dolan Career & Rehabilitation Consulting, Ltd., 307 Henry Street,
Suite 407, Alton, IL 62002
Phone: 618-474-5328 Fax: 618-462-3359
Contact: J. Stephen Dolan, M.A., C.R.C.,
Career & Rehabilitation Consultant
eMail: dolanrehab@piasanet.com

Grauer, Barbara Kabcenell, M.A., NCC,
1370 Sheridan Road,
Highland Park, IL 60035
Phone: 708-432-4479

Grimard Wilson Consulting,
111 N. Wabash Ave., Suite 2005,
Chicago, IL 60602
Phone: 312-201-1142
Contact: Diane Grimard Wilson, M.A.

Harper College Career Transition Center,
Building A, Room 124, Palatine, IL 60067
Phone: 708-459-8233
Mary Ann Jirak, Coordinator

Helfand, David P., Ed.D., NCCC,
250 Ridge, Evanston, IL 60202
Phone: 847-328-2787

*__Lansky Career Consultants,__
330 N. Wabash #2905, Chicago, IL 60611
Phone: 312-494-0022
Contact: Judith Lansky, M.A., M.B.A.,
President; Julie Benesh, Adjunct Consultant

LeBrun, Peter, Career/Life Counselor
Phone: 312-281-7274

*__Life/Career Planning Center for Religious__ (Roman Catholic), 10526 W. Cermak
Rd., Suite 111, Westchester, IL 60153
Phone: 708-531-9228
Contact: Dolores Linhart, Director

LifeScopes, 427 Greenwood St.,
Suite 3W, Evanston, IL 60201
Phone: 847-733-1805
Contact: Barbara H. Hill,
Career Management Consultant
eMail: LifeScopes@aol.com

Living by Design, 1010 Lake Street,
Suite 502A, Oak Park, IL 60302
Phone: 708-386-2505
Contact: Barbara Upton, LCSW

*__Midwest Career Development Service__
(An Interdenominational Church Career
Development Center),
1840 Westchester Blvd.,
Westchester, IL 60154
Phone: 708-343-6268

Midwest Women's Center, 828 S. Wabash,
Suite 200, Chicago, IL 60605
Phone: 312-922-8530

Moraine Valley Community College,
Job Placement Center, 10900 S. 88th Ave.,
Palos Hills, IL 60465
Phone: 708-974-5737

Right Livelyhood$,
23 W. 402 Green Briar Dr.,
Naperville, IL 60540
Phone: 708-369-9066

Skorupa, Jessica, Ph.D., NCCC,
16335 S. Harlem #423, Tinley Park, IL 60477
Phone: 708-614-7664
eMail: dr@jessicaskorupa.com

The Summit Group, P.O. Box 3794,
Peoria, IL 61612-3794
Phone: 309-681-1118
Contact: John R. Throop, D.Min., President

Widmer & Associates,
1510 W. Sunnyview Dr., Peoria, IL 61614
Phone: 309-691-3312
Contact: Mary F. Widmer, President

INDIANA

Career Consultants,
107 N. Pennsylvania St., Suite 400,
Indianapolis, IN 46204
Phone: 317-639-5601
Contact: Al Milburn,
Career Management Consultant

Jones, Sally, Program Coordinator/
Developer, Indiana University, School
of Continuing Studies, Owen Hall,
Room 202, Bloomington, IN 47405
Phone: 812-855-4991

KCDM Associates, 10401 N. Meridian St.,
Suite 300, Indianapolis, IN 46290
Phone: 317-581-6230
Contact: Mike Kenney

Performance Development Systems, Inc.,
312 Iroquois Trail, Burns Harbor, IN 46304
Phone: 219-787-9216
Contact: William P. Henning, Counselor

IOWA

Beers Consulting, 5505 Boulder Dr.,
West Des Moines, IA 50266
Phone: 515-225-1245
Contact: Rosanne Beers

Sudak-Allison, Jill, 3219 SE 19th Court,
Des Moines, IA 50320
Phone: 515-282-5040

University of Iowa, Center for Career Development and Cooperative Education, 315 Calvin Hall, Iowa City, IA 52242
Phone: 319-335-3201

Wendroff, Gloria, Secrets to Successful Job Search, 703 E. Burlington Ave., Fairfield, IA 52556
Phone: 515-472-4529

Zilber, Suzanne, 801 Crystal St., Ames, IA 50010
Phone: 515-232-9379

KANSAS

***Midwest Career Development Service** (An Interdenominational Church Career Development Center), 754 N. 31st St., Kansas City, KS 66110-0816
Contact: Ronald Brushwyler, Director

KENTUCKY

Career Span, 2465-C Nicholasville Rd., Suite 201, Lexington, KY 40503
Phone: 859-543-0343
Contact: Carla Ockerman-Hunter, M.A., NCCC
eMail: careerspan@aol.com

The Epoch Group, 6500 Glenridge Park Place, Suite 12, Louisville, KY 40222
Phone: 502-326-9122
Contact: Phillip A. Ronniger

LOUISIANA

Aptitude Assessment of Louisiana, Inc.
7912 Wrenwood Boulevard, Suite C, Baton Rouge, LA 70809
Phone: 504-927-8678 Fax: 504-927-6153
Contact: Ursula B. Carmena

Career Planning and Assessment Center, Metropolitan College, University of New Orleans, New Orleans, LA 70148
Phone: 504-286-7100

MAINE

Career Perspectives, 75 Pearl St., Suite 204, Portland, ME 04101
Phone: 207-775-4487
Contact: Deborah L. Gallant

Heart at Work, 261 Main St., Yarmouth, ME 04096
Phone: 207-846-0644
Contact: Barbara Sirois Babkirk, M.Ed., NCC, L.C.P.C., Licensed Counselor and Consultant
eMail: heartwork@javanet.com

Suit Yourself International Inc., 120 Pendleton Point, Islesboro, ME 04848
Phone: 207-734-8206
Contact: Debra Spencer, President

Women's Worth Career Counseling, 9 Village Lane, Westbrook, ME 04092
Phone: 207-856-6666
Contact: Jacqueline Murphy, Career Counselor

MARYLAND

***Call to Career**, 8720 Georgia Ave., Suite 802, Silver Spring, MD 20910
Phone: 301-961-1017
Contact: Cheryl Palmer, M.Ed., NCC, NCCC, President

Career Perspectives, 510 Sixth St., Annapolis, MD 21403
Phone: 410-280-2299
Contact: Jeanne H. Slawson, Career Consultant

Careerscope, Inc., One Mall North, Suite 216, 1025 Governor Warfield Pkwy., Columbia, MD 21044
Phone: 410-992-5042 or 301-596-1866
Contact: Constantine Bitsas, Executive Director

Career Transition Services, 3126 Berkshire Rd., Baltimore, MD 21214-3404
Phone: 410-444-5857
Contact: Michael Bryant

College of Notre Dame of Maryland, Continuing Education Center, 4701 N. Charles St., Baltimore, MD 21210
Phone: 410-532-5303

Friedman, Lynn, Ph.D, Clinical Psychologist & Work-life Consultant 4401 East-West Highway, Ste. 306, Bethesda, Maryland 20814
Phone: 301-656-9650
eMail: mail@drlynnfriedman.com

Goucher College, Goucher Center for Continuing Studies, 1021 Dulaney Valley Rd., Baltimore, MD 21204
Phone: 410-337-6200
Contact: Carole B. Ellin, Career/Job-Search Counselor

Headley, Anne S., M.A., 7100 Baltimore Ave., Suite 208, College Park, MD 20740
Phone: 301-779-1917

Kensington Consulting, 8701 Georgia Ave., Suite 406, Silver Spring, MD 20910
Phone: 301-587-1234
Contact: David M. Reile, Ph.D., NCCC, or Barbara H. Suddarth, Ph.D., NCCC

Maryland New Directions Inc., 2220 N. Charles St., Baltimore, MD 21218
Phone: 410-235-8800
Contact: Rose Marie Coughlin, Director

Mendelson, Irene N., NCCC, BEMW, Inc., Counseling and Training for the Workplace, 7984 D Old Georgetown Rd., Bethesda, MD 20814-2440
Phone: 301-657-8922

Positive Passages Life/Career Transition Counseling and Coaching, 4702 Falstone Ave., Chevy Chase, MD 20815
Phone: 301-907-0760
Contact: Jeanette Kreiser, Ed.D
eMail: jkreiser@earthlink.net

Prince George's Community College, Career Assessment and Planning Center, 301 Largo Rd., Largo, MD 20772
Phone: 301-322-0886
Contact: Margaret Taibi, Ph.D., Director

TransitionWorks, 10964 Bloomingdale Dr., Rockville, MD 20852-5550
Phone: 301-770-4277
Contact: Stephanie Kay, M.A., A.G.S., Principal; Nancy K. Schlossberg, Ed.D., Principal

MASSACHUSETTS

Alumni and Community Career Services, P.O. Box 35310, Amherst, MA 01003
Phone: 413-545-0742
Contact: Karen D. Knight, Associate Director
eMail: kdk@acad.umass.edu

Boston Career Link, 281 Huntington Ave., Boston, MA 02115
Phone: 617-536-1888

Career Development Center, Northern Essex Community College, Elliott Street, Haverhill, MA 01830
Phone: 978-556-3722
Contact: M.J. Pernaa, Director of Career Counseling

Career Link, Career Information Center, Kingston Public Library, 6 Green St., Kingston, MA 02364
Phone: 781-585-0517
Contact: Sia Stewart, Library Director

*__Career Management Consultants__, Thirty Park Ave., Worcester, MA 01605
Phone: 508-853-8669
Contact: Patricia Stepanski Plouffe, President

Career Resource Center, Worcester YWCA, 1 Salem Square, Worcester, MA 01608
Phone: 508-791-3181

Career Source, 185 Alewife Brook Pkwy., Cambridge, MA 02138
Phone: 617-661-7867
(Inherited the Radcliffe Career Services Office's library, after that office closed permanently. Also offers career counseling.)

*__Center for Career Development & Ministry__, 70 Chase St., Newton Center, MA 02159
Phone: 617-969-7750
Contact: Stephen Ott, Director

Center for Careers, Jewish Vocational Service, 105 Chauncy St., 6th Fl., Boston, MA 02111
Phone: 617-451-8147
Contact: Lee Ann Bennett, Coordinator, Core Services

Changes, Career Counseling and Job-hunt Training, 2516 Massachusetts Ave., Cambridge, MA 02140
Phone: 617-868-7775
Contact: Carl J. Schneider

Jewish Vocational Service, Mature Worker Programs, 333 Nahanton St., Newton, MA 02159
Phone: 617-965-7940

Linkage, Inc., 110 Hartwell Ave., Lexington, MA 02173
Phone: 781-862-4030
Contact: David J. Giber, Ph.D.

Miller, Wynne W., Coaching & Career Development, 15 Cypress St., Suite 200, Newton Center, MA 02459-2242
Phone: 617-527-4848 Fax: 617-527-2248
eMail: wynne@win-coaching.com

Murray Associates, P.O. Box 312, Westwood, MA 02090
Phone: 617-329-1287
Contact: Robert Murray, Ed.D., Licensed Psychologist

Neville Associates, Inc., 10 Tower Office Park, Suite 416, Woburn, MA 01801
Phone: 781-938-7870
Contact: Dr. Joseph Neville, Career Development Consultant

Smith College Career Development Office, Drew Hall, 84 Elm St., Northampton, MA 01063
Phone: 413-585-2570
Contact: Jane Sommer, Associate Director

Stein, Phyllis R., 59 Parker St., Cambridge, MA 02138
Phone: 617-354-7948
(Former Director of Radcliffe Career Services)

Wellness Center, 51 Mill St., Unit 8, Hanover, MA 02339
Phone: 781-829-4300
Contact: Janet Barr

MICHIGAN

*__C3 Circle__, Grand Rapids, MI 49544
Phone: 616-677-1952
Contact: Lois Dye, L.M. Dye, M.A., LPC

Jewish Vocational Service, 29699 Southfield Road, Southfield, MI 48076-2063
Phone: 248-559-5000

Keystone Coaching & Consulting, 22 Cherry St., Holland, MI 49423
Phone: 616-396-1517
Contact: Mark de Roo
eMail: crdesign@macatawa.org

Lansing Community College, 2020 Career and Employment Development Services, PO Box 40010, Lansing, MI 48901-7210
Phone: 517-483-1221 or 517-483-1172
Contact: James C. Osborn, Ph.D., LPC, Director, Career and Employment Services

*__Life Stewardship Associates__, 6918 Glen Creek Dr. SE, Dutton, MI 49316
Phone: 616-698-3125
Contact: Ken Soper, M.Div., M.A., Director

New Options: Counseling for Women in Transition, 2311 E. Stadium, Suite B-2, Ann Arbor, MI 48104
Phone: 313-973-0003
Contact: Phyllis Perry, M.S.W.

Oakland University, Continuum Center for Adult Counseling and Leadership Training, Rochester, MI 48309
Phone: 313-370-3033

University of Michigan, Center for the Education of Women, 330 East Liberty, Ann Arbor, MI 48104
Phone: 313-998-7080

Women's Resource Center, 252 State St. SE, Grand Rapids, MI 49503
Phone: 616-458-5443

MINNESOTA

Andrea, Richard E., Ph.D., 1014 Bartelmy Lane, Maplewood, MN 55119-3637
Phone: 612-730-9892

Associated Career Services, 3550 Lexington Ave. N., Suite 120, Shoreview, MN 55126
Phone: 612-787-0501

Career Dynamics, Inc., 8400 Normandale Lake Blvd., Suite 1220, Bloomington, MN 55437
Phone: 612-921-2378
Contact: Joan Strewler, Psychologist

Human Dynamics, 3036 Ontario Rd., Little Canada, MN 55117
Phone: 612-484-8299
Contact: Greg J. Cylkowski, M.A., founder

*__North Central Career Development Center__ (An Interdenominational Church Career Development Center), 516 Mission House Lane, New Brighton, MN 55112
Phone: 612-636-5120
Contact: Kenneth J. McFayden, Ph.D., Director

Prototype Career Services, 626 Armstrong Ave., St. Paul, MN 55102
Phone: 800-368-3197
Contact: Amy Lindgren and Julie Remington, Counseling Psychologists

Sizen, Stanley J., Vocational Services, P.O. Box 363, Anoka, MN 55303
Phone: 612-441-8053

Southwest Family Services, Career Planning Services, 10267 University Ave. North, Blaine, MN 55434
Phone: 612-825-4407
Contact: Kathy Bergman, M.A., LP.

Working Opportunities for Women, 2700 University Ave., #120, St. Paul, MN 55114
Phone: 612-647-9961

MISSISSIPPI

Mississippi Gulf Coast Community College, Career Development Center, Jackson County Campus, P.O. Box 100, Gautier, MS 39553
Phone: 601-497-9602
Contact: Rebecca Williams, Manager

Mississippi State University, Career Services Center, P.O. Box P, Colvard Union, Suite 316, Mississippi State, MS 39762-5515
Phone: 601-325-3344

MISSOURI

Career Center, Community Career Services, 110 Noyes Hall, University of Missouri, Columbia, MO 65211
Phone: 573-882-6801 Fax: 573-882-5440
Contact: Craig Benson
eMail: umccppc@missouri.edu

Career Management Center, 8301 State Line Rd., Suite 202, Kansas City, MO 64114
Phone: 816-363-1500
Contact: Janice Y. Benjamin, President

Forest Institute of Professional Psychology, 2885 West Battlefield Rd., Springfield, MO 65807
Phone: 417-823-3477
Contact: Rod C. Cannedy, Ph.D.

The Job Doctor, 505 S. Ewing, St. Louis, MO 63103
Phone: 314-863-1166
Contact: M. Rose Jonas, Ph.D.

*__Midwest Career Development Service__ (An Interdenominational Church Career Development Center), 754 N. 31st St., Kansas City, KS 66110-0816
Contact: Ronald Brushwyler, Director

Women's Center, University of Missouri-Kansas City, 5100 Rockhill Rd., 104 Scofield Hall, Kansas City, MO 64110
Phone: 816-235-1638

MONTANA

Career Transitions, 321 E. Main, Suite 215, Bozeman, MT 59715
Phone: 406-587-1721
Contact: Estella Villasenor, Executive Director; Darla Joyner, Assistant Director

NEBRASKA

Career Management Services, 5000 Central Park Dr., Suite 204, Lincoln, NE 68504
Phone: 402-466-8427
Contact: Vaughn L. Carter, President

*__Olson Counseling Services__, 8720 Frederick, Suite 105, Omaha, NE 68128
Phone: 402-390-2342
Contact: Gail A. Olson, P.A.C.

Student Success Center,
Central Community College,
Hastings Campus, Hastings, NE 68902
Phone: 402-461-2424

NEVADA

Career/Lifestyles, Alamo Plaza,
4550 W. Oakey Blvd., Suite 111,
Las Vegas, NV 89102
Phone: 702-258-3353
Contact: Carol J. Cravens, M.A., NCC

Greener Pastures Institute,
6301 S. Squaw Valley Rd., Suite 1383,
Pahrump, NV 89048-7949
Phone: 800-688-6352
Contact: Bill Seavey

NEW HAMPSHIRE

Individual Employment Services,
90-A Sixth St., P.O. Box 917, Dover, NH 03820
Phone: 603-742-5616
Contact: James Otis, Employment Counselor

Tucker, Janet, Career Counselor, M.Ed., NCCC, 10 String Bridge, Exeter, NH 03833
Phone: 603-772-8693
eMail: jbtucker@nh.ultranet.com

NEW JERSEY

Adult Advisory Service, Kean College of New Jersey. Administration Bldg.,
Union, NJ 07083
Phone: 908-527-2210

Adult Resource Center,
100 Horseneck Road, Montville, NJ 07045
Phone: 201-335-6910

Arista Concepts Career Development Service, P.O. Box 2436, Princeton, NJ 08540
Phone: 609-921-0308
Contact: Kera Greene, M.Ed.

Baskin Business & Career Services,
P.O. 956, Springfield, NJ 07081
Phone: 973-379-4393
Contact: Beverly Baskin,
M.A., LPC, NCCC, CPRW
eMail: bbcs@att.net

Behavior Dynamics Associates, Inc.,
34 Cambridge Terrace,
Springfield, NJ 07081
Phone: 201-912-0136
Contact: Roy Hirschfeld

Career Options Center, YWCA Tribute to Women and Industry (TWIN) Program,
232 E. Front St., Plainfield, NJ 07060
Phone: 908-756-3836 or 908-273-4242
Contact: Janet M. Korba, Program Director

Center for Life Enhancement,
1156 E. Ridgewood Ave.,
Ridgewood, NJ 07450
Phone: 201-670-8443
Contact: David R. Johnson,
Director of Career Programs

Cohen, Jerry, M.A., NCC, NCCC,
Chester Professional Bldg.,
P.O. Box 235, Chester, NJ 07930
Phone: 908-789-4404

Collins, Loree, 3 Beechwood Rd.,
Summit, NJ 07901
Phone: 908-273-9219

Douglass College, Douglass Advisory Services for Women, Rutgers Women's Center, 132 George St.,
New Brunswick, NJ 08903
Phone: 908-932-9603

Dowd, Juditha,
440 Rosemont Ringoes Road,
Stockton, NJ 08559
Phone: 609-397-9375 Fax: 609-397-9375
eMail: jdowd@blast.net

Grundfest, Sandra, Ed.D., Licensed Psychologist & Certified Career Counselor,
35 Clyde Road, Suite 101, Somerset,
NJ 08873
Phone: 609-921-8401 Fax: 609-921-9430

Guarneri Associates,
Career and Job-search Counseling,
1101 Lawrence Rd., Lawrenceville, NJ 08648
Phone: 609-771-1669
Contact: Susan Guarneri,
LPC, CPRW, JCTC, NCCC;
Jack Guarneri, M.S., NCC, NCCC
eMail: resumagic@aol.com

The Job Club, Princeton Unitarian Church,
Cherry Hill Rd., Princeton, NJ 08540
Phone: 609-924-1604
(Free service, open to the community)

JobSeekers in Princeton N.J. Trinity Church, 33 Mercer Street,
Princeton, NJ 08542
Phone: 609-924-2277
(Meets Tuesdays, 7:30–9:30 p.m.)

Job Seekers of Montclair,
St. Luke's Episcopal Church,
73 S. Fullerton Ave, Montclair, NJ 07042
Phone: 201-783-3442
(Meets Thursdays, 7:30-9:30 p.m.)

Lester Minsuk & Associates,
29 Exeter Rd., East Windsor, NJ 08520
Phone: 609-448-4600

Mercer County Community College,
Career Services, 1200 Old Trenton Rd.,
Trenton, NJ 08690
Phone: 609-586-4800, ext. 304

Metro Career Services,
784 Morris Turnpike, Suite 203,
Short Hills, NJ 07078
Phone: 973-912-0106
Contact: Judy Scherer, M.A.
eMail: metcareer@aol.com

*__Northeast Career Center__
(An Interdenominational Church Career Development Center),
407 Nassau Street, Princeton, NJ 08540
Phone: 609-924-9408
Contact: Linda Mumford, M.A., Director
eMail: nccc@nerc.com

Princeton Management Consultants, Inc., 99 Moore St., Princeton, NJ 08540
Phone: 609-924-2411
Contact: Niels H. Nielsen, M.A., Job and Career Counselor

Resource Center for Women, 31 Woodland Ave., Summit, NJ 07901
Phone: 908-273-7253

Sigmon, Scott B., Ed.D., 1945 Morris Ave., Union, NJ 07083
Phone: 908-686-7555

NEW MEXICO

Career Camp, P.O. Box 5, Taos, NM 87571
Phone: 505-751-3255
Contact: Laurel Donnellan, Director
eMail: info@careercamp.com

Young Women's Christian Association, YWCA Career Services Center, 7201 Paseo Del Norte NE, Albuquerque, NM 87113
Phone: 505-822-9922

NEW YORK

Allen, Carol, Consultant, 560 West 43rd St., Suite 5G, New York, NY 10036
Phone: 212-268-5182

Bernstein, Alan B., CSW, PC, 122 East 82nd St., New York, NY 10028
Phone: 212-288-4881

Career 101 Associates, 230 West 55th St., Suite 17F, New York, NY 10019
Phone: 212-333-4013
Contact: L. Michelle Tullier, Ph.D., Director

Career Development Center, Long Island University, C.W. Post Campus, Brookville, NY 11548
Phone: 516-299-225
Contact: Pamela Lennox, Ph.D., Director

Career Resource Center, Bethlehem Public Library, 451 Delaware Ave., Delmar, NY 12054
Phone: 518-439-9314
Contact: Denise L. Coblish, Career Resources Librarian

Career Strategies, Inc., 350 West 24th St., New York, NY 10011
Phone: 212-807-1340
Contact: "CB" Bowman, President

Careers by Choice, Inc., 205 E. Main St., Huntington, NY 11743
Phone: 631-673-5432
Contact: Marjorie ("MJ") Feld

Careers In Transition, A Private Career Advisory Service, Glenmont, NY 12077
Contact: Thomas J. Denham, Ed.M.
eMail: tdenham@siena.edu

Celia Paul Associates, 1776 Broadway, Suite 1806, New York, NY 10019
Phone: 212-397-1020
Contact: Celia Paul, President; Dr. Stephen Rosen, Chairman
eMail: srosenc@ix.netcom.com
(Specializing in Lawyers, Doctors, and Scientists)

Center for Creativity and Work, P.O. Box 9158, Woodstock, NY 12498
Phone: 212-490-9158 or 914-336-8318
Contact: Allie Roth, President
(Offices in Manhattan and Woodstock)

Janice La Rouche Associates, 333 Central Park W., New York, NY 10025
Phone: 212-663-0970

The John C. Crystal Center, 152 Madison Ave., 23rd Fl., New York, NY 10016
Phone: 212-889-8500 or 800-333-9003
Contact: Nella G. Barkley, President
(John Crystal, the original founder of this center, died ten years ago; Nella, his business partner for many years, now directs the center's work.)

*__Judith Gerberg Associates__, 250 West 57th St., New York, NY 10107
Phone: 212-315-2322

Hofstra University, Career Counseling Center, Room 120, Saltzman Community Center, 131 Hofstra, Hempstead, NY 11550
Phone: 516-463-6788

Kingsborough Community College, Office of Career Counseling and Placement, 2001 Oriental Blvd., Rm. C102, Brooklyn, NY 11235
Phone: 718-368-5115

Livelyhood Job Search Center, 301 Madison Ave., 3rd Floor, New York, NY 10017
Phone: 212-687-2411
Contact: John Aigner, Director

McPherson, James E., 101 Ives Hall, Cornell University, Ithaca, NY 14853-3901

New Options, 960 Park Ave., New York, NY 10028
Phone: 212-535-1444

Onondaga County Public Library, The Galleries of Syracuse, 447 South Salina St., Syracuse, NY 13202-2494
Phone: 315-435-1895
Contact: Holly Sammons, Librarian
eMail: sammons@ocpl.lib.ny.us.
(Information Services. Has Info Trac, a computerized index and directory of over 100,000 companies, plus other job-hunting resources)

Orange County Community College, Counseling Center, 115 South St., Middletown, NY 10940
Phone: 914-341-4070

Personnel Sciences Center, Inc., 276 Fifth Ave., Suite 401, New York, NY 10001
Phone: 212-683-3008 Fax: 212 683-3436
Contact: Dr. Jeffrey A. Goldberg, Ph.D., President, Licensed Psychologist

The Prager-Bernstein Group,
441 Lexington Ave., Suite 1404,
New York, NY 10017
Phone: 212-697-0645
Contact: Leslie B. Prager, M.A., C.M.P., Senior Partner
eMail: Leslie-PBG@eMail.msn.com

Psychological Services Center,
Career Services Unit, University at Albany, SUNY, Husted 167, 135 Western Ave.,
Albany, NY 12222
Phone: 518-442-4900 Fax: 315-446-5869
Contact: George B. Litchford, Ph.D., Director
(Individual and group career counseling)

RLS Career Center,
Career Development Specialist,
770 James Street, Syracuse, NY 13203
Phone: 315-446-0500 Fax: 315-446-5869
Contact: Rebecca A. Livengood, Executive Director
eMail: rls@borg.com

Schenectady Public Library,
Job Information Center,
99 Clinton St., Schenectady, NY 12305
(Has weekly listings, including job-search listings of companies nationwide)

Scientific Career Transitions,
Science & Technology Advisory Board,
1776 Broadway, Suite 1806,
New York, NY 10019
Phone: 212-397-1021
Contact: Stephen Rosen, Ph.D.
eMail: srosenc@ix.netcom.com
(Specializes in scientists and engineers)

Vehicles, Inc., Life Skills and Career Training, 1832 Madison Ave., Room 202, New York, NY 10035-2707
Phone: 212-722-1111
Contact: Janet Avery

Volunteer Consulting Group, Inc.,
6 East 39th St., 6th Floor,
New York, NY 10016
Phone: 212-447-1236

WIN Workshops (Women in Networking),
1120 Avenue of the Americas, Fourth Floor,
New York, NY 10036
Phone: 212-333-8788
Contact: Emily Koltnow

NORTH CAROLINA

Career Consulting Associates of Raleigh,
P.O. Box 17653, Raleigh, NC 27619
Phone: 919-782-3252
Contact: Susan W. Simonds, President

Career, Educational, Psychological Evaluations, 2915 Providence Rd., Suite 300, Charlotte, NC 28211
Phone: 704-362-1942

Career Focus Workshops,
8301 Brittanis Field Road,
Oakridge, NC 27310
Phone: 336-643-1025
Contact: Glenn Wise, President
eMail: glwise2@cs.com

Career Management Center,
3203 Woman's Club Dr., Suite 100,
Raleigh, NC 27612
Phone: 919-787-1222, ext. 109
Contact: Temple G. Porter, Director

***The Career and Personal Counseling Service** (An Interdenominational Church Career Development Center),
4108 Park Rd., Suite 200,
Charlotte, NC 28209
Phone: 919-276-3162 or 704-523-7751
Fax: 704-523-7752
Contact: Sue M. Setzer, Executive Director
eMail: career@trellis.net

The Intensive Life/Career Planning Workshop, 131 Chimney Rise Dr.,
Cary, NC 27511
Phone: 919-469-5775
Contact: Mike Thomas, Ph.D.; Steve Mulliner, Ph.D.
eMail: mikethomas@nc.rr.com

Joyce Richman & Associates, Ltd.,
2911 Shady Lawn Dr.,
Greensboro, NC 27408
Phone: 910-288-1799

Kochendofer, Sally, Ph.D.,
Charlotte, NC 28211
Phone: 704-362-1514
eMail: drsallyk@mindspring.com

Lambeth, Diane E., M.S.W.,
Career Consultant. P.O. Box 18945,
Raleigh, NC 27619
Phone: 919-828-3286

Life Management Services, LC,
301 Gregson Dr., Cary, NC 27511
Phone: 919-481-4707
Contact: Marilyn and Hal Shook
(The Shooks originally trained with John Crystal, though they have evolved their own program since then)

Truax, Bonnie M., Ed.D., NCCC,
Career/Life Planning and Relocation Services,
2102 N. Elm St., Suite K1,
Greensboro, NC 27408
Phone: 910-271-2050
(Free support group)

Women's Center of Raleigh,
128 E. Hargett St., Suite 10,
Raleigh, NC 27601
Phone: 919-829-3711

NORTH DAKOTA

Business & Life Resources Career Development Center,
112 North University Dr., Suite 3300,
Fargo, ND 58103
Phone: 800-950-0848
Contact: Gail Reierson

OHIO

Adult Resource Center, The University of Akron, Buckingham Center for Continuing Education, Room 55, Akron, OH 44325-3102
Phone: 216-972-7448
Contact: Sandra B. Edwards, Director

Career Initiatives Center,
1557 E. 27th St., Cleveland, OH 44114
Phone: 216-574-8998
Contact: Richard Hanscom, Director

Career Point, Belden-Whipple Building, 4150 Belden Village St., N.W., Suite 101, Canton, OH 44718
Phone: 216-492-1920
Contact: Victor W. Valli, Career Consultant

Cuyahoga County Public Library InfoPLACE Service, Career, Education & Community Information Service, 5225 Library Lane, Maple Heights, OH 44137-1291
Phone: 216-475-2225

*__Diversified Career Services, Inc.__,
2490 Edington Rd., Columbus, OH 43221
Phone: 614-481-0508
Contact: Laura Armstrong, LPC, NBC, Owner & President;
Robert J. Armstrong, M.Div., Ph.D., LPC
eMail: armstrong@creatingfutures.org

The Human Touch
Phone: 513-772-5839
Contact: Judy R. Kroger, LPC, Career and Human Resources Counselor
eMail: judykroger@aol.com

J&K Associates and Success Skills Seminars, Inc.,
607 Otterbein Ave., Dayton, OH 45406-4507
Phone: 937-274-3630 or 937-274-4375
Contact: Pat Kenney, Ph.D., President

*__KSM Careers & Consulting__,
1655 W. Market St., Suite 506, Akron, OH 44313
Phone: 330-867-0242
Contact: Kathryn Musholt, President

*__Midwest Career Development Service__ (An Interdenominational Church Career Development Center), 1520 Old Henderson Rd., Suite 102B, Columbus, OH 43221-3616
Phone: 614-442-8822

New Career, 328 Race St., Dover, OH 44622
Phone: 216-364-5557
Contact: Marshall Karp, M.A., NCC, LPC, Owner

*__Professional Pastoral Counseling Institute, Inc.__, 8035 Hosbrook Rd., Suite 300, Cincinnati, OH 45236
Phone: 513-791-5990
Contact: Judy Kroger, Counselor

Pyramid Career Services, Inc.,
2400 Cleveland Ave., NW, Canton, OH 44709
Phone: 330-453-3767
Contact: Maryellen R. Hess, Executive Director

Woods, Anne, 8225 Markhaven Ct., W. Worthington, OH 43235
Phone: 614-888-7941

OKLAHOMA

Resonance and the YMCA Women's Resource Center of Tulsa,
1608 S. Elwood, Tulsa, OK 74119
Phone: 918-587-3888
Contact: Penny Painter, Executive Director, Resonance; Jane Vantine, Site Director, YMCA Women's Resource Center; Nancy Weber, M.A., Career Counselor

Stoodley, Martha, Rt. #1, Box 575, Checotah, OK 74426-9742

Transitions Counseling Center,
6216 S. Lewis Ave., Suite 148, Tulsa, OK 74136
Phone: 918-742-4877
Contact: Michelle Jones, M.S., Owner/Career Counselor

OREGON

Career Development, P.O. Box 850, Forest Grove, OR 97116
Phone: 503-357-9233
Contact: Edward H. Hosley, Ph.D., Director

Career Pathways, 4037 NW Elmwood Dr., Corvallis, OR 97330-1068
Phone: 541-754-1958
Contact: Peggy Carrick, M.A., LPC, NCC
eMail: panda@proaxis.com

Verk Consultants, Inc., 1190 Olive St., P.O. Box 11277, Eugene, OR 97440
Phone: 541-687-9170
Contact: Larry H. Malmgren, M.S., President

PENNSYLVANIA

Beck Associates/ Susquehanna Institute, East Shore Medical Center, 2405 Linglestown Road, Harrisburg, PA 17110-9429
Phone: 717-545-5500 Fax: 717-545-5858
Contact: Dr. Edward S. Beck
eMail: esb1@juno.com

Career by Design, 1011 Cathill Rd., Sellersville, PA 18960
Phone: 215-723-8413
Contact: Henry D. Landes, Career Consultant

Career Development Center, Jewish Family & Children's Service, 5743 Bartlett St., Pittsburgh, PA 15217
Phone: 412-422-5627
Contact: Linda Ehrenreich, Director

Career Strategies, 1845 Walnut St., 7th Floor, Philadelphia, PA 19103-4707
Phone: 215-854-1824

Center for Adults in Transition, Bucks County Community College, Newtown, PA 18940
Phone: 215-968-8188

Center for Career Services / Jewish Employment and Vocational Service, 1845 Walnut St., 7th floor, Philadelphia, PA 19103-4707
Phone: 215-854-1800 Fax: 215-854-1880
Contact: Joyce Zawodny, Director

Eikleberry, Carol, Ph.D., 1376 Freeport Rd., Suite 3A, Pittsburgh, PA 15238
Phone: 412-963-9008

Forty Plus of Philadelphia, Inc., 1218 Chestnut St., Philadelphia, PA 19107-4810
Phone: 215-923-2074

Haynes, Lathe, Ph.D., 401 Shady Ave., Suite C107, Pittsburgh, PA 15238
Phone: 412-361-6336

Kelly, Jack, Career Counselor, Career Pro Resume Services, 251 DeKalb Pike, Suite E608, King of Prussia, PA 19406
Phone: 610-337-7187

Kessler, Jane E., M.A., Licensed Psychologist, 252 W. Swamp Rd., Suite 56, Doylestown, PA 18901
Phone: 215-348-8218 Fax: 215-348-0329

***Mid-Atlantic Career Center**, 1401 Columbia Ave., Lancaster, PA 17603
Phone: 717-397-7451
Contact: Dennis K. Hall, Executive Director
eMail: macctr@belatlantic.org

Options Career and Human Resource Consulting, 225 S. 15th St., Suite 1635, Philadelphia, PA 19102-3916
Phone: 215-735-2202 Fax: 215-735-8097
eMail: info@optionscareers.org

Priority Two, P.O. Box 343, Sewickley, PA 15143
Phone: 412-935-0252
Contact: Pat Gottschalk, Administrative Assistant
(Five locations in the Pittsburgh area; call for addresses. No one is turned away for lack of funds)

RHODE ISLAND

Career Designs, 104 Rankin Ave., Providence, RI 02908-4216
Phone: 401-521-2323
Contact: Terence Duniho, Career Consultant

SOUTH CAROLINA

Career Counselor Services, Inc., 138 Ingleoak Lane, Greenville, SC 29615
Phone: 864-242-4474
Contact: Al A. Hafer, Ed.D., NCCC, NCC, LPC

Greenville Technical College, Career Advancement Center, P.O. Box 5616, Greenville, SC 29606
Phone: 864-250-8281
Contact: F.M. Rogers, Director

SOUTH DAKOTA

Career Concepts Planning Center, Inc., 1602 Mountain View Rd., Suite 102, Rapid City, SD 57702
Phone: 605-342-5177, or toll free: 800-456-0832
Contact: Melvin M. Tuggle, Jr., President

***Coleman, Barb**, Bethesda Christian Counseling Midwest, Inc., 231 S. Phillips Ave., Suite 350, Sioux Falls, SD 57104-6326
Phone: 605-334-3739

University of Sioux Falls, The Center for Women, 1101 W. 22nd St., Sioux Falls, SD 57105.
Phone: 605-331-6697
Contact: Tami Haug-Davis, Director

TENNESSEE

***Career Achievement**, NiS International Services, 1321 Murfreesboro Road, Suite 610, Nashville, TN 37217
Phone: 615-367-5000
Contact: William L. (Bill) Karlson; Harry McClure, Manager

***Career Resources**, 2323 Hillsboro Rd., Suite 508, Nashville, TN 37212
Phone: 615-297-0404
Contact: Jane C. Hardy, Principal

***Miller, Dan,** The Business Source, 7100 Executive Center Dr., Suite 110, Brentwood, TN 37027
Phone: 615-373-7771

***RHM Group**, P.O. Box 271135, Nashville, TN 37227
Phone: 615-391-5000
Contact: Robert H. McKown

World Career Transition, P.O. Box 1423, Brentwood, TN 37027-1423
Phone: 800-366-0945
Contact: Bill Karlson, Executive VP

YWCA of Nashville and Middle Tennessee, Career/Life Planning Program, 1608 Woodmont Blvd., Nashville, TN 37215
Phone: 615-269-9922

TEXAS

Austin Career Associates, 901 Rio Grande, Austin, TX 78701
Phone: 512-474-1185
Contact: Maydelle Fason, Licensed Career Counselor

Career Action Associates P.C., 8350 Meadow Rd., Suite 272, Dallas, TX 75231
Phone: 214-378-8350
Contact: Joyce Shoop, LPC; Rebecca Hayes, M. Ed, CRC, LPC
(Office also at 1325 8th Ave., Ft. Worth, TX 76104. Phone: 817-926-9941)

Career Management Resources,
2602 River Oaks, Irving, TX 76006
Phone: 817-261-5308
Contact: Mary Holdcroft, Career Coach, M.Ed., LPC, NCC, NCCC

Career and Recovery Resources, Inc.,
2525 San Jacinto, Houston, TX 77002
Phone: 713-754-7000
Contact: Vernal Swisher, Director

Citrin, Richard S., Ph.D., Psychologist, Iatreia Institute, 1152 Country Club Ln., Ft. Worth, TX 76112
Phone: 817-654-9600

Counseling Services of Houston,
1964 W. Gray, Suite 204, Houston, TX 77019
Phone: 713-521-9391
Contact: Rosemary C. Vienot, M.S., LPC

Employment/Career Information Resource Center, Corpus Christi Public Library, 805 Comanche, Corpus Christi, TX 78401
Phone: 512-880-7004
Contact: Lynda F. Whitton-Henley, Career Information Specialist

Fason, Maydelle, Employment Consultant, 1607 Poquonock Road, Austin, TX 78703
Phone: 512-474-1185

New Directions Counseling Center,
8140 North Mopac, Bldg. II, Suite 230, Austin, TX 78759
Phone: 512-343-9496
Contact: Jeanne Quereau, M.A., LPC

***New Life Institute**, P.O. Box 4487, Austin, TX 78765
Phone: 512-469-9447
Contact: Bob Breihan, Director

Ragland, Chuck, Transformational Consultancy, 2504 Briargrove Dr., Austin, TX 78704-2704
Phone: 512-440-1200

San Antonio Psychological Services,
6800 Park Ten Blvd., Suite 208 North, San Antonio, TX 78213
Phone: 210-737-2039

***Southwest Career Development Center** (An Interdenominational Church Career Development Center), Box 5923, Arlington, TX 76005
Phone: 817-640-5181
Contact: Jerry D. Overton, Director-Counselor

***Stedham, Mary**, Counseling/Consulting Services, 2434 S. 10th, Abilene, TX 79605
Phone: 915-672-4044

Vocational Guidance Service, 2600 S.W. Freeway, Suite 800, Houston, TX 77098
Phone: 713-535-7104
Contact: Beverley K. Finn, Director

***Worklife Institute Consulting**,
7100 Regency Square, Suite 210, Houston, TX 77036
Phone: 713-266-2456
Contact: Diana C. Dale, Director

UTAH

University of Utah, Center for Adult Development, 1195 Annex Bldg., Salt Lake City, UT 84112
Phone: 801-581-3228

VERMONT

Career Networks and ProSearch,
1372 Old Stage Rd., Williston, VT 05495
Phone: 800-918-WORK or 802-872-1533

VIRGINIA

The BrownMiller Group,
312 Granite Ave., Richmond, VA 23226
Phone: 804-288-2157
Contact: Sally Brown, Bonnie Miller

Change & Growth Consulting,
6220 Old Franconia Rd., Alexandria, VA 22310
Phone: 703-569-2029
Contact: Barbara S. Woods, M.Ed., NCC, LPC, Counselor

Educational Opportunity Center,
121 College Place, Suite 200, Norfolk, VA 23510
Phone: 757-683-2312
Contact: Agatha A. Peterson, Director

Fairfax County Office for Women,
The Government Center,
12000 Government Center Pkwy., Suite 38, Fairfax, VA 22035
Phone: 703-324-5735
Contact: Elizabeth Lee McManus, Program Manager

Hollins College, Women's Center, P.O. Box 9628, Roanoke, VA 24020
Phone: 703-362-6269
Contact: Tina Rolen, Career Counselor

Mary Baldwin College, Rosemarie Sena Center for Career and Life Planning, Kable House, Staunton, VA 24401
Phone: 703-887-7221

McCarthy & Company, Career Transition Management, 4201 South 32nd Rd., Arlington, VA 22206
Phone: 703-761-4300
Contact: Peter McCarthy, President

Psychological Consultants, Inc.,
6724 Patterson Ave., Richmond, VA 23226
Phone: 804-288-4125

Virginia Commonwealth University, University Career Center, 907 Floyd Ave., Room 2007, Richmond, VA 23284-2007
Phone: 804-367-1645

The Women's Center, 133 Park St., NE, Vienna, VA 22180
Phone: 703-281-2657
Contact: Conda Blackmon

Working from the Heart,
1309 Merchant Lane, McLean, VA 22101
Contact: Jacqueline McMakin and Susan Gardiner, Co-Directors

WASHINGTON

Bridgeway Career Development,
1800 Westlake Avenue N., Suite 110,
Seattle, WA 98101
Phone: 206-789-5222
Contact: Janet Scarborough, M.Ed.,
C.M.H.C., President
eMail: js@bridgewaycareer.com

Career Management Institute,
8404 27th St. W., University Place, WA 98466
Phone: 253-565-8818
Contact: Ruthann Reim, M.A., NCC,
CMHC
eMail: careermi@nwrain.com

***Center for Career Decisions,**
Career Counseling and Consulting,
3121 East Madison St., Suite 209,
Seattle, WA 98112
Phone: 206-325-9093
Contact: Larry Gaffin

Centerpoint Institute for Life and Career Renewal, Career Consultants,
603 Stewart St., 1018 Lloyd Bldg.,
Seattle, WA 98101
Phone: 206-622-8070
Contact: Carol Vecchio, Career Counselor

Churchill, Diane, 508 W. Sixth, Suite 202,
Spokane, WA 99204
Phone: 509-458-0962

***Haldane, Bernard,**
900 University Street #17E, Seattle, WA
98101
Phone: 206-382-3658
(A pioneer in the clergy career management and assessment field, Bernard teaches seminars and trains volunteers to do job-search counseling. This individual service is not to be confused with the agency that bears his name, of which he gave up ownership long ago.)

The Individual Development Center, Inc.
(I.D. Center), 1020 E. John, Seattle, WA
98102
Phone: 206-329-0600
Contact: Mary Lou Hunt, NCC, M.A.,
President

Lue, Keith, P.O. Box 1554,
Issaquah, WA 98027
Phone: 425-415-2744.
eMail: keithlue@keydiscovery.com

***People Management Group International,** 924 First St., Suite A,
Snohomish, WA 98290
Phone: 206-563-0105
Contact: Arthur F. Miller, Jr., Chairman

WEST VIRGINIA

Jepson, Ed, 2 Hazlett Court,
Wheeling, WV 26003
Phone: 304-232-2375

Ticich, Frank, M.S., LPC, CRC, CVE,
Career Consultant, 153 Tartan Drive,
Iollanbee, WV 26037
Phone: 304-748-1772
(Free Service Available)

WISCONSIN

Making Alternative Plans,
Career Development Center,
Alverno College, 3401 S. 39th St.,
P.O. Box 343922, Milwaukee, WI 53234-3922
Phone: 414-382-6010

Swanson, David, Career Seminars and
Workshops, 7235 West Wells St.,
Wauwatosa, WI 53213-3607
Phone: 414-774-4755
eMail: dswanson@wi.rr.com
(David was on staff at my two-week workshop twenty times)

WYOMING

Gray, Barbara W., Career Consultant,
P.O. Box 9490, Jackson, WY 83002
Phone: 307-733-6544

University of Wyoming,
Career Planning and Placement Center,
P.O. Box 3195/Knight Hall 228,
Laramie, WY 82071-3195
Phone: 307-766-2398

U.S.A. -- NATIONWIDE

Forty Plus Clubs: A nationwide network of voluntary, autonomous nonprofit clubs, manned by its unemployed members (who must give a certain number of hours of service per week on assigned committees), paying no salaries, supported by initiation fees (often around $500) and monthly dues (often around $60 per month). Varying reports, as to their helpfulness. However, one reader gave a very good report on them recently: "I would just like to let you know that 40+, for me, has been a really big help. They provide good job search training.... But even more importantly, for me, is the professional office environment they provide to work out of, and the fellowship of others who are also looking for work.... As they say at 40+, 'It's hell to job search alone.'"

If you have Internet access, a list of the North American 40+ chapters is to be found at:

`http://www.fp.org/chapters/htm`

Eleven of these chapters have their own Web sites; in my opinion, the best and most up-to-date one belongs to the Greater Washington chapter:

`http://www.fp.org/`

For those who lack Web access, at this writing there are clubs in the following cities (listed alphabetically by States): *California*: San Diego, Orange, Los Angeles, Oakland; *Colorado*: Lakewood, Ft. Collins, Colorado Springs; *District of Columbia*: Greater Washington; *Hawaii*: Honolulu; *Illinois*: Chicago; *Minnesota*: St. Paul; *New York*: New York, Buffalo; *Ohio*: Columbus; *Oregon*: Beaverton; *Pennsylvania*: Philadelphia; *Texas*:

Houston, Dallas; *Utah*: Salt Lake City; *Washington*: Bellevue; *Wisconsin*: Brookfield; and in *Canada*: Toronto.

If you live in or near any of these cities, you can check the white pages of your phone book (under "Forty Plus") for their address and phone number.

CANADA

Alberta

Work from the Heart, 8708 136 St., Edmonton, Alberta T5R 0B9
Phone: 403-484-8387
Contact: Marguerite Todd

British Colombia

CBD Network Inc., #201-2033 Gordon Dr., Kelowna, B.C. V1Y 3J2
Phone: 250-717-1821

Conscious Career Choices, 402-2277 West 2nd Ave, Vancouver, B.C. V6K 2G3
Phone: 604-737-3955
Contact: Marlene Haley, B.A., M.Ed., Career Counselor
Web: www.Findworkyoulove.com

Curtis, Susan, M.Ed., 4513 West 13th Ave., Vancouver, B.C. V6R 2V5
Phone: 604-228-9618

R. Morin & Co., Ltd., 1503–1625 Hornby St., Vancouver, B.C. V6Z 2M2
Phone: 604-688-7212
Contact: Rita Morin

Manitoba

Job-Finding Club, 516-294 Portage Ave., Winnipeg, Manitoba R3C 0B9
Phone: 204-947-1948

New Brunswick

Careerguide, Ryan Bldg., 3rd Floor, 57 Carleton St., Fredericton, New Brunswick
Phone: 506-459-4185
Contact: Elspeth (Beth) Leroux, B.A., B.Ed., M.Ed.

Nova Scotia

Enhancing Your Horizons Consulting, 25 Birchwood Terr., Dartmouth, Nova Scotia B3A 3W2
Phone: 902-464-9110
Contact: Sue Landry

People Plus, PLA Centre, 7001 Mumford Rd., Halifax Shopping Centre, Tower 1, Suite 101, Halifax, Nova Scotia B3L 4N9
Phone: 902-454-2809

Ontario

After Graduation Career Counseling, 73 Roxborough St. West, Toronto, Ontario M5R 1T9
Phone: 416-923-8319
Contact: Teresa Snelgrove, Ph.D., Director

André Filion & Associates, Inc., 151 Slater Street, Suite 500, Ottawa, Ontario K1P 5H3
Phone: 613-230-7023
Contact: Kenneth Des Roches

Career Partners International/Hazell & Ass., 1220 Yonge St., 3rd Floor, Toronto, Ontario M4T 1W1
Phone: 416-961-3700
eMail: mhazell@hazell.com

Career Strategy Counseling, 2 Briar Hill Place, London, Ontario N5Y 1P7
Phone: 519-660-0622
Contact: David H. Wenn, B.A., M.Ed.
eMail: clarkes@wwdc.com

Changes by Choice, 190 Burndale Ave., North York, Ontario M2N 1T2
Phone: 416-590-9939
Contact: Patti Davie

Donner & Wheeler and Associates, Career Development Consultants, Health and Social Services Sector, 1055 Bloor St. East, Mississauga, Ontario L4Y 2N5
Phone: 905-949-5954
Contact: Mary M. Wheeler
(Offers workshops particularly for those in the health and social services sector)

Human Achievement Associates, 22 Cottonwood Crescent, London, Ontario N6G 2Y8
Phone: 519-657-3000
Contact: Mr. Kerry A. Hill

Mid-Life Transitions, 2 Slade Ave., Toronto, Ontario M6G 3A1
Phone: 416-653-0563
Contact: Marilyn Melville

The Precision Group, 400 Matheson Blvd. East, Unit 18, Mississauga, Ontario L4Z 1N8
Phone: 905-507-8696
Contact: Harold Harder, B.Sc., B.Admin.St.

Puttock, Judith, B.B.A., C.H.R.P., Career Management Consultant, Strategic Career Options, Planning & Education (SCOPE), 913 Southwind Court, Newmarket, Ontario
Phone: 905-898-0180

Steinberg, Susan, M.Ed., 74 Denlow Blvd., Don Mills, Ontario M3B 1P9
Phone: 416-449-6936

YMCA Career Planning & Development, 42 Charles Street East, Toronto, Ontario M4Y 1T4
Phone: 416-928-9622.

Quebec

Jewish Vocational Service, Centre Juif D'Orientation et de L'Emploi, 5151, ch. de la Côte Ste-Catherine, Montréal, Quebec, H3W 1M6
Phone: 514-345-2625
Contact: Alta Abramowitz, Director, Employment Development Services.
(Uses both French and English versions of Parachute)
(Utilise des versions françaises et anglaises de parachute)

Longpre, Jean-Marc,
3-600 Odette-Oligny, Lavel,
Quebec, Canada H7N 5Z2
Phone: 450-967-9849

Roy, Marie-Carmelle,
1281 LasalleLongueil, Quebec,
Canada, J4K 3H6
Phone: 450-442-2648
eMail: mcroy@vidiotron.ca

Saskatchewan

People Focus, 712 10th St. East,
Saskatoon, S7H OH1
Phone: 306-933-4956
Contact: Carol Stevenson Seller

OVERSEAS

(Listed by country and city, which are in **bold type***.)*

Cabinet Daniel Porot, 1, rue Verdaine,
CH-1204 **Geneva, Switzerland**
Phone: 41 22 311 04 38
Contact: Daniel Porot, Founder
(Daniel was co-leader with me each summer at my international Two-Week Workshop for twenty years)

Kessler-Laufbahnberatung,
Alpenblickstr. 33, CH-8645,
Jona b. **Rapperswil, Switzerland**
Phone: 055 211 0977
Contact: Peter Kessler, Counselor

•Lernen•Beraten•Begleiten•, Maria
Bamert-Widmer, Churerstrasse 26,
CH-8852, **Altendorf, Switzerland**
Phone: 055 442 55 76

Hans-U. Sauser, Beratung und Ausbildung,
Rosenauweg 27, CH-5430 **Wettingen, Switzerland**
Phone: 056 426 64 09

Honegger Career Mgmt., Scheeitergasse 3,
CH-8001 **Zuerich, Switzerland**
Phone: 01 790 18 46
Contact: Urs W. Honegger

Peter Baumgartner, Lowen Pfaffikon,
Postfach 10, 8808 **Pfaffikon, Switzerland**
Phone: 055 415 66 22

Madeleine Leitner, Dipl. Psych.
Ohmstrasse 8, 80802 **Munchen, Germany**
Phone: 089 33 04 02 03

Career Development Seminars, offered
at Westfalische Wilhelms-Universitat
Muenster, Dez. 1.4 Wissenschafliche
Weiterbildung, Schlossplatz 2, 48149
Muenster, Germany
Phone: 0251 832 4762;
and at Universitat Bremen, Zentrum fur
Weiterbildung, 28359 **Bremen, Germany**
Phone: 0421 Brunnenweg 10,
48153 Muenster, Germany.

John Lees Associates, 37 Tatton St.,
Knutsford **Cheshire, England** WA16 6hauk
Phone: (UK): 01565 631625
Fax: 01565 650950
Contact: John Lees
eMail: johnlees.jla@dial.pipex.com

Bridgeway Associates Ltd.,
Career Consultants, P.O. Box 16,
Chipping Campden GL55 6ZB
London and Midlands
Phone: 01386 841840
Contact: Jane Bartlett

The Chaney Partnership, Hillier House,
509 Upper Richmond Rd. West, SW14 7EE
London, England
Phone: 020 8878 3227
Contact: Isabel Chaney, B.A.

Career Shaman, 119 The Street, Adisham.
Canterbury, **Kent** CT3 3JS
Phone: 01304 84279
eMail: careers@career-shaman.com

Anne Radford, 303 Bankside Lofts,
65 Hopton Street, SE1 9JL **London, England**
Phone: 020 7633 9630

PASSPORT, 8 Ashness Road, SW11 6RY
London, England
Phone: 020 7228 1982
Contact: Janie Wilson

Career Development, 10 York Pl.,
Brandon Hill, BS1 5UT **Bristol, England**
Phone: 0117 925 4363
Contact: Philip Houghton

Executive Partnership, Ltd., Henry James
Leeke House, 3 Links Court, Links
Business Park, St. Mellons, Cardiff CF3 0LT
South Wales, UK
Phone: 44 (0) 29 20839500
Contact: Philip Houghton

John Lees Associates, The Ruskin Rooms,
Drury Lane, Knutsford,
Cheshire WA16 6HA, **England**
Phone: 01565 631625
Contact: John Lees, Director

Castle Consultants International,
9 Drummond Park, Crook of Devon,
Kinross, KY13 7UX, **Scotland**
Phone: 0171 798 8804
Also at: 140 Battersea Park Road, SW11
4NB **London, England**
Phone: 44 1577 840 122 Fax: 44 207 6811 445
Contact: Walt Hopkins,
Founder and Director
eMail: Walt@Hopkins.net

Brian McIvor & Associates, Newgrange
Mall, Slane, **County Mead, Ireland**
Phone: 00 353 41 988 4035
(Brian has been on staff at my international Two-Week Workshop for four years)

Adigo Consultores, Av. Doria 164,
Sao Paulo SP 04635-070 **Brazil**
Phone: 55 11 530 0330
Contact: Alberto M. Barros, Director

Worklife, The Center for Worklife Counselling, Suite 2, 4 Bond St., Mosman, P.O. Box 407, **Spit Junction** NSW 2088 **Australia**
Phone: 612 9968 1588
Contact: Paul Stevens, Director
eMail: worklife@ozeMail.com.au
(Paul has been the dean of career counseling in Australia for many years)

The Growth Connection, Suite 402, 4th Floor, 56 Berry St.,
North Sydney NSW 2060 **Australia**
Phone: 61 2 9954 3322
Contact: Imogen Wareing, Director

Life by Design, Suite 19, 88 Helen St.,
Lane Cove 2066 NSW **Australia**
Phone: 61 2 9420 8280
Contact: Ian Hutchinson

Narelle Milligan, Career Consultant, 4 McLeod Place, **Kambah** ACT 2902 **Australia**
Phone: 61 2 6296 4398

Designing Your Life, 10 Nepean Pl.,
Macquarie ACT 2614 **Australia**
Phone: 61 6 253 2231
Contact: Judith Bailey

New Zealand Creative Career Centre, Ltd., 4th Floor, Braemar House, 32 The Terrace, P.O. Box 3058, **Wellington, New Zealand**
Phone: 64 4 499 8414
Contact: Felicity McLennan

Life Work Career Counselling,
P.O. Box 2223, **Christchurch, New Zealand**
Phone: 64 03 379 2781
Contact: Max Palmer

Career Makers, P.O. Box 277-95, Mt. Roskill, **Auckland, New Zealand**
Phone: 649 817 5189
Contact: Liz Constable

Find A Job You Can Love, 2/8 Hatton St., Karori, **Wellington, New Zealand**
Phone: 64 4 476 2554
Contact: Tim Martin

Transformation Technologies Pte Ltd.
122 Thomson Green, 574986 **Singapore**
Phone: 65 456 6358
Contact: Anthony Tan, Director

Byung Ju Cho, Seocho-Ku Banpo-dong
104-16 Banpo Hyundai Villa A-402,
Seoul, 137-040, **South Korea**
Phone: 011-9084-6236

Readers often write to ask us which of these overseas counselors are familiar with my approach to job-hunting and career-changing. The answer is: *every one of the counselors listed above*, have attended my two-week workshop, and therefore know my approach well.

Other overseas counselors not trained by me, but who may still be quite helpful to you, since they are experienced counselors, and are familiar with *Parachute*, are:

Judy Feierstein, M.A.,
46/2 Derech Bet Lechem, 93504
Jerusalem, Israel
Phone: 02 71 06 73

Lori Mendel, 19/6 Emanuel Haromi,
62645 **Tel-Aviv, Israel**
Phone: 972-3-524-1068

Johan Veeninga, Careers by Design, Business Park "De Molenzoom,"
P.O. Box 143, NL-3990 DC,
Houten/Utrecht, **The Netherlands**
Phone: 31 (0) 3403 75153

Employment Agencies for Overseas Jobs:
Safe Jobs in Japan, 56 Northwood Ave.,
Bridgewater, NJ 08807
Phone: 908-231-0994.
Web: www.safejobsinjapan.com
(Located in Japan, they place college graduates who wish to teach conversational English in Japan. This address is their U.S. administrative support office.)

Dick Bolles' Two-Week Workshop is no longer offered. Begun in 1974, it was discontinued in 2001. A shorter 4-day workshop will eventually be offered, according to present plans, in California, each year. Contact Norma Wong, Registrar, by phone: 925-837-3002 (12 noon–5 p.m. West Coast Time) or by fax: 925-837-5120 (anytime, 24/7) for information about times, dates, etc.

APPENDIX C

How To Choose A Career Coach Or Counselor

HOW TO CHOOSE A CAREER COACH OR COUNSELOR, IF YOU DECIDE YOU NEED ONE

LET'S START OUT with some simple definitions:

Career Coach. A person can be certified as a career coach after as little as three days training.

Career Counselor. A person can call themselves a career counselor, in some parts of the U.S., without any training.

• NCCC Counselor. NCCC means a"Nationally certified career counselor." There are currently over 850 in the U.S.

• NCC Counselor. NCC means "Nationally certified counselor." There are over 20,000 such in the U.S. This can mean general counseling expertise, not necessarily career counseling expertise.

• LPC Counselor. LPC means a "Licensed professional counselor" -- and often refers to state licensing. Again, this does not necessarily mean expertise with career counseling. There are a number of states, now, that have some sort of licensing regulation of all counselors. In some states getting this licensing is mandatory, in others getting it is optional.

I wish I could say that everyone who hangs out a sign saying they are now a career coach or counselor could be completely trusted. Nope, they can't all be. As you can see from the definitions above, the career counseling field is largely unregulated. And even where there is certification, certification doesn't tell you much.

For, as is the case in many professions, all coaches and counselors divide basically into three groups: a) those who are honest and know what they're doing; b) those who are honest but inept; and c) those who are dishonest, and merely want your money -- in lump sums, and up front.

You, of course, want a list of those in the first category -- those who are honest and know what they're doing. Well, unfortunately, no one (including me) has such a list. You've got to do your own homework, or research, here, and your own interviewing, in your own geographical area, or you will deserve what you get.

Why is it that *you* and only *you* can do it? You, you, and nobody else but you? Well, let's say a friend tells you to go see so-and-so. He's a wonderful coach or counselor, but unhappily he reminds you of your Uncle Harry, whom you detest. Bummer! But, no one except you knows that you've always hated your Uncle Harry. That's why no one else can do this research for you -- because the real question is not "Who is best?" but "Who is best for you?" Those last two words demand that it be you who 'makes the call,' that it be you who does the research.

Of course, you're tempted to skip this research, aren't you? *"Well, I'll just call up one place, and if I like the sound of them, I'll sign up. I'm a pretty good judge of character."* Right. I've heard this refrain from so many job-hunters who called me, after they'd lost all their money in a bad "pay-up-front" contract, because they had been *taken*, by slicker salespeople than they had ever run into before. As they tell me their stories, they cry over the telephone. I express, of course, my sympathy and compassion (I once got *taken* myself, the same way), but then I add, "I'm terribly sorry to hear that you had such a heartbreaking experience, but -- as the Scots would say -- 'Ya dinna do your homework.' Often you could easily have discovered whether a particular counselor was competent or not, before you ever gave them any of your money, simply by doing the preliminary research that I urge upon *everybody*."

Another way people try to avoid this research is by saying, "Well, I'll just see who Bolles recommends." That's a stretch, because I never have recommended anyone. Some try to claim I do, including, over the years, some of the people listed in the preceding Sampler, arguing that their very listing here constitutes a recommendation from me. Nice try! Inclusion in this book does NOT constitute an endorsement or recommendation by me -- as I have been at great pains to make clear for the past thirty years. Never has meant that. Never will. *(Anyone listed here who claims that it does, gets removed from this Sampler the following year.)* This is just a *sampler* of names *who have asked to be listed*, not a "hall of fame." With them, as with all others, you must do your own homework. You must do your own research.

COLLECT THREE NAMES THAT YOU CAN RESEARCH

So, how do you go about finding a good career coach or counselor? Well, you start by collecting three names of career counselors in your geographical area.

How do you find those names? Several ways:

First, you can get names from your friends: ask if any of them have ever used a career coach or counselor. And if so, did they like 'em? And if so, what is that coach's or counselor's name?

Secondly, you can get names from the Sampler that precedes this section (beginning on page 374). See if there are any career coaches or counselors who are near you. They may know how you can find still other names in your community. But I repeat what I said above: just because they're listed in the Sampler *doesn't* mean I recommend them. It only means they asked to be listed, and professed familiarity with the contents of this book (current edition). You've still got to research these people.

Need more names? Try your telephone book's Yellow Pages, under such headings as: Aptitude and Employment Testing, Career and Vocational Counseling, Personnel Consultants and (if you are a woman) Women's Organizations and Services.

Once you have three names, you need to go do some comparison shopping. You want to go talk with all three of them face-to-face, and decide which of the three (if any) you want to hook up with.

Don't try to do this over the telephone, please! There is so much more you can tell, when you're looking the person straight in the eyes.

What will this initial interview cost you, with each of the three? The answer to that is easy: when setting up an appointment, *ask*. Some, a few, will charge you nothing for the initial interview. One of the best counselors I know of makes this a part of her policy: *I don't charge for the first interview because I want to be free to tell them I can't help them, if for some reason we just don't hit it off.* In most cases, however, if it's an individual coach or counselor, you *are* going to have to pay them for this exploratory hour, or part of an hour -- even if it's only five or ten minutes. Do not expect that most individual counselors can afford to give you this exploratory interview for nothing! If they did that, and got a lot of requests like yours, they would never be able to make a living. You do have the right, however, to inquire ahead of time how much they are going to have to charge you for the exploratory interview. On the other hand, if this is not an individual counselor, but a firm trying to sell you a package 'up front,' I guarantee you they will give you the initial interview for free. They plan to use that first interview to sell you their program.

THE QUESTIONS TO ASK

When you are face-to-face with the individual coach or counselor, (or firm) you ask each of them the same questions, listed on the form below. (Keep a little pad or notebook with you, so you can write their answers down.)

MY SEARCH FOR A GOOD CAREER COUNSELOR

Questions I Will Ask Them	Answer from counselor #1	Answer from counselor #2	Answer from counselor #3
1. What is your program?			
2. Who will be doing it with me? And how long has this person been doing it?			
3. What is your success rate?			
4. What is the cost of your services?			
5. Is there a contract up front? If so, may I see it please, and take it home with me?			

After visiting the three places you chose for your comparison shopping, you have to go home, sit down, put your feet up, look over your notes, and compare those places.

You need to decide a) whether you want none of the three, or b) one of the three (and if so, which one). Remember, you don't have to choose any of the three counselors, if you didn't really care for any of them. If that is the case, then go choose three new counselors out of the Yellow Pages or wherever, dust off the notebook, and go out again. It may take a few more hours to find what you want. But the wallet, the purse, the job-hunt, the life, you save will be your own.

As you look over your notes, you will realize there is no definitive way for you to determine a career counselor's expertise. It's something you'll have to *smell out*, as you go along. But here are some clues. These are primarily clues about *firms* rather than individual coaches or counselors, but many clues apply to both:

BAD ANSWERS

If they give you the feeling that everything will be done for you, by them (including interpretation of tests, and decision making about what this means you should do, or where you should do it) -- rather than asserting that you are going to have to do almost all the work, with their basically assuming the role of coach,

(Give them **15 bad points**)

You want to learn how to do this for yourself; you're going to be job-hunting again, you know.

If they say they are not the person who will be doing the program with you, but deny you any chance to meet the counselor you would be working with,

(Give them **75 bad points**)

You're talking to a salesperson. My advice after talking to job-hunters for thirty years, is: avoid any firm that has a salesperson.

If you do get a chance to meet the counselor, but you don't like the counselor as a person,

(Give them **150 bad points**)

I don't care what their expertise is, if you don't like them, you're going to have a rough time getting what you want. I guarantee it. Rapport is everything.

If you ask how long the counselor has been doing this, and they get huffy or give a double-barreled answer, such as: "I've had eighteen years' experience in the business and career counseling world,"

(Give them **20 bad points**)

What that may mean is: seventeen and a half years as a fertilizer salesman, and one half year doing career counseling. Persist.

"How long have you been with this firm, and how long have you been doing formal career counseling, as you are here?" You might be interested to know that some executive or career counseling firms hire yesterday's clients as today's new staff. Such new staff are sometimes given training only after they're "on-the-job." They are practicing on you.

If they try to answer the question of their experience by pointing to their degrees or credentials,

(Give them **3 bad points**)

Degrees or credentials tell you they've passed certain tests of their qualifications, but often these tests bear more on their expertise at career assessment *than on their knowledge of creative job-hunting techniques.*

If, when you ask about their success rate, they say they have never had a client that failed to find a job, no matter what,

(Give them **5 bad points**)

They're lying. I have studied career counseling programs for over thirty years, have attended many, have studied records at State and Federal offices, and I have hardly ever seen a program that placed more than 86% of their clients, tops, in their best years. And it goes downhill from there. A prominent executive counseling firm was reported by the Attorney General's Office of New York State to have placed only 38 out of 550 clients (a 93% failure rate). If they make it clear that they have had a good success rate, but if you fail to work hard at the whole process, then there is no guarantee you are going to find a job, give them three stars.

If they show you letters from ecstatically happy former clients, but when you ask to talk to some of those clients, you get stone-walled,

(Give them **45 bad points**)

I quote from one job-hunter's letter to me: "I asked to speak to a former client or clients. You would of thought I asked to speak to Elvis. The Counselor stammered and stuttered and gave me a million excuses why I couldn't talk to some of these 'satisfied' former clients. None of the excuses sounded legitimate to me. We went back and forth for about thirty minutes. Finally, he excused himself and went to speak to his boss, the owner. The next thing I knew I was called into the owner's office for a more 'personal' sales pitch. We spoke for about 45 minutes as he tried to convince me to use his service. When I told him I was not ready to sign up, he became angry and asked my Counselor why I had been put before 'the committee' if I wasn't ready to commit? The Counselor claimed I had given a verbal commitment at our last meeting. The owner then turned to me and said I seemed to have a problem making a decision and that he did not want to do business with me. I was shocked. They had turned the whole story around to make it look like it was my fault. I felt humiliated. In retrospect, the whole process felt like dealing with a used car salesman. They used pressure tactics and intimidation to try to get what they wanted. As you have probably gathered, more than anything else this experience made me angry."

If it is a *firm*, and they claim they only accept 5 clients out of every hundred who apply, and your name will have to be put before 'The Committee' before you can be accepted,

(Give them **1000 bad points**)

This is one of the oldest tricks in the book. You're supposed to feel 'special' before they lift those thousands of dollars out of your wallet. Personally, the minute I heard this at a particular agency or service, I would run *for the door and never look back.*

If you ask what is the cost of their services, and they reply that it is a lump sum that must all be paid "up front" before you start or shortly after you start, either all at once or in installments,

(Give them **100 bad points**)

I have many friends among career coaches and counselors who charge one lump sum up front, and I know them to be very competent, sincere, and helpful. The trouble is, I have run into many charlatans in this field, over the years, who have also charged one lump sum up front, and were revealed to be incompetent, insincere, and (basically) crooks. And the trouble is, you won't know which one you've run into, until they have all your money. I have tried for twenty-five years to think of some way around this, and

I've concluded there basically is none. So now I say, if it were me, anytime I run into a coach, counselor, or executive counseling firm that charges a lump sum up front, I would go elsewhere. It's just a risk I can't afford to take. If you on the other hand can *afford to gamble that much money, and lose it, then go ahead and do what you decide to do. But, I've listened to too many people who got taken, and couldn't afford to lose all that money.*

If it's a firm, and they asked you to bring in your partner or spouse with you,

(Give them **45 bad points**)

This is a well-known tactic of some of the slickest salespeople and firms on the face of the earth, who want your spouse or partner there so they can manipulate them if they can't manipulate you, to reach a decision on the spot, while they have you in their 'grasp.'

If it is a firm, particularly an executive counseling firm, and they ask you to sign a contract 'up front',

(Give them **1000 bad points**)

With firms that have a bad track record, there is always a written contract. And you must sign it, before they will help you. (Often, your partner or spouse will be asked to sign it, too.) The fee normally ranges from $1000 on up to $10,000 or more. You are told you can get the fee back (or some of it at least) if you are dissatisfied. Yeah, just try!! They have more ways around ever giving you your money back than you can possibly imagine, no matter what their verbal promises (or even written ones) claim.

Sometimes, for example, the written contract will claim to provide for a partial refund, at any time, until you reach a cut-off date in the program, which the contract specifies. Unfortunately, many crafty fraudulent firms bend over backwards to be extra nice, extra available, and extra helpful to you until that cut-off point is reached. So, when the cut-off point for getting a refund has been reached, you let it pass because you are very satisfied with their past services, and believe there will be many more weeks of the same. Only, there aren't. At fraudulent firms, once the cut-off point is passed, the career counselor becomes virtually impossible for you to get ahold of. Call after call will not be returned. You will say to yourself "What happened?" Well, what happened, my friend, is that you paid up in full, they have all the money they're ever going to get out of you, and now they don't want to give you any more time.

Over the last twenty years, I have had to listen to grown men and women cry over the telephone, all because they signed a contract. Most often they were executives, or senior managers, who never had to go job-hunting before, and unknowingly signed up with some executive counseling firm that was fraudulent, or at least on the edge of legality. They thought the high fee guaranteed excellence. It didn't.

You may think I am exaggerating: I mean, can there possibly be such mean men and women, who would prey on job-hunters,

when they're down and out. Yes, ma'am, and yes, sir, there are. That's why you have to do this preliminary research so thoroughly.

I quote from the late Robert Wegmann, former director of the UHCL Center for Labor Market Studies: "One high-charging career counseling firm went bankrupt a few years ago. They left many of their materials behind in their former office. A box of what they abandoned has come into my possession. Going through the contents of the box has been fascinating.

"Particularly interesting are several scripts used to train their salespeople. The goal of the sales pitch is to convince the

unemployed (or unhappily employed) person that he or she can't find a good job alone, but can do it with professional help. Hiring us, they argue, is just like hiring a lawyer . . .

"Then, at the end of the pitch, comes the 'takeaway.' The firm may not accept your money, you are warned! There will have to be a review board meeting at which your application is considered. Only a minority of applicants are accepted. The firm only wants the right kind of clients.

"That's the pitch. But the rest of the documents tell a very different story. In fact, the firm is running a series of sales contests with all the 'professionalism' of a used car lot . . .

"These salespeople were paid on commission. The higher the sales the higher the percentage of the customer's fee they got to keep.

"There are sales contests. The winner receives a handsome green Master's jacket. Each monthly winner qualifies for a Grand Master's Tournament, with large prizes . . .

"So take this one piece of advice . . . If someone offers to help you find a great job as long as you'll pay several thousand dollars in advance, do as follows:

"A. Find door

"B. Walk out same

"C. Do not return."

GOOD ANSWERS

Well, those are the bad answers that may help you determine whether this is the coach, counselor or firm that you want. How about the good answers? Yes, there are such things: career coaches or counselors or firms who charge by the hour. With them, there is no written contract. You sign nothing. You pay only for each hour as you use it, according to their set rate. Each time you keep an appointment, you pay them at the end of that hour for their help, according to that rate. Period. Finis. You never owe them any money. You can stop seeing them at any time, if you feel you are not getting the help you wish.

What will they charge? You will find, these days, that the best career coaches or counselors *(plus some of the worst)* will charge you whatever a really good therapist or marriage counselor charges per hour, in your geographical area. Currently, in large metropolitan areas, that runs up to $150 an hour, sometimes more. In suburbia or rural areas, it may be much less -- $40 an hour, or so.

That fee is for *individual time* with the career coach or counselor. If you can't afford the fee, ask whether they also run groups. If they do, the fee will be much less. And, in one of those delightful ironies of life, since you get a chance to listen to problems which other job-hunters in your group are having, the group will often give you more help than an individual session with a counselor would. Not always; but often. It's always ironic when *cheaper* and *more helpful* go hand in hand.

If the career counselor in question does offer groups, there should (again) never be a contract. The charge should be payable at the end of each session, and you should be able to drop out at any time, without further cost, if you decide you are not getting the help you want.

There are, incidentally, some career counselors who run free (or almost free) job-hunting workshops through local churches, synagogues, chambers of commerce, community colleges, adult education programs, and the like, as their community service, or *pro bonum* work (as it is technically called). I have had reports of such workshops from a number of places in the U.S. and Canada. They surely exist in other parts of the world as well. If money is a big problem for you, in getting help with your job-hunt, ask around your community to see if such workshops as these exist in your community. Your chamber of commerce will likely know, or your church or synagogue.

Index

U

V

W

Y

Update 2003

TO: PARACHUTE
P.O. Box 379
Walnut Creek, CA 94597

I think that the information in the 2002 edition needs to be changed, in your next revision, regarding (or, the following resource should be added):

____

____

____

____

____

____

I cannot find the following resource, listed on page __________:

____

____

____

____

____

____

Name ______________________________

Address ______________________________

Please make a copy.

Submit this so as to reach us by February 1, 2002. Thank you.

Other Resources

Additional materials by Richard N. Bolles to help you with your job-hunt:

The What Color Is Your Parachute? Workbook
This handy workbook leads the job-seeker through the process of determining exactly what sort of job or career they are most suited for, easily streamlining this potentially stressful and confusing task. $9.95

Job-Hunting on the Internet,
Third Edition, revised and expanded.
This handy guide has quickly established itself as the ideal resource for anyone who's taking the logical step of job-hunting on the Internet. $12.95

The Three Boxes of Life, And How to Get Out of Them
An introduction to life/work planning. $18.95

How to Find Your Mission in Life
Originally created as an appendix to *What Color Is Your Parachute?*, this book was written to answer one of the questions most often asked by job-hunters. $14.95

Job-Hunting Tips for the So-Called Handicapped
A unique perspective on job-hunting and career-changing, addressing the experiences of the disabled in performing these tasks. $12.95

The Career Counselor's Handbook
(with Howard Figler)
A complete guide for practicing or aspiring career counselors. $17.95